COMPUTER EDUCATION FOR TEACHERS

6 EDITION

Integrating Technology into Classroom Teaching

COMPUTER EDUCATION FOR TEACHERS

6 EDITION

Integrating Technology into Classroom Teaching

Vicki F. Sharp

California State University, Northridge

WILEY
JOHN WILEY & SONS, INC.

*This book is dedicated to
my husband, Richard Malcolm Sharp,
my son, David Allen Sharp,
and the dedicated teachers
that I have had the privilege to know!*

VICE PRESIDENT & PUBLISHER   Jay O'Callaghan
ACQUISITIONS EDITOR   Robert Johnston
SENIOR PRODUCTION EDITOR   Nicole Repasky
PHOTO EDITOR   Hilary Newman
PHOTO RESEARCHER   Teri Stratford
MARKETING MANAGER   Danielle Torio
SENIOR DESIGNER   Madelyn Lesure
PRODUCTION MANAGEMENT SERVICES   Pine Tree Composition, Inc.
SENIOR MEDIA EDITOR   Lynn Pearlman
EDITORIAL ASSISTANT   Carrie Tupa
COVER PHOTO AND OPENERS   © Jose L. Pelaez/Corbis

This book was set in Times Ten Roman by Laserwords Private Limited, Chennai, India and printed and bound by R.R. Donnelley/Jefferson City. The cover was printed by R.R. Donnelley/Jefferson City.

This book is printed on acid free paper. ∞

To order books or for customer service please, call 1-800-CALL WILEY (225-5945).

Library of Congress Cataloging-in-Publication Data
Sharp, Vicki F.
  Computer education for teachers : integrating technology into classroom teaching /
Vicki Sharp.—6th ed.
      p. cm.
  Includes index.
  ISBN 978-0-470-14110-6 (pbk.)
1. Education—Data processing. 2. Computers—Study and teaching.
3. Computer-assisted instruction. I. Title.
LB1028.43.S55 2009
370.285—dc22

                                                     2008006157

Printed in the United States of America

10 9 8 7 6 5 4 3 2 1

About the Author

Vicki F. Sharp is Professor Emeritus at California State University. She received a PhD in Quantitative Research from St. Louis University and a BA from Washington University. She teaches math/science methods courses and computer courses, and she supervises student teachers. She has been the author of more than 43 books, including *Statistics for the Social Sciences* (Little, Brown), the *HyperStudio in an Hour* series, *PowerPoint in an Hour* and *Best Web Sites for Teachers* (ISTE), and the *Make It with Office* series and *Make It with Inspiration* (Visions Technology in Education). She serves as a computer consultant and trainer for software publishers and school districts in southern California. She speaks at computer conventions such as Computer User Educators (CUE) and the National Education Computer Conference (NECC). Her special interests include integrating the computer into the classroom, teacher education, digital photography, and school improvement.

When I wrote the first edition of *Computer Education for Teachers*, I had an Apple IIc computer with an internal floppy drive and I stored text and pictures on a 5-1/4 inch floppy disk. The textbook was considered ahead of its time. Looking back, the book is antiquated and technology is changing so fast it is hard to keep up with all the new innovations.

Our machines are now smaller, contain terabyte hard drives, and have gigabyte processing speeds. We use the Internet as a huge library resource, and electronic mail has proliferated. (In fact, we communicate by e-mail to such an extent that I am relieved when our server breaks down.) We are using the Internet for distance learning producing Podcasts, creating videos for YouTube, engaging in social networks, and spending our time in virtual worlds. Computers are being used to help students with special needs realize their potential. In the next 10 years, the computer and the Internet will become even more pervasive influences on how we teach and what happens in the classroom. It will be a more exciting time for teachers and students. The new edition of this text contains many useful new features, which I hope you enjoy!

Approach and Features of This Text

Computer Education for Teachers: Integrating Technology into Classroom Teaching is designed to introduce future teachers to computer technology in a meaningful, practical fashion. It is written for undergraduate and graduate students who want an up-to-date, readable, practical, concise introduction to computers for teachers. Covering a large range of topics, this book should help you acquire the knowledge and skills necessary to integrate computers into your classroom in ways that will be of most use to you and of greatest service to your students.

Throughout its previous five editions, *Computer Education for Teachers* has maintained the key features that contributed to the success of the very first edition:

- **Accessibility:** Readers need not have had any prior experience with computers. The clear, straightforward writing style of the text makes the topics accessible to all.

- **Extensive illustrations:** A wealth of illustrations and screen shots clearly convey the salient features of the latest and best software, help computer novices identify hardware, and help explain concepts.

- **Learning tools:** Proven learning support features include each chapter's *Introduction, Objectives, Summary, Chapter Mastery Test, Key Terms*, and *Suggested Readings and References*. Practical resources of use to teachers

include evaluation *Checklists, Classroom Lesson Plans, Web Links*, and *Computer Lab Activities*.

- **Current research:** The inclusion of the latest research on computers provides readers with an understanding of effective and ineffective uses of computer hardware and software and promising new directions for computer use in the classroom.

- **Discussions of advances in computer technology:** These explorations keep readers on the cutting edge of computer knowledge.

- **Annotated web site listings:** Online lists of annotated web sites provide readers with additional sources of lesson plans, tutorials, historical information, and classroom tools.

- **End-of-chapter references:** These reference lists provide readers with books and articles to launch detailed investigations into many aspects of educational software and hardware and learning theory.

New to the Sixth Edition

Computer Education for Teachers remains true to its original purpose: to provide meaningful and practical guidance in bringing computers into the classroom. However, this edition has been extensively rewritten, with new chapters. It contains many exciting new features. Among them are:

- Online video tutorials demonstrating projects such as creating a newsletter and producing a Podcast

- Digital photography chapter and expanded section on using a video camera

- The latest innovations discussed, such as Podcasts, Google Earth, Skype, Twitter, Moodle, Wikis, Blogs, Second Life, YouTube, MySpace, Clickers, Open Journaling, Mapping Mashups, and Screencasting

- Online project templates and examples

- Numerous evaluation and checklists in PDF format for downloading

- Interactive self-study tests

- New online instructor's test manual

- New illustrations

- Chapter PowerPoint presentations

- Practical classroom activities

- Software Reviews

- Best Educational Web Sites by Dr. Richard Malcolm Sharp, Professor Emeritus

- Papers by distinguished individuals such as Dr. David Moursund, Dr. George Friedman, Jane Caughlin, Tony Brewer, and Dr. Warren Buckleitner

- Sample Digital Photography chapters from Dr. Arnie Abrams
- Podcasts by Don Johnston, Anita McAnear, and Robert Sachs
- Hardware reference guide online
- Article on computer theorists online by Dr. David Kretschmer
- Article on computer robotics by Dr. Kenneth Berry

Supplements for Teaching and Learning

This edition of *Computer Education for Teachers* features new and expanded supplements for course instructors and readers/students online.

FOR THE INSTRUCTOR

Instructors using this book will find additional teaching support at the *Instructor's Companion Site*, at http://www.wiley.com/college/sharp. This version includes an online instructor's manual by Dr. David Kretschmer, *PowerPoint*

slides, video tutorials, projects and examples, software reviews, evaluation checklists, and websites, and additional teaching resources.

FOR THE STUDENT

Education students will find their learning supported by the *Student Companion Site*, http://www.wiley.com/college/sharp. This version features video tutorials, Internet sites with links to lesson plans, self-quizzes, projects and examples, software reviews, evaluation checklists, and much more.

A Message to Readers

If you would like to see some topic in a future edition or have any comments or questions, please send your thoughts to me at

Internet address: vicki.sharp@csun.edu

University address:

Dr. Vicki Sharp, California State University, Northridge, School of Education, 18111 Nordhoff, Northridge, CA 91330-8265

Acknowledgments

What a monumental effort this book was. If it were not for some very special people, it would never have been completed.

First, I would like to thank my husband, Dr. Richard Malcolm Sharp, for his invaluable contributions. He not only gave me emotional support, but he also contributed to the book's resources. He compiled excellent annotated Web sites online at http://www.wiley.com/college/sharp.

Second, I would like to thank Robert A. Sachs and Marsha Lifter. Bob is Instructional Technology Application Facilitator for Los Angeles Unified School District C Schools. He made numerous suggestions, created some beautiful photos for the book, and did an outstanding Podcast. Marsha Lifter—writer, lecturer, and university teacher at California State University, San Luis Obispo—provided information and background.

Third, I want to express my appreciation to Robert Johnston, Acquisitions Editor, Education at John Wiley & Sons and Carrie Tupa, Editorial Assistant. Robert believed in my ability to produce a good product. He gave me direction and was always available to help with the project. Carrie had excellent insights and suggestions. She was very knowledgeable about the education technology field. The John Wiley team is an exceptional group of people to work with and I am proud to be a part of this team. Patty Donovan (Pine Tree Composition, Inc.) was an outstanding

Project Manager and Teri Stratford, freelance photo researcher, was a miracle worker.

Fourth, I give special thanks to Dr. David Moursund, Founder of the ISTE and Professor Emeritus at the College of Education at the University of Oregon; Janet Caughlin, technology book series writer and speaker; Tony Vincent, handheld expert and fifth-grade teacher; Anthony Nguyen, Director of Technology at California State University, Northridge (CSUN); Dr. Richard Malcolm Sharp, Professor Emeritus at California State University, Northridge; Dr. David Kretschmer, Chair of the Elementary Department at CSUN; Anita McAnear, Acquisitions Editor for *Learning & Leading* magazine, ISTE; Dr. Warren Buckleitner, Editor of *Children's Technology Review*; Dr. Arnie Abrams, a professor at Oregon University, contributed sample chapters on digital photography; Dr. Ken Berry, professor of Secondary Education at CSUN; Don Johnston, owner of Don Johnston, Inc.; and, last but not least, Dr. George Friedman, adjunct professor at the University of Southern California, formerly research director at the Space Studies Institute, Princeton. Each person's special contribution appears online.

Fifth, I thank all the terrific individuals who critiqued this book and offered many wonderful suggestions that were incorporated into this new edition:

Wren M. Bump, *University of Houston–Clear Lake*
Phillip Horton, *Covenant College*
Daniel J. Glisczinski, *University of Minnesota Duluth*
David A. McCarthy, *University of Minnesota Duluth*
Julie M. Reitinger, *Webster University*
Jana M. Willis, *University of Houston–Clear Lake*
Wanjira Kinuthia, *Georgia State University*
Norma Wheat, *Campbellsville University*
Lynne Packnowski, *Akron University*

Finally, I thank the many software houses that contributed to the completion of this textbook:

Barnum Software: Christopher Wright

BIAS, Inc.: Zac Wheatcroft, Sales & Marketing Associate

Centron: http://www.centronsoftware.com/

Creative Learning Systems: Matt Dickstein, Chief Executive Officer

Don Johnston, Inc.: Valerie Chernek, Mindy Brown (Director of Marketing), Cathy Kostrzeski, Inbound Inside Sales, Melessa Abraham (Marketing), and Melissa Reynolds (Marketing)

Digital Frog International: Celcia Clark, President, and Tracie Treahy, Marketing Coordinator

Edelman and Associates: Erika Gallardo and Rosalie Duryee

Educational Resources: Martin Smith

Edware: Luke M. Curley, BSc

Encore: Kelly Finnerty, product manager

Equilibrium: Dave Pola, Corporate Communications Manager, and Chris Caracci, technical expert

FableVision: Kelly Fischbach, Vice President of Educational Publishing

FileMaker Inc.: Kevin Mallon

FTC Publishing: Mike Kessler, President, and Zac Lancaster, Vice President

Gamco: Greg Koenig, Manager of Marketing Communication

Grolier Electronic Publishing: Veronica Scheer

Harmonic Vision: Joel Brazy, and Skip Nesbit, Harmonic Vision Sales

Houghton Mifflin: Bill Kearney, Account Manager (Riverdeep)

Inspiration: Ava Ryherd, Training Resource Specialist, Megan Murphy, Product Manager, and Crystal Miller

Jackson Software: Andrew Cohn

Learning Enhancement Corporation (Brainware): Betsy Hill, Chief Operating Officer

Learning Services, Inc.: Don McNeill, Territorial Sales Manager

Optimum Resources, Inc.: Christopher J. Gintz, Chief Operating Officer

Software Express: Lisa Lane

Software MacKiev: Jack Minsky, President and Jackie Specht, Education Sales Manager, Debra Barrows, Education Sales Manager

Studio eWorks Inc.: Bonnie Saliba, Contact person (video tutorials) at http://www.studioworks.com, Robert Thell, presenter, 1-800-432-2082

Sunburst Communications: Christine Pearse, Marketing Manager

Tom Snyder Productions: Alicia Gregoire-Poirier, and Rick Abrams, General Manager

Tech4Learning: Melinda Kolk and David Wagner

Terrapin Logo: Bill Glass

Viva Media: Eve Seber

Visions Technology in Education: John Crowder, president, and Tim Yost, graphic designer

Waggener Edstrom: Jocelyn Boudreaux, account executive, and Erica Harbison, senior account executive.

BRIEF CONTENTS

CONTENTS

11 Multimedia and Video Technology   216

12 Selecting Software and Integrating It into the Classroom   242

13 Technology in Special Education: Assistive Technology   265

Historical Past

Computer Literacy

It is only by studying our past that we gain perspective and are able to prepare for the future. In reading this chapter, you will learn what led to the development of modern-day computers, and what part education played in this history. What are the current educational milestones? Why are educational technology standards important?

Using the computer, students and teachers can do the following:

students can

- do library investigations on the Internet,
- get math tutorial help,
- create electronic portfolios,
- view science simulations,
- write research papers, and
- do desktop publishing.

teachers can

- create an electronic spreadsheet grade book,
- find lesson plans and instruction material,
- use technical Internet chat rooms,
- create PowerPoint presentations,
- communicate with students by e-mail, and
- create newsletters for parents.

objectives

Upon completing this chapter, you will be able to do the following:

1 Differentiate among the generations of computers according to their technological advances.

2 Identify and place in proper sequence three of the major developments in the history of computing.

3 Discuss succinctly the contributions of each of the following individuals to the field of computing:
(a) Charles Babbage,
(b) Herman Hollerith,
(c) Howard Aiken,
(d) John Atanasoff, and
(e) John Mauchly and J. Presper Eckert.

4 Be able to identify the ISTE Educational Technology Standards.

Before the Modern Computer

Before the modern computer primitive people found it necessary to count using their fingers as a natural instrument. With their fingers, they could show how many animals they had killed on a hunt or the number of people in a village. To indicate large numbers, they used all 10 fingers; since humans have 10 fingers, 10 became the basis of our number system.

As time passed, life became more complex, and people needed a more sophisticated way to keep track of their possessions. Some of the instruments that they used during this period were the abacus, the pascaline, and the stepped reckoner. These calculating devices preclude the introduction of computers.

Though not a calculating device, Jacquard's loom (Figure 1.1), invented in 1804, was a significant invention in the development of computers. Joseph Maria Jacquard used punched cards to create patterns on fabric woven on a loom. This device was a forerunner of the keypunch machine.

However, it wasn't until 1854, nearly two centuries later, that George Boole devised what became known as **Boolean algebra**, a system of logic based on the binary system. In the late 1930s, inventors were then able to build a computer that used this binary system, the standard internal language of today's digital computers.

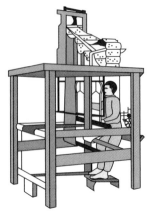

Figure 1.1
Jacquard's Loom

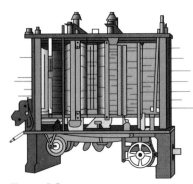

Figure 1.2
Babbage's Analytical Engine

Figure 1.3
Hollerith's Tabulating Machine

Check online at
http://www.wiley
.com/college/sharp
for a PDF file on early calcu-
lating devices.

Beginning of the Computer

The official beginning of the computer can be traced to Charles Babbage, a mathematics professor, when he constructed the Analytical Engine in 1835 (Figure 1.2).

A close personal friend of Babbage, Augusta Ada Byron, Countess of Lovelace, the only legally recognized daughter of Lord Bryon, raised money for his invention and wrote a demonstration programmer for the Analytical Engine. Because of this program, she is considered the first computer programmer, and the programming language **Ada** was named after her.

Babbage designed a system with provision for printed data, a control unit, and an information storage unit, but the Analytical Engine was never completed because construction of the machine required precision tools that did not exist at the time. For this achievement he is called the "father of computers," and historians have even said that all modern computers were descended directly from Babbage's Analytical Engine. In his day, however, Babbage was considered a failure, and he died in poverty.

A mere 19 years later, the punched-card element of the Analytical Engine (Figure 1.3) appeared in a working machine, a tabulator built by Herman Hollerith, an American inventor.

Because of Hollerith's invention, the census was completed in just two years, compared to the seven years it took for the 1880 census. Eventually, Hollerith organized his own company, called the Tabulating Machine Company. In the 1900s, he leased out his more sophisticated tabulating machines for the census. His business prospered and merged with other companies. The company went through a series of name changes, and the last name change came in 1924 when it became known as International Business Machines, or IBM. Table 1.1 summarizes the achievements of the inventors.

In the 20th century, the Census Bureau bought a machine designed by James Powers, which replaced Hollerith's machines.[1] The machines being produced were primarily for the business community. The scientific community's need for more complex processing remained unmet.

The Modern Computer

In 1944, the age of the modern computer began. World War II created a need for better data handling, which encouraged advances in technology and the development of computers.

Table 1.1 Computing Devices Before the 20th Century

Inventor	Invention	Year
Unknown	Abacus	approx. 3000 B.C.
John Napier	Napier's Bones	1617
Blaise Pascal	Pascaline	1642
Gottfried Leibniz	Stepped Reckoner	1674
Joseph Marie Jacquard	Punched Card Loom	1804
Charles Babbage	Analytical Engine	1835
Herman Hollerith	Tabulating Machine	1887

[1] Powers founded a company called Powers Accounting Machine Co., which merged with others to become know as Remington Rand and then Sperry Rand. Today, these companies are part of the Unisys conglomerate.

MARK I

During the war, a brilliant team of scientists and engineers (among them Alan Turing, Max Newman, Ian Fleming, and Lewis Powell) gathered at Bletchley Park, north of London, to work on a machine that could solve the German secret code. They designed the Colossus, an electronic computer that was used to break the German Enigma cipher. Much of their innovative work remains classified.

In 1937, Howard Aiken was to complete his research for his PhD at Harvard University. Faced with tedious calculations on nonlinear, differential equations, he decided that he needed an automatic calculating machine to make the chore less arduous. Initially, Aiken found little support at Harvard for his machine, so he turned to private industry. IBM was impressed with Aiken's idea and agreed to back him in his effort. Aiken headed a group of scientists whose task was to build a modern equivalent to Babbage's Analytical Engine. In 1943, the Mark I, also called the IBM Automatic Sequence Controlled Calculator, was completed at IBM Development Laboratories in Endicott, New York. The Mark I (Figure 1.4) could perform three calculations per second, weighed 5 tons, was 51 feet long, and printed its results on an electric typewriter. The first electromechanical computer was responsible for making IBM a giant in computer technology. After the completion of the Mark I, IBM produced several machines that were similar to the Mark I, and Howard Aiken also built a series of machines (the Mark II, Mark III, and Mark IV).

Figure 1.4
Harvard Mark I
(*Source:* Courtesy of the Computer History Museum)

In 1945, the Mark II was housed in a building without air conditioning. Because the computer generated tremendous heat, the windows were left open. One day this giant computer suddenly stopped working, and everyone tried frantically to discover the source of the problem. Grace Hopper and her coworkers found the culprit: a dead moth in a relay of the computer. They removed the moth with tweezers and placed it in the Mark II logbook. When Aiken came back to see how things were going with his associates, they told him they had had to **debug** the machine, thus coining the term for fixing a computer problem.[2]

THE ABC

While Aiken was working on his Mark I in 1939 at Iowa State University, John Atanasoff designed and built the first electronic digital computer with Clifford Berry, a graduate student. Atanasoff and Berry then went to work on an operational

---

[2] Today the Mark II logbook is preserved in the Naval Museum in Dahlgren, Virginia.

model called the ABC, the Atanasoff-Berry Computer. In 1941, John Mauchly, a physicist and faculty member at the University of Pennsylvania, stayed five days as Atanasoff's houseguest. During his stay, he had an opportunity to read and study Atanasoff's handbook explaining the electronic theories and construction plans of the ABC (Mollenhoff, 1990).

The First Generation of Computers

With the start of World War II, the military needed an extremely fast computer that would be capable of performing the thousands of computations necessary for compiling ballistic tables for new naval guns and missiles. John Mauchly and J. Prespert Eckert, an electrical engineer, believed the only way to solve this problem was with an electronic digital machine, so they worked on this project together. In 1946, they completed an operational electronic digital computer called the ENIAC (Electronic Numerical Integrator and Calculator), derived from what Mauchly had gleaned from Atanasoff's unpatented work. The ENIAC worked on a decimal system and had all the features of today's computers.[3] The ENIAC, shown in Figure 1.5, was tremendous in size, filling up a very large room and weighing 30 tons. It conducted electricity through 18,000 vacuum tubes.

Figure 1.5
ENIAC

    The ENIAC was the first to introduce vacuum tube technology (Figure 1.6) and it was classified as the first generation of computers.[4] The ENIAC's limitation was a small memory and difficulty shifting from one program to another, which required rewiring the machine. Maybe it took the ENIAC two minutes to compute a result, but it took individuals days to set up the problem. There needed to be a way to store the computer's program in the computer's memory. The EDVAC, completed in

---

[3] In 1973 Judge Earl R. Larson invalidated the ENIAC patent when he said that Eckert and Mauchly had derived some of their ideas from Atanasoff's unpatented work. Atanasoff then received recognition as one of the fathers of computing.

[4] Since its inception, the computer has gone through several stages of development. Generally, these technological advances are classified by *generations*, a marketing term. Even though there is some overlap among generations, it is convenient to view the computer's technological development terms of this classification.

1952, could store information in memory in the same form as data and was one of the first machines to use binary notation. Before 1951 the computer was not manufactured on a large scale. In 1951, with the arrival of the UNIVAC, the era of **commercial computers** began.

Figure 1.6
Vacuum Tubes
(*Source:* Sergey Goruppa/iStockphpto)

The Second Generation of Computers

We perceive the **second generation of computers** as beginning when the **transistor** (Figure 1.7) replaced the vacuum tube in the late 1950s. In 1947, John Bardeen, Walter H. Brattain, and William Shockley, a team of physicists working at Bell Labs, invented the transistor. They shared the Nobel Prize for this invention in 1956. The transistor, an electrically operated switch similar to an old-fashioned relay, was a landmark in the development of the computer. Transistors conduct electricity more efficiently, consume less energy, need less space, and generate less heat than vacuum tubes. In addition, they do not burn out as tubes do. The computer with transistors became smaller, more reliable, faster, and less expensive than a computer with vacuum tubes. Small- and medium-size businesses now found it more economical to buy computers.

Figure 1.7
Transistor

The Third Generation of Computers

The **third generation of computers** uses integrated circuits, online terminals, and disk storage. The beginning of the **third generation of computers** is marked by the 1964 introduction of the IBM 360, the computer that pioneered the use of **integrated circuits** on a chip. In that year, computer scientists developed tiny integrated circuits and installed hundreds of these transistors on a single silicon chip, which was as small as a fingertip (Figure 1.8.) The computer became smaller, more reliable, and less expensive than ever before.

They were almost a thousand times faster than the first generation of computers, and manufacturers mass-produced them at a low price, making them accessible to small companies.

Figure 1.8
Actual Silicon Chip Size

The Fourth Generation of Computers—The Microcomputer

The development of microprocessor technology launched the **fourth generation of computers**. The **microprocessor chip** (Figure 1.9) is a central processing unit, the brains of the computer, built on a single chip.

Figure 1.9
Microprocessor Chip
(*Source:* ©2008 Jupiterimages Corporation)

Edward "Ted" Hoff designed the microprocessor in 1968 while working at Intel. Three years later, Intel introduced the Intel 8080 microprocessor version, which was capable of running the processing unit of a computer. The journal *Radio Electronics* published an article in 1974 on a home-built computer that used this technology. In June 1975 *Popular Electronics* ran a story on Altair, a microcomputer that ran on the 8080 chip. The article mentioned that Micro Instrumentation Technology Systems (MITS) was selling kits for this computer. The public response and interest in Altair kits was overwhelming, and they inspired other companies to develop similar products.

Bill Gates and Paul Allen were just college students when they wrote the first BASIC interpreter for the Intel 8080 microprocessor. The language they created, called MBASIC, was licensed to MITS and sold with the Altair computer. In 1975 Bill Gates and Paul Allen (Figure 1.10) founded Microsoft. Years later, Microsoft became a leader in programming languages by supplying IBM PCs with DOS (**D**isk **O**perating **S**ystem) and non–IBM PCs with the MS-DOS operating system.

At about the same time that Gates and Allen were launching Microsoft, Steve Wozniak and Steve Jobs were working inside a garage selling their Apple computers for $666.66 (Figure 1.11). Figure 1.11 shows the Apple I. Steve Wozniak and Steve Jobs placed ads in hobbyist publications with the money that they raised by selling their personal possessions. They provided software for their machines free of charge. In 1977 a historic movement for computers occurred when Wozniak and Jobs introduced a new fully assembled version of their Apple machine called the Apple II. The Apple II was the first computer widely accepted by business users because of its spreadsheet simulation program, *VisiCalc*. In addition, it was compact, it came with 4 kilobytes (4K) of memory, and it was priced at $1,298.

(*Source:* Doug Wilson/©Corbis)

Figure 1.10
Bill Gates and Paul Allen

Figure 1.11
(a) Apple I Computer.
(*Source:* Courtesy Apple Computer, Inc.)

(b) Steve Jobs and Steve Wozniak.
(*Source:* Bettmann/©Corbis)

Four years later, IBM entered the personal computer market with the IBM PC. This computer quickly became a best seller. Because of IBM's successful entrance in the field, other computer makers chose to capitalize on its popularity by developing their own "clones." These personal computers had many of the same features as the IBM machines and could run the same programs. With the IBM PC, widespread use of personal computers became a reality. In 1977, computers even began appearing in schools. The following timeline shows these important events.

MODERN COMPUTER TIME LINE

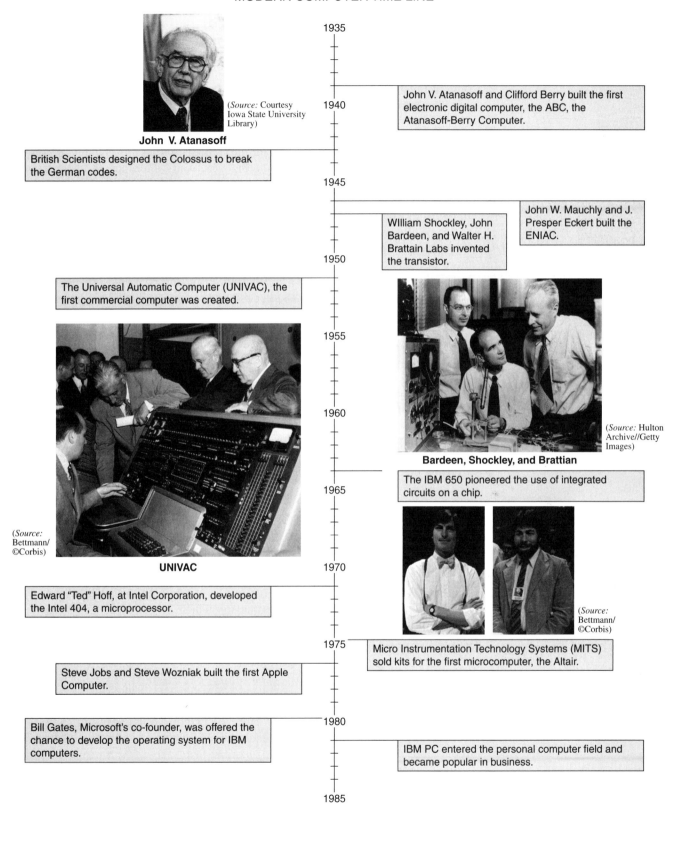

John V. Atanasoff

(*Source:* Courtesy Iowa State University Library)

John V. Atanasoff and Clifford Berry built the first electronic digital computer, the ABC, the Atanasoff-Berry Computer.

British Scientists designed the Colossus to break the German codes.

John W. Mauchly and J. Presper Eckert built the ENIAC.

WIlliam Shockley, John Bardeen, and Walter H. Brattain Labs invented the transistor.

The Universal Automatic Computer (UNIVAC), the first commercial computer was created.

Bardeen, Shockley, and Brattian

(*Source:* Hulton Archive//Getty Images)

UNIVAC

(*Source:* Bettmann/©Corbis)

The IBM 650 pioneered the use of integrated circuits on a chip.

Edward "Ted" Hoff, at Intel Corporation, developed the Intel 404, a microprocessor.

(*Source:* Bettmann/©Corbis)

Micro Instrumentation Technology Systems (MITS) sold kits for the first microcomputer, the Altair.

Steve Jobs and Steve Wozniak built the first Apple Computer.

Bill Gates, Microsoft's co-founder, was offered the chance to develop the operating system for IBM computers.

IBM PC entered the personal computer field and became popular in business.

1935

1940

1945

1950

1955

1960

1965

1970

1975

1980

1985

The Fifth Generation of Computers

The **fifth generation of computers**, marked from the mid-1990s to now, heralded super-fast computer chips capable of carrying out trillions of calculations per second. IBM's Blue Gene/L supercomputer is capable of 280 trillion operations a second during continuous operation (CNETNews.com).

Computers now feature voice recognition, natural and foreign language translation, fiber optic networks, and optical discs. Computers are smaller with increased data storage and memory. Many systems now have touch screens and handwriting recognition software that let the user employ a pencil-like stylus as the input device. There are developments in artificial intelligence, logical inference, and parallel processing. Today, the voice synthesizers that are used in computers sound more human than those used a few years ago. Navigation systems in cars use voice synthesizers to tell us in what direction to travel.

Presently, printers and computers are communicating through wireless networks. In addition, machines employ parallel processing; that is, a computer performs two or more operations simultaneously. Computers come with flat-panel displays that are larger, in color, and detachable. The **Internet**, a worldwide system for linking small computer networks, is exerting an increasingly pervasive influence on our everyday lives.

Teachers and students are finding new ways to work from their homes and in schools. Through the use of wireless telecommunication services, they are spending less time in the classroom and more time on the Internet via voice, data, and video conferencing. Teachers and students are using Internet's research tools, and many communicate through online course software almost exclusively. Exciting new technologies will deliver huge increases in bandwidth capacity, making Internet access occur with lightning-fast speed. With these exciting new developments come new forms of interactive content, realistic 3-D virtual reality[5] multiplayer games, and interactive education video forums. In Chapter 17, we will discuss the many new advances in computer technology and speculate on its future.

Computers in Education

For years scientist and engineers used computers but it wasn't until the 1950s that the computer came into the schools. As an avid computer enthusiast, I watched the computer evolve and adopted it as an instructional tool early. In the following paragraphs I discuss the history of educational computing through an ordinary teacher's perspective.

AN EDUCATOR'S PERSPECTIVE

We have come a long way from the 1940s when computers consisted of vacuum tubes, data were recorded on magnetic tapes and magnetic drums, and primarily scientists and engineers used the machines. In 1950, this all changed when the first documented instructional use of the computer occurred at Massachusetts Institute of Technology (MIT). Teachers used a computer flight simulator to train pilots. Nine years later, the first documented instructional use of computers with elementary school students occurred in New York City when an IBM 650 computer was used to teach schoolchildren binary arithmetic. I was an elementary school student myself and this event went unnoticed. During the 1960s computers were inaccessible to most students, including me. This situation changed in 1964 when John Kemeny and Thomas Kurtz, both at Dartmouth College, designed BASIC (Beginners All-Purpose

---

[5] Virtual reality (VR) is a computer system that can immerse the user in the illusion of a computer generate word. The user can navigate throughout this world at will (Pfaffenberger, 2003). See Chapter 11 for further discussion.

Symbolic Instruction Code), which required minimal instruction to learn. After BASIC's introduction, word spread about the new language designed for Dartmouth's time-sharing system. **Time-sharing** permitted several students to interact with a machine at the same time.

Check online at
http://www.wiley
.com/college/sharp
for a BASIC and Logo primer.

During this time period, Patrick Suppes and Richard Atkinson, at Stanford University, did some research and development on **computer-assisted instruction (CAI)** in reading and mathematics. CAI involves students in instructional activity on a computer. Suppes and Atkinson produced math drill-and-practice software on **mainframe**[6] computers. The computer would display a problem, the student would respond, and the computer would give immediate feedback.

In 1969, when I was working on my PhD, I used a keypunch machine to type on cards that were then read by a mainframe computer that filled a large room. Also that year was famous for the Department of Defense (DOD) creating ARPAnet, which later became known as the **Internet**. The ARPAnet was a large network of computers with links to smaller computer networks, which connect the Pentagon with defense researchers in academia and business.

In the early 1970s, when I started teaching at the University, Seymour Papert (Figure 1.12), an MIT professor, utilized a different approach to computers in education. Papert developed a programming language called Logo to encourage thinking about mathematics. As a beginning college teacher I really wasn't involved with Logo until the microcomputer came into my life. During this time period, Don Bitzer, along with a team of specialists, developed an instructional system called Programmed Logic for Arithmetic Teaching Operations (PLATO). This system featured a terminal with a plasma screen, a specially designed keyboard, and an authoring system called Tutor. This authoring system developed tutorial lessons and complete courses. Some of my colleagues experimented with Tutor and then dropped it.

Figure 1.12
Seymour Papert
(*Source:*Bill Pierce/Time Life Pictures Getty Images)

In 1977, Steve Jobs and Steve Wozniak introduced a fully assembled version of their Apple computer, called the Apple II. I thought this small desktop computer with its 4K of memory, priced at $1,298, was a marvel. At California State University, we had an Apple II in a special room next to the administrative offices. We were excited about this computer with its two 5-$\frac{1}{4}$ inch disk drives (Figure 1.13). My colleagues and I learned how to use this machine and how to program in BASIC. There was a scarcity of software and BASIC was built into the old Apple IIs so it was convenient to teach our students programming. While we were working on our Apple II computer, software publishers emerged. The Minnesota Educational Computing Consortium (MCC) was the largest microcomputer software provider and others followed in its footsteps.

Figure 1.13
Apple II
(*Source:* Courtesy Apple Computer, Inc.)

---

[6] In the early 1960s all computers were called mainframes in reference to the cabinet that held the central processing unit. As time progressed, very large computers began to be called mainframe computers.

In the early 1980s I wanted to bring computers to elementary teachers, so I bought 35 pocket Sharp PC-1211 computers and taught programming off campus. Using the Apple IIe as a demonstration machine, I showed how to use software such as *Lemonade Stand* and use a word processor program called *Bank Street Writer*. At that time, educational software was limited and inadequate, and the focus was still on teaching the programming language BASIC, followed shortly thereafter by Logo. Many teachers wanted to design their own software language using authoring programs such as Pilot and SuperPilot. Over time, interest in this type of software waned as we discovered how much time and expertise were needed to develop good courseware. Instead, many of us decided it would be more productive to purchase packaged software programs.

Networking emerged in the 1980s and 1990s when administrators and school districts began to see the value of connecting computers and users. **Networking** consists of connecting a group of computers and peripherals to a communication system. School districts realized that computers networked to a central server could provide instruction more efficiently and at a lower cost than stand-alone machines.

In 1992, I was using the Internet with UNIX commands to do library research. This type of usage made the Internet difficult for my students. Around this time, Swiss researchers developed the **World Wide Web**[7], a system that enables the user to move smoothly through the Internet, jumping from one document to another. Software tools called *browsers* were developed that made access to Internet resources uncomplicated. With the introduction of Mosaic browser Figure 1.14 in 1994, the Internet became easy for everyone to use. This browser allowed users to view pictures and documents by simply clicking on a mouse. Educators all over the world quickly became interested in the computers and began to see the potential for this powerful technology. Also with the production of quality software, the computer's role had changed from a device used for computer programming to an instrument that could efficiently be integrated into the curriculum. We used computers for word processing, database management, spreadsheets, graphics generation, and desktop publishing.

In the last half of the 1990s the emphasis has once more shifted and teachers and students began using the Internet as a huge library resource, and electronic mail proliferated. (In fact, my colleagues and students communicate by e-mail to

Figure 1.14
Mosaic
(*Source:* Credit NCSA/
University of Illinois)

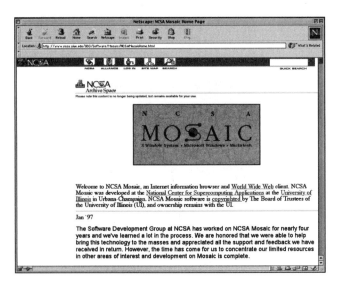

[7]"The World Wide Web is made up of "Web servers" that store and disseminate "Web pages," which are "rich" documents that contain text, graphics, animations, and videos to anyone with an Internet connection." (Freedman, 2008)

such an extent that I am relieved when our server breaks down.) Because of the interest in technology, in 1998, the International Society for Technology in Education (ISTE) developed the National Educational Technology Standards (NETS) for teachers, students, and administrators. These standards discuss what students should know and be able to accomplish with technology. Furthermore, accreditation standards for teacher education institutions discussed expectations for teacher competency in preparation programs. You will find this document at ISTE's Web site, http://cnets.iste.org/teachers/t_stands.html. The following timeline shows these important educational milestones. The National Educational Technology Standards for Students are listed on the back inside cover

TIME LINE OF EDUCATIONAL MILESTONES

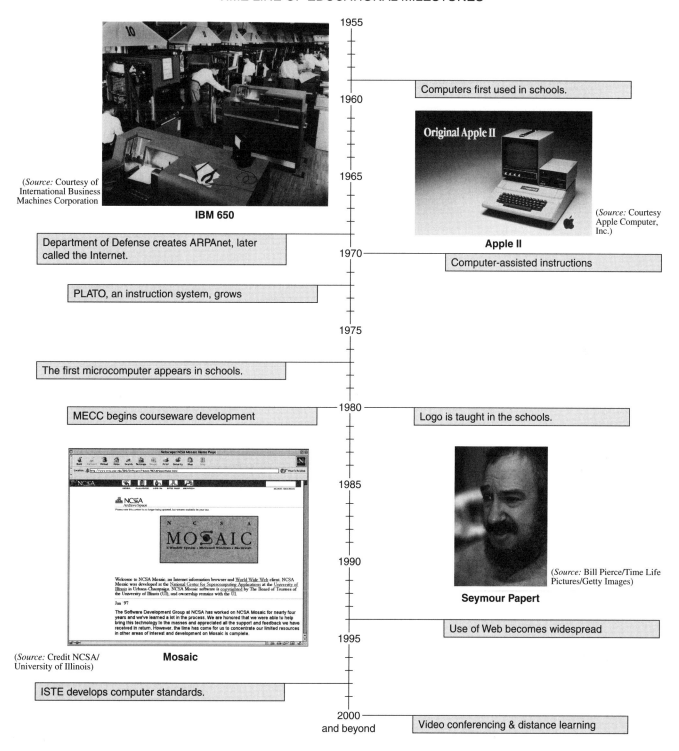

(*Source:* Courtesy of International Business Machines Corporation

IBM 650

(*Source:* Courtesy Apple Computer, Inc.)

Apple II

Original Apple II

(*Source:* Bill Pierce/Time Life Pictures/Getty Images)

Seymour Papert

(*Source:* Credit NCSA/ University of Illinois)   **Mosaic**

1955

1960 — Computers first used in schools.

1965

Department of Defense creates ARPAnet, later called the Internet.

1970 — Computer-assisted instructions

PLATO, an instruction system, grows

1975

The first microcomputer appears in schools.

1980 — MECC begins courseware development   Logo is taught in the schools.

1985

1990

Use of Web becomes widespread

1995

ISTE develops computer standards.

2000 and beyond   Video conferencing & distance learning

of this textbook. The National Educational Standards for Teachers are listed on the front inside cover of this textbook.

In the 21st century computers are being used to help students with special needs realize their potential. Presently, there are more online and distance learning courses in higher education and the K–12 schools. Students and teachers are increasingly using computerized electronic organizers such as the Palm and Blackberry. I am presently showing my students how to do Podcasts, and my colleagues are delivering their lecture notes through this media. We are doing video conferencing and the iPod is being used as a hard drive, music, and lecture note delivery system. I can only speculate on what the next generation of educational computers will bring (see Chapter 17).

SUMMARY

The origin of computers can be traced back to inventors who were interested in processing information and developing devices to simplify tedious arithmetic calculations. In the 1900s, inventors constructed the earliest electro-mechanical computer, quickly replaced by the faster electronic computer. At first the computers filled large rooms and electricity was conducted using vacuum tubes. Transistors then replaced the vacuum tubes, which were replaced by integrated circuits and then large-scale integrated circuit chips. Recently there have been developments in artificial intelligence, logical inference, and parallel processing and radical changes in the Internet. Along the way, computers have become an indispensable tool for teachers, students, and administrators—starting with PLATO, an instructional system, and recently the widespread use of the World Wide Web. Like a snowball rolling down a hill, expanding as it speeds up, the use of the computer in education is certain to avalanche.

STUDY AND ONLINE RESOURCES

CHAPTER 1 ONLINE RESOURCES

In the **student section** of the book's online site at **http://www.wiley.com/college/sharp**, you will find PDFs on BASIC, Logo, and calculating devices along with top-rated Web sites and a chapter quiz. (To read or print the PDFs, open them with Adobe Reader.) Watch the video tutorial online and learn how to conduct an Internet search.

CHAPTER MASTERY TEST

Lets check for chapter comprehension with a short mastery test. Key Terms, Computer Lab, and Suggested Readings and References follow the test.

1. Discuss briefly the contributions made to the computer field by the following individuals: (a) Howard Aiken, (b) Charles Babbage, (c) Herman Hollerith, and (d) John Atanasoff.

2. Identify and place in correct order two of the major inventions in the field of computing.

3. Explain the importance of transistors and microprocessors in the development of modern computers.

4. What computer opportunities would a sixth grader have in 1953 as opposed to a sixth grader in 2008?

5. Why was Hollerith's Tabulating Machine developed for the 1890 census significant for the future of computing?

6. Explain the discovery that made personal computers possible.

7. Explain why Charles Babbage might be considered to have been born at the wrong time.

8. What are Steve Jobs's and Steve Wozniak's major achievements in the computer field?

9. Explain why Ada Lovelace deserves an important place in the history of computers.

10. What spearheaded the development of the electronic digital computer?

11. What are Bill Gates's and Paul Allen's major achievements in the computer field?

12. What was George Boole's lasting contribution to computer history?

13. Why did the Internet suddenly become popular?

14. Name two major events that increased the use of the computer in education.

15. Why did programming suddenly fall out of favor?

16. What are the Educational Technology Standards for teachers and students?

17. Why did BASIC become so popular in the 1980s?

18. Name two ways that teachers can integrate the computer into their classrooms.

KEY TERMS

Ada p. 4
BASIC p. 8
Boolean algebra p. 3
Commercial computer p. 7
Computer-assisted instruction (CAI) p. 11

Debug p. 5
Fifth generation of computers p. 10
First generation of computers p. 6
Fourth generation of computers p. 7
Integrated circuits p. 7

Internet p. 11
Mainframe p. 11
Microprocessor chip p. 7
Networking p. 12
PLATO p. 11
Second generation of computers p. 7

Third generation of computers p. 7
Time-sharing p. 11
Transistor p. 7
World Wide Web p. 12

 COMPUTER LAB: Activities for Mastery And Your Portfolio

1.1 Interactive Time Line: The Modern History of Computers Test your knowledge of the history of computers with this time line.

1.2 Prepare a paper on the 1973 court trial between Sperry Rand and Honeywell. In this case, Judge Larson ruled that "Eckert and Mauchly did not themselves invent the electronic digital computer, but instead derived the subject matter from one John V. Atanasoff."

1.3 Using a computer time line program such as Tom Snyder's *TimeLiner 5.1*, list at least 10 significant computer events from 1863 to 2008.

1.4 Prepare an in-depth research report on the life of an important inventor and his or her contribution to the history of computers. Watch the video tutorial online and learn how to conduct an Internet search.

1.5 Write three biographical sketches on important women in the computer field, discussing their achievements.

1.6 Use three magazines to investigate developments in educational computing that occurred during the last five years. Write a brief summary of the findings.

SUGGESTED READINGS AND REFERENCES

Asimov, Isaac. *How Did We Find Out About Computers?* New York: Walker, 1984.

Aspray, William. "John Von Neumann's Contributions to Computing and Computer Science." *Annals of the History of Computing* 11, no. 3 (1989): 165.

Austrian, G. *Herman Hollerith: Forgotten Giant of Information Processing.* New York: Columbia University Press, 1982.

Bernstein, J. *The Analytical Engine.* New York: Morrow, 1981.

Bruce, Linda. "The Standards Approach: Planning for Excellence in Distance Education." *Syllabus* 17, no. 2 (September 2003): 29–31.

Freedman, A. *The Computer Desktop Encyclopedia.* New York: American Management Association, 2008, at http://www.com puterlanguage.com/techweb.html

Gates, Bill, Nathan Myhrvold, and Peter Rinearson. *The Road Ahead.* New York: Viking Penguin, 1996.

Goldstine, H. *The Computer from Pascal to Von Neumann.* Princeton, N.J.: Princeton University Press, 1972.

Macintosh, Allan R. "Dr. Atanasoff's Computer." *Scientific American* 259, no. 2 (August 1, 1988): 90.

McDonald, Glenn, and Cameron Crotty. "The Digital Future." *PC World,* January 1, 2000, pp. 116–134.

Metropolis, N., J. Howlett, and G. C. Rota, eds. *A History of Computing in the Twentieth Century.* New York: Academic Press, 1980.

Mollenhoff, Clark R. "Forgotten Father of the Computer." *The World & I* (March 1990): 319–332.

Molnar, Andrew R. "Computers in Education—a Brief History." *T.H.E. Journal* 24, no. 11 (June 1997): 59–62.

Moore, Johanna D. "Making Computer Tutors More Like Humans." *Journal of Artificial Intelligence in Education* 7, no. 2 (1996): 181–214.

Morrison, P., and E. Morrison, eds. *Charles Babbage and His Calculating Engines.* New York: Dover, 1961.

Naisbitt, John. *Megatrends: Ten New Directions Transforming Our Lives.* New York: Warner Books, 1982.

Naisbitt, John. *Megatrends 2000: Ten New Directions for the 1990s.* New York: Morrow, 1990.

Niemiec, Richard P., and Richard J. Walberg. "From Teaching Machines to Microcomputers: Some Milestones in the History of Computer-Based Instruction." *Journal of Research on Computing in Education* 21, no. 3 (Spring 1989): 263.

Palfreman, Jon, and Doron Swade. *The Dream Machine.* London: BBC Books, 1991.

Papert, Seymour. *Mindstorms: Children, Computers and Powerful Ideas.* New York: Basic Books, 1980.

Papert, Seymour, and Nicholas Negroponte. *The Connected Family: Bridging the Digital Generation Gap.* Atlanta: Longstreet Press, 1996.

Pfaffenberger, Bryan. *Webster's New World Dictionary Computer Dictionary,* 10th ed. New York: Que, 2003.

Pfaffenberger, Bryan, Bill Daley, and Roberta Baber. *Computers in Your Future 2004,* 6th ed. Upper Saddle River, NJ: Prentice Hall, 2003.

Pullan, J. M. *A History of the Abacus.* New York: Praeger, 1968.

Resick, Rosalind. "Pressing Mosaic." *Internet* (October 1994): 81–88.

Ritchie, David. *The Computer Pioneers: The Making of the Modern Computer.* New York: Simon and Schuster, 1986.

Roblyer, M. D. *Integrating Educational Technology into Teaching,* 4th ed. Columbus, Ohio: Pearson Merrill Prentice Hall, 2006.

Takahashi, D. "A Dogged Inventor Makes the Computer Industry Say: Hello, Mr. Chip." *Los Angeles Times,* October 21, 1990, p. C1.

Waldrop, M. Mitchell. "The Origins of Personal Computing." *Scientific American* 285, no. 6 (December 2001): 84–91.

Getting Started on the Computer

Integrating Computer Hardware into the Classroom

A typical computer system found in any classroom has a monitor, keyboard, mouse, printer, hard disk drive, CD-ROM drive or DVD drive, modem, and speakers. Before you buy educational software, you should know this and more about computer hardware. In the process of reading the chapter, you will learn how to pick out hardware for the classroom by using specific criteria. You will review a checklist designed to help you select the right computer or monitor for your classroom. You will examine the hardware that is the most frequently used in the classroom. Finally, you will learn how to use the Online Hardware Reference Guide, designed especially for teachers.

Using the computer, students and teachers can do the following:

students can

- learn about basic computer components,
- learn about output devices,
- use a hardware reference guide,
- learn about input devices,
- write hardware reviews and,
- use a hardware evaluation checklist.

teachers can

- create a hardware reference guide,
- devise a hardware checklist,
- find lesson plans and instructional material,
- discuss different hardware sites,
- demonstrate different hardware devices.

objectives

Upon completing this chapter, you will be able to do the following:

1 Discuss how the basic components of a computer system operate.

2 Describe the major input devices and explain how each works.

3 Describe the major output devices and explain how each works.

4 Choose appropriate hardware in terms of established criteria.

What is a Computer?

A computer is a machine that can handle huge amounts of information at an incredible speed. Computers do not have brains, feelings, or the ability to solve their own problems; they can solve only those problems they have been programmed to solve. A common computer system found in a typical classroom might have a monitor, keyboard, mouse, printer, hard disk drive, central processing unit (CPU), CD-ROM or DVD drive, microphone, digital camera, modem, and speakers. Figure 2.1 is an example of a computer and its different components.

A computer performs four tasks:

1. receiving input such as figures, facts, or sets of instructions;
2. storing information by placing it in its memory;
3. processing the data by acting on the information; and
4. outputting the information by generating the results of the processing.

An example may shed some light on how the computer performs its four basic tasks. Imagine that Professor Friedman is conducting research. She has collected her data carefully and now wants the computer to do some statistical analysis on the data. She installs her statistical program onto the hard drive of her computer. Next, using the keyboard, she enters her data into the spreadsheet of the statistical program and chooses "Analysis of Variance" from the statistical procedures.

Figure 2.1

The Computer and Its Components

(*Source:* © 2008 Jupiterimages Corporation)

The computer stores the data she enters in memory and then processes this information by performing the necessary statistical calculations in its central processing. The professor sees the results of the analysis on the screen or on a printout from the printer.

Elements of a Computer

A computer system consists of a central processing unit and the peripheral devices connected to it, along with the computer's operating system. The central processor, or CPU, is contained on a single chip called a **microprocessor**. The memory, RAM (random access memory), and ROM (read only memory) of the computer are also stored on computer chips.

COMPUTER CHIPS

A **computer chip** is a silicon wafer, approximately 1/16-inch wide and 1/30-inch thick, that holds from a few dozen to millions of electronic components. The term *chip* is synonymous with *integrated circuit.* Computer chips are encased in plastic to protect them. Metal pins on the chips enable them to be plugged into a computer circuit board. Figure 2.2 shows a chip encased in its plastic protection. If you look carefully at this chip, you can see tiny circuits etched on the metal. The process of putting these circuits on one chip and connecting them together is called **large-scale integration (LSI)** or **very-large-scale integration (VLSI)**. This complex procedure, which involves engineering, plotting, photography, baking, and magnetism, permits silicon chips to be produced in large quantities at a very low cost.

Today, a single chip can hold hundreds of millions of transistors. With wafer scale integration, eventually these circuits will be built in overlapping layers, and they will hold billions of transistors.

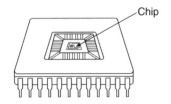

Figure 2.2

Computer Chip Encased in Plastic

CIRCUIT BOARDS

In the microcomputer, the RAM chips, ROM chips, CPU chips, and other components are plugged into a flat board called a **printed circuit board** (Figure 2.3). The other side of this board is printed with electrical conductive pathways among the components. A circuit board in 1960 connected together discrete components; today the boards connect chips that each contains one thousand to hundreds of millions of transistors with only a few components (Freedman, 2008).

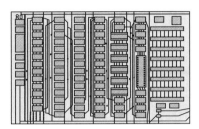

Figure 2.3
Printed Circuit Board

CENTRAL PROCESSING UNIT

The **central processing unit (CPU)**, also called the *processor*, is the brains of the computer. A personal computer's central processor is contained on a single chip called a *microprocessor*, which is smaller than a fingernail. This unit is essential because it controls the way the computer operates. Whenever a programmer designs software that gives instructions to the computer, it is the processor that executes these instructions. The central processor gets instructions from memory and either carries out the instructions or tells other components to follow the instructions. Then it follows the next set of instructions. This procedure is repeated until the task is completed. The central processing unit (Figure 2.4) consists of three components: the control unit, the arithmetic unit, and the logic unit. In the majority of microcomputers, the arithmetic unit and the logic unit are combined and are referred to as the **arithmetic logic unit (ALU)**.

The **control unit** verifies that the computer carries out instructions, transfers instructions to the main memory for storage, and relays information back and forth between the main memory and the ALU. The arithmetic logic unit carries out all the arithmetic operations and logical decisions. Since the central processing unit can work only on small amounts of information at a time, it needs a way to store information, or memory, while it is not being processed.

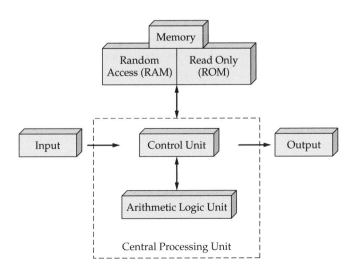

Figure 2.4
Central Processing Unit

MEMORY

Two types of chips take care of a computer's internal memory: **read only memory (ROM)** chips and **random access memory (RAM)** chips. ROM chips store information permanently in a computer's memory, and this memory supplies the computer with a list of operating instructions. These instructions are burned into the computer during the manufacturing process. For example, most computers have a program in ROM that uploads the screen symbols, such as a cursor (usually in the form of a blinking square or line). ROM is called *nonvolatile memory* because it does not disappear when the computer is turned off. There is nothing an ordinary computer user can do to remove or replace the instructions of ROM. BASIC was stored in the ROM of the Apple II line of computers, and today there are ROM chips in microwave ovens, watches, and calculators.

Unlike the information on ROM chips, the information stored in RAM can be modified; users can write, read, and erase this information. This type of memory needs a constant power supply so that the data are not lost. RAM is referred to as *volatile memory* because of its temporary nature. Whenever a user turns off the computer, he or she loses whatever information is in RAM. The basic unit for RAM storage is a **byte**, the space available to hold letters, numbers, and special characters.[1]

In the 1970s, a computer user normally manipulated thousands of characters at a time so RAM size was measured in **kilobytes**, or thousands of bytes (the symbol for kilobytes is K). For example, a computer that had 512K was capable of holding approximately 512,000 numbers, symbols, and letters.[2] In the early 1980s, computers usually had a memory size of 64K, which was considered more than adequate for a personal computer. Today, RAM size is discussed in terms of **megabytes (MB)**, or millions of bytes, **gigabytes (GB)**, or billions of bytes, and **terabytes**, or trillions of bytes.

The amount of RAM chips a computer has determines the amount of information that can be retained in memory, the size and number of programs that can be run simultaneously, and the amount of data that will be processed immediately. Programs vary in their memory requirements; for example, the software *Inspiration* 8 needs 5 MB of RAM to run on a Macintosh with System OS X or later, while 512 MB of RAM or higher is recommended for Microsoft Office 2007. Fortunately, the RAM size of most computers can be expanded by adding RAM chips.

BINARY NOTATION

All computer input is converted through **binary notation** into binary numbers consisting of two digits, 0 and 1. An instruction that is read as a 1 tells the computer to turn on a circuit, and an instruction read as a 0 tells the computer to turn off the circuit. The digits 0 and 1 are called **bits**, short for *b*inary dig*its*. The computer can represent letters, numbers, and symbols by combining these individual bits into a binary code. Each character or letter typed is translated into a byte by turning circuits off and on. This whole procedure happens at lightning speed whenever a user hits a key on the computer keyboard. For example, when the user types the letter *Z,* the computer translates it into 01011010. When the user types the number 1, it is translated into 00110001. Every character on the keyboard has a different code combination.

---

[1] Bytes are discussed in more detail in the *Binary Notation* section of this chapter.
[2] The accurate number is 524,288 ($512 \times 1{,}024$) because the computer uses powers of 2, and 2^{10} is 1,024. A kilobyte then represents 1,024, or approximately 1,000, bytes.

OPERATING SYSTEMS

In the early days of computing, a person operated a computer with an elaborate control panel. Later, computer programmers designed a program that would allow the computer to control its own operation. This control program is the **operating system** of the computer, and its major task is to handle the transfer of data and programs to and from the computer's disks. The operating system can display a directory showing the names of programs stored on the disk, it can copy a program from one disk to another, and it can display and print the contents of any file on the screen. The operating system controls the computer components and allows them to communicate with each other. There are many other functions that an operating system performs; the computer's system manual enumerates them.

Different computers have different operating systems. The same computer, moreover, may have more than one operating system available to it. Two recent well-known operating systems are Macintosh OS X–Leopard and Windows Vista.

Lacking a single standard operating system, all computers are not compatible. Companies have sought ways to solve this incompatibility problem by producing emulation programs and cards that were placed in the computers. In 2006 Apple introduced its Intel-powered Macintoshes with *Boot Camp* software, which let you run Windows software on the Macintosh. You cannot run multiple operating systems but just one system at a time. *Parallels Desktop for Mac* software (Parallels) went a step further and a user could run Windows alongside the Macintosh OS X on the Intel-powered Apple computers.

In the past, different models of computers varied in the way their operating systems were supplied to them. Presently, the majority of computers have hard disk drives, and their operating systems are installed from a DVD onto the hard disks. Previously, when operating systems were stored on floppy disks, the user would insert the disk into a disk drive, turn on the computer, and wait for it to run a small program usually stored in the ROM of the computer. This program's purpose was to *load* the operating system into the main memory of the computer and then turn over its authority to the operating system. The procedure of starting the computer so that it could load its operating system became known as **booting the system**, because the small program that helped it do this was called a *bootstrap loader*, as the initial loading was analogous to "lifting yourself by your own bootstraps."

Since its inception, the Macintosh's trademark has been its ease of use. It had the most workable operating system, a characteristic that distinguished it from other systems. Practically every Macintosh application program used the same user interface, so the user did not have to relearn commands each time he or she used a different application. The success of the Macintosh interface led Microsoft to introduce its similar interface known as Windows. Both Apple Macintosh OS X–Leopard and Microsoft's Windows Vista feature **graphical user interfaces (GUIs)** in which the user points with the mouse to a picture or icon to select a program instead of typing commands.

Let us take a look at the opening screens of these particular versions of the Macintosh and Windows operating systems and a third operating system known as Linux.

Macintosh OS X–Leopard.   The new Macintosh operating system referred to as Mac OS X combines UNIX with the ease of use of the Macintosh. This system has translucent buttons and an aqua interface. At the bottom of the screen, Mac OS X shows icons of folders, applications, and documents (Figure 2.5). The system's Finder gives users an extremely fast means of finding files, running applications, and communicating with people. This version offers enhanced speech recognition, Internet functionality, and multimedia capabilities.

Figure 2.5
Macintosh Opening Screen
(*Source:* Reprinted with permission from Apple, Inc.)

Windows Vista.   The Windows Vista operating system features an easy user interface, more security, and unique support services. The system is built to take advantage of the Internet and provide support for mobile users. This version has brand new tools, and the ability to see what your files contain without opening them. As you can see from Windows' opening screen in Figure 2.6, the system is more attractive visually. There is a Windows Sidebar that gives users access to gadgets, such as the Windows Media Player controls or picture slide shows.

Figure 2.6
Windows Opening Screen
(*Source:* Reprinted with permission from Microsoft Corporation)

Linux.   In 1991, Linux, a version of UNIX, was developed by Linus Torvalds at the University of Helsinki in Finland. Torvalds, a computer science student, turned Minix, a classroom teaching tool, into Linux. Numerous programmers have contributed to this system. Today, Linux is developed under the GNU General Public License, and its source code is freely available to anyone. This does not mean Linux is free. Companies and developers may charge money for Linux as long as the source code remains available. Linux runs on a variety of hardware platforms including Alpha, PowerPC, × 86 PCs, and IBM's product line. The distribution of Linux along with technical support and training are available for a fee from sellers such as Red Hat Software (www.redhat.com) and The SCO Group (www.sco.com). Linux is a very stable, cost-effective, and secure operating system and that is why it has gained popularity, and its usage is expected to grow. Linux can be used for networking and software development. VA Linux Systems has a Web site that discusses Linux (www.linux.com), and Antone Gonsalves has written a good reference text. For further discussion of the

Macintosh and Microsoft Windows operating systems, consult operating system manuals or visit the Internet sites listed online at http://www.wiley.com/college/sharp.

Hardware Overview

The **hardware** of a computer system includes the electronic components, boards, wires, and peripherals. Buying hardware for your classroom is a complicated and time-consuming job that requires an examination of many factors.

Before you begin the process of selecting hardware, you first must choose the software that meets the needs of your class. The **software** instructs the computer hardware to perform various tasks. If you have only hardware, you are powerless to accomplish anything with the computer, much as if you had a car without fuel. Selecting software is no easy task either. First, you must determine your primary needs and then you must estimate your future needs. For example, you might be satisfied initially with software such as *PrintShop*, but in time you will require a sophisticated desktop program such as *Quark XPress*. If you want to use an advanced program like *Quark XPress* you will need computer hardware with ample memory.

Regardless of your software needs, however, you will benefit from spending time learning about available hardware, its capabilities, and its functions. Current computer magazines (such as *MacWorld* or *PC Magazine*) will alert you to the latest hardware developments. You can save time and money by being prepared to ask the right questions.

We will look at some of the factors that most influence a teacher or student's hardware decisions. We briefly examine some of the basic hardware equipment available for classrooms.

HARDWARE REFERENCE GUIDE FOR TEACHERS

Use the *Hardware Reference Guide for Teachers* to help answer questions in this chapter and broaden your knowledge about hardware devices that are available in the classroom. This picture reference guide is available online at **http://www.wiley.com/college/sharp**. You can download it as a PDF file.

INPUT DEVICES

An input device gives information to the computer system so that it can perform its tasks. Years ago, the keypunch machine was the major means of input; today, it is the keyboard (Figure 2.7). However, the keyboard suffers from some drawbacks.

(*Source:* iStockphoto)

Figures 2.7
Keyboard

It is not ideal for making screen selections and an inexperience typist is more likely to make mistakes when using the keyboard for screen selection. As a result, computer manufacturers created pointing devices that lessen the need for a keyboard.

Today, most computers use both a keyboard and supplemental pointing devices such as a joystick, mouse, trackball, and trackpad (Figure 2.8).

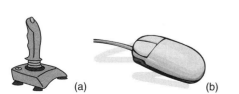

(a)   (b)   (c)   (d)

(*Source*: Courtesy Kensington Computer Product Group)

Figures 2.8
(a) Joystick, **(b)** Mouse, **(c)** Trackball **(d)** Trackpad
(*Source:* © 2008 Jupiterimages Corporation)

In addition to pointing devices, many other input devices are used in the classroom. These devices include optical scanning devices that utilize laser capabilities. The laser searches for groups of dots that represent marks, characters, or lines. These input devices differ from each other in terms of the programs used and the way the computer massages the data.

Optical Mark Reader. The optical mark reader (OMR) was designed initially to read penciled or graphic information on exam answer sheets. Many schools and school districts use the optical mark reader to grade standardized tests. With the proper software, the OMR will also keep library and attendance records and report grades.

Scanners. The scanner is enjoying popularity in schools because of its affordability and its usefulness in desktop publishing, electronic portfolios, faxing, and optical character recognition (OCR). OCR is machine recognition of typed or printed text. By using OCR software such as Omini Page Pro (ScanSoft) with a scanner, a student can rapidly enter a printed page into the computer. The scanner can also transform images into electronic images. Figure 2.9 is a photograph of my husband and son that was scanned into the computer.

Scanners digitize photographs or line art and stores the images as files that can be transferred into paint programs or directly into word processing programs. If you create a newsletter and want to insert a picture into the text, you scan the picture, copy it, and then "paste" it into the document. Scanners used for this purpose come in a variety of forms; the most common in the classroom are flatbed and handhelds. The film scanner is used to a lesser degree (Figure 2.10).

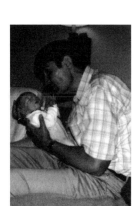

Figure 2.9
Scanned Photograph

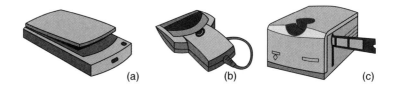

Figure 2.10
(a) Flatbed, **(b)** Handheld, and **(c)** Film Scanner
(*Source:* © 2008 Jupiterimages Corporation)

(a)   (b)   (c)

Digital Cameras. Currently, interest in digital cameras is increasing in schools all over the country. The digital camera records images in a digital format. The digital camera is a quick way to get photos into computer-readable form, which can be used for school reports, desktop publishing, security badges, pictures for Web pages, or parents' notes. (See Chapter 10 for complete coverage of digital photography in the classroom.)

Video Conferencing or Webcam Cameras. Webcams are small cameras that teachers and students can use to take pictures for newsletters or Web sites, to make live video, and to take simple e-mail videos and pictures to share with other classes or other school districts. Students can also use these live cameras to see and interact with people and places around the world through a Web browser. An easy way to find live Webcams is by typing "Webcam" in your search engine.

(*Source:* iStockphoto)

HANDHELD COMPUTERS

Students and teachers are increasingly using electronic organizers, Personal Data Assistants (PDAs), and handheld computers. They have become quite affordable compared to desktop computers. These devices enable you to take notes, conduct scientific data collection and analysis, see photos and video clips, send and receive faxes, send e-mail, search the Internet, listen to MP3s, keep a calendar, and collect information from distant databases. For the education market, some machines provide computer access for every student in the classroom and are quite inexpensive. For example, students can use the NEO (AlphaSmart) (Figure 2.11) to do most of their work wherever they happen to be—in a classroom, in the lab, on a field trip, or at home.

 See the online site to find authors Janet Caughlin and Tony Vincent's article on handheld computers.

(*Source:* Courtesy Renaissance Learning, Inc.)

Figure 2.11
NEO in the Classroom

OUTPUT DEVICES

One of the most essential output devices is the **printer**, which gives users a permanent record of their work by producing a printout, or hard copy. For years, the dot-matrix printer was the most widely used printer. With the price reduction of laser printers and the advances in inkjet technology, this situation has changed and the dot-matrix printer has disappeared from the majority of classrooms. The two types of printers most often found in the classroom are the inkjet and laser (Figure 2.12). Even though the cost of the color inkjet printer has been decreasing steadily, there is a significant cost associated with the purchase of the ink cartridges. The color laser printer has become almost as popular as the inkjet because of its price (under $300) and near-professional quality print.

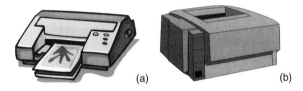

(a)   (b)

Figure 2.12
(a) Inkjet and **(b)** Laser
(*Source:* © 2008 Jupiterimages Corporation)

SCREEN DISPLAYS

The computer could function without peripherals such as digital cameras or speakers, but the monitor is an essential piece of equipment. The most frequently used types of monitors in the classroom are the **cathode ray tube** (CRT) monitor (Figure 2.13a) and the **liquid crystal display (LCD)** monitor (Figure 2.13b).

(a)   (b)

Figures 2.13
(a) Cathode Ray Tube Monitor
and **(b)** LCD Monitor

(*Source:* Courtesy ViewSonic Corporation)   (*Source:* iStockphoto)

A CRT is "a vacuum tube used as a display screen in a computer monitor or TV" (Freedman, 2008). Recently, the CRT is disappearing from the classroom and being replaced by the LCD monitors. The LCD is created by positioning a liquid crystal material between two sheets of polarizing material squeezed between two glass panels. LCD monitors have a smaller footprint, lower power consumption, and less radiation and screen glare. Teachers and students are constantly using laptops with LCD displays for presentation, networking, and carrying their work with them. In the future, other displays such as the organic light-emitting diodes (OLED) display will become popular (see Chapter 17).

CLASSROOM PRESENTATION DEVICES

The classroom teacher needs a way to use the computer to demonstrate a program or concept to the entire class. Presentation tools are becoming very popular with teachers who want to share information with small and large groups of students. Currently, four methods are used: interactive whiteboard, LCD projection panel, projector, and video scan converter. We will only discuss the interactive whiteboard. (Refer to the online *Hardware Reference Guide for Teachers* for the rest of these hardware devices.)

The Interactive whiteboard is a touch-sensitive screen that is commonly white and resembles a dry-erase board (Figure 2.14). Where the blackboard is just a simple board needing nothing other than chalk and eraser, the interactive whiteboard needs a computer, a projector, interactive whiteboard, and special markers. When this hookup is complete, users can then look at images, manipulate them, and add comments using a special pen or highlighter. The teacher can use his or her finger like a mouse and run applications like PowerPoint from this board.

Figure 2.14
Interactive Whiteboard
(*Source:* ©2001-2008 SMART Technologies ULC. All rights reserved)

These boards are colorful, motivating, and can accommodate different age groups and motor skills. Teachers can share lessons with other individuals outside the classroom. She or he can save and post these lessons. An English teacher can display writing and have a group of students brainstorm and edit the material and save it for future use. The history teacher can use this device to display pictures, videos, and maps to motivate students. The possibilities for this technology in the classroom are promising. However, these boards are expensive and may need someone with expertise to make technical adjustments.

STORAGE DEVICES

There are (a) floppy disks, (b) zip disks, (c) USB drives, (d) hard drives, and (e) optical discs typically found in a classroom (Figure 2.15). The laser discs have all but disappeared.

The **floppy disk**, introduced by IBM in 1971, was for a long time the most prevalent means of storage. Today, the majority of new laptop computers come without a

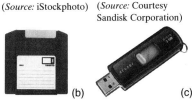

(*Source:* iStockphoto) (*Source:* Courtesy Sandisk Corporation)

(a)   (b)   (c)   (d)   (e)

Figure 2.15
Storage Devices
(*Source:* © 2008 Jupiterimages Corporation)

floppy drive. With the advent of Iomega's **Zip disk**, storage media changed forever. The Zip disk became popular because of its ability to store much more data than the floppy disk. The first Zip disks stored 100 MB. Now they store 750 MB.

The latest rage is the **USB drive**, or flash drive, which is capable of storing more information than Zip disks. The USB mini flash drives, usually the size of a fat pen, largely fulfill data-exchange needs for USB-equipped PCs. You can easily store digital photos, MP3 files, PowerPoint presentations, and Word documents on them.

The **hard drive** stores huge amounts of data. Teachers can even use portable hard drives as backup. The major flaw with a hard drive is it can wear out in three to five years.

The **optical disc**, which has a 30-year life expectancy, is the hard drive's likely successor. Optical storage currently found in schools consists of compact discs (CDs), compact disc read only memory (CD-ROMs), and digital versatile discs (DVD-ROM). Table 2.1 shows the storage capabilities of these media.

There are discs that can be recorded on once for archival purposes such as CD-Rs (CD-recordable). DVDs, which hold more information, consist of DVD-Rs (DVD-recordable) and DVD+Rs (DVD+recordable). In addition, there are erasable optical discs.

Table 2.1   Storage Capabilities of Current Media*

Compact disc	74 minutes of stereo audio
Floppy disk	Up to 1.44 MB
Hard drive	20 GB and above 3 Terabytes
Zip disk	Up to 750 MB
USB drive	64 MB to 12 GB
CD-ROM	650 MB
DVD-ROM	4.7–17 GB

*For more information on the storage mentioned here, consult the online *Hardware Reference Guide for Teachers*.

(*Source:* © 2008 Jupiterimages Corporation)

FAX MACHINE AND MODEM

The facsimile (fax) machine and the modem are two more input/output devices. The **fax machine** enables users to transmit text and images between distant locations. The **modem** enables two computers to communicate with each other over communications lines, such as telephone lines. (Refer to Chapter 3 for a discussion of the modem.)

iPOD

Because of the **iPod's** (Figure 2.16a) popularity as a music player, educators began using the iPod in the K–12 classroom and at the college level. Students with special needs who formerly had test content read aloud to them could download their test, listen on their earphones, and see the test on their video iPod. In schools across the country students created **Podcasts** or non-music audio broadcasts for fellow students to download to their iPods. University students began using the iPod to download Podcasts of a professor's lectures, listen to foreign language lessons and music selections from music courses, and download well-known classical books. In addition, students used their iPod as a storage drive, recorder, to share digital content, and listen to travel logs.

At the MacWorld 2007 conference, Apple introduced a breakthrough device called the iPhone, which combined three devices in one. The iPhone (Figure 2.16b) as it was called combined a widescreen iPod with a mobile phone and an Internet device for e-mail, Web browsing, and maps.

Figure 2.16
(a) iPod and **(b)** iPhone

(a)   (b)

(*Source:* Courtesy Apple Computer, Inc.)

(*Source:* Courtesy Apple Computer, Inc.)

Computer Selection Criteria

The following guidelines will help you purchase a desktop, portable, or handheld computer.

ABILITY TO RUN SOFTWARE APPLICATIONS

The software applications you will be using will determine the computer that you select. You may not be able to buy a certain computer because it does not run the particular software that you need to use in your district. Software programs also have memory and storage requirements as well as additional input/output device needs, which are factors that influence buying decisions. Most computers come bundled with software such as browser or word processing software.

TYPE OF COMPUTER

Is the computer compatible with other computers in the school district? How easy is it to use the equipment? Is the documentation well written? Are the weight and size of the machine important considerations? How durable is the machine? Is it too delicate for classroom use? One of your main decisions is whether to buy a computer equipped with a Windows system or a Macintosh system. The Macintosh is still easier to use, set up, and expand than is a Windows computer. However, Windows computers have a wider selection of peripherals and software. If you are interested in ease of use and expansion, graphics, multimedia, and video, buy a Macintosh; if you need spreadsheets and databases and a wider assortment of peripherals, buy a Windows system.

MEMORY

A very important consideration during the hardware selection process is the computer's random access memory, the working memory. In the early 1980s, 64K of RAM was considered more than adequate for running educational software. Today, many applications need 32 MB or more of memory, and these memory requirements are continually increasing. For example, *Timeliner 5.1* (Tom Snyder) requires 32 MB to run its Windows version effectively. Every time software publishers upgrade programs, they add more features requiring more memory. The amount of RAM a computer has affects the kind of software it is capable of running. Any new system you are purchasing should have a minimum of 2–4 Gigabytes of memory of RAM. Buy as much RAM as you can afford because you can never have too much.

EXPANDABILITY

Consider these questions when your computer system is not powerful enough for your needs: Can you upgrade the processor chip? Can the memory of the computer be increased? Can special equipment be added to the machine for the student with disabilities? Is the computer designed so that extra peripherals such as a scanner can be added easily? Does your computer have **expansion slots**? In other words, does your computer have a receptacle inside that will accept expansion boards or printed circuit boards? These boards, or *cards*, as they are called, expand the computer's ability so that it can accept other peripheral devices such as sound cards.

SPEED

The speed at which a microcomputer accesses its instructions is another important consideration. Speed depends on clock speed and word size. **Clock speed** is the number of electronic pulses per second, measured in megahertz (MHz) up to gigahertz (GHz). The more pulses the computer has per second, the faster it executes the instructions. The clock speed on a microcomputer can vary. For example, the old Apple II had a clock speed of 1 MHz. For a typical classroom you see clock speeds of 1 to 3.2 GHz. Some programs, such as sophisticated spreadsheet programs, require more speed than others.

KEYBOARD

You should test out the keyboard feel by sitting at the computer and checking how comfortable it is to type on the keys. Keyboards today have many different ergonomic designs. One computer might have impressive specifications, but typing on its keyboard may be uncomfortable. See if an extended keyboard is available. Extended keyboards have additional keys that can be programmed to perform different functions and numeric pads that speed up number entry.

HARD DISK SPACE

Like everything else on computers, hard disk space has gotten larger and less expensive. Most new computers are being sold with a minimum of 250 GB. You need a gigantic hard disk if you plan to store digitized photographs or edit videos; the bigger the better!

VIDEO OUTPUT

When it comes to the computer monitor, the cathode ray tube (CRT) is the most economical for word processing, spreadsheets, and educational software. The higher the resolution of the screen, linear dots, or **pixels** (picture elements), the clearer the screen's display. The **l**iquid **c**rystal **d**isplay (LCD) monitors are replacing the CRT monitors and should be a first choice for the classroom. These displays use liquid crystals and are found in laptop and desktop computers. The size of your desktop monitor should not be smaller than 15 inches; for a few dollars more you can buy a 17-inch monitor.

VIDEO RAM (VRAM)

Video RAM, also called **VRAM**, "is the type of memory used in a display adapter" (Freedman, 2008). Video RAM simultaneously refreshes the screen while text and images are drawn in memory. Make sure you have at least 32 MB of graphic memory. If you play multimedia software and video games, 128 MB is preferred.

SOUND

The quality of sound is very important for playing musical compositions or educational games. Ask about the number of voices the system has. You should get a minimum of 32 voices. A high-quality sound card can have more than 64 MIDI (Musical Instrument Digital Interface) voices,[3] the "number of musical notes that can be played back simultaneously in a MIDI sound device" (Freedman, 2008). If you want a realistic sound, purchase more voices. Find out the octave ranges of the voices. Most computers offer speech synthesizers capable of pronouncing words.

PERIPHERALS

Study the peripherals that you need and know the features that are available. Read magazines to determine which peripherals are best to purchase. Find out which peripherals have the lowest rate of repair and the fastest access time.

HARDWARE RELIABILITY AND DEALER SUPPORT

Are local dealers reputable? Find a local store that can easily service the machine. Does the store give free training on newly purchased machinery? Is there a service contract? Is the equipment warranted for a year, and is there quick turnaround on computer repair? Is the machine relatively easy to operate? Do you need hours to study its thick manuals? For a young student or an easily frustrated adult, these considerations are important. Is there quality documentation for the computer?

COST

Prices that are quoted by manufacturers are discounted, so check *Computer Shopper*, Internet, local newspaper ads, and magazines to determine the price structure of a system. There are educational discounts from most computer manufacturers. Is the machine too costly compared to similar machines? Does the manufacturer include free software? Is there a warranty on the product, on-site repair, or, at the very least, a place to ship the machine for quick repair? For computer equipment it is important to get an extended warranty. The hardware checklist on page 31 should serve as a handy guide for analyzing your hardware needs.

---

[3] "A standard protocol for the interchange of musical information between musical instruments, synthesizers, and computers" (Freedman, 2008).

Hardware Checklist

Directions: Examine the following items and determine which ones you feel are important for your particular class situation. Evaluate the hardware and place an *X* on each line where it meets your needs.

Computer Type _____ **Model** _____ **Manufacturer** _____

Features

___ 1. Ability to run software
___ 2. Screen size
___ 3. Text/graphics display
    ___ a. Number of lines
    ___ b. Characters per line
    ___ c. Resolution
    ___ d. Number of colors
___ 4. Sound
    ___ a. Number of voices
    ___ b. Number of octaves
    ___ c. Loudness
___ 5. Portability
___ 6. Keyboard design
    ___ a. Number of keys
    ___ b. Numeric keypad
___ 7. Ease of expansion
___ 8. Color capabilities
___ 9. Equipment compatibility
___ 10. Networking
___ 11. Memory (RAM)
___ 12. Memory (video RAM)
___ 13. Hard disk capacity
___ 14. CD-ROM drive (8 X, 16X, 24 X, 32 X, etc.)
___ 15. DVD drive
___ 16. CD-RW or DVD-RW drive
___ 17. Central processing speed

Ease of Use

___ 1. Easy program loading
___ 2. Flexibility
___ 3. Easy equipment setup
___ 4. Tutorial manual

Consumer Value

___ 1. Cost of basic unit
___ 2. Cost of peripherals
    ___ a. Hard drive
    ___ b. Interfaces/cables
    ___ c. Memory expansion
    ___ d. Modem
    ___ e. Monitor
        ___ (1) Included in price
        ___ (2) Size
    ___ f. Printer
    ___ g. Other
    ___ h. Software included
    ___ i. Speech synthesizer
___ 3. Total investment

Support

___ 1. Service contract
___ 2. Nearby dealer support
___ 3. Readable manuals
___ 4. Tutorial
___ 5. Index
___ 6. Warranty period (carry-in or on-site)
___ 7. Teacher training

Rating Scale

Rate the hardware by placing a check in the appropriate box.

Excellent_____ Very good _____ Good _____ Fair _____ Poor _____

Comments:

SUMMARY

In education, the student uses the computer to perform three functions: logic comparisons, arithmetic operations, and storage and retrieval. The computer accomplishes these functions at high speed, storing huge amounts of data in a binary format. The central processing unit, the brain of the computer, controls what is happening; an arithmetic logic unit (ALU) performs the arithmetic and logic operations; and primary memory, ROM and RAM, store all data and instructions necessary for operation. ROM, read only memory, cannot be changed and is hardwired into the machine. RAM, random access memory, is temporary memory that stores data and programs that need processing. Because of its erasable characteristics, RAM allows a program to be executed as many times as the user needs. Since RAM is temporary, disks are very important permanent storage media.

The operating system, the control program that handles the transfer of data and programs to and from computer disks, makes it possible to enter and run programs.

Every computer has input, output, and input/output devices that add functionality to the machine. This chapter has explored the functions of the major input, output, and input/output devices. We also considered criteria for hardware selection.

STUDY AND ONLINE RESOURCES

CHAPTER 2 ONLINE RESOURCES

 In the **student section** of the book's online site at **http://www.wiley.com/college/sharp**, you will find the *Hardware Reference Guide for Teachers*, PDFs, handheld and hardware checklists, top-rated Web sites, and chapter quizzes. Access these resources to learn about technology and integrating it into the classroom. Watch the video tutorial online and learn how to conduct an Internet search.

CHAPTER MASTERY TEST

Lets check for chapter comprehension with a short mastery test. Key Terms, Computer Lab, and Suggested Readings and References follow the test.

1. Contrast RAM and ROM.

2. Explain how the different components of a central processing unit work.

3. What is an operating system and what function does it perform?

4. Discuss the microprocessor, the CPU, and memory and explain how they function independently and as a complete unit.

5. Is it important to have enough RAM for your computer?

6. Define and explain the following terms: *bit, byte, kilobyte, megabyte, and terabyte.*

7. What does "to boot a computer" mean?

8. Why are erasable optical discs the wave of the future?

9. Explain the difference between a CD-ROM and a DVD-ROM.

10. Name two input and two output devices. Explain how each works.

11. Name four factors to consider when examining hardware.

12. Name three ways the iPod is being used in the classroom.

13. What is an interactive whiteboard? Give two uses for it in the classroom.

14. What is a digital camera and what are two uses for it in the classroom?

KEY TERMS

Arithmetic logic unit
 (ALU) p. 19

Binary notation p. 20

Bit p. 20

Booting the system
 p. 21

Byte p. 20

Cathode ray tube
 (CRT) p. 25

Central processing unit
 (CPU) p. 19

Circuit boards p. 19

Clock speed p. 29

Computer chip p. 18

Control unit p. 19

Digital camera p. 24

Expansion slots p. 29

Fax machine p. 27

Floppy disk p. 26

Gigabyte (GB) p. 20

Graphical user interface
 (GUI) p. 21

Hard drive p. 27

Hardware p. 23

Inkjet printer p. 17

Interactive whiteboard
 p. 26

iPod p. 28

Joystick p. 27

Keyboard p. 23

Kilobyte (K) p. 20

Large-scale integration
 (LSI) printer p. 18

Laser printer p. 25

Liquid crystal display
 (LCD) p. 25

Megabyte (MB) p. 20

Microprocessor p. 18

Modem p. 27

Mouse p. 23

Operating system p. 21

Optical character recog-
 nition (OCR) p. 24

Optical disc p. 27

Optical mark reader
 (OMR) p. 24

Pixel p. 29

Podcasts p. 28

Printed circuit board
 p. 19

Printer p. 25

Projection panel p. 26

Projector p. 26

Random access memory
 (RAM) p. 20

Read only memory
 (ROM) p. 20

Scanner p. 24

Software p. 23

Terabyte p. 20

USB drive p. 27

Very-large-scale
 integration (VLSI)
 p. 18

Videoconferencing
 cameras p. 24

Video RAM
 (VRAM) p. 30

Video scan converter
 p. 26

Webcam p. 24

Zip disk p. 27

 COMPUTER LAB: Activities for Mastery and Your Portfolio

2.1 Hardware Review Test your visual recognition of computer hardware.

2.2 Take a field trip to a local school that uses digital cameras and report how they are incorporated in student writing projects.

2.3 At the library, find a recent article on microchips and discuss recent developments in this technology.

2.4 Interview a local school district and write a report on how the district uses computers.

2.5 Visit a computer retail store and write a report on the different hardware devices that could enrich the use of computers in the classroom.

2.6 Using a program like Tom Snyder's *Timeline 5.1*, prepare a time line on the evolution of the computer.

2.7 Have the students use the Hardware Checklist on page 31 and go online to make a hypothetical purchase of a computer system. Watch the video tutorial online and learn how to conduct an Internet Search.

SUGGESTED READINGS AND REFERENCES

American National Standards Institute. *American National Standard Code for Information Interchange.* New York: ANSI, 1986.

Batane, Tshepo. "Technology and Student Collaboration." *T.H.E. Journal* 30, issue 3 (October 2002): 16.

Beauchamp, G., and Parkinson, J. "Beyond the wow factor: Developing interactivity with the interactive whiteboard." *School Science Review* 316, no. 86 (2005): 97–103.

Breen, Christopher. "The iPod on TV." *MacWorld* April 2006, pp. 74–75.

Brooks, Jason. "Vista Scales New Heights." *eWeek Labs*, December 4, 2006, pp. 55–58.

Butterfield, Eric. "Color Lasers Get Down to Business." *PC World* 24, issue 6 (June 2006): 60–63.

Dvorak, John C. "Inside Track." *PC Magazine* 24, issue 16, September 20, 2005, pp. 61–101.

Friedman, Tomas L. *The World is Flat.* New York: Farrar, Straus and Giroux, 2005.

Freedman, Alan. *Computer Desktop Encyclopedia CD-ROM.* Penn. Point Pleasant: The Computer Language Company, 2008. http://www.computerlanguage.com

Fryer, Wesley A. "Room with a View." *Technology & Learning* 25, issue 8, March 2005, pp. 13–16.

Galli, Peter. "Ballmer: "Vista's Strong." *eWeek*, December 4, 2006, pp. 13–14.

Glover, D., and Miller, D., Averis, D., and Door, V. The interactive whiteboard: A literature survey. *Technology, Pedagogy and Education* 2, no. 14 (2005): 155–170.

Gonsalves, Antone. "The Linux Alternative." *Teaching and Learning* 23, no. 8 (March 2003): 9–12.

Hayes, Frank. "The iPhone Idea." *Computerworld* 41, issue 3, January 15, 2007, p. 38.

Jasper, Paul. "Color Lasers Get Affordable." *PC World* 23, issue 12, December 2005, pp. 133–140.

Keller, Jeff. "This Month in Digital Cameras." *MacWorld* 20, issue 2 (February 2003): p. 48.

Kent, Lynette. *Teach Yourself Visually Mac OS X Leopard*. New York: John Wiley & Sons, 2007.

McFarland, Scholle Sawyer. "The Digital Classroom." *MacWorld,* April 2006, p. 23.

McFedries, Paul. *Teach Yourself Visually Windows Vista*. New York: John Wiley & Sons, 2007.

Michaels, Philip. "More of Leopard Revealed." *MacWorld*, June 2007, pp. 18–19.

Pownell, David, and Gerald D. Bailey. "The Next Small Thing." *Learning and Leading with Technology* 27, no. 8 (May 2000): 47–49.

Ray, David. "Conquering Space with LCD Monitors." *eWeek* 23, issue 36, September 11, 2006, p. 36.

Smith, H. J., Higgins, S., Wall, K., and Miller, J. "Interactive Whiteboards: Boon or Bandwagon? A Critical Review of the Literature." *Journal of Computer Assisted Learning* 21, issue 2 (2005): 91–101.

Supon, Viola. "Using Digital Cameras for Multidimensional Learning in K–12 Classrooms." *Journal of Instructional Psychology* 33, issue 2 (June 2006): 154–156.

Tomlinson, Howard. "Educational PDA Games Engage Students, Teach Essential Language Skills." *T.H.E. Journal* (September 2003): 2–44.

Walthes, Scott. "Using Handhelds in K–12 Classrooms." *Media & Methods* 42, issue 1 (September/October 2005): pp. 9–11.

Zepke, Nick, and Linda Leach. "Appropriate Pedagogy and Technology in a Cross-Cultural Distance Education Context." *Teaching in Higher Education* 7, no. 3 (July 2002): 309–321.

Networking, Internet, and Distance Learning

CHAPTER

3

The Internet in the Classroom

Having access to the Internet means that you could tap into thousands of databases and communicate electronically with experts all over the world on any topic. Students can explore this giant library with millions of sites and obtain information on any curriculum area, participate in online discussion groups, download lecture notes, and do research. They can create Web pages to showcase their own work and share information. Students can also study online using distance learning, which offers them a great opportunity for an education. This chapter introduces you to the Internet where you learn about its many classroom uses. Exercises will help you integrate the Internet into the classroom. We also present Internet sites that include articles on Internet origins, online encyclopedias, and online dictionaries.

Using the computer, students and teachers can do the following:

students can

- do research for projects,
- do homework and seek tutorial help,
- take practice quizzes,
- participate in collaborative science investigations, and
- video conference with other students.

teachers can

- post exams online,
- find lesson plans and instructional material,
- share common problems with other teachers,
- work on collaborative projects, and
- communicate with e-mail and video conferencing.

objectives

Upon completing this chapter, you will be able to do the following:

1 Describe *networking* and explain how it operates.

2 Discuss the Internet's historical background

3 Explain what video conferencing is and how it is being used.

4 Discuss distance learning and its implications for education.

5 List the advantages and disadvantages of distance learning.

What is Networking?

In order to understand what the Internet is all about you must first have a clear understanding of **networking** and what it is. In simple terms, a network lets you transmit video, voice, and/or data between individual users (Freedman, 2008). Networking is another way that computers communicate with each other. In a network, numerous computers are connected together. A computer network (Figure 3.1) generally requires one or more computers and a **file server**, which is a computer with a large data capacity that serves as a repository for information. The file server directs the flow of information to and from the computers in the network. You also need a network card, if the networking capabilities are not built or plugged into the computer, and cables, wires, hookups, and operating system software (available from companies such as Novell, Apple, and Microsoft) that gives access to the file server. Besides this special software and equipment, you need "networkable" software that runs on the network. In addition, a network needs a variety of devices to connect parts of the network and handle traffic among the various components. A **hub** is a central connecting device that joins communication lines together on a network. **Switches** and **routers** are devices used to organize the traffic along the correct pathway. They forward this information from one network to another. A network can have a permanent connection such as a cable or a temporary connection made through the telephone or another communication device.

Figure 3.1
A Simple Computer Network

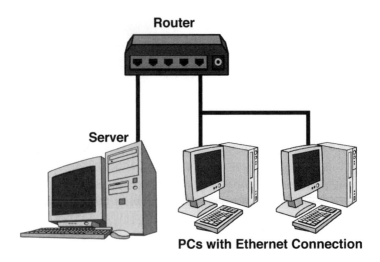

The computer's network cable connection can be either copper or fiber optic. The more expensive fiber optic cables, a transmission medium consisting of glass fibers, transmit digital signals in the form of pulses of light produced by a laser. Using this type of cabling, the network can handle more messages simultaneously than it could with copper wiring or coaxial cable.

Networks

Local area networks (LANs), **wide area networks (WANs)**, and telephones are three types of networks. LANs provide communication within a local area, usually within 200 or 300 feet, such as in an office building. A school might have its card catalog stored on a file server's hard disk, accessible by other computers throughout the building through a LAN. WANs provide communication for a larger area and require miles of communication linkage. A telephone network connects computers via telephone. The only difference between a WAN and a telephone network is the fact that the telephone's communication is intermittent, but the wide area network communicates all the time. Networks not only use cables but are also being connected without wires.

WIRELESS NETWORKS IN THE SCHOOLS

A **wireless network** enables you to transmit data "between computers, servers, and other network devices without the use of a physical cable or wire" (Freedman, 2008). The different means used to provide wireless transmission are infrared, cellular, microwave, and satellite. Presently, infrared transmission is being used in small networks of either one room or to connect computers from room to room. This type of transmission has become popular in the classroom, because it is very easy to install. In using this type of network, all the user has to worry about is making sure the signal is not blocked from the computers or deflected. Current portable computers have infrared transceivers so they can send files to their printer, a desktop computer, or a handheld computer.

Apple's *Airport Extreme Wireless* is an example of a wireless technology that uses radio signals to communicate and does not require an unobstructed line of sight to make a connection. *Airport Extreme* also delivers fast, affordable wireless technology to the home or classroom without cables or complicated networking hardware. Students can communicate up to 150 feet away, and the communication is fast, at 54 megabits per second (Mbps). *Airport Wireless* Internet access requires an *Airport Extreme* card, an *Airport Extreme* base station (Figure 3.2), and Internet access (http://www.apple.com).

Another example of a wireless network comes from Bluetooth special interest groups (http://www.bluetooth.com). *Bluetooth* is short-range radio communication

Figure 3.2
Apple's Airport Extreme
Wireless Technology
(*Source:* Courtesy Apple Computer, Inc.)

that uses radio waves that can transmit through walls and nonmetal objects. This technology enables a variety of devices, such as laptops, PCs, phones, personal data assistants (PDAs) (Chapter 2), and printers, to communicate with each other without cables. A small group of users can also use this technology to create their own personal area network. Data can be sent from 750 Kb to 1 Mb per second across distances of up to 100 meters.

Wireless networks eliminate expensive cabling and add flexibility, permitting users to move the machines freely around a room. It also reduces the cost of running cables throughout the buildings and upgrading computer equipment. Quite a few colleges provide wireless-network access but leave it to students to purchase laptop computers with wireless-network cards to use the network. Using wireless networking, students and faculty can access this network from different areas of the campus. The network relies on wireless access points (base stations) that are connected to the server. These base stations transmit radio frequency over the campus. When a user leaves the transmitting area of one station, he or she enters that of another. As the cost of wireless decreases and the speed of computers increases, wireless networks will proliferate schools across the country. That is when we will see the possibility of every classroom being connected to the Internet (Nguyen, Personal Communication, December 18, 2007).

ADVANTAGES AND DISADVANTAGES OF NETWORKING

The advantages of networking computers are communication, speed and accuracy, expense, and file sharing. When you network computers you can work with individuals on different floors or in different buildings. You can communicate faster and more accurately because messages are not so easily misplaced. Networking can save money because users share software and equipment such as word processing programs and laser printers. Finally, networking enables individuals to share files with one another for classroom research.

Unfortunately, networking has potential disadvantages, among them training cost, competent technicians, down time, and security. The cost to network requires computer training, and usually high maintenance. This requires expertise that may not always be readily available. Also school districts must consider the frustration level of teachers faced with the extra burden of learning a new system. If there are crashes the teacher might be faced with long down time and no one to help them. The necessary network software is not always available. Finally, the user must be mindful of system security; an unauthorized individual can access all information if the network is unprotected.

The Internet

Now that we have examined the upside and downside of networking, let us discuss the largest world network, the Internet. The Internet Usage and World Population Statistics report for December 31, 2007 shows the Internet has over 1 billion users (Internet World Stats, 2008). This population is expected to grow at 50-fold by 2015 (Technology & Democracy Project, 2008). In 1969 the U.S. Department of Defense created the Internet for military research purposes. The department's major concerns were to ensure mass communication of information while providing for maximum security. The original network was called ARPAnet because the Advanced Research Projects Agency designed it. As the years went by the name was shortened to the Internet and it was widely used for academic and commercial research.

RECENT GROWTH OF THE INTERNET

For many years people used command-line UNIX utilities to interact with the Internet. This type of usage made the Internet difficult for the novice. However, this all changed when Swiss researchers developed the **World Wide Web**, a system that enables the user to move smoothly through the Internet (see the Internet history writeup at http://www.wiley/college/sharp). Software tools called web *browsers* were developed that made access to Internet resources uncomplicated.

In the last half of the 1990s, two developments led to a surge in the Internet's growth. First, with the new graphics-based Web browsers such as Microsoft's *Internet Explorer* and *Netscape Navigator*, the World Wide Web exploded. Students and teachers found the Web easy to use, and it was no longer the private domain of scientists and hackers. Delphi was the first online service to offer access to the Web. Simultaneously, new Internet service providers offered access to individuals and companies. Internet service providers (ISPs) such as the Microsoft Software Network (MSN) provided Internet access and e-mail, and EarthLink Network, the world's largest independent ISP, provided network access and home pages. Many school districts gave students free ISP connection. Some commercial ISPs provide free connections to users. Liquid Slate lists free Internet service providers (http://www.liquidslate.com/).

The second development was the proliferation of e-mail, which made the Internet more popular. As online services such as America Online and CompuServe connected to the Internet, the Internet came to function as a central gateway linking users of different services.

To learn more about the Internet's history, visit our online site at **http://www.wiley.com/college /sharp**. You can download a brief Internet history in PDF format or look at numerous award-winning Web sites.

INTERNET 2

Because of the Internet's congestion, academic and scientific users of the Internet again developed their own network. Led by 205 universities, **Internet 2** is an association that works together with government and industry to develop advanced network applications and technologies. Internet 2 is designed primarily to exchange multimedia data, real time, at high speeds. If you want to learn more about this network, visit the association's home page at http://www.internet2.edu/.

Connecting to the Internet

To access the Web, you need a connection to the Internet and a computer that is powerful enough to handle the memory requirements for most browsers. PC computers need to run Windows with at least a Pentium processor and Macintosh computers need to run System 9 or higher. You should have at least 512 MB of RAM. You will also need a modem, digital subscriber line (DSL), or a satellite data service.

THE MODEM

A **modem** lets two computers communicate over some type of communications line such as a telephone line. The word *modem* is a contraction of MOdulator/ DEModulator. The modem *modulates* the computer output to an acceptable signal for transmission and then *demodulates* the signal back for computer input. The modem on the transmitting computer converts the digital signals to modulated, analog signal tones and transmits them over telephone lines. The receiving computer's modem transforms the incoming analog signals back to their digital equivalents in order to understand them. Figure 3.3 illustrates this modem-to-modem transmission.

The above modem definition applies to the dial-up 56 Kbps modem, which gives slow speed access to the Internet. The dial-up modem is quickly being replaced

Figure 3.3
Modem-to-Modem Transmission

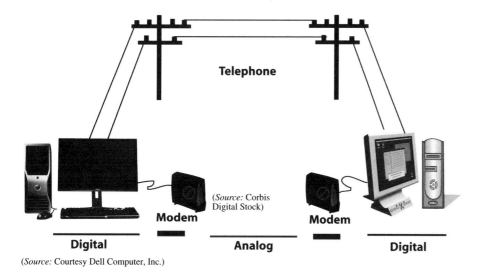

Telephone

(Source: Corbis
Digital Stock)

Modem   **Modem**

Digital   **Analog**   **Digital**

(Source: Courtesy Dell Computer, Inc.)

by the cable modem because of the speed factor and the lack of hardware support from Internet service providers. The cable modem gives users high-speed access to the Internet.

CABLE MODEM

A **cable modem** enables you to connect to the Internet with the same cable that attaches to a standard television set. Cable modems offer a greater **bandwidth**, in simple terms, you can send more data through the modem than DSL or dial-up modems. The more bandwidth you have the more information you can transfer in a fixed time period. Even though this is the case, a cable modem is limited by the amount of use of the line, because the cable line is shared among many users. The speeds for cable vary, and heavy downloads are faster when few people are online. In the near future, we will see faster cable modems.

DIGITAL SUBSCRIBER LINES

Digital subscriber lines (DSLs) and cable modems are different technologies, but both provide dedicated multimegabit connections to a service, and they are both always on, unlike dial-up modems. DSL is a digital point-to-point technology that offers high-speed transmission over standard copper telephone wiring. Downloading occurs at speeds up to 8 Mbps. DSL can carry both voice and data signals at the same time, in both directions. There are many versions of DSL with varying transmission speeds. The percentage of homes in the United States with **broadband**, or high speed–transmission Internet access, is expected to be 80 percent in 2010. Presently, 47% of Americans have high speed Internet access (Internet World Stats, 2007). Broadband growth will be driven by an increase in consumer adoption of cable modem and DSL technology (Deveaux, 2000). Recently, companies providing DSL have been competing with cable companies to provide faster service.

A benefit of DSL is that you can use the phone at the same time you use the Web, so you do not need a separate telephone line. However, DSL speeds are tied to the distance between the user and the central office. Also, DSL may not be available in your area.

SATELLITE DATA SERVICE

Satellite data service uses a satellite dish to connect your computer to the Internet. A satellite data service can provide speeds of 400 Kbps for downloading. Computers connect to this service via a modem, and the installation charges are high. Of the technologies briefly described here, it is impossible to know which will dominate in the years to come. However, it is certain that the connection speeds will be faster, and more users will be using high-speed digital lines.

Internet Service Providers (ISPs)

An ISP is an organization that provides access to the Internet. A customer is usually charged a fixed amount of money per month, but there can be other charges involved. Small service providers usually just give access to the Internet, whereas large service providers such as America Online (AOL) (http://www.aol.com) provide forums, services, and proprietary databases as well. America Online gives members access to the Internet as well as to special content including e-mail, instant messaging, chat rooms, customized news information, financial information and stock quotes, movie information, maps and driving directions, and local entertainment information (Figure 3.4).

Figure 3.4
America Online
(*Source:* Reprinted with permission from AOL)

Microsoft Network (http://www.msn.com/) is another popular service provider. Subscribers to these ISPs can access some specialized members-only services through their browsers.

Several resources can help you find an ISP to fit your needs. If you already have access to the Internet through an online service, you can check out a list of providers at http://www.thelist.com/. *The List* enables you to search for providers by country, state, or area code. In the *ISP Directory of Internet Access* (http://findanisp.com/) you can find dial-up or other Internet access services in the United States, organized by local phone calling areas. Another place to find information about ISPs is in the local Yellow Pages. You might also contact a local computer user group.

Internet Resources

Online you will find a table of other resources that range from Archie Server to Multiple User Dimension.

The resources available through a connection to the Internet range from e-mail to searchable databases. We discuss electronic mail and a few other notable resources in this chapter.

ELECTRONIC MAIL

Electronic mail, or **e-mail**, can be used to send messages to individuals at local or distant locations in a matter of seconds. What makes this system unique is the fact that the message recipient does not have to be present to receive a message. A host computer stores in memory any messages received; when the recipient logs on to the system, the screen displays a message informing him or her about the mail. There are many additional advantages to e-mail. You can quickly address an issue via e-mail without time-consuming social interaction. E-mail also conquers the problems of long-distance communication. People all over the world can easily communicate with each other instantly. E-mail can generate answers quickly and inexpensively. A typical e-mail address has two parts: (1) the user's identification followed by the *at* (@) symbol and (2) the domain information consisting of the site name and type of organization.

For example, the author's e-mail address is vicki.sharp@csun.edu. The user's name identified in this example is *vicki.sharp*. The site name or domain name is *CSUN* (California State University, Northridge), and the domain type is *edu* (educational institution).

Other domain types are government organization (*gov*), nonprofit organization (*org*), and commercial organization (*com*). Figure 3.5 shows an electronic mail message sent via America Online. Electronic mail also lets the sender send attachments, which are separate files containing graphics or documents. Standalone commercial e-mail programs such as *Eudora Pro* (Qualcomm) are loaded with features. Students who need fewer bells and whistles can download a freeware program (software that is disseminated without a charge) such as *Eudora Light* or *Pegasus* (David Harris, publisher) and use these programs without restrictions. Both programs include basic components such as sending and receiving messages, forwarding, replying, and setting up an address book. In addition, there are free Web-based mail services such as *Yahoo! Mail* and *Hotmail. Yahoo! Mail* enables the user to navigate by pointing and clicking. In addition, it offers nice features such as a signature file and mail filters.

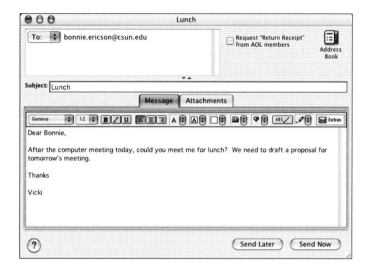

Figure 3.5
E-mail Message on America Online

Hotmail, one of the newest members to the Microsoft Network, besides being easy to use, includes an antivirus scanner provided by McAfee. The *Free E-mail Address* site reviews some of these e-mail services (http://www.free-email-address .com/). *Gaggle.Net* is a monitored Internet e-mail service for children. The advertising-supported version of Gaggle is free (http://www.gaggle.net/learn.html). Teachers can sign up entire classes to use it.

Netiquette.   Getting along in the electronic environment is called **netiquette.** Here are a few suggestions for proper online behavior:

1. Keep your messages to the point and brief.

2. Do not use ALL UPPERCASE LETTERS; this is considered shouting.

3. Never criticize a person's writing or spelling.

4. Do not overreact to items you see online.

5. Do not send excessive messages to multiple groups (cross-posting), in disregard of the members' interests.

6. Do not post items that are offensive.

7. Use discretion by not getting too personal with anyone.

8. Do not lie about your identity.

You can find further suggestions on netiquette at the Netiquette Home Page (http:// www.albion.com/netiquette/) and at Master the Basics: Netiquette (http://www .learnthenet.com/english/html/09netiqt.htm).

CHAT ROOMS

The **chat room** is a discussion by keyboard on a specific topic. The chat takes place in real time; that is, it occurs instantly. When you type a text message on the computer screen your words are seen on the screen by other people in the chat room. Chat rooms are available from services such as America Online, Web sites such as *Yahoo!,* and the Internet relay chat system.

INSTANT MESSAGING

Instant messaging is a feature enabling two or more people to swap messages in real time. In addition, instant messaging systems enable users to transfer files, and some systems enable users to send messages even if they are not online. Three major services that offer this system are Yahoo! Messenger, AOL's Instant Messenger (AIM), and Microsoft's MSN Messenger.

With instant messaging you can share photos and sounds with friends. If you set up a buddy list of the names of people you want to send messages to, when people on your list log on to the Internet with the Instant Messaging software, you are notified that they are online. When they log off, you are also notified. With a Web cam and a headset (Figure 3.6), you can chat with friends by speaking to them and seeing them.

Figure 3.6
Web Cam and Headset
(*Source:* © 2008 Jupiterimages Corporation, WebCam courtesy Sony Electronics)

What follows is an example of an instant messaging session between me and my son.

Figure 3.7
Instant Messaging Session
(*Source:* Reproduced with permission of Yahoo! Inc. © 2008 by Yahoo! Inc. YAHOO And the YAHOO! Logo are trademarks of Yahoo! Inc.)

Text messaging is a cousin of instant messaging. In this case, individuals send their short text messages via a personal data assistant, a smart phone, pager, or some other type of handheld device. Text messages have become so popular they are used to order products and participate in television contests.

INTERNET RELAY CHAT (IRC)

Internet relay chat (IRC) is computer conferencing on the Internet. IRC channels on a wide range of topics take place on IRC servers around the world. After you join a channel, your messages are broadcast to everyone listening on that particular channel.

SKYPE

Skype (Skype Technologies) is a very popular free Internet phone service. This service is software based. A user just needs a microphone and he or she can talk free as long as the other person has Skype. For example, I used Skype to talk to my friends in Brazil. If you want to use Skype to dial a telephone, there is a per-minute cost.

NEWSGROUPS

Newsgroups are Internet discussion groups that focus on a particular topic. Newsgroups are like public bulletin boards where you can read messages that others have written and write your own thoughts. An example of a Web site with a wide variety of newsgroups is Yahoo Groups at http://www.egroups.com/.

World Wide Web

Finally, World Wide Web (WWW) is a collection of computers containing documents accessed with special software that enables users to view text, graphics, video, and photos and to link to another document on the Web. The next chapter is devoted entirely to the WWW. Because of the Internet and the WWW, distance learning has surged forward.

Distance Education and Distance Learning Defined

In the past, experts made a distinction between distance education and distance learning. **Distance education** referred to institutions or instructors delivering knowledge using telecommunication or remote capabilities. **Distance learning** is defined as "obtaining education and training from a remote teaching site via TV or computer" (Freedman, 2008). In other words, distance education was about the instructor, and distance learning was about the student. These terms have since become interchangeable and we will use the term "distance learning."

Distance Learning: A Brief History

The first attempt at distance learning was through correspondence. In 1873, Ann Ticknor made an important contribution to distance learning by establishing the Society to Encourage Studies at Home in Boston. In a 24-year period, the Society provided correspondence instruction to 10,000 women of all social classes. From 1883 to 1891, Chautauqua College of Liberal Arts granted academic degrees to students who successfully finished work by correspondence (Nasseh, 1997).

Distance learning entered our university via the "extension" division of the University of Chicago in 1892. The University of Chicago had the first major correspondence program in the United States where teachers and students were learning in different places. With the development of radio after World War I and television in the 1950s, educators found new ways to deliver distance learning. However, with all this interest in distance learning, progress in the United States was slow except for the University of Phoenix who delivered distance learning through television, satellite, and the Internet.

Recently the need for distance learning has increased and there are a variety of reasons for this. In today's society family life has become overscheduled and people have lengthy commute times and work longer hours. Because of the technological world we live in, individuals need more than a high school education. The emergence of the Internet and the evolving new technologies have made it easier for distance learning to become popular.

Distance Learning Technologies

There are many possible ways of delivering distance learning to the user such as correspondence courses through postal mail, fax, videotape or prerecorded audio tape, radio, audio conferencing via telephone, television, Web-based course management (WebCT), or video conferencing. Often one or more of these methods of delivery are used in conjunction with each other. Table 3.1 shows these technologies.

Table 3.1 Technologies for Distance Learning

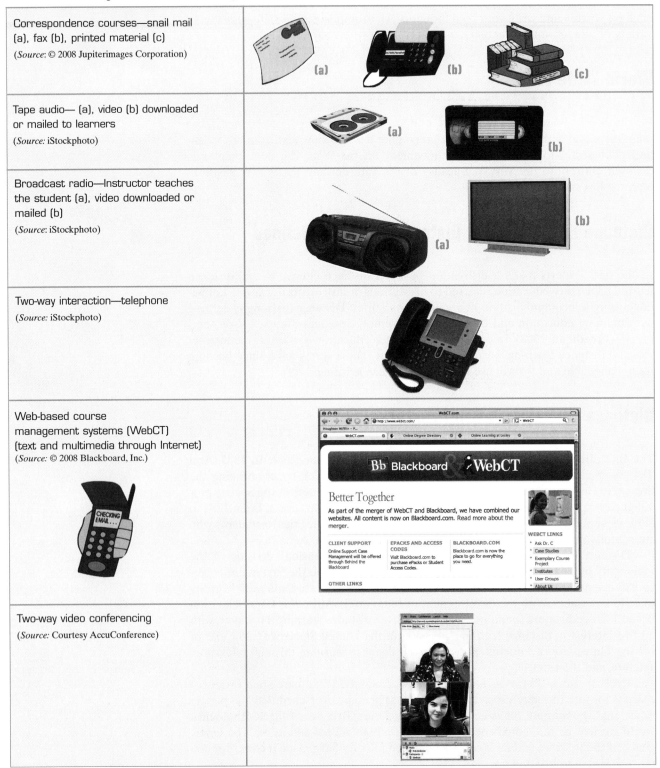

Correspondence courses—snail mail (a), fax (b), printed material (c)
(*Source:* © 2008 Jupiterimages Corporation)

Tape audio— (a), video (b) downloaded or mailed to learners
(*Source:* iStockphoto)

Broadcast radio—Instructor teaches the student (a), video downloaded or mailed (b)
(*Source:* iStockphoto)

Two-way interaction—telephone
(*Source:* iStockphoto)

Web-based course management systems (WebCT) (text and multimedia through Internet)
(*Source:* © 2008 Blackboard, Inc.)

Two-way video conferencing
(*Source:* Courtesy AccuConference)

As you can see from Table 3.1, the Internet is still the principal way of delivering distance learning. Distance learning usually occurs through either Web-based courses or video courses. An example of Web-based learning is WebCT in Figure 3.8.

Figure 3.8
Web-Based Training (WBT)
(*Source:* © 2008 Blackboard, Inc.)

WebCT, which has merged with Blackboard (http://www.blackboard.com/) is a strong presence in providing software to facilitate distance learning.

Their customers include K–12, higher education, textbook publishers, government, and corporations. WebCT offers prospective users free download and trial of its software. However, once you upload your courses online, you pay a license fee based on your projected enrollment.

A free alternative is the **open source** course management program called "Moodle" (Modular Object-Oriented Dynamic Learning Environment) (http://moodle.org/). Created by a development community, this open source software application's source code is publicly distributed and it lets users have the freedom to modify it. Using "Moodle," educators can create online courses that include online quizzes, class assignments, participant lists, and forums. School districts are increasingly using these kinds of programs.

VIDEO COURSES

Video courses, or telecourses, are based on a series of television programs that are supplemented by text, study guides, readings, and lectures by local faculty. The students view the broadcast on local television stations or view program tapes.

DESKTOP VIDEO CONFERENCING

Video conferencing enables you to be in two places at the same time. Instead of moving large sums in an armored car, a bank can relay video messages on how much money it wants to transfer. A teacher can confer with an ill student at home without leaving the classroom. A businessman can attend a long-distance conference without leaving the office. This industry is expanding because of better data compression, miniaturization, lower costs, wider availability of digital telephone lines, and faster processors.

Because of technological improvements, desktop video conferencing is becoming common in schools and classrooms across the United States. If you have the proper hardware and software, you can engage in **desktop video conferencing**. You need a network or modem connection, speakers, microphone, video camera, and computer. You can use software such as White Pine's *CU-SeeMe, Yahoo! Messenger, iChat* AV (Figure 3.9), or Microsoft's *NetMeeting*. When you use *iChat* AV with the *iSight* camera you and another person are able to talk to and see each other as if you were in the same room. (Apple's *iSight* camera is a combination camera and microphone.)

Figure 3.9
Teachers Having a Video
Conference
(*Source:* Screenshot of iChat®. Reprinted
with permission from Apple, Inc.)

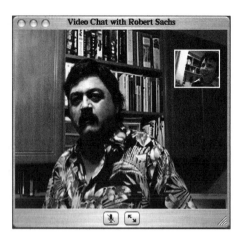

For a student at home this is a great convenience; he or she can communicate with a teacher to get an explanation of a problem. This technology is also a great asset for a student with hearing difficulties. Not only can the student read the text spoken by the teacher but he or she also can read the lips of the teacher. You need special high-speed connections for it to work well. The demand for higher bandwidth is increasing; however, soon this problem will be resolved.

Different Approaches to Distance Learning

Some independent study courses rely on computer-based student contact and feedback. Some distance learning programs have students communicate with teachers through electronic mail, attend some class sessions, and meet in small groups on weekends. Some undergraduate and graduate degree programs rely on cable networks, providing video courses accompanied by a textbook and other materials.

You may wonder what approach to distance learning is the most effective. Regardless of the technology used, the best approach focuses first on the needs of the students, the content requirements, and the constraints of the situation. The delivery system is secondary. Good printed instructional materials such as readings and a syllabus can give students most of what they need. Technology can then be used to provide face-to-face or voice-to-voice interaction, access to experts in the field, student feedback, information about assignments, and audiotape or videotape lectures on topics that require explanation.

The Future of Distance Education

As the number of individuals using the Internet increases, more people will be engaging in distance education. Presently, distance education is being used in medicine, law, education, and business. For years, doctors, lawyers, and engineers have used it to continue their studies. Many of these professionals are too busy with work to participate in classroom study, and they find home study their only option. Distance learning also reaches students who are in remote, rural locations. Some schools may not be able to spend money on a teacher to teach an advanced physics or chemistry course, and distance learning addresses this problem. Additionally, learners who are homebound due to serious illness or physical disability may not be able to travel to educational institutions. Furthermore, through distance learning technology the teacher can bring experts or special individuals into a classroom. Distance learning can also link two classrooms so that students can communicate with each other.

Throughout the United States, professors are engaging in electronic instruction. Higher-education institutions have used distance education to reach a diverse audience that would not be accessible through traditional classroom instruction. Many universities are offering degrees via the Internet. Duke University was one of the first schools to offer a master's degree in nursing online. The University of Illinois at Urbana–Champaign (UIUC) offers any student in the state the chance to take engineering courses without having to attend classes on campus. At Curtain University in Australia, teachers use distance learning to reach students in Western Australia. Walden University (Figure 3.10) is a leading online university. This school provides degrees in education, health and human services, engineering, computer science, business, and other academic areas. It is an outstanding accredited university that has been in existence over 35 years. It has helped working individuals achieve their educational goals. Lesley University prepares women and men for professional careers in education, the arts, human services, management, environmental activism, and liberal arts. Other fine schools are Kaplan University, Ellis College, and Capella University.

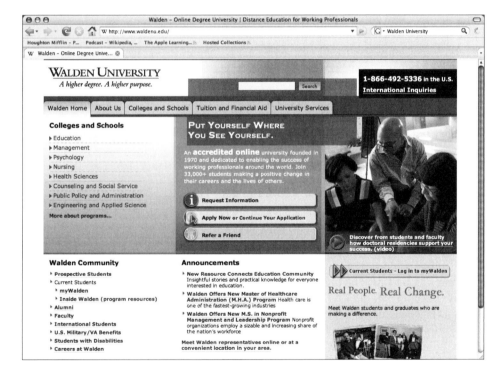

Figure 3.10
Walden University
(*Source:* Courtesy of Walden University at http://www.waldenu.edu/. The telephone number is 1-866-492-5336 in the U.S.A.)

 Check online at **http://www. wiley.com/ college/sharp** *for numerous sites on distance learning. Read* Dr. George Friedman's article online. He is adjunct professor in the School of Engineering at the University of Southern California, research director at the Space Studies Institute at Princeton, and is a founder, fellow, and former president of the International Council on Systems Engineering

The majority of states provide Web-based online courses for high schools. If you go to the Education Portal site at http://education-portal.com/pages/Online_ High_Schools.html, you can see a listing of states with online high school diploma programs. Many advanced and core subjects are taught in courses such as French, calculus, etc. A principal can enroll students who need a particular course. The course may not be offered at their particular school or it may not fit in with the student schedules.

"The Virtual High School" TEAMS distance learning, a service of the Los Angeles County Office of Education (LACOE), brings learning opportunities to K–8 students, teachers, and parents across the United States through nationally televised satellite broadcasts and the Internet. Many elementary teachers create their own Web pages (Figure 3.11), which provide resources online to help students in their classroom. Parents can access these sites to check on homework, activities, and more. "The Teacher's Desk" is designed by Angela A. Ackley, a teacher at St. John and St. Paul School in Ashtabula, Ohio. This site offers more than 250 fifth- and sixth-grade lesson plans that cover reading, grammar, creative writing, and other language arts.

Figure 3.11
The Teacher's Desk
(*Source:* Reprinted by permission Angela Ackley. http://www.teachersdesk.org/)

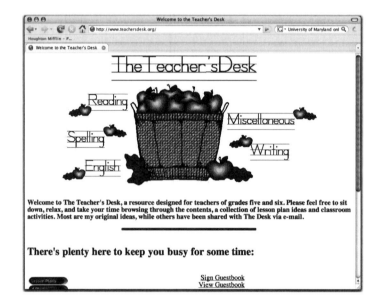

Drawbacks of Distance Education

The main drawback of distance education is that its technology is expensive. Two-way interactive can be very costly because the equipment needed is expensive and the cost of connecting two sites can be quite high. The cost of transmitting over telephone lines is high because of the huge bandwidth that the signal requires.

Another disadvantage is that the technology is difficult to set up. Video conferencing requires an expert to coordinate personnel, vendors, technicians, and the telephone company. Extensive planning—scheduling of equipment and rooms—is needed. The rooms have to be planned in advance, and the equipment must be checked.

In addition, people need to learn how to use this technology. Teachers need to redesign their lessons and activities to take advantage of distance learning technology, but first they need to be trained. A lot of work is involved in distance learning, and only those who are able to expend the extra time, effort, and resources should undertake it. The quality of distance learning depends on the instructor's attitude and preparation.

Another problem that occurs is misuse of the technology. An instructor may not use it to its full potential because of a lack of training. A poor technician might unfavorably influence the educational environment by building anxiety in the students and failing to help the teacher.

Frequently, equipment problems cause delays in instruction. Poor sound or audio quality can impede learning and teaching. Severed connections can frustrate all participants.

Finally, a series of drawbacks involve more subtle concerns. The advantage of eye-to-eye contact is limited in or missing from a distance learning context. Finally, not all subjects are best taught through distance education, and not all students are suited for this type of learning.

Despite its drawbacks, the trend toward distance education continues. In the process, the way we view the traditional school may change forever. Technology will certainly change the way students learn and the time they spend in school. See Chapter 16 for a discussion of research in distance education.

Suggestions for Integrating the Internet into the Classroom

The Internet offers some exciting possibilities for the classroom. Because teachers and students have access to this huge library of information, teachers need to develop skills for determining the most relevant and best quality information. Here are a few suggestions on how to enhance students' learning experiences:

1. Students can conduct online research using databases and online resources. They can find information and visual and auditory data on topics such as whales, pandas, educational statistics, laws, teenage smoking, and the Civil War.

2. The class can track current events through online magazines and newspapers. Students are no longer limited to hometown newspapers and magazines. Access to the Internet gives students access to critical stories in a variety of places. Students can compare local newspaper stories with what is being written by national and world news organizations.

3. New and experienced teachers can access databases of lesson plans, teaching methods, and instructional approaches. Students can find information on what to teach, hands-on experiments, drama techniques, and lesson plans.

4. Students can even access information on job possibilities, job contacts, and résumé preparation.

SAMPLE CLASSROOM LESSON PLANS

I. E-MAIL

Subject: Language Arts

Grade(s): 2 and up

Objective: Students will e-mail letters to other students.

Standards
• NCTE English Language Arts Standards 4, 5, 12
• ISTE NETS for Students 1, 2, 3, 4

Materials
You will need a computer, a word processing program, and a connection to the Internet.

Procedures

1. Introduce the students to the Internet.

2. Demonstrate how the computer, software, modem, and printer work.

3. Discuss terms such as *newsgroups* and *electronic mail.*

4. Show examples of completed pen pal letters.

5. Have students type and transmit letters to students at another school using the Internet.

II. ECONOMICS

Subject: Math

Grade(s): 5 and up

Objective: Students will improve their research skills and learn about the Stock Exchange.

Standards
• National Council of Teachers of Math 1, 5, 8, 10
• ISTE NETS for Students 1, 2, 4, 5, 6

Materials
You will need a computer with access to the Internet.

Procedures

1. Teach a unit on the stock market.

2. Have students research a minimum of six stocks (three for the New York Stock Exchange and three for the NASDAQ).

3. Have students use the library and the Internet to find information.

4. Give the students $3,000 in play money to make pretend purchases.

5. Have the students maintain a stock portfolio for the entire semester.

6. At the end of the semester, ask students to write reports using graphs, charts, and spreadsheets to describe the results of their purchases.

III. CHEMICAL AND PHYSICAL WEATHERING

Subject: Science

Grade(s): 4 and up

Objective: Students will identify and explain causes of chemical and physical weathering.

Standards
• National Science Education Standards A1, A2, D1, D3
• ISTE NETS for Students 1, 2, 4, 5, 6

Materials
You will need a computer with access to the Internet.

Procedures

1. Teach a unit on current environmental issues.

2. Have students measure local rainfall and its acidity level.

3. Access the Internet and have students use it to discover patterns of acidity in the rainwater across the continent.

4. Ask students to post their results online for other schools to use.

5. Have students download information from other students and draw maps and charts.

IV. LESSON PLANS

Subject: General

Grade(s): 9 and up

Objective: Using the Internet, students will find online activities or lessons.

Standards
- ISTE NETS for Students 1, 2, 4, 5

Materials
You will need a computer and access to the Internet.

Procedures

1. Have the students search the Internet for useful sites.

2. Ask students to choose a lesson plan for a specific topic in a subject area that consists of an online interactive activity.

3. Have students print the lesson plan and discuss or demonstrate it to the class.

V. PRESIDENTS

Subject: Social Studies

Grade(s): 4 and up

Objective: Students will learn about the American presidency by searching a site such as *The American Presidency,* found at http://gi.grolier.com/. You can also use Google and type Presidents in its search field. You will find many other excellent sites.

Standards
- National Council for the Social Studies Curriculum Standards 3, 4, 5, 6
- ISTE NETS for Students 1, 2, 4, 5

Materials
You will need a computer and access to the Internet.

Procedures

1. Discuss in class how to search the site.

2. Divide the students into small groups.

3. Next, have the students use *The American Presidency* site or one like it to make up questions on the presidency.

4. Have the groups exchange questions and tell them to find the answers in a 15-minute time period. (Vary the time period according to the number and complexity of questions.)

5. The first group that answers the question correctly earns the same number of points as the number of groups that there are, the second group to finish earns one less, and so on.

6. Have the groups exchange questions again and continue the activity until every group has seen all the questions.

7. The winner is the group with the most points.

VI. FAMOUS ART TREASURES

Subject: Art

Grade(s): 6 and up

Objective: Students will use a site such as *Treasures of the Louvre,* located at http://www.paris.org/Musees/Louvre/Treasures/, to learn about the different art treasures found in a museum.

Standards
• ISTE NETS for Students 1, 2, 4, 5, 6

Materials
You will need a computer and access to the Internet.

Procedures
1. Discuss some of the art treasures that people see in the Louvre.
2. Divide the students into small groups.
3. Have each group research on the Internet a treasure that is located at the museum and write a description of this art object.
4. In class, have each group discuss the art treasure it researched.
5. Each week e-mail a set of clues to each group to help them find a particular art treasure.
6. The first group to come up with the answer gets a point.

SUMMARY

In this chapter, we discussed the Internet, the mother of networks, including its history and the many resources it offers, such as e-mail. We discussed how the Internet is being used more and more for distance education, which has become a key in improving instruction and classes. We discussed reasons for this trend, from an increase in homebound students to a shortage of teachers. Finally, we examined six classroom activities.

STUDY AND ONLINE RESOURCES

CHAPTER 3 ONLINE RESOURCES

In the **student section** of the book's online site at **http://www.wiley.com/college/sharp**, you will find PDFs, articles, top-rated Web sites, and chapter quizzes. Access these resources to learn about technology and integrating it into the classroom. Watch the video tutorial online at **http://www.wiley.com/college/sharp** and learn how to refine your Internet search.

CHAPTER MASTERY TEST

Lets check for chapter comprehension with a short mastery test. Key Terms, Computer Lab, and Suggested Readings and References follow the test.

1. How did the Internet begin and what led to its growth?
2. Define *networking*.
3. Discuss the advantages and disadvantages of using networking in the classroom.
4. Describe the Internet and discuss three of its resources.
5. Explain the differences among e-mail, chat rooms, and instant messaging.
6. What is the World Wide Web and why is it an invaluable resource?
7. Distinguish between dial-up modems and cable modems.
8. What is Internet 2 and why was it necessary?
9. What are some advantages of a wireless network?
10. What are some of the advantages and disadvantages of distance education?

KEY TERMS

Bandwidth p. 41
Broadband p. 41
Cable modem p. 41
Chat room p. 44
Desktop video conferencing p. 47
Digital subscriber lines (DSLs) p. 41
Distance education p. 45

Distance learning p. 45
E-mail p. 42
File server p. 37
Hub p. 37
Instant messaging p. 44
Internet p. 39
Internet 2 p. 40
Internet relay chat (IRC) p. 44

Internet service provider (ISP) p. 42
Local area networks (LANs) p. 38
Modem p. 40
Netiquette p. 43
Network p. 38
Networking p. 37
Newsgroup p. 45
Open source p. 47

Routers p. 37
Satellite data service p. 41
Switches p. 37
Text messaging p. 44
Wide area networks (WANs) p. 38
Wireless network p. 38
World Wide Web (WWW) p. 40

 ## COMPUTER LAB: Activities for Mastery and Your Portfolio

3.1 Understanding the Internet Take a quiz to test your knowledge of Internet-related terms.

3.2 E-mail someone in your class or at another school.

3.3 Take a field trip to a school that uses networking. Find out what type of network and what software is being utilized and how students are using networking in the classroom. Evaluate this school's program, listing its strengths and weaknesses.

3.4 Examine the different online services and compare their costs and benefits. Watch the video tutorial online and learn how to conduct an Internet search.

SUGGESTED READINGS AND REFERENCES

Altschuler, Glenn C., and Ralph Janis. "Promise and Pitfalls in Distance Education for Alumni." *Chronicles of Higher Education* 46, issue 41 (June 16, 2000): PB8.

Andrews, Paul. "A Tech Rebirth?" *U.S. News & World Report* 134, issue 1 (January 13, 2003): 28–31.

Charp, Sylvia. "Technology for All Students." *T.H.E. Journal* 30, issue 9 (April 2003): 8.

Coffee, Peter. "Internet's 20th Anniversary Is Not Worth All the Hype." *eWeek* 20, issue 2 (January 13, 2003): 53–54.

Computer Industry Almanac http://www.clickz.com/showPage.html?page=stats/web_worldwide

Craig, Dorothy, and Jaci Stewart. "Mission to Mars." *Learning and Leading with Technology* 25, no. 2 (October 1997): 22–27.

Crosby, Shelley. Netiquette and Teen Safety Online. *School Library Media Activities Monthly* 23, issue 4 (December 2006): 18–22.

Davis, Bob. "Internet in Schools: A National Crusade Backed by Scant Data." *Wall Street Journal Eastern Edition*, June 19, 2000, A1.

Dede, Chris. "The Evolution of Distance Education: Emerging Technologies and Distributed Learning." *American Journal of Distance Education* 10, no. 2 (1996): 4–36.

Deveaux, Sarah, "Cable vs. DSL Is No Battle." *InfoWorld,* July 11, 2000, http://www.infoworld.com.

Dyril, Odvard, E. "Stats Making News." *Technology and Learning* 18, no. 7 (March 1998): 64.

Finn, Robin. "A Visionary Seeking to Connect the World, Wirelessly." *New York Times*, July 14, 2006, B2.

Fletcher, Geoffrey H. "Igniting the Internet Revolution." *T.H.E. Journal* 30, no. 4 (November 2002): 1–23.

Freedman, Alan. *Computer Desktop Encyclopedia,* Point Pleasant, Penn: The Computer Language Company, 2008.

Globus, Sheila. "Good, Bad and Internet." *Current Health 2* 28, issue 6 (February 2002): 13–15.

Gowan, Michael. "The Future Web." *PC World* 19, issue 4 (April 2001): 105–117.

Harris, Judy. "Ridiculous Questions! The Issue of Scale in Netiquette." *Learning and Leading with Technology* 25, no. 2 (October 1997): 13–16.

Hoffman, Tony. "The Best Free Software." *PC Magazine*, February 20, 2007, pp. 61–71.

"Internet Service Fiber joins the fray." *Consumer Reports* 72, issue 2 (February 2007): 24–28.

Internet World Stats, http:www.internetwordstats.com/, Internet Statistics Study, "Broadband Adoption," July 6, 2007.

Kaufman, Roger, and Ryan Watkins. "Assuring the Future for Distance Learning." *Quarterly Review of Distance Education* 1, no. 1 (Spring 2000): 59–68.

Kennedy, David M. "Dimensions of Distance: A Comparison of Classroom Education and Distance Education." *Nurse Education Today* 22, no. 5 (July 2002): 409–416.

Kirk, Rea. "A Study of the Use of a Private Chat Room to Increase Reflective Thinking in Pre-Service Teachers." *College Student Journal* 34 (March 2000): 115.

Kniffel, Leonard. "Internet 2 Marks 10th Anniversary with Tenfold Speed Increase." *American Libraries* 38, issue 1 (January 2007): 30–30.

Kurland, Daniel, Richard Sharp, and Vicki Sharp. *Introduction to the Internet for Education.* Belmont, Calif.: Wadsworth, 1997.

Ladau, Gary. "Tuning in to Wireless." *Campus Technology*, January 2007.

Maning, Stephen. "Lots of scope with Skype." *Times Educational Supplement*, January 5, 2007, p. 58.

Merritt, Mark. "Videoconferencing." *Presentation* (June 2000): 72–74.

Milner, Jacob. "Warming Up to Wireless." *T.H.E Journal* 33, no. 4 (November 2005): 29–35.

Moore, Michael G., and Greg Kearsley. *Distance Education: A Systems View, 2nd* ed. Belmont, Calif: Wadsworth, 2005.

Nasseh, Bizhan. "A Brief History of Distance Education," 1997, http://www.seniornet.org/edu/art/history.html.

Peha, Jon M. "Debates via Computer Networks: Improving Writing and Bridging Classrooms." *T.H.E. Journal* 24, no. 9 (April 1997): 65–68.

Resick, Rosalind. "Pressing Mosaic." *Internet* (October 1994): 81–88.

Shaw, Micheal "Buddy, can you spare a lesson?" *Times Educational Supplement*, June 23, 2006, p. 5.

Sullivan, Brian. "Netiquette." *Computerworld* 36, issue 10 (March 2, 2002): 48.

Technology Democracy Projects, 2008, http://www.discovery .org/a/4444

Van Horn, Royal. "Technology." *Phi Delta Kappan* 81, no. 10 (June 2000): 795.

Tunstall, Jeremy. *The Open University Opens.* London: Routledge, 1974.

Watkins, Ryan, Roger Kaufman, and Ingrid Guerra. "The Future of Distance Learning: Defining and Sustaining Useful Results." *Educational Technology* 41, no. 3 (May–June 2001): 19–26.

Weise, Elizabeth. "Successful Net Search Starts with Need." *USA Today*, January 24, 2000, 3D.

Woolley, Scott. "Wider-Fi." *Forbes* 171, issue 8 (April 14, 2003): 201–205.

Wireless Laptops in the Classroom and the Sesame Street Syndrome Communication of the ACM 49, issue 9 (September 2006): 25–27.

Young, Jefferey R. "The Fight for Classroom Attention: Professor vs. Laptop." *Chronicle of Higher Education* 52, issue 39 (June 6, 2006): A27–A29.

The Web

Integrating the Web into the Classroom

There are many ways to integrate the World Wide Web into the classroom. One way is to build a Web page using HTML. In creating this Web page, students can learn about any academic subject and simultaneously express themselves through the Web page. Students can learn to use a search engine to find specific information. Teachers can have students team with each other and do WebQuests on a variety of topics such as "What would Abraham Lincoln think about how teenagers live today?" In this chapter you will learn about the criteria for selecting Web sites. In addition, you will read about some Web utility programs, and review a useful collection of Web lesson plans.

Using the computer, students and teachers can do the following:

students can

- investigate different search engines,
- learn how to search the Internet,
- use criteria to investigate different Web sites,
- design a Web page,
- do a WebQuest.

teachers can

- find Web sites for students to investigate,
- demonstrate how to search the Internet,
- give examples of different WebQuests,
- find lesson plans and instructional material,
- communicate with students by e-mail, and
- devise a Web site evaluation form.

objectives

Upon completing this chapter, you will be able to do the following:

1 Name two search engines and describe their strengths.

2 Develop some strategies for searching the Web.

3 Identify four criteria for selecting Web sites.

5 Follow guidelines for Web page design

6 Explain what a WebQuest is and how it can be useful in the classroom.

7 Distinguish between Web 1.0 and Web 2.0.

What is the World Wide Web?

"The World Wide Web is a major service on the Internet" (Freedman, 2008). The World Wide Web (WWW) consists of **Web servers** that store and deliver Web pages or documents that contain text, graphics, animation, sound, and video. A **Web site** is a place where Web pages reside. When you access a Web site, the first page of the site is referred to as the **home page**. Using software called *browsers*, such as *Microsoft Internet Explorer* or *Safari*, you access these Web pages and are able to see them on your computer screen. Each Web site has its own unique **Uniform Resource Locator (URL)**, or address, to help you locate it. For example, when you type the URL http://www.paris.org/Musees/Louvre/Treasures/ in Microsoft's *Internet Explorer*'s address text box (Figure 4.1) and then press Enter, after a few seconds the home page corresponding to the URL, the Treasures of the Louvre, appears.

Figure 4.1
Internet Explorer's
Address Text
(*Source:* Reprinted with
permission from Microsoft
Corporation)

URL

On this page, you have specific items called *links* or connections to other Web pages (Figure 4.2). The World Wide Web gets its name from these links, which are like threads in a spider's web. Links, or *hot spots*,[1] are words that are displayed in a different color or pictures that are boxed by a colored border. When you click on a live link the cursor (or arrow) becomes a hand, and you can jump to another page, whether on the same computer or on another computer on the other side of the world.

Figure 4.2
Treasures of the Louvre
(*Source:* Reprinted by
permission Norman Barth. http://paris.org/)

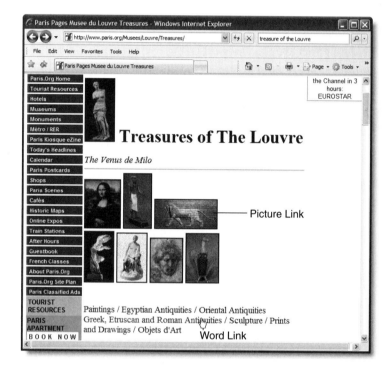

The size of the text on the Web page as well as the color of the links can be changed using the Preferences or View menu. This type of modification helps the individual who is colorblind or has trouble seeing small print.

A Brief History

Before the World Wide Web came into existence, people used text commands to communicate on the Internet. In 1989, Tim Berners-Lee, who worked at the European Particle Physics Laboratory, wrote a proposal that led to the development of the World Wide Web. In 1991, a math student by the name of Nicola Pellow created a browser that would work on any device (Berners-Lee, 2000). Scientists and academics created other browsers to surf the Net. Among these individuals were Marc Andreessen and Eric Bina who developed ***Mosaic*** at the University of Illinois' National Center for Supercomputing Applications (NCSA). Andreessen later went

---

[1] A location on the computer screen, usually inside a hypermedia program, that causes an action when a person uses his or her mouse to click on it.

into partnership with Jim Clark, founder of Silicon Graphics, to create the first mainstream browser Netscape Navigator, or Netscape. This browser was more advanced than other browsers in the way it handled graphics (Jones, Elgan, & Potter, 2006). In a short period of time, more browsers were developed, such as Microsoft's *Internet Explorer*; these browsers made it unnecessary to learn the UNIX commands that people had previously used on the Internet.

World Wide Web 1.0 and World Wide Web 2.0

In its early days the World Wide Web was referred to as Web 1.0. During this time period Web content was static and consisted mainly of fixed pages. The Web changed when computers became faster and bandwidth increased. The consumer could download multimedia files, and view Web pages containing pictures and video. Because of these changes, Web 2.0, not to be confused with Internet 2, came into existence.

Web 2.0 is "an umbrella term for the second wave of the World Wide Web, which was coined by O'Reilly Media (www.oreilly.com) and CMP Media (www.cmp.com) in their 2004 and subsequent conferences on the subject" (Freedman, 2008). Web 2.0 has user-generated content where individuals express themselves on a variety of topics. We saw the rise of instant messaging (Chapter 3), wikis, blogs, social networking sites such as MySpace (Chapter 10), people-generated movies on YouTube (Chapter 11), and a virtual world site called Second Life (Chapter 11). In addition, people created Web-based applications such as Google Docs (Chapter 6). (Web 3.0 is the next stage of development for the web.)

Finding a Web Page

When teachers or students want to visit a site, they usually type its URL in a browser window. But what happens when the browser cannot locate the address? One way to handle this problem is to physically modify the URL to get the page you desire. For example, when you try to call up the *Medical Matrix* home page at http://www.medmatrix.org/SPages/Patient_Education_and_Support.stm you get an error message. Try deleting the final segment (Patient_Education_and_Support. stm) and press *Return* or *Enter*. Continue removing segments from the URL up to the forward slashes until it works. For this example, the functional URL is http://www.medmatrix.org/. If this method of trying to find the URL does not work, try using a search engine to find the site.

To learn more about finding a Web page, visit our online site at http://www.wiley.com/college/sharp. Watch the video tutorial online at http://www.wiley.com/college/sharp and learn how to refine your Internet search.

Search Engines

Because the Web has millions of searchable pages, finding information is a difficult task. **Search engines** are software programs that help you locate information in a database on the Internet. Search engines have only become important since the explosion of the World Wide Web (Freedman, 2008). Search engines locate Web pages on a subject or locate a specific page when you are lacking its URL. To use a search engine, type a word or phrase called a *keyword* or *search term* in the search engine's text box. For example, you might type *Fort Sumter* as your searching term. The search engine then returns results in the form of links to relevant sites.

Well-known search engines are *Google*, *Yahoo*, *MSN*, *AOL*, and *Ask*. The kind of search site you use depends on the information you need. *Yahoo!*, launched in 1994, was the first major online Web-based subject directory and search engine to gain attention.

Many of the search engine sites automatically send **spider programs** out on the Web to collect the text of the relevant Web pages. These spiders are automated electronic software programs that follow the links on a page and put all the text into one huge database. You then search this database when you use the site. Some search engines are combination directories and search engines. **Metasearch engines** do nothing but search other sites. For example, an excellent metasearch engine is *Metacrawler*. These sites simultaneously bring you the results from many search engines. Many sites have become **portals**, sites that do not link to other sites but contain the information you seek. For a list of all major search engines, how they work, and their significant features, visit http://www.searchenginewatch.com. Table 4.1 on pages 61–62 lists some popular search engines that enable you to look for any topic.

HOW TO SEARCH

To be a good searcher, you must have the mind of a detective and think creatively. After all, the Internet is a big database with thousands of links that vary in quality. The search tool you choose is determined by what you are trying to find. If you just want to browse, directories such as *Yahoo!* are a good place to begin. If you are a beginner and want to ask a simple question, Ask.com might be very useful. If you need a special type of database, try *Open Directory* (http://dmoz.org). Finally, if you are doing advanced searches, begin with *Google*.

Here are a few general rules to follow when you search:

1. Narrow your search and avoid thousands of unnecessary results or hits. When using *Yahoo!*, for example, click the advanced search link and try using an exact phrase match.

2. When searching, avoid generic or commonly used words. For instance, a search for the *Civil War* is too general and will deliver a tremendous number of matches. In *Google,* for example, using the search term *Civil War* on March 4, 2008, delivered 46,300,000 pages. By limiting the search to Civil War court martial Fitz John Porter, you will be given only 68,200 pages.

3. Most search engines enable you to link your search terms with Boolean Operators such as *AND (Italy + Paris), OR, (Italy OR Paris)* or *NOT (Italy – Paris)* as well as to search for phrases by placing the words in quotation marks, which causes the engine to search for *all* the terms enclosed in the quotation marks. For example, searching for "To be, or not to be," would give you only information that addressed that phrase. The connectors vary with the search engines. Check your search engine's help page for more tips and tricks.

4. Use wildcards if the search engine allows it. Wildcards will turn up results on all terms containing the wildcard. For example, surg* will yield results on *surgery*, *surgeries*, and *surgical.*

5. To get an answer to a question, try Ask.com. For example, if you type "What is the capital of Turkey?" into the search textbox you will get the answer to your question (Ankara).

6. Enter singular terms. Many search engines will find the substring and include plural terms in the results.

7. To search the Blogosphere, try using Google Blog (blogsearch.google.com), and try Amazon (Amazon.com) for books.

8. If you want to find hundreds of maps with integrated information, try using Programmable Web (www.programmableweb.com). Click on their Mashups tab. A mashup is a Web page that combines data from multiple sources (Freedman, 2008).

9. Microsoft's site (search.live.com) has an excellent Web site which lets you search for images, video, news, maps, and more.

10. You can search library sites like the New York Public Library (http://www.nypl.org/) or a University library like California State University,

Northridge (http://library.csun.edu/). To avail yourself of all these library services you will need a library card number or some access identification.

11. To find old Web pages try using the Wayback Machine, a Web site that lets people visit archived versions of Web sites. The URL for this site is http://www.archive.org.

- The University of California at Berkeley recommends specific search tools and search strategies, including advanced searching techniques. Go to http://www.lib.berkeley.edu/TeachingLib/Guides/Internet/

- The University of South Carolina's Bare Bones 101 (http://www.sc.edu/ beaufort/library/pages/bones/bones.shtml) offers a basic Web search tutorial, including definitions, search strategies, and specific information about top directories and search engines.

- *Awesome Library* (http://www.awesomelibrary.org/help.html) shows simple as well as advanced searching techniques.

Table 4.1 Some Popular Search Engines

Search Engine	URL	Description
About.com	http://about.com/	Real people offer expert guidance on the Internet's best. They search in a wide range of subject areas.
AltaVista	http://www.altavista.com/	A database of Internet resources including Web pages and some Usenet newsgroups.
Ask.com (formerly AskJeeves)	http://www.ask.com/	Asks you to type in an actual question. The software identifies a variety of possible answers to your question. A kid's version called Ask for Kids is available at http://www.askforkids.com/.
Clusty	http://clusty.com/	Groups results into topics.
Dogpile	http://www.dogpile.com	Searches 26 databases simultaneously and supports Boolean searches.
Excite	http://www.excite.com	Collects the "most popular," frequently accessed Internet sites. It is unique because it searches by concept.
Fast Search	http://alltheweb.com	One of the largest indexes of the Web. The site is also known as All The Web.
Google	http://www.google.com	Searches for sites based on popularity, and these sites are ranked by how many sites have links to them.
Google Web Directory	http://directory.google.com	A database of sites organized by subject categories. This directory has over 1.5 billion pages and is considered the largest database.
ixquick	http://ixquick.com	Brings forth the best engines on the Internet and merges the results. It removes

(continued)

Table 4.1 *continued*

Search Engine	URL	Description
		redundancies and puts the results into a grouping.
Kartoo	http://www.kartoo.com/	A visual search engine that gives results in interactive maps.
KidsClick!	http://www.kidsclick.org/	Created by a group of librarians, shows students sites for grades K–8.
LookSmart	http://www.looksmart.com/	A searchable, category-based Web directory.
Lycos	http://www.lycos.com	Cross between Yahoo! and AltaVista. It also enables you to search for images.
MetaCrawler	http://www.metacrawler.com	Searches many search engines quickly and simultaneously. It also offers MiniCrawler, which performs searches in a window on the desktop.
Open Directory Project	http://dmoz.org	One of the most comprehensive search engines, with millions of sites.
Yahoo!	http://www.yahoo.com	A popular hierarchical directory. A kid's version called Yahoo! kids is available at http://www.kids.yahoo.com.
Web Crawler	http://www.webcrawler.com	Searches content areas and is also a Web directory.
Windows Live Search	http://www.live.com	A new search engine that eliminates scrolling. It is very useful for image searching.

Multimedia via the Internet

With the explosion of the World Wide Web came a surge in the number of Web sites created by individuals and organizations. Web site authors included graphics, animation, and sound in their sites. Students and teachers used visual images to communicate in distance learning, including clip art, animation, photos, and scans on their Web pages. Students shot movies with their camcorders and downloaded these movies to the Internet. Users of all ages began using the Web to listen to music. With this increase in users and usage came an increase in Internet multimedia applications. We review some here.

STREAMING VIDEO

Streaming video is a compressed movie sent in real time via the Internet. The receiving users can play these streaming movies with a streaming video player such as *RealVideo* or *QuickTime*. Streaming video begins playing as soon as you start to download. The quality of the movie depends on the speed of the computer connection. Videomaker's site on streaming video, found at http://www.streamingvideos .com, gives complete answers to frequently asked questions about streaming video.

STREAMING AUDIO

Streaming audio is one-way audio transmission over the data network. *Real One* is a multimedia player that plays streaming audio and streaming video in real time.

PLUG-INS

Web browsers come with plug-in extensions for video, audio, telephony, 3-D animation, and video conferencing. A **plug-in** is a separate program that works with a browser to enhance its capabilities. Table 4.2 lists popular plug-ins.

Table 4.2 Some Popular Plug-ins

Name	Web site	Description
Acrobat Reader	http://www.adobe.com/	Displays and prints Adobe Acrobat documents (PDFs)
Apple QuickTime	http://www.apple.com	Plays animation, music, MIDI, audio, video, and VR panoramas and objects.
Flash Player	http://www.macromedia.com	Displays animation and graphics.
Java	http://developers.sun.com/	Lets you run applications that use Java technology.
RealPlayer	http://www.real.com	Plays audio and video.
Shockwave	http://www.macromedia.com	Plays interactive games, multimedia, and streaming audio and displays graphics.
Windows Media Player	http://www.microsoft.com/	Plays streaming audio, video, animations, and multimedia presentations.

Web Site Evaluation

Sifting through sites on the Internet is a complex process; it is important to be able to distinguish a good Web site from one that is mediocre. Users must be cautious, because anyone can have a Web page and include on it information that is inaccurate, false, or just plain fantasy. The following criteria will help you evaluate Web sites.

DOWNLOAD TIME

Does the home page download fast enough to use during full-class instruction? Does this page download efficiently enough to keep students focused during small-group and independent study? Does the page download too slowly because it has too many graphics?

NAVIGATION EASE

Are your students able to move easily from page to page? Is the page designed in such a way that the students do not get confused or lost? Are the links and descriptions clearly labeled so the students have no trouble keeping on task? Do the majority of the links work?

APPEARANCE

Is the home page's design attractive and appropriate for students? Is the students' first impression positive, and will they be motivated to return repeatedly? Is the design clear so that the students can explore the page effectively? Are the screens easy to read?

GRAPHICS, VIDEOS, AND SOUNDS

Do the graphics, videos, and sounds have a clear purpose, and are they appropriate for the intended students? Do the graphics, videos, and sounds help the students reach their objectives? Do they enhance the content?

CONTENT

Does the site offer information that meets the learning objective? Is this information clearly labeled and accurate? How is the site organized? Is the information at an appropriate grade level, and can the student easily understand it? Are the related links worthwhile and appropriate? Is the content free of bias and stereotype? Does the site provide interactivity that increases its instructional value?

CURRENCY

Is the site updated on a regular basis?

CREDIBILITY

Is the site a trustworthy source of information? Does it provide author and source citations as well as a contact person to answer students' questions?

Now you have an idea of what is important when examining a website on the Internet. You might want to use the checklist form on page 65 and use its criteria to rate a site to see if it meets your curriculum objectives.

 Visit our online site at http:// www.wiley.com/ college/sharp where you can download a checklist in PDF format.

Integrating the Web into the Classroom

In this section, you will find Web sites that are particularly useful for teachers and students. They cover all curriculum areas and include an excellent collection of lesson plans. The sites were chosen for their currency, ease of use, comprehensiveness, and organization. They met the criteria listed in the form on page 65. The sites are updated frequently and contain the latest information. Many of the sites are award winners and have been cited for their authoritative and reliable information. Also online you will find a collection of these award-winning sites.

Web Sites to Use in the Classroom

MULTISUBJECT

Scholastic's Teacher Section

http://teacher.scholastic.com/

Scholastic provides standards-based lesson plans and reproducible materials for grades Pre-K–8. Under Teacher Resources, click on Lesson Plans for Web-based, ready-to-use curriculum materials. The science lesson plan seen in Figure 4.3 is an example of what you will find at this site. Use the site's search engine to find a specific lesson plan.

Web Site Rating Scale

Site Title: _____

Subject: _____

URL (address): _____

Grade Level and Class: _____

Objective: _____

URLs for individual site pages (addresses): Evaluate the Web site according to the following criteria. Circle the number that you feel the site deserves, 5 being outstanding and 1 being the worst.

1. Download Speed

Quickly loads text	5	4	3	2	1
Quickly loads graphics	5	4	3	2	1

2. Navigation Ease

Easy movement link to link	5	4	3	2	1
Links clearly labeled	5	4	3	2	1
Links to other sites operate effectively	5	4	3	2	1
Links for backward and forward movement	5	4	3	2	1
Adequate number of links	5	4	3	2	1
Links are apropos and helpful	5	4	3	2	1

3. Appearance

Visual appeal	5	4	3	2	1
Clarity	5	4	3	2	1

4. Content

Information that meets objectives	5	4	3	2	1
Clearly organized and labeled	5	4	3	2	1
Linked to worthwhile sites	5	4	3	2	1
Accurate and useful	5	4	3	2	1
Provides interactivity	5	4	3	2	1
Free of bias and stereotype	5	4	3	2	1
Site author clearly identified	5	4	3	2	1
Sufficient worthwhile information	5	4	3	2	1
Authoritative source	5	4	3	2	1
Readable by student at grade level	5	4	3	2	1
Students collaborate with other sites	5	4	3	2	1
Teachers share with others	5	4	3	2	1

5. Graphics, Videos, and Sound

Use clearly identified	5	4	3	2	1
Clear purpose and appropriate	5	4	3	2	1
Aids students to achieve objectives	5	4	3	2	1
Relevant for the site	5	4	3	2	1
Graphics enhance content	5	4	3	2	1

6. Currency (Frequency of Updating)   5   4   3   2   1

7. Credible Source of Information

Author and source citation	5	4	3	2	1
Contact person	5	4	3	2	1

Add the total number of points that the site earns to determine the overall rating.

Overall rating: _____

_____**150–133 points: This site is of sound content, and I can let the students freely explore.**

_____**132–111 points: This site contains good instructional material, but the students will need very specific instructions to explore the site.**

_____**110–94 points: This site contains some worthwhile information, but students will need more specific links and a list of bookmarks, along with frequent discussions, to progress.**

_____**93–63 points: Although some useful information exists at this site, the best way to effectively use this site is through whole-class instruction and guiding the students.**

_____**62–52 points: This site contains some useful information, but other sites would be more appropriate, and I must supervise the students.**

Figure 4.3
Scholastic Lesson Plans and Reproducibles
(*Source:* Screenshots from teacher .scholastic.com. Copyright © 2008 by Scholastic Inc. Used by permission.)

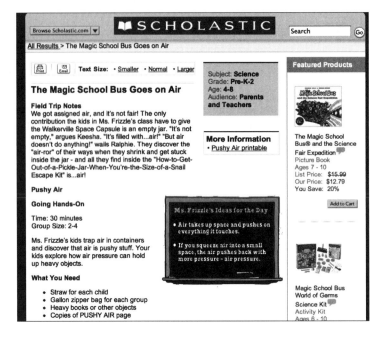

CanTeach

http://www.canteach.ca

CanTeach offers hundreds of lesson plans, thousands of links, and tons of other resources for elementary school teachers. The physical science lesson plan "Making a Pinhole Camera #2" is shown in Figure 4.4 (http://www.canteach.ca/elementary/physical4.html).

Figure 4.4
CanTeach
(*Source:* Courtesy CanTeach)

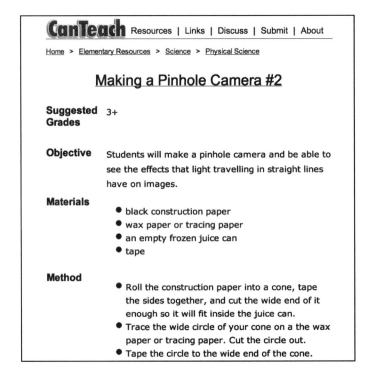

LANGUAGE ARTS

Pals Activities

http://pals.virginia.edu/Virginia/Activities/

This site offers an assortment of activities for reinforcing readiness-reading skills. Concepts covered are letter sounds, alphabet recognition, word concepts, word recognition, rhymes, beginning sounds, and blending. For beginning sounds, one of the game activities is the "Follow-the-Path Game" shown in Figure 4.5.

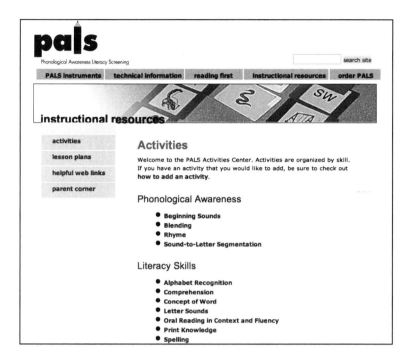

Also refer to *The Teacher's Desk* (http://www.teachersdesk.org) for a collection of over 150 Language Arts lesson plans for grades 5–6.

CyberGuides: Teacher Guides and Student Activities

http://www.sdcoe.k12.ca.us/score/cyberguide.html

CyberGuides are supplementary, standards-based, Web-delivered units of instruction centered on core works of literature. Each *CyberGuide* contains a student and teacher edition, standards, a task, a method for completion, teacher-selected Web Sites, and a rubric. A sample lesson plan for the book *The Door in the Wall* is seen in Figure 4.6 (http://www.sdcoe.k12.ca.us/score/door/doortg.html).

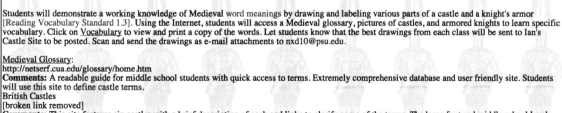

Student Activity 1: Illustrate/label parts of a castle and a knight in armor

Students will demonstrate a working knowledge of Medieval word meanings by drawing and labeling various parts of a castle and a knight's armor [Reading Vocabulary Standard 1.3]. Using the Internet, students will access a Medieval glossary, pictures of castles, and armored knights to learn specific vocabulary. Click on Vocabulary to view and print a copy of the words. Let students know that the best drawings from each class will be sent to Ian's Castle Site to be posted. Scan and send the drawings as e-mail attachments to nxd10@psu.edu.

Medieval Glossary:
http://netserf.cua.edu/glossary/home.htm
Comments: A readable guide for middle school students with quick access to terms. Extremely comprehensive database and user friendly site. Students will use this site to define castle terms.
British Castles
[broken link removed]
Comments: This site features six castles with a brief description of each and links to clarify some of the terms. The large font and middle school level readability are added benefits. Click on the forward arrow at the bottom of each page to learn about siege warfare and visit other castle sites. Use this site for ideas when drawing the castle.
Arms and Armory Glossary
http://www.chronique.com/Library/Glossaries/glossary-AA/armsindx.htm
Comments: Consists of a comprehensive glossary of terms with good readability. Use this site to define armor terms.
Armor and Weapons
[broken link removed]
Comments: Provides great illustrations of various types of armor and weapons with brief descriptors. Use this site for ideas when drawing the armored knight.

Figure 4.6
Door in the Wall
(*Source:* San Diego County office of Education)

The story "The Door in the Wall" takes place in the Middle Ages. Life during this time period is revealed through the experiences of Robin, a 10-year-old boy who hopes to become a knight. After becoming ill and losing the use of his legs, he struggles to overcome his handicap and proves himself a hero.

MATH

SCORE Mathematics Lessons

http://score.kings.k12.ca.us/

SCORE Mathematics Lessons reflect California's and the National Council of Teachers of Mathematics' standards. Excellent sample lesson plans are "What's My Number?" (http://score.kings.k12.ca.us/lessons/100board.html) and "Shopping for Toys" (http://score.kings.k12.ca.us/lessons/shop4toy.htm). For "What's My Number?" students seek information on the Internet to find facts needed to arrive at a number on the 100 board, a number known only to the author. Students use the information to work math problems. In "Shopping for Toys" (Figure 4.7), students have won a $100 gift certificate and can spend up to that amount to buy some toys. They then make a display consisting of drawings of some of the toys they chose and a few sentences explaining why they chose those toys. They answer teacher-made questions and fill in their order forms.

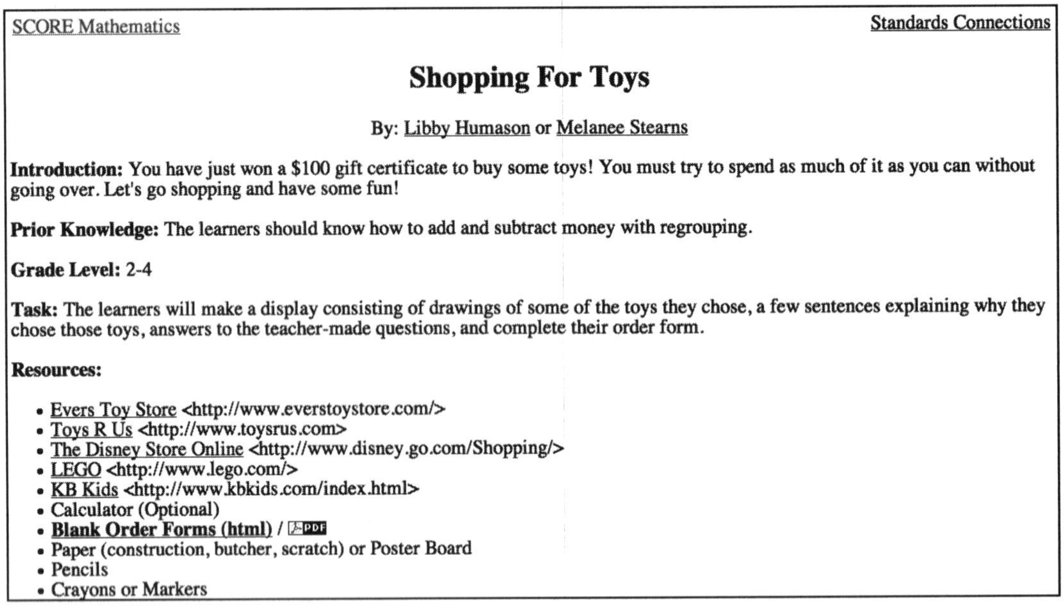

Figure 4.7
Shopping for Toys
(*Source:* Kings County office of Education)

SCORE Mathematics	Standards Connections

Shopping For Toys

By: Libby Humason or Melanee Stearns

Introduction: You have just won a $100 gift certificate to buy some toys! You must try to spend as much of it as you can without going over. Let's go shopping and have some fun!

Prior Knowledge: The learners should know how to add and subtract money with regrouping.

Grade Level: 2-4

Task: The learners will make a display consisting of drawings of some of the toys they chose, a few sentences explaining why they chose those toys, answers to the teacher-made questions, and complete their order form.

Resources:

- Evers Toy Store <http://www.everstoystore.com/>
- Toys R Us <http://www.toysrus.com>
- The Disney Store Online <http://www.disney.go.com/Shopping/>
- LEGO <http://www.lego.com/>
- KB Kids <http://www.kbkids.com/index.html>
- Calculator (Optional)
- **Blank Order Forms (html)** / [PDF]
- Paper (construction, butcher, scratch) or Poster Board
- Pencils
- Crayons or Markers

Math Forum Internet Mathematics Library

http://mathforum.org/library/resource_types/lesson_plans/

This immense collection offers hundreds of topics from many sources, including Suzanne Alejandre's *Understanding Algebraic Factoring* (Figure 4.8) (http://mathforum.org/alejandre/algfac.html).

SOCIAL STUDIES

Archiving Early America

http://www.earlyamerica.com

This site links to many primary sources of historical documents and portraits from 18th-century America. It includes portraits of famous 18th-century figures, original historical documents with abstracts, and chapters from books such as *The*

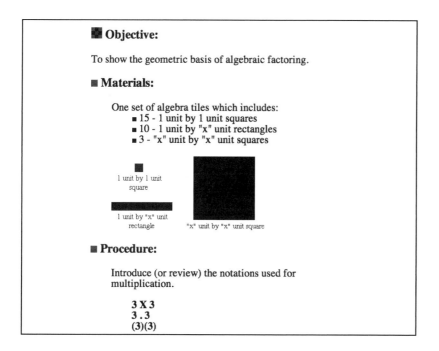

Figure 4.8
Algebraic Factoring
(*Source:* Reproduced with permission from
Drexel University, copyright 2008 by The
Math Forum @ Drexel (http://mathforum
.org/). All rights reserved.)

Autobiography of Benjamin Franklin. It also has a script that scrolls to what happened on a particular day in history. Click on Freedom Documents to see documents such as *The Declaration of Independence* (Figure 4.9).

Figure 4.9
Archiving Early America
(*Source:* Courtesy Archiving Early
America)

Shotgun's Home of the Civil War

http://www.civilwarhome.com/

This site contains a range of information on Civil War battles, Civil War biographies, Civil War medicine, Civil War potpourri, essays on the Civil War, letters about the Civil War, and much more. Click on *Civil War Biographies* to find the biography on Ulysses Simpson Grant shown in Figure 4.10. The biographical information covers the subject's participation in the Civil War, and in many instances pictures are included.

Ulysses Simpson Grant
(1822-1885)

The best evidence of the changes that had occurred in warfare from Jomini to Clausewitz can be found in the campaigns of Robert E. Lee and Ulysses S. Grant. The latter was born Hiram Ulysses Grant in Ohio but through confusion at West Point he became Ulysses Simpson Grant. Appointed to the military academy, he found it distasteful and hoped that Congress would abolish the institution, freeing him. He excelled only in horsemanship for that he had displayed a capability early in life and graduated in 1843, 21st out of 39 graduates. Posted to the 4th Infantry, since

SCIENCE

CEEE GirlTECH Lesson Plans

http://teachertech.rice.edu/Lessons/

GirlTECH has offered Internet science and math lesson plans for grades 7–12 since 1995. Use the site's search engine to find the lesson plan you want. You will find lesson plans that are similar to "Balancing Chemical Equations" (Figure 4.11).

Figure 4.11
Balancing Chemical Equations
(*Source:* Funbasedlearning.com)

FunBased Learning Lesson plans > Balancing Chemical Equations

Chemistry Dc	**School Mate Planners**
Get Matched Based on Science and Compatibility at Chemistry.com® www.Chemistry.com/DC	Affordable planners help students set goals and manage time. www.schoolmate.com
Ads by Google	Advertise on this site

Lesson plan for balancing equations   by Sulan Dun

Teaching balancing equations to high school students is difficult, because often some of the students are still at Piaget's concrete rather than abstract reasoning stage. That is, they can't just see the molecules in their head and/or draw them correctly. This lesson plan makes use of an online app (http://funbasedlearning.com/chemistry/default.htm) which makes that abstraction concrete – all of my grade 9 class mastered balancing equations in an hour (including the remedial students) using an early prototype of this app.

Directions:
1. Go to http://funbasedlearning.com/chemistry/default.htm. Click on the Classic Chembalancer worksheet link, print it out, and photocopy as needed for your class.
2. Go down to the computer lab (if you have internet access* for all those machines), hand out the worksheet, and have the students play the Classic Chembalancer game at

It includes an interactive quiz, links to other resources, a description of the project, project requirements, and Internet links that will enable the student to access the information needed to complete the project.

Access Excellence Activities Exchange

http://www.accessexcellence.org/AE

Access Excellence Activities Exchange, sponsored by Genentech, contains an archive of hundreds of lessons and activities submitted by high school biology and life science teachers participating in the Access Excellence Program. The site is suitable for grades 9–12. Scroll and then click on "The Brain: Understanding Neurobiology Through the Study of Addiction", a module developed by BSCS, Copyright© 2000 by BSCS and Video Discovery, Inc., then the "Teacher's Guide" to find lesson plans on Addiction (Figure 4.12).

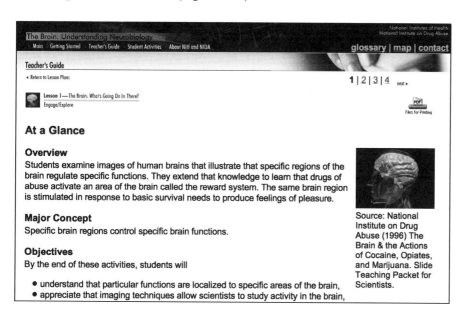

Figure 4.12
Access Excellence
(*Source:* BSCS, Copyright © 2000 by BSCS and Video Discovery, Inc. All rights Reserved)

I Can Do That!

http://www.eurekascience.com/ICanDoThat/

I Can Do That! is an amusing site that helps students learn about DNA, RNA, cells, protein, cloning, and other biotechnology topics (Figure 4.13).

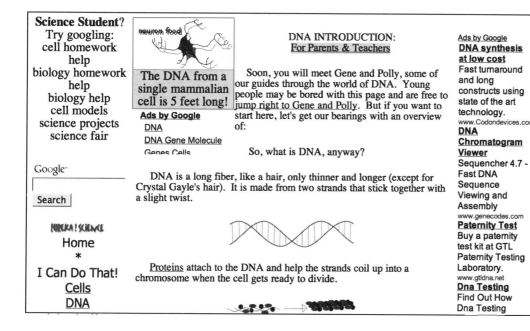

Figure 4.13
I Can Do That!
(*Source:* Reprinted by permission of Eureka! Science Corp.)

Newton's Apple

http://www.newtonsapple.tv/

This site contains a complete collection of teacher's guides from the TV show *Newton's Apple*. There are over 300 video clips. Try the fun experiments by clicking on "Science Try Its" or try science fair projects by clicking on "Science Fair Projects" (Figure 4.14).

Figure 4.14
Newton's Apple
(*Source:* Reprinted Courtesy of Twin Cities Public Television. Inc. www.newtonsapple.tv)

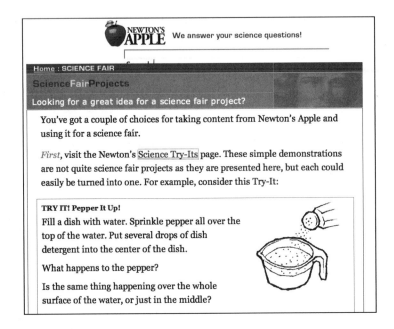

Another excellent site is *AskERIC Lesson Plans* (The Educator's Reference Desk) found at http://www.eduref.org/Virtual/Lessons/. This site has a large collection of lesson plans contributed by teachers for grades pre-K to higher education.

Sample Classroom Lesson Plans

I. COMBINING GEOGRAPHY WITH ART

Students will learn how to use a map site such as *MapQuest* (http://www.mapquest.com) and a drawing or painting program such as *Frames* or *Adobe PhotoShop Elements*. They will find a map at *MapQuest* that covers an area they would like to visit. Next, they will copy and paste this map into their paint or draw program. Finally, they will add text, arrows, and pictures to illustrate their map.

II. WEATHER TRACKERS

Students will use an Internet weather site such as Weather.com (http://www.weather.com) to track the weather conditions around the world. They can create charts and graphs using a program such as *Excel*. Finally, they will discuss the results with their classmates.

III. WACKY STORIES

Students will make up a list of words to be used at *Education Place's Wacky Web Tales* site (http://www.eduplace.com/tales/index.html). This site will generate wacky stories, or "mad libs." Students can then share their funny stories with their classmates.

IV. HISTORY PUZZLES

Students will use a puzzle site such as *PuzzleMaker* (http://puzzlemaker.discovery education.com/) to create a crossword puzzle for their history vocabulary words. They will then exchange puzzles to see if their classmates can solve them. They can also use one of many crossword puzzles from the existing database.

V. BUILDING A HOME PAGE

Students will make their own home pages using an existing Web page builder such as *GeoCities* at http://geocities.yahoo.com/.

VI. SCAVENGER HUNTS

Students will form groups to make up a scavenger hunt in science, social studies, music, art, or science. Their objective is to find a picture of a hawk or find out who the first American woman astronaut was. Next, students will exchange their scavenger hunts and search online for the required answers. (Table 4.3 shows a sample Scavenger Hunt.)

 Visit our online site at http://www.wiley.com/college/sharp and you will find a Scavenger Hunt Lesson Plan PDF.

Table 4.3 **Scavenger Hunt Form**

1. What is Michigan's state tree?

http://www.michigan.gov/

2. What animal made Jane Goodall famous?

http://www.janegoodall.org

3. Why do leaves change color in the fall?

http://www.sciencemadesimple.com/

4. Who was the first American woman astronaut to orbit the earth?

http://www.kidskonnect.com/Astronauts/AstronautsHome.html

5. Which president served the shortest term in the White House?

http://www.whitehouse.gov/history/presidents/

6. What was the name of the Supreme Court decision that overturned legalized segregation?

http://www.infoplease.com/history.html

7. What is the currency in Zambia?

http://www.xe.com/ucc/

8. In what year was the last star sewn on our present-day flag?

http://www.ushistory.org/betsy/

9. How many immigrants were processed at Ellis Island from 1892 to 1924?

http://www.ellisisland.org/

10. Starting from the foot of the pedestal, how many steps must you climb to reach the torch of the Statue of Liberty?

http://www.nps.gov/stli/

Variation.   Students can use a scavenger hunt online to see who can solve it the fastest. For example, if they are studying Black History Month they might use *Dr. Martin Luther King, Jr., Scavenger Hunt* (http://tstrong.com/mlking/).

WebQuests

In 1995, at San Diego State University, Professor of Educational Technology Bernie Dodge developed and coined the concept **WebQuest** while teaching preservice teachers. He gave the students a format for online lessons that would foster higher-order thinking. Shortly thereafter, Tom March, working for Pacific Bell, developed the first

WebQuest. Dr. Dodge's format for Web-based lessons was later published in *The Distance Educator Journal* (http://webquest.sdsu.edu/about_webquests.html). This paper, "Some Thoughts About WebQuests," defined a WebQuest as "an inquiry oriented activity where most or all of the information that the students use comes from the Web."

The WebQuest can consist of a single class session or a month-long unit. It usually involves a group of students who divide their labor. The lessons consist of materials selected by the teachers and used by the students. WebQuests can be done on a variety of topics that are not well defined and that require creativity and problem-solving skills. Some examples are "What was it like to live during the American Revolution?" "What would Benjamin Franklin think about how teenagers live today?" WebQuests are not meant to prompt simple recall but foster inquiry and logical constructivism incorporating collaborative learning.

What you need to create a WebQuest is the ability to design a Web page with links. Of course, if you are not talented this way, there are plenty of templates available on the Web. A server is not necessary, because you can copy the WebQuest on the hard drive. If you see a WebQuest that you want to use, you can use a program such as *Grab-a-Site 5.0* (Blue Squirrel) to load it on your hard drive. (Naturally, you need to get the author's permission to grab the page.)

In a WebQuest there are six important components: (1) introduction, (2) task, (3) process, (4) resources, (5) evaluation, and (6) conclusions. The *introduction* gives students background information and assigns roles for them to play. For example, a student might be a member of a research team or an astronaut. The teacher also gives students an overview of the learning objectives. The *task* tells the students what they will accomplish by the end of the WebQuest. For example, using *Planetary WebQuest* (Figure 4.15) (http://www.djusd.k12.ca.us/emerson/Staffpgs/Nancy Chatteinier/PlanetaryWebQuest.htm), students analyze the different planets and decide which planet to colonize.

Figure 4.15
Planetary WebQuest
(*Source:* Courtesy Nancy Chatteinier)

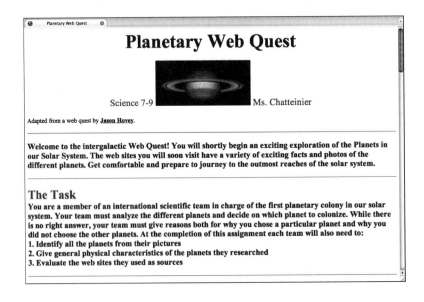

At the end of the assignment, each team has to identify the planets, give general physical characteristics, and evaluate its sources. The *process* consists of step-by-step instructions the students go through to accomplish the task that is set. The *resources* section should consist of a list of resources, either printed or bookmarked Web sites that the students need to complete the task. The resources are either listed separately or embedded in the process section. The students can also use other resources such as videos, audiocassettes, or maps. Each WebQuest must have some method for *evaluation*. The method should be fair and consistent for the tasks set. Finally, the *conclusion* component has students discuss what they discovered and the teacher summarize what has transpired.

Since the beginning of WebQuests, teachers, curriculum specialists, and teacher educators at the university level have used Bernie Dodge's *WebQuest Page* at San Diego State University. He now maintains this database of WebQuest examples at http://webquest.org (Figure 4.16). Click on **Find WebQuest** and search using the curriculum and grade to find hundreds of sites.

Figure 4.16
WebQuest Portal
(*Source:* © Bernie Dodge, PhD)

Over time, the *WebQuest Page* has grown and developed links to WebQuests all over the world. Thousands of teachers have created WebQuest lessons on the Web. To find them, simply search with any search engine by typing in the search term *WebQuest*. Your search may turn up the WebQuest lesson Art of Geometry (http://216.101.114.8/Young), which connects geometry with art, or *EcoQuest: Desert Edition* (http://members.aol.com/QuestSite/1/2.html), an interactive WebQuest designed for teachers in search of middle school science curricula. Finally, Tom March, a WebQuest originator, has a *Best WebQuests* site (http://bestwebquests.com) ranging from art to science.

Web Page Creation

With the growth of the Internet, computer-literate people everywhere have expressed themselves by creating Web pages. The building of Web pages has increased exponentially, and these pages range from the informative to the ridiculous. Because of the popularity of Web pages, many programs were designed to create them. Using HTML code was difficult for the ordinary computer user, so software companies produced Web publishing programs that had a simple graphical interface for Web pages and that automatically generated the HTML code. Word processing programs such as *Word Perfect* and *Microsoft Word* enable you to create a Web page and export it as HTML. *PowerPoint* 2007 lets you save your presentation as a Web page. There are organizer programs like *Inspiration* that have HTML features built into their programs.

Web creation programs like iWeb (Apple) and WebBlender (Tech4Learning) are designed for the novice adult or younger student. iWeb is a template-driven program where you first choose a design and then add movies, pictures, and text. WebBlender is a simple drag-and-drop Web creation program. The tools are intuitive and the interface is simple. Figure 4.17 shows a WebBlender screen.

Higher-level programs such as *Dreamweaver* (Macromedia) or *GoLive Studio* (Adobe) are for the advanced student. *Dreamweaver MX* and *GoLive Studio* enable you to create professional Web sites. They feature visual layout tools and extensive code editing.

 To learn more about award-winning Web creation software programs, visit our online site at http://www.wiley.com/college/sharp.

Figure 4.17
Tech4Learning Web Page
(*Source:* WebBlender is a registered trademark of Tech4Learning, Inc.)

Furthermore, sites such as Yahoo's! *GeoCities* (http://geocities.yahoo.com/) and Class Homebuilder (Scholastic) (http://teacher.scholastic.com/homepagebuilder/index.htm) enable you to build your own Web pages. You can use page wizards at these sites to create a Web page in a matter of minutes. You simply answer a few questions, and the wizard builds a professional-looking page according to your answers (Figure 4.18). In addition, you can create pages from scratch using a page builder. With a page builder, you drag and drop items.

Figure 4.18
Quick Start Web Page Wizard
(*Source:* Reproduced with permission of Yahoo! Inc.® 2008 by Yahoo! Inc. YAHOO! and the YAHOO! logo are trademarks of Yahoo! Inc.)

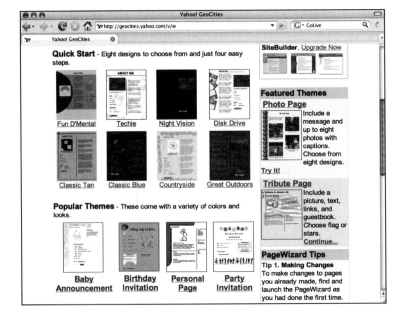

HTML editors are less intuitive but are available as shareware programs that can be purchased for a fraction of the cost of the others. Programs of this kind include SiteSpinner 2.7 (Windows) Virtual Mechanics Inc., and *PageSpinner* (Macintosh) (Jerry Aman, Optima System). If you are a purist and want to work close to the code, you will have to learn hypertext markup language and programming languages.

HYPERTEXT MARKUP LANGUAGE

Hypertext markup language (HTML) is the formatting language behind the documents that you see on the World Wide Web. The Web pages are created with code that has embedded text, for example, the <title>California State University <title> (Figure 4.19). HTML is not a programming language. In the early days Web pages were simple documents, but today this has changed because of the multimedia nature of the Web. You now have programming languages like Java Script that are embedded in these Web pages.

```
Source of: http://www.calstate.edu/
<html xmlns="http://www.w3.org/1999/xhtml">
<head>
<meta http-equiv="Content-Type" content="text/html; charset=iso-8859-1" />
<title>The California State University</title>
<link href="/css/cointernet-structure-temp.css" rel="stylesheet" type="text/css"/>
<script language="JavaScript" type="text/javascript" src="/js/top_nav_menu.js"></script>
<script language="JavaScript" type="text/javascript" src="/js/ranImg.js"></script>
<script src="http://www.google-analytics.com/urchin.js" type="text/javascript">
</script>
```

Figure 4.19
California University Northridge's Home Page (*Source:* California University Northridge's home page)

GUIDELINES FOR CREATING A WEB PAGE

Before creating your own Web page, read the following guidelines:

1. Plan ahead, that is, decide what type of information you want to put on the Web. Then outline your ideas, write your text, and revise it. You need to present the information in a logical order and make every word count. Be sure to run your spell checker and proofread carefully.

2. Organize your information. Create a sketch so you can see where you will place your text and graphics. In other words, storyboard your ideas. You can use a concept mapping program such as *Inspiration* (Inspiration Software, Inc.) for this purpose.

3. To help you decide where you want to place your navigational buttons,[2] create a map and experiment by putting these buttons in different locations on the map. Rather than spending time scrolling, your reader should be able to jump easily from one location to another.

4. Read your home page carefully. Does it communicate well, set a good tone, and catch people's attention? Good first impressions count in Web pages as well as in life.

5. Use graphics wisely to enhance content. Do not overload your page with pictures; no user enjoys long waits for graphics to load. Use an **interlaced GIF**, which displays graphics with one set of alternative lines at a time. (GIF stands for *graphic interchange format.*)

6. Be sure your site contains appropriate, relevant, timely, and engaging material.

7. Check the information on your site for reliability.

8. Be careful not to clutter the page with too many elements. Use of too many typefaces detracts from the general feeling of the writing.

9. Break up your text so it is more readable.

10. Keep the content interesting by using a variety of items so as not to bore the audience. An example of a good Web site is *Cells Alive!* (Figure 4.20; http://www.cellsalive.com/). This site is a primer on cellular biology featuring a fascinating collection of pictures and animation with clear explanations. You can actually see how penicillin destroys bacteria and can view microscopic parasites.

To learn more about HTML, visit our online site at http://www.wiley.com/college/sharp. There is also a brief guide that will give you some of the basics for creating an HTML document as well as award-winning Web sites.

---

[2] A location on the computer screen, usually inside a hypermedia program, that causes an action when a person uses his or her mouse to click on it.

Figure 4.20
*Cells **Alive!***

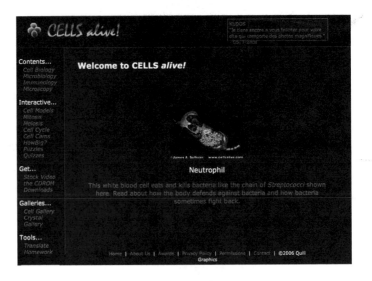

WEB DEVELOPMENT TOOLS

Since Web page creation has become such a popular phenomenon, a cottage industry has developed around it. Web animation programs such as *Flash* (Macromedia) (Figure 4.21) and *Frames* (Tech4Learning) and image-editing programs such as *ImageBlender* (Tech4Learning) are being used more and more in the schools.

Figure 4.21
Flash
(*Source:* Authors photo, software used with permission from Macromedia)

WEB UTILITIES

Some Web utilities that teachers find very useful are off-line browsers and **URL managers**. With an **off-line browser,** students can examine Web sites without an Internet connection. With a good URL manager, the teacher or student can organize URLs so they can easily find them when he or she wants. Table 4.4 shows a few of these programs.

SUBSCRIPTION-BASED SITES

Subscription-based Web sites such as Learning.com, *NetTrekker*, *QuickMind Online*, *Imagine Learning English*, and *Gizmos* contain lesson plans, state standards, and tutorials. They are aligned with ISTE's National Educational Technology Standards (NETS) and also reinforce the state core curriculum standards. The sites usually have a trial period, and they cost from $1,000–$1,200 a year for a class.

Table 4.4 Web Utilities

Title, Publisher	Description
URL Manager Pro, Kagi Shareware by Alco Blom http://www.url-manager.com	This utility is a professional **bookmark manager** for the Kagi Shareware Macintosh. Enables you to organize and collect URLs in a hierarchical manner, organize bookmarks between folders with drag and drop, and access URLs on the Web.
Bookmark Buddy, OSoLis www.bookmarkbuddy.net	This program is a professional bookmark manager for Windows.
Grab-a-Site 5.0, Blue Squirrel http://www.bluesquirrel.com/	Enables you to save Web sites to your hard drive. It works on numerous Windows operating systems. This utility is ideal for browsing off line.
WebWacker 4.0, Blue Squirrel http://www.bluesquirrel.com/	*WebWacker* is an off-line browser for the Macintosh that saves Web sites to a hard drive.

Learning.com

http://learning.com/

Learning.com website *EasyTech* is a subscription-based curriculum solution that provides online instruction for grades K–8. EasyTech integrates technology into the classroom and reinforces core curriculum concepts. It covers the national technology standards and enables teachers to use their own states' core curriculum standards. Through interactive online tutorials (Figure 4.22) students learn to use word processing, database, spreadsheet, and presentation software. They learn by using these applications as tools in core curriculum areas such as science, language arts, social studies, and math. *EasyTech* comes with e-mail support as well as a management system with which teachers can assign lessons and assess how well students are achieving the educational objectives. The teacher is provided with class reports, student reports, and lesson reports.

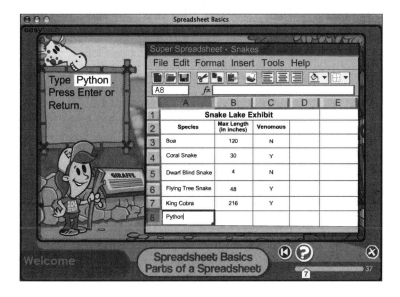

Figure 4.22
Spreadsheet Basics

netTrekker

http://www.nettrekker.com/frontdoor

netTrekker is a search engine for schools that gives easy access to 180,000 K–12 online educational resources that are aligned with every state's standards. Each site is rated (Figure 4.23) by educators and librarians and comes with its own individual description. This is a safe way for students to search the Web, because they can be sure that the sites contain only academic content that is organized around the K–12 curricula. Using *netTrekker* you can access your state's standards; find online lesson plans, learning exercises, and Web sites; and use interactive history time lines.

Figure 4.23
netTrekker
(*Source:* Courtesy netTrekker, www.netTrekker.com)

Finally, there is QuickMind.net (http://www.quickmind.net/), Imagine Learning English (http://www.imaginelearning.com), and Gizmos (http://www.explorelearning.com). QuickMind.net, created by Sunburst, is a site for grades K–12. This database contains a rich variety of resources and tools with which teachers and students can share, print e-mail, publish, or download. *Imagine Learning English* has vocabulary activities for 4- to 7-year-olds and acts as each student's individual tutor. Finally, *Gizmos* is an award-winning math and science site developed for grades 6–12. This site has a large collection of math and science simulations with accompanying ready-made lessons (Figure 4.24).

Figure 4.24
Gismos
(*Source:* Courtesy ExploreLearning)

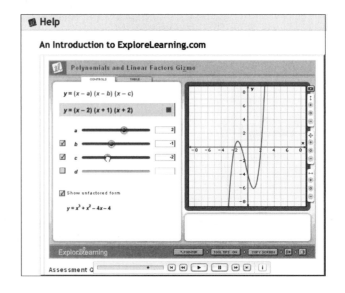

SUMMARY

In this chapter, we discussed the World Wide Web, and especially Web page creation, hypertext markup language (HTML), and guidelines for creating a Web site. In the process, we discussed some useful Web utilities such as *Grab-a-Site 5.0* and *URL Manager Pro*. We examined the WebQuest and considered some examples. Furthermore, we looked at the various search engines and explored a few pointers on how to search. We examined criteria for selecting Web sites and a Web site evaluation scale. Finally, we considered ways to integrate the Web into the classroom.

STUDY AND ONLINE RESOURCES

CHAPTER 4 ONLINE RESOURCES

 In the **student section** of the book's online site at **http://www.wiley.com/college/sharp**, you will find an Internet searching guide, PDFs, templates, an Internet checklist, articles, top-rated Web sites, and chapter quizzes. Watch the video tutorial online at **http://www.wiley.com/college/sharp** to learn how to refine your Internet search.

CHAPTER MASTERY TEST

Lets check for chapter comprehension with a short mastery test. Key Terms, Computer Lab, and Suggested Readings and References follow the test.

1. Identify four criteria for selecting Web sites.

2. Offer a few generalized suggestions for searching the Web.

3. Explain what a *search engine* is and give an example.

4. Give three general rules to follow when creating a Web page.

5. What is the World Wide Web and why is it an invaluable resource?

6. Give an example of a browser and explain why you need to use one.

7. Name two ways you can use Web sites in the classroom.

8. Define the following terms: *HTML, Web1,* and *Web2*.

9. What is a WebQuest and why is it a valuable learning tool?

10. Define the following terms: *home page* and *URL*.

11. What are *streaming audio* and *streaming video* and how are they being used on the Web?

KEY TERMS

Home page p. 57
Hypertext markup language (HTML) p. 77
Interlaced GIF p. 77
Metasearch engines p. 60
Mosaic p. 58

Off-line browsers p. 78
Plug-in p. 63
Portals p. 60
Search engines p. 59
Spider programs p. 60

Streaming audio p. 63
Streaming video p. 62
Uniform resource locator (URL) p. 57
URL managers p. 78
Web 1 p. 59

Web 2 p. 59
WebQuest p. 73
Web servers p. 57
Web site p. 57

COMPUTER LAB: ACTIVITIES FOR MASTERY AND YOUR PORTFOLIO

4.1 Internet Searching Strategies Test your understanding of how to search the Internet. Watch the video tutorial online and learn how to refine your Internet search. Search for lesson plans on math, science, social studies, and language arts.

4.2 Create a Teacher Web Page Create a Web page for your classroom. Watch the video tutorial online and learn how to create a Web page.

4.3 Create a Student Web Page Use these directions to help your students create Web pages.

4.4 Use the Web site evaluation form to rate five Web sites.

4.5 Investigate five different search engines and explain the advantages and disadvantages of each one.

4.6 Create a simple Web page that displays a graphic, has a link, and has text.

4.7 Create multimedia projects or reports on the Web using applications such as *PowerPoint*. Some invaluable telecommunications tutorials accompany products such as *Microsoft Word* and *Pages*. Watch the video tutorial online and learn how to create a PowerPoint presentation.

SUGGESTED READINGS AND REFERENCES

Andreessen, Marc. NCSA Mosaic Technical Summary. National Center for Supercomputing Applications, Urbana, Illinois, February 20, 1993.

Belicove, Mikal E., and Joe Kraynak. *Internet Yellow Pages, 2007 ed.* (Indianapolis: Que Publishing, October 20, 2006).

Berners-Lee, Tim, with Mark Fischetti. *Weaving the Web: The Original Design and Ultimate Destiny of the World Wide Web.* New York: HarperCollins, 2000.

Bunz, Ulla. "Web Site Creation as a Valuable Exercise: Seven Steps to Communicating Significance Online." *Technology Teacher* 62, issue 5 (February 2003): 7–10.

Carroll, Sean. "How to Find Anything Online." *PC Magazine,* vol. 22, issue 9 (May 27, 2003): 80–82.

Freedman, Alan. *Computer Desktop Encyclopedia.* Point Pleasant, Penn.: Computer Language Company, 2008.

Gesing, Ted, and Jeremy Schneider. *Java Script for the World Wide Web.* Berkeley, CA: Peachpit Press, 1997.

Hardman, Justin, and David Carpenter. "Breathing fire into Web 2.0." *Learning and Leading with Technology* 34, no. 5 (February 2007): 18–25.

Hawkridge, David. "The Human in the Machine: Reflections on Mentoring at the British Open University." *Mentoring and Tutoring: Partnership in Learning* 11, issue 1 (April 2003): 15–25.

Henke, Karen Greenwood. "5 Web 2.0 Time Savers." *Technology & Learning,* 27 (June 2007): 32–33.

Hock, Ran. "Search Engines: From Web 0.0 to Web 2.0 and Beyond." *Online* 31, issue 1 (January/February 2007): 26–30.

Jones, George, Elgan, Mike, and Valerie Potter. "Fifteen World-Widening Years." *InformationWeek* (September 18, 2006): 41–47.

Kelly, Rebecca. "Working with WebQuests." *Teaching Exceptional Children* 32, no. 6 (July/August 2000): 4.

McLester, Susan. "Web 2.0: Web 2.0 for Educators." *Technology and Learning* 27, no. 9 (April 2007): 18–23.

Mehta, Seema. "New K–12 elective: class online." *Los Angeles Times,* February 4, 2007, A1, A21.

Metz, Cade. "Web 3.0." *PC Magazine,* April 10, 2007, pp. 74–76.

Milstein, Sarah. "Find the Good Stuff Fast." *MacWorld,* February 2007, pp. 70–71.

Sharp, Vicki, and Richard Sharp. *Best Web Sites for Teachers, 7th ed.,* Eugene, Oregon: Visions Technology in Education, 2006–7.

Warlick, David. "A Day in the Life of Web 2.0." *Technology and Learning* 27, no. 3 (October 2006): 18–23.

Williams, Robin. *The Non-Designer's Web Book, 2nd ed.* Berkeley, Calif.: Peachpit Press, 2003.

Internet Issues

Internet Dangers

The Internet offers a dishonest person the opportunity to steal your identity. And it offers a virus the opportunity to infect your computer files. In this chapter, you will learn about all sorts of Internet-related problems including identity theft, spam, phishing attacks, plagiarism, unequal access, computer piracy, and copyright infringement. Online you will find Internet sites and articles on viruses, identity theft, and related computer topics.

Using the computer, students and teachers can do the following:

students can

- learn about computer hackers on the Internet,
- search the Internet for ways to improve unequal access,
- visit sites such as "Turnitin" in order to write about plagiarism,
- create a checklist on how to avoid Internet Viruses and Worms.

teachers can

- discuss computer hackers,
- give examples of different computer problems such as unequal access,
- show students Web sites devoted to plagiarism,
- find lesson plans and instructional material,
- demonstrate ways students can improve computer security.

objectives

Upon completing this chapter, you will be able to do the following:

1. Describe Internet issues such as ethics violation, crime, viruses, plagiarism, and copyright infringement.

2. Describe three factors related to software piracy.

3. List some practical ways a teacher can improve computer security.

4. Discuss problem of unequal access.

Internet Problems

Computers have benefited us in many ways. Computers have improved education, medical care, and business operations. Computers have also helped artists be more creative and enabled factories and businesses to operate more efficiently and effectively. As we have seen in our discussion on distance learning (Chapter 4), no advance comes without disadvantages. In this section, we examine some of the problematic issues associated with using the Internet. We talk about problems that range from invasion of privacy to copyright infringement.

INTERNET SECURITY PROBLEMS

There are quite a few security drawbacks on the Internet. People can use it to steal information. Some companies have had clients' correspondence violated. It is for this reason that Chrysler, Chevrolet, and Ford will not send designs over the Internet. Even though data are encrypted or encoded, it is difficult to verify a user's identity. Experts such as Taso Devetzis, a Bellcore lab researcher who does encryption work on the Internet, feels that the Internet is still not 100 percent secure.

Because of security problems, many school districts are using a security system called a **firewall** to protect their schools' networks against threats from hackers from other networks. A firewall is usually a combination of software and hardware that prevents computers in a school's network from communicating directly with computers outside the network. By using this protection schools lessen the possibility of receiving spam.

SPAM

Spam is sending unsolicited junk e-mail. Besides sending e-mail spam messages, people send spam through mobile phones, instant messaging, newsgroups, blogs, and fax transmissions.

On May 3, 1978, Gary Thuerk became the first person to send **spam.** He sent an e-mail ad to 600 people over a network of university and government computers (Streitfeld, 2003). In 2006, the amount of spam sent daily was estimated at 12.4 billion (Evett, 2006). Adding to this problem is software that lets the user harvest e-mail. Software like *Ada Email Address Search XP* searches and finds your target e-mail addresses from more than 3 billion Web pages.

Anyone using e-mail has been personally affected by spam. My spam messages outnumber my legitimate e-mails. Just yesterday, I received 225 e-mail messages. The majority of these messages were spam, ranging from pornography to advertisements for miracle pills, phony degrees, pyramid schemes, low-interest loans and mortgages, to chain letters. Oh, I forgot. I also received a West African–based e-mail (Figure 5.1) that informed me how I would receive a share of an unclaimed fortune. I have not bought my multimillion-dollar estate yet.

Figure 5.1
Eight-Million-Dollar Letter

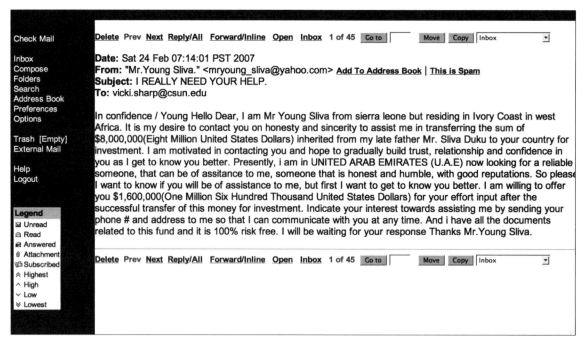

In 2003, the House of Representatives passed an antispam bill. Soon, it will be common for the courts to impose civil penalties on spammers. Industry groups will find more ways to block, authenticate, or otherwise filter bulk mailers. But all of these remedies may not solve the problem right away because there are so many groups that have an investment in this issue.

Until this problem is cleared up, you need to safeguard your e-mail addresses, use the delete key, without opening the message, and complain to your ISPs and e-mail service. You will need to learn to use your browser's filtering feature or buy a spam-filtering product such as *SpamKiller* by McAfee or *Spam Sleuth* by Blue Squirrel. This software will filter out a great deal of spam from your mailbox.

PHISHING ATTACKS

Phishing refers to e-mail scams that try to get your credit card numbers, Social Security numbers, and personal passwords. You receive an official-looking email that pretends to come from a legitimate organization like a bank or retail store. The sender then asks for personal information. These emails lead individuals to counterfeit Web sites that trick them into divulging their financial information. In 2006 the number of phishing attacks against companies increased to one or more a day. Even though this sounds minor compared to millions for spam and e-mail viruses, it is very disturbing. What this means is the people that perpetrate these attacks have information on the organizations they want to penetrate (Roberts, 2006).

SAFETY CONCERNS

Filtering and monitoring software helps ensure a safer online experience by blocking access to inappropriate sites. Filtering programs include *CyberPatrol* (SurfControl, Inc.) and *Net Nanny* (ContentWatch). With *Cyber Patrol*, the teacher can customize lists of sites appropriate for individual students. *CyberPatrol* also comes with an extensive array of fully researched Web sites that are updated on a daily basis. *Net Nanny* (Figure 5.2) keeps a list of multiple users. This product is user-friendly and maintains a list of approved and blocked Web sites. Furthermore, users can view full Web site lists. *Net Nanny* integrates with popular search engines such as Google, Yahoo, and Dogpile.

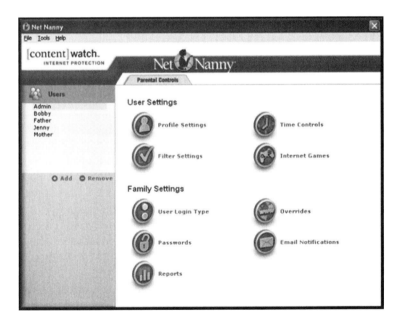

Figure 5.2
Net Nanny
(*Source:* Net Nanny® ContentWatch®)

In addition to software programs, there are search engines such as *Ask for Kids* (http://www.askkids.com/) and Yahoo! Kids (http://kids.yahoo.com/) that are specially designed for students. These databases contain no sex or pornography sites. There are sites such as Kids' Rules for Online Safety that offer online safety guides where you can browse for Internet safety products (http://safekids.com/).

PRIVACY VIOLATION

The concern for privacy is an issue that is not unique to computerized systems, but such systems increase the likelihood that an individual's privacy will be invaded. Computerized systems have proliferated in recent years, and these systems contain many different types of information. If a person lives in the United States, his or her name appears in federal, state, and local government data banks and in many private-sector files.[1] The Internal Revenue Service keeps records on everyone who files tax returns. State and local governments maintain files concerning taxes and law enforcement; public and private institutions keep records on students' educational performance; and medical data banks store medical records. It is hard to determine exactly who has what information and how this information will be used. According to the American Management Association's annual 2005 Electronic Monitoring & Surveillance Survey, 50 percent of major U.S. companies track employees by looking at their employees' e-mail, and 76 percent monitor their employees' Web connections (http://www.amanet.org/research). Personal information—such as addresses, telephone numbers, and maps to homes—is accessible through the Internet. For a few dollars you can find out where a person lives, as well as intimate personal information. Many people have unwanted visitors at their doorsteps because of the Internet.

A technology called a **cookie** keeps records of the online activities on your hard drive. A cookie gives the server the name of the site you visited and information about your choices, and when you return to the site, it requests information from your cookie file and gathers even more data on your habits.

With so many different types of computerized systems, financial or academic indiscretions of 10 years ago may return to haunt you. Information that you provided for one purpose may be used for another. The computer poses a threat to our privacy, and we should be concerned about the possibility of unauthorized persons or groups gaining access to personal information simply by entering a system. By looking at statements of charges from Nordstrom's, Ticket Master, Toys 'R Us, Apple Inc., and Foreign Automotive Services, a "computer detective" can deduce that you like to go shopping in an upscale store, go to the theater, have children, and own a computer and a foreign automobile. If bills are examined over an extended period, a personal, psychological, and economic profile can be developed, and this information could be used to swindle you out of huge sums of money—or even to blackmail you.

Another concern regarding invasion of privacy is computer record matching, the comparison of files stored in different governmental agencies on the same individual. Law enforcement agencies use computer matching to find a criminal by comparing Medicare files and Social Security benefits files to identify individuals who are believed deceased but are still receiving Social Security checks. Supporters of this use of the computer argue that people who break the law should be punished, and this procedure saves the taxpayers money. Opponents argue that it uses information for a purpose different from what was originally intended. If the people who supplied the information thought that it would be used against them, they might falsify data or not supply the needed information, impeding the operation of the asking agencies and costing taxpayers money.

In the 1970s and 1980s, a series of laws was enacted to protect privacy by controlling the collection and dissemination of information. The Freedom of Information Act (1970) gave individuals access to information about themselves collected by federal agencies. (Unfortunately, the government can still continue to collect information and, under many circumstances, can refuse to release it or release only edited versions.) The Privacy Act of 1974 stated that data collected for one purpose could not be used for another. This restriction only applied to federal agencies. The Family Education Rights and Privacy Act (1974) regulated access to public and private school grades and anecdotal records stored on computer. Because of this law, parents or students could gain access to a student's records, and unauthorized parties were blocked from this information. Finally, the Comprehensive Crime Control Act (1984) made it illegal for private individuals to modify, destroy, disclose, or use information stored in a government computer.

---

[1] A data bank is an electronic storehouse for data.

VIRUSES AND WORMS

Another harmful force in computing today is the **virus**, a set of instructions that infects computer files by duplicating itself. A malicious individual writes a code and buries it in an existing program. When the program is loaded into the computer, the virus attaches itself to other programs on the person's computer. This creates a chain reaction. When a person installs an infected program on his or her computer or downloads an infected program from the Internet, the person also installs the virus. Computers can become infected electronically when a hacker creates a virus and sends it over phone lines to a local network. Since the network is connected to thousands of computers, the infection is carried to all the connected computers. When the virus arrives at each of these computers, it performs the assignment it was created to do. E-mail attachments have become a quick way to spread viruses. In 2000, federal agencies experienced attacks by malicious e-mails spreading the "I LOVE YOU" virus. At least 14 agencies were affected, including the CIA and the Department of Energy. Strange as it may seem, an industry group had warned about the "I LOVE YOU" and "Love Letter" e-mail viruses, but there was an eight-hour delay before this information was given to federal agencies. This virus was so destructive that it cost an estimated $15 billion worldwide.

(*Source:* © 2008 JupiterImages Corporation)

A virus program can be nearly harmless, simply producing an obscene or silly message unexpectedly on the computer screen. But it also can be a very destructive force, wiping out huge amounts of data. For example, a recent version of a popular utility program contained a virus that destroyed all the data on the user's hard disk. (Of course, the company that created the program rectified the situation by shipping a new version without the virus.) A virus can also find bank accounts with certain names and give the owners large sums of money (Figure 5.3).

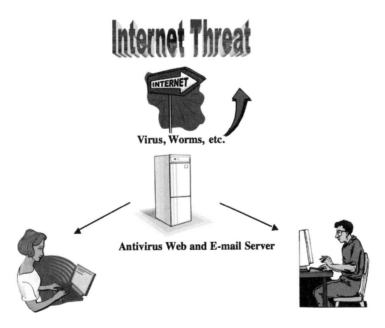

Virus, Worms, etc.

Antivirus Web and E-mail Server

Figure 5.3
Internet Viruses
and Worms

Viruses are very hard to detect because they can be programmed to wreak havoc immediately or to lie dormant until a given future date. Viruses that are programmed to go off at a certain time are called *time bombs*. For example, the famous Michelangelo virus, named after the artist, activated itself on Michelangelo's birthday.

Another enemy of the computer user is the **worm**, which is sometimes confused with a virus. A virus is a piece of code that adds itself to other programs and cannot run independently. A worm is "A destructive program that replicates itself throughout a single computer or across a network, both wired and wireless" (Freedman, 2008). After the worm is finished with its work, the data usually are corrupted and irretrievable. A famous example, called the Internet Worm, occurred on November 2, 1988. This program, authored by Robert T. Morris (Figure 5.4), a graduate student in computer science at Cornell, was responsible for disrupting the operations of between 6,000 and 9,000 computers nationwide. In early August 2003, the SoBig.F computer worm infected computers by filling email in-boxes and jamming networks. SoBig.F sent e-mail messages to personal computers with titles like "Thank you! Your details," "Re: Your application," "Re: Wicked screensaver," and "Re: That movie," with each message containing an attachment. This computer mass-mailing worm was designed to turn machines into robots capable of delivering spam to thousands of machines. In one day, my husband received 8,500 e-mail messages as a result of this worm.

Figure 5.4
Robert T. Morris
(*Source:* ©J. L. Atlan/Sygma/Corbis)

A large industry of virus protection software such as McAfee Security's *Virex*, Symantec's *Norton AntiVirus*, and Intego's *VirusBarrier X4* (Figure 5.5) has come into existence to combat the different types of viruses. The software scans for viruses, repairs damaged files, and prints status reports. McAfee recently reported that there are over 180,000 viruses, and the number is growing at an unprecedented rate (http://vil.nai.com). Unfortunately, these antivirus programs are imperfect at best, because new, undetectable viruses pop up all the time. In 1986 there was only one unknown virus. Presently, between 3 to 6 new viruses are discovered every day (http://www.sarc.com). Thank goodness most are low-level threats. The WildList Organization keeps track of viruses all over the world (http://www.wildlist.org). The best protection against virus infection involves taking certain precautions. Table 5.1 shows some of these safety tips.

Figure 5.5
Intego VirusBarrier
X4
(*Source:* ©INTEGO)

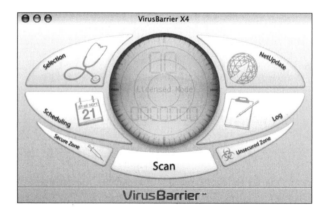

Some warnings about computer viruses are hoaxes. In 1997, many people received a warning that said, "Beware of e-mail bearing the title Good Times." It went on to say, "Don't open this message; delete it immediately. If you read the message it will unleash a virus that will damage your computer hard drive and destroy your computer." The warning then told people to e-mail their friends to tell them about this threat. Even some of the experts were scared, and big corporations fell for the hoax. In reality, the e-mail did not contain a computer virus but instead a

Table 5.1 Precautions Against Viruses

- Back up your hard disk frequently.
- Download into a single computer as opposed to a networked system.
- Use virus protection programs to check every piece of software for a virus before loading it onto your computer's memory.
- Always lock your USB drive or zip disk so that it cannot be destroyed.
- Do not open attachments unless you know the sender, because viruses can be attached to what is now considered "regular" e-mail.

self-replicating e-mail virus. People were tricked into replicating the e-mail message. Another popular hoax, sent by e-mail to Windows users, told the receiver that an infected computer file had been downloaded on their computer. The hoax gave directions on how to delete the file. If the unsuspecting person deleted the file, they unknowingly deleted a valid part of the Windows operating system.

CRIME

According to the FBI, computer crime cost $67 billion (Evers, 2006). Criminals steal computers from people's homes and department stores, manipulate financial accounts, break into secret governmental computer files, and even use computer online services to lure young people to their homes.

In the early 1980s, there were no clear laws to prevent individuals from accessing military computers or White House computers. Ian Murphy, a 24-year-old hacker called *Captain Zap* (Figure 5.6), changed this situation when he and three companions used a home computer and telephone lines to hack into electronics companies, merchandise order records, and government documents. (A **hacker** is a computer programming expert or someone who illegally accesses and tampers with computer files.) The group was caught and indicted for receiving stolen property. Murphy was fined $1,000 and sentenced to jail for two and one-half years.

Figure 5.6
Ian Murphy, Captain Zap
(*Source:* Michael A. Smith/Time Life Pictures/Getty Images)

After this case, legislators spent several years in research and discussion. The culmination of their efforts was the Computer Fraud and Abuse Act of 1986, "a U.S. federal law that criminalizes the abuse of U.S. government computers or networks that cross state boundaries" (Pfaffenberger, 1997). Fines and prison sentences are given for illegal access, theft of credit data, and spying. The case of Herbert Zinn, a high school dropout, was the first to test this law. He was convicted on January 23, 1989, under the Computer Fraud and Abuse Act, of breaking into AT&T and the Department of Defense systems. He destroyed $174,000 worth of files, copied programs worth millions of dollars, and published passwords and ways to circumvent computer security systems. Because Zinn was not yet 18, he was sentenced to only nine months in prison and fined $10,000. However, if Zinn had been 18, he would have received a 13-year prison sentence and a fine of $80,000.

Unfortunately, hacking is now associated with theft and fraud, but this was not always the case. In the beginning, the majority of computer hackers were not considered crooks or pranksters but computer geeks who had a curiosity about how things operated. Some of these programmers created "hacks"—programming shortcuts to complete computing tasks faster. The best-known hack was created in 1969 when Dennis Ritchie and Ken Thompson (Figure 5.7), two employees at Bell Labs' think tank, came up with a standard operating system called UNIX. Today, hacking is more prevalent than ever, but the hackers have gone underground because of fear of prosecution. As you have probably surmised, only estimated statistics on computer crime are available. Many people are unaware that their rights have been violated by crime, because their data were transferred electronically. In addition, individuals who are aware hesitate to take claims to court because of the inevitable exposure of their private lives. Furthermore, companies prefer to handle computer crime internally to avoid embarrassment and unfavorable publicity.

Figure 5.7
Dennis Ritchie
and Ken Thompson
(*Source:* Courtesy AT&T Archives and
History Center)

IDENTITY THEFT

(*Source:* © 2008
Jupiterimages Corporation)

Identity theft is the stealing of a person's identity by using his or her Social Security number, driver's license, or other types of identification. The thief uses the information to purchase items, open new charge accounts, and access the person's existing accounts, running up large bills. The thief can commit all sorts of crimes using the person's identity without the person's knowledge. In many cases it is extremely difficult for the victim to prove that he or she was not the one who ran up charges or committed a crime. According to International Data Group, "IDC believes that $715.6 million was made in the trafficking of stolen and compromised identities in 2005."

If you want to prevent this from happening to you, do the following: (1) make sure your passwords are not easy to guess or obtain; (2) be careful to make physical access to your computer difficult; (3) be careful who you are talking to on the Internet; and (4) update your antivirus program and run firewalls for protection. You can report cases of identity theft through the FTC's identity theft Web site at http://www.ftc.gov/bcp/edu/microsites/idtheft (Rupley, 2003).

PLAGIARISM ON THE INTERNET

Webster's New World College Dictionary defines **plagiarism** as the taking of ideas, writings, and so on from another and passing them off as one's own. Plagiarism via the Internet is an escalating problem. It is very easy for a student to copy information and then paste it into a document. Prior to the Internet, it was easier to check whether a student's work was plagiarized. A teacher had only to research in the library or textbooks. Today, students have access to a gigantic amount of information. Teachers do not want to spend hours looking at Web sites to find out if a paper has been plagiarized.

Unethical students are violating copyright at the elementary, high school, and college levels. Eighty percent of college students admit to cheating, and 90 percent believe that students who cheat are not caught and that when they are they are not properly disciplined. *Education Week* published a national survey that showed that 54 percent of students admitted that they had plagiarized at least once via the Internet (http://www.plagiarism.org). In 1996, Turnitin.com was one of the first sites to help educators combat digital plagiarism. To use Turnitin.com (Figure 5.8), the teacher must register for the service and submit a request for a quote. The cost varies depending on the institution or school. Instructors create a profile, class list, and assignments. Students also create a profile and enroll in their instructor's class. After registration is complete, students can submit their papers to the site, or teachers can collect the students' papers and submit them all at once to the site. Turnitin then analyzes student work by comparing it to billions of pages of content found via the Internet and then gives the teacher an evaluation (http://www.turnitin.com).

Figure 5.8
Turnitin
(*Source:* iParadigms, LLC – developers of Turnitin and iThenticate)

To avoid plagiarism, you must give credit for a person's theory, opinion, idea, graphic, drawings, or statistics. You must give credit for anything that is spoken or written by another individual or that you paraphrase from what they said or wrote.

COPYRIGHT INFRINGEMENT

According to *Webster's New World College Dictionary*, **copyright** is "the exclusive right to the publication, production, or sale of the rights to literary, dramatic, musical, or artistic work, or the use of a commercial print or label, granted by law for a specified period of time to an author, composer, artist, distributor, etc." In short, copyright gives the author the right to do the following:

- reproduce the work,
- permit copies to be made by others,
- prepare derivative works, and
- publicly display the copyrighted work (Brewer, 2003).

When students copy information from the Internet, they should cite it, whether it is an e-mail message, a photograph, a video file, a music file, an audio file, or content from a Web site. Students should check the fine print on Web sites before borrowing their content. When in doubt, students should cite work.

Copyright laws not only protect against downloading material from the Internet, but they also protect books, videos, newspapers, reference materials, magazines, and software. Teachers should understand the Copyright Act of 1976 and be able to explain the concept of fair use, which refers to the guidelines that regulate how educators can copy and otherwise use copyrighted materials for nonprofit educational purposes in their classrooms. In 1998, the Conference on Fair Use (CONFU) wrote a report that expanded these guidelines to include audio, film, digital technologies, and multimedia as well as print. To determine whether a use would constitute infringement of the copyright law, the teacher should look at the

1. purpose and character of the use,
2. nature of the copyrighted work,
3. portion used of the work, and
4. effect of the use on the marketplace.

What this all means is tread carefully when dealing with copyrighted material.

(*Source:* © 2008 Jupiterimages Corporation)

Software Piracy

Thomas Jefferson once said, "Some are born good, some make good, some are caught with the goods." Another issue related to computer use in the schools, besides an inadequate supply of computers and security concerns, is software piracy. **Piracy**—the illegal copying of software—occurs by the thousands of incidents each year.

In 2006 a Business Software Alliance (BSA) study showed that 35 percent of all the software installed on personal computers worldwide is pirated and that the losses suffered total $40 billion. The United States suffered the highest loss at $7.3 billion considering its market share. Countries such as Russia, China, and India have made some progress (http://www.bsa.org/usa/research). We are gaining ground in the battle against software piracy, but we have not won the war.

Software copies work as well as the originals and sell for less money. Piracy is easy and only the large piracy rings are caught. The Software Piracy Association (SPA) a division of the Software and Information Industry Association (SIIA), reports finding many forms of software piracy on the Internet (SPA, 2007), and the Business Software Alliance reports an increase in Internet piracy (http://www.bsa.org/usa/research). Internet sites offer pirated software for free downloading, and bulletin boards give links to these sites. For example, the well-known Pirates with Attitude (PWA) piracy ring was guilty of copyright infringement. PWA operated a Web site named *Sentinel*, which enabled members to download 5,000 copyrighted software programs for free. The Web site owner, Robin Rothberg, was arrested in February 2000, and a grand jury later indicted the other 16 members of the group (Software & Information Industry Association, http://www.siia.net).

The SIIA is the principal trade association of the software code and information content industry. SIIA represents more than 1,000 leading companies that develop and distribute software and electronic content for business, education, consumers, and the Internet. Visit the SIIA antipiracy home page at http://www.siia.net/piracy. You can call its hotline to report software violations at (800) 388-7478 (Figure 5.9).

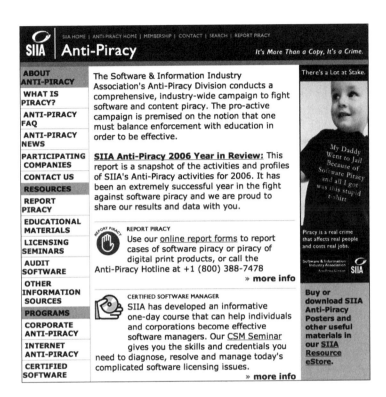

Figure 5.9
SIIA Anti-Piracy Home Page
(*Source:* Courtesy SIIA)

In the 1980s, one of the most popular computer programs was a copy program that was able to duplicate protected software. It is speculated that 30–50 percent of a typical school's software has been illegally copied. One teacher sent an illegally copied piece of software to the software manufacturer for repair. People who would never think of stealing from a department store freely make illegal copies of software, justifying their dishonesty with the following rationalizations: (1) software developers receive free publicity for their products through illegal copies; (2) software is grossly overpriced and therefore fair game for piracy; and (3) the cost of copying software is borne by the developer and not the customer, and developers have money to spare. The truth is that software developers never condone illegal copying; they expect buyers to use the original copies of their products and make backups only as legally stipulated; software is very expensive to produce and market; and the cost of copying software is borne initially by the developers, but it is ultimately paid for by the legitimate buyer. (Guglielmo, 1992)

The unauthorized duplication of software violates federal copyright law and deprives developers of the revenue they richly deserve. The law clearly states that "anyone who violates any of the rights of the copyright owner is an infringement of the copyright" (Federal Copyright Law, Section 501). Reproducing computer software without the proper authorization is a federal offense. The money paid for software represents a fee for one copy and does not give the user the right to copy freely. Civil damages for unauthorized copying can amount to as much as $150,000. Criminal penalties include jail and fines (Federal Copyright Law, Title 18, Section 2319[b]). Many bills have been introduced in Congress to strengthen copyright laws and increase penalties for illegal copying. The software piracy issue is certain to receive continued legal attention.

Software developers have produced elaborate copy protection schemes to combat the piracy problem. One method is to build instructions into the program that will override any command to copy the software. The problem with this method is that hackers can easily create a program that gets around the copy protection. Another method uses software fingerprints. Fingerprinting is a technique that examines a computer system's individual configuration to collect information that can be used as the system's unique identification. The data are selectively encrypted together to build a unique identifier that sets off a "time bomb" in the software program if the user does not pay, making the program erase itself, along with any files that it created. Another method used is to program the software so it is linked to serial numbers inside the chips or logic board of the computer unit. Presently networks have serial numbers and there is electronic registration offered by almost every software house. Microsoft requires a product key and limits the number of times that this key can be activated on different personal computers. Yet for every scheme that is devised, a copy buster program is developed to override it.

Unfortunately, schools are a major culprit in educational software piracy. Why do schools copy illegally? Many schools and districts are eager to integrate the computer into the classroom. They have limited funds, and one copy for 32 students is not enough for group participation. Teachers want many copies so that they can have a group of students using the same software simultaneously. They view copying software as equivalent to photocopying teacher-made tests for their classrooms. They also justify the piracy as being for the greater good of students. In the end, the educator is the loser.

Companies cannot make a profit selling educational software, so they divert their money to manufacturing products that are more economically lucrative. Software pirates ultimately drive smaller companies out of business.

What can school districts do to dissuade teachers or students from illegally copying software? They can warn teachers about illegally duplicating software and institute disciplinary action when violations occur. Furthermore, schools can keep software locked away in restricted areas and limit student and teacher access. They can appoint a person or committee to be responsible for keeping records on the software purchased and how it is being used. This person or committee would maintain a log of the software purchased and the machine on which the software resides. In addition, districts can require that teachers supervise students when they use software. In the classroom, teachers can discuss recent criminal cases or related movies such as the classic movie *War Games* to make students aware of the problems involved. Teachers can explain the federal and state laws and the differences between a felony, a crime punishable by a year in prison, and a misdemeanor, a crime punishable by a fine or a prison term. After the students have an understanding of the seriousness of computer crimes, they can devise a computer break-in policy for the school. The teacher can give each student a copy of this policy to read and study. The teacher can then present hypothetical cases concerning computer ethics breaches and ask the students what punishment according to the break-in policy they would recommend for the offender. Teachers should find better ways to combat their budget constraints. Buying lab packs or multiple copies of software is one answer. Another is using a 30-day trial version of software to try it out before you buy it and find out if it is inappropriate. A district can be encouraged to buy on-site licenses for selected programs, allowing the schools to make legal multiple copies and do multiple loadings of a program.[2] Schools should also move toward networking their machines, which enable them to run a networkable piece of software over multiple machines. Finally, teachers should involve students, parents, and the community in raising money for software. In the long term, it is better to purchase the software than to steal it because the legitimate buyer receives technical support and upgrades from the publisher. Most important, it is the honorable and ethical way to operate.

---

[2] Multiple loadings refers to the practice of loading a program from one disk onto several computers.

SECURITY

One of the major issues related to computer use in the schools is security. Computer owners, including schools, must take steps to prevent theft and inappropriate use of their equipment. According to Safeware Insurance Agency, computer theft is the number-two cause of computer losses (http://www.safeware.com/). Computer theft is a growing global problem costing billions annually (Computer Crime Research Center, http://www.crime-research.org/0204.html). Today, most computer facilities have some sort of security system. These facilities have means of confirming the identities of persons who want to use the system so that unauthorized users do not gain access. Usually, authorized users are issued special cards, keys, passwords, or account numbers. In elementary schools and high schools, this identification system may consist of a simple list of names. Each person on this list has a key that provides access to a computer room with bolted-down machines. Unfortunately, some users lend their keys and share their passwords. Often, when computer users are allowed to choose their passwords, they choose easy-to-guess and easy-to-remember passwords. The problem is what can be done. Passwords are really not the answer. If a password is secure it is difficult to remember and you will usually misplace it. Sam Tuohey, CTO of Stanford Federal Credit Union, performed an audit of password strengths and his cracking team found that "approximately 80 percent of the values could be cracked in about a second" (Roberts, 2006).

One way to avert these problems is to assign access codes that are read by the computer from pass cards. The user does not have to remember this number, so the number can be complex. Even if the card is stolen, the code can be changed when the theft is reported. U.S. computer makers offer **smart cards** as a security feature for laptop computers. A smart card can be used as an identification badge, consolidating different systems into one card. For example, an enabled smart card can be used for building access, network log-in, credit card, and remote and Web access. Figure 5.10 shows (A) the cardholder's picture, (B) the bar code, (C) the seal, and (D) the microchip on a smart card.

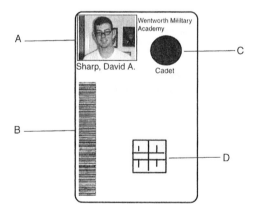

Figure 5.10
Smart Card

Another way businesses and schools are increasing security is by requiring every individual to enter a special code with his or her card. Experts advise going a step further by checking any available personal files for problems and restricting the number of people with access and the type of access they have to the computer. For instance, at most universities, students and professors use the same computer center, but they are not given the same access. Typically, the students have fewer privileges than the professors do.

Fingerprint recognition is another technology that can be used to control access to a computer or network. Fingerprints are unique identification and are difficult to fake or lose. Before access is granted, the individual's fingers are scanned by a fingerprint reader and matched with the stored images of his or her fingerprints.

Figure 5.11

Mouse Fingerprint Scanner
(*Source:* Courtesy Microsoft)

The Fingerprint scanner is being utilized in police stations, personal computer keyboards, and computer mice. Figure 5.11 shows a Microsoft computer mouse with a built-in fingerprint scanner. Another security problem concerns the protection of the operating system and data on the computer. It is essential that security measures protect all operating systems.

Unscrupulous individuals have found ways to circumvent such systems to print out a list of users' passwords, to give themselves access rights they are not officially assigned, and to spread viruses. For these reasons, all sensitive data should be stored and locked up when not in use. Some large companies use data encryption to store data in scrambled form, meaningless to anyone without a special data item called a *key*.

Computer labs are prone to abuse by students who may unintentionally or deliberately alter computer files, trash programs, and create all sorts of havoc. Teachers can safeguard their computers from tampering by purchasing desktop security programs such as *Fortres 101* (Fortres Grand Corporation) and *SmartFilter*, Bess Edition (Secure Computing). *SmartFilter* prevents users from deleting critical files and applications and blocks access to inappropriate sites (Figure 5.12).

Figure 5.12

SmartFilter, Bess Edition
(*Source:* Copyright © 1997–2007 Secure Computing Corporation. All rights reserved.)

SmartFilter also prevents making unauthorized changes to the desktop, saving unwanted programs, running disallowed programs, or corrupting the operating system, whether accidentally or maliciously. This software has a broad set of categories that include education–specific categories that are designed for schools.

Computers should also be safeguarded against natural disasters such as power surges, fires, and earthquakes. At the fundamental level, a good surge protector will rule out most power surges. If you have crucial data, a battery backup is essential because it gives you time to save your data. However, disks do wear out and fire destroys, so it is important even with battery backup to make backup disks and store them in a different location. Use a USB flash drive or rewriteable CD-ROMs to transfer the files.

From this discussion, it should be evident how important security is. How far one goes in implementing a system for security is related to cost. Usually, the more complicated the system, the more costly it is to carry out. Security will continue to be a problem because the number of computers and users continues to grow.

Eventually, there will be a computer on each student's desk. The teacher's main job will be to determine how to use this technology as a powerful tool for education. The teacher will also have to provide appropriate security.

Presently, there is a trend for students to purchase their own computers for home use or to bring them to college. A student who does not have access to a computer is definitely at a disadvantage in this technological world.

UNEQUAL ACCESS

Still another issue related to computer use in the schools and a major challenge to education in the 21st century is unequal access to computers. As it is often called, the **digital divide** "is the difference between those who have computers and high-tech gadgets in general and those who do not" (Freedman, 2003). Often, the divide runs along economic and racial/ethnic lines.

A computer gives a student the ability to search the Internet for the answers to questions or to use a word processing program to correct spelling and check grammar. Students can create better reports with graphics and sound and create electronic portfolios and multimedia presentations. With computer access, students are more motivated to work harder in school, and they make greater strides in learning and developing technology skills. They can use distance learning to get an education from the privacy of their homes. Unequal access to computers can widen the division between the wealthy and the poor. Cattagni and Farris (2001) showed that the ratio of students to computers with Internet access was higher for schools with the greatest poverty levels (6.8–1.0) than for other schools (4.5 or 5.6–1.0; National Center for Educational Statistics, http://nces.ed.gov/pubs2002/internet/4.asp). The Commerce Department report *Falling Through the Net: Toward Digital Inclusion* states that more and more individuals are using computers, but a digital divide still exists because digital access is still uneven. The report shows that the more money that a household earns, the higher the rate of computer access. Furthermore, the study shows that minorities, people with disabilities, and people with less education do not have as much access to computers.

By being aware of these problems of unequal access, teachers can be more sensitive to the needs of the students. Teachers can use their expertise to integrate technology into the classroom more effectively. They can tell students who do not own computers how to get access after school hours. They may want to be an advocate and raise money for more computers or talk to local businesses for help. There really is no easy answer to this issue in an era when the cost of education is increasing and budget cuts are too. Fortunately, private foundations have tried to alleviate this problem by donating computers to libraries. The Federal Commerce Commission offers a discounted price (e-rate) for Internet service, which applies to schools and libraries. There are many initiatives that are trying to make sure that all students have equal access to technology. Ideally this situation will change in the years to come, and the computer will be as commonplace as the cell phone.

Health Risks Using Computers

Along with an inadequate supply of computers, security and piracy concerns, and unequal access, is the issue of health risks. Every computer store offers a variety of injury-reducing equipment in the form of wrist pads, antiglare screens, and ergonomic keyboards and trackballs. Unfortunately, it is very easy to use computer equipment improperly to the point of damaging your body. **Repetitive strain injuries** are a serious medical problem. According to the Bureau of Labor Statistics (http://www.bls.gov/), computer monitors, like other electrical devices, generate electric and magnetic fields at a very low frequency. There is scientific debate over whether low-level electromagnetic emissions cause health problems such as cancer. Even though this debate is unresolved, the computer industry has moved to reduce these emissions. Most manufacturers support a standard for Maximum Video Terminal Radiation (MPR-II), which were established in 1990 by the Swedish Government. Recently, school districts have begun to purchase liquid crystal display monitors instead of RGB monitors. The liquid crystal display monitor does not have emissions problems.

You can lessen the chances of computer-related injury by following these 10 suggestions:

1. Position yourself in front of the screen like a concert pianist, relaxing your shoulders and keeping your forearms and hands in a straight line. Make sure your lower back is supported and your thighs are horizontal to the ground. The top of the computer monitor should be slightly below eye level, and it should be positioned to prevent any type of glare. Finally, your feet should rest flat on the floor, and there should be clearance under the work area, between your legs and the desk (Figure 5.13).

Figure 5.13
Correct Posture for Computer Use

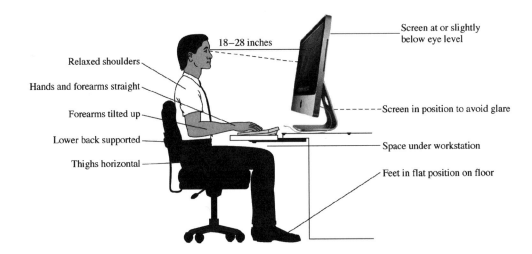

2. Always work 18–28 inches from the monitor. Electromagnetic emissions from the front of any display should be negligible at 28 inches. Furthermore, the left side of the computer and the back usually generate the strongest emissions, so try to stay clear of these areas.

3. Avoid unnecessarily turning up the brightness on the monitor because you may be exposing yourself to higher emissions than the MPR-II guidelines allow.

4. Do not overwork. Take frequent breaks from the computer, at least once an hour. Move around and exercise your legs, arms, and neck. Do not stare at the monitor continually, but look around every 5 or 10 minutes. Remain relaxed.

5. Spend time finding a proper chair for your computer. Try it out and make sure you have ways of adjusting it to suit your individual needs.

6. The equipment you use most often should be close enough that you do not have to stretch to reach it.

7. Check to make sure the keys on your keyboard are not too difficult to press. The keys should give some tactile feedback; do not press too hard on the keyboard. Use function keys to help cut down on keystrokes.

8. Do not grip the mouse too tightly because it will increase the risk of injury. Additionally, choose a mouse that is comfortable for your hand.

9. Never brace your wrists against mouse pads when you are typing because this will eventually cause injury.

10. Finally, if you continually work with graphics, buy an appropriate input device such as a drawing tablet.

SUMMARY

The Internet is a wonderful, rich resource that enables individuals to find a variety of important and useful information. However, the Internet is also used for less-noble purposes. Computers are involved in new types of crime as well as some variations on traditional crimes. We delved into problems such as Internet security, spam, safety concerns, invasion of privacy, identity theft, plagiarism, software privacy, and copyright infringement. We talked about the Web site Turnitin where teachers can check to see if students' papers are plagiarized. We also discovered that even though the computer is prominent in our society, there is still unequal access to computer technology. We spent time discussing health risks using computers and we examined safety guidelines to follow while using the computer.

STUDY AND ONLINE RESOURCES

CHAPTER 5 ONLINE RESOURCES

 In the **student section** of the book's online site at **http://www.wiley.com/college/sharp**, you will find PDFs templates, and articles, along with top-rated Web sites on the Internet about child safety, acceptable use policies, filtering, and content management. Watch the video tutorial online at **http://www.wiley.com/college/sharp** to learn how to refine your Internet search.

CHAPTER MASTERY TEST

Lets check for chapter comprehension with a short mastery test. Key Terms, Computer Lab, and Suggested Readings and References follow the test.

1. Explain the conflict between the computer user and the software publisher.

2. What can ordinary persons do to protect their data from fire, theft, and storage media failure?

3. What does copyright give to its creator and what is *plagiarism*?

4. Discuss two issues related to computer privacy.

5. Discuss the Herbert Zinn case and explain why it was important.

6. Why are computer viruses destructive? List some precautions you can take to prevent one from infecting your computer system.

7. What is *spam* and why is it causing havoc?

8. What happens when you are a victim of identity theft?

9. What is a *computer cookie* and why should we be concerned about what it does?

10. What is the *digital divide* and why is it an important issue?

11. Discuss three ways to reduce the risks of computer-related injuries.

KEY TERMS

Cookie p. 86
Copyright p. 91
Digital divide p. 97
Filtering and monitoring software p. 85

Firewall p. 83
Hacker p. 89
Phishing attacks p. 85
Piracy p. 92

Plagiarism p. 91
Repetitive strain injuries p. 97
Smart cards p. 95
Spam p. 84

Virus p. 87
Worm p. 87

COMPUTER LAB: Activities for Mastery and Your Portfolio

5.1 Understanding Copyright Laws Use this exercise to determine your understanding of copyright law.

5.2 Research an example of a recent computer crime and prepare a short report. In this report, describe (a) what happened, (b) how the crime was discovered, and (c) how the crime could have been prevented. Watch the video tutorial online and learn how to refine your Internet search.

5.3 Prepare a report on two types of computer viruses. Explain how they affected your computer and how they were discovered.

5.4 Find three current examples of how computers were used to invade a person's privacy. How could these violations have been prevented?

5.5 Set up a security system for a hypothetical computer lab.

5.6 Ergonomics Test your understanding of correct computer posture and computer health risks.

SUGGESTED READINGS AND REFERENCES

Bell, Mary Ann. "The Elephant in the Room." *School Library Journal* 53, issue 1 (January 2007): 40–42.

Breen, Christopher. "Spa, Fighters." *Macworld* (June 2007): 32–40.

Brewer, Tony. *Technology Integration in the 21st Century Classroom.* Eugene, Ore.: Visions Technology in Education, 2003.

Brooks, Jason. "Wireless LAN Security Crackdown." *eWeek* 19, issue 18 (May 6, 2002): 45–47.

Cattagni, Anne, and Elizabeth Farris. "Internet Access in U.S. Public Schools and Classrooms: 1994–2000." *Education Statistics Quarterly* 3, no. 2 (Summer 2001): 54–61.

Christiansen, Christian A., Allan Carey, Sally Hudson, and Rose Ryan "Worldwide Identity Theft Black Market 2006–2010 Forcast." December 2006, Doc #204834, http://www.idc.com/getdoc.jsp?containerId=204834

Darden, Edwin C. "Trouble on the Line." *American School Board Journal* 194, issue 1 (January 2007): 36–37.

D'Errico, Richard. "Slam Spam, Propose Solutions." *Business Review* (May 19, 2003): 1–2.

Dyrli, Odvard Egil. "Online Privacy and the Cookies Controversy." *Technology and Learning* (March 1997): 20.

Evers, Jodi. "Computer crime costs $67 billion (FBI 2005 crime survey)." CNET.com, January 19, 2006.

Evett, Don. "Spam Statistic 2006." http://spam-filter-review.toptenreviews.com/spam-statistics.html

Freedman, Warren. *The Right of Privacy in the Computer Age.* New York: Quorum Books, 2003.

Friedlander, Emily. "Access Denied." *FamilyPC* 7, no. 7 (July 2000): 28.

Goodman, Joshua, Gordon V. Cormack, and David Heckerman. "Spam and the Ongoing Battle for the Inbox." *Communications of the ACM* 50, issue 2 (February 2007): 25–31.

Guglielmo, Connie. "Managers Clamp Down on Software Piracy." *MacWeek* 6, no. 2 (January 13, 1992): 60–63.

Hulme, George V. "Networks Without a Safety Net." *Information Week,* issue 894 (June 24, 2002): 70–72.

Kanabar, Dina, and Vijay Kanabar. "A Quick Guide to Basic Network Security." *Computers in Libraries* 23, issue 5 (May 2003): 25–27.

Kandra, Anne. "Don't Let Them Steal Your Good Name." *PC World* 20, issue 10 (October 2002): 43–46.

Keizer, Gregg. "WLAN Security: Reducing the Risks." *Tech-Web*, April 13, 2003, http://www.techweb.com/tech/mobile/20030407_mobile

Larkin, Erik. "The Internet's Public Enemy Number One." *PC World* 25, issue 12 (December 2007): 67–68.

Levy, Steven, and Brad Stone. "Hunting the Hackers." *Time*, February 21, 2000, pp. 39–44.

Livingston, Brian. "There's Life Left in IIS." *InfoWorld,* January 2003.

Menn, Joseph. "Virus Fails to Hit Microsoft, But Users Are Not So Lucky." *Los Angeles Times,* Saturday, August 16, 2003, Business Section, C1, C3.

Pfaffenberger, Bryan. *Webster's New World Dictionary of Computer Terms, 6th ed.* New York: Que, 1997.

Pike, Sarah. "What's in Your Inbox?" *PC Magazine*, Feb 2008, vol. 27 Issue 3 Pages 104–104.

Roberts, Paul J. " Building Smarter Authentication." *InfoWorld*, September 24, 2006, pp. 27–32.

Robinson, LeAnne K., Abbie Brown, and Tim Green. "The Threat of Security." *Learning and Leading with Technology,* ISTE, September/October 2007, pp. 19–23.

Rubenking, Janet. "Identity theft: What, me worry?" *PC Magazine*, March 2, 2004, pp. 75–77.

Rupley, Sebastian. "Identity Theft: The Scary Truth." *PC Magazine,* September 3, 2003.

Schwartz, John. "Decoding Computer Intruders." *New York Times*, April 24, 2003, E1.

Shiver Jr., Jube. "Teenager Charged in Blaster Attacks."*Los Angeles Times,* August 31, 2003, Business Section, C1, C2.

Snell, Jason. "College via Podcast." *Macworld* 24, issue 1, (January 2007): 128–129.

Streitfield, David. "Opening Pandora's In-Box." *Los Angeles Times/Business/Technology*, May 11, 2003.

Word Processing

Integrating Word Processing into the Classroom

Word processing programs are the most widely used computer application in the office, home, and classroom (Pfaffenberger, 2003). Students at all grade levels can use word processing software to create book reports, letterhead stationery, flyers, and newsletters. In the lower grades students can use large-size fonts to create stories, alphabet books, and journals. Teachers can have students write letters to people in the class and across the country. This chapter discusses how to select a word processor for the classroom. We consider the general features of a word processor. A checklist helps you choose the right word processor. Exercises help you integrate word processing into the classroom.

Using the computer, students and teachers can do the following:

students can

- create a research report,
- prepare a resumé,
- design letterhead stationery,
- create a class newsletter,
- write a letter,
- create a Web page, and
- create a flyer.

teachers can

- create a certificate,
- create a brochure,
- design place cards for the classroom,
- create a newsletter,
- make a book report form, and
- write a mail merge letter for parents.

objectives

Upon completing this chapter, you will be able to do the following:

1 Define the term word processor.

2 Describe the features and functions of a word processor.

3 Demonstrate how a word processing program operates.

4 Evaluate word processing software based on standard criteria.

5 Utilize and create a repertoire of word processing activities for the classroom.

6 Evaluate a word processing program utilizing the criteria given in this book.

7 Explore the offerings of Internet sites on word processing, which range from creative writing tips to lesson plans.

8 After viewing video tutorials you will be able to create newsletters, flyers, resumés, and more.

Historical Background

Word processing grew out of a desire to automate the writing process. In 1961, IBM introduced the elite Selectric typewriter, a fast electric model that was the elite typewriter of its day. Ten years later, Wang Laboratories inaugurated the Wang 1200, a small-screen typing workstation capable of reading output and storing information on a cassette tape. With the advent of disk storage, we saw the development of word processing programs—first *Word Star* (1979), then *WordPerfect* (1980). Word processing took a leap forward in 1981, when IBM introduced its personal computer, the PC. Now we saw the computer being merged with word processing.

The years between 1981 and 1985 saw a flurry of word processing program introductions: *EasyWriter* (Unlimited Software), *Volkswriter*[1], *MacWrite* (Apple), *Microsoft Word* (Microsoft Corporation), *Bank Street Writer* (Scholastic), and *PFS Write* (Software, Inc.). The 1980s marked the beginning of a trend away from stand-alone word processing programs toward comprehensive products incorporating several software tools in one package. Manufacturers began selling two types of these packages: **integrated programs** such as *AppleWorks* and *Microsoft Works* and **software suites** such as *Microsoft Office* and *Lotus SmartSuite*. Integrated programs usually consist of a word processor, a spreadsheet, a database, graphic tools, and

[1] Lifetree is now called Writing Tools Groups, a subsidiary of WordStar International.

communication software that work through the same launching platform. The **soft-ware suite** is a group of bundled programs including utilities that can exchange data. (See Chapter 9.)

What is a Word Processor?

A **word processor** is a software program designed to make the computer a useful electronic writing tool for editing, storing, and printing documents. Before the computer, the typewriter was the principal tool used for writing reports, and a typist had to take great pains to avoid making mistakes because correcting and revising were tedious tasks. Word processing programs enable users to make changes quickly and efficiently simply by pressing a few keys on the keyboard. Users can easily save a document on a flash drive, make multiple copies, and store disks for safekeeping.

Today, when writers discuss word processing they usually are talking about personal computers with word processing software. Such software programs are for sale at local software stores, usually on CD-ROM. The buyer installs the program on a computer and can then create documents, edit text, underline, and delete. In addition, there are Web-based programs, which are available at Internet sites.

Components of Word Processing

A word processor usually involves interaction among the components shown in Figure 6.1. Through the software, the user types in text on the keyboard, views it on the monitor, changes it as necessary, saves the document on the hard drive or to a Zip disk or flash drive, and prints it on the printer.

Figure 6.1
Word Processing Components
(*Source:* © Jupiterimages corporation)

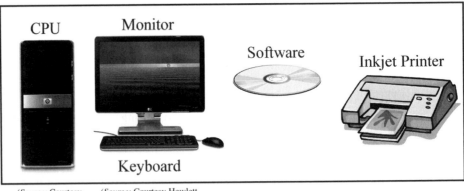

(*Source:* Courtesy Hewlett-Packard Company)   (*Source:* Courtesy Hewlett Productions)

The word processing packages on the market today come with every imaginable feature. Among these programs are word processors that are well suited for classroom use. For elementary school students, software reviewers recommend programs such as *Write:OutLoud, Clicker 5, Scholastic Keys: MacWrite, Kid Works Deluxe*, and *Storybook Weaver Deluxe* because they have fewer features and are easier to use. *(Macwrite* has a simple interface for *Microsoft Word.)* The features in most programs for children include *delete*, which removes unwanted text, and *insert*, which inserts lines or passages. *Writer's Companion, Pages, Microsoft Works, WordPerfect*, and *Microsoft Word* are for junior high, high school, and college students, and they are more complicated, offer multiple features, and occupy more disk space and memory. A case in point is *Microsoft Word*, which contains many desktop publishing features, macros, charting tools, and custom toolbars.

Standard Word Processing Features

Most word processors feature *cursor control*, *word wrap*, and *page breaks*.

CURSOR CONTROL

A **cursor** is a blinking (usually white) block of light that shows the position of a character.

The computer user positions the cursor where he or she wants to correct text or enter text. The equivalent on a typewriter is the place on the paper where the next keystroke will strike. As you type, the cursor stays just ahead of the last character you have typed. The cursor can move one character at a time, line by line, or over a block of text. You can also move it with the mouse.

WORD WRAP

Word wrap lets you type as much as you want without paying attention to the end of lines. When you reach the right-hand margin, the cursor automatically moves to the beginning of the next line; you do not have to hit the return key. If the word you are typing does not fit at the end of a line, word wrap automatically moves it to the next line. You need to hit the return key only to start a new paragraph or to move down a line.

PAGE BREAKS

Most word processors display some mark on the screen that tells where the pages in the document break. Before printing your document you can use this feature to check to make sure there are no bad breaks, such as those that strand a single word on a page.

Basic Word Processing Editing Features

Word processors vary in their editing capabilities, but have the same common editing features: *insert*, *delete*, *find and replace*, *cut*, *paste*, *copy*, and *drag-and-drop*.

INSERT

The **insert** function allows you to insert lines of text, words, and paragraphs anywhere in the document.

DELETE

The **delete** function allows you to erase words, lines, or paragraphs of text. After you delete the material, the text closes up around the remaining space.

FIND AND REPLACE

The **find and replace** function (Figure 6.2) in *Microsoft Word* allows you to search a document for a word or phrase and replace it with another. For example, if you want to replace the word *costly* with *expensive*, you can instruct the computer to find every incident of *costly* so you can replace it with *expensive*.

CUT AND PASTE

With the **cut and paste** feature the user selects letters, words, or blocks of text and removes them from their location and then "pastes" them in a new location. This is how it works:

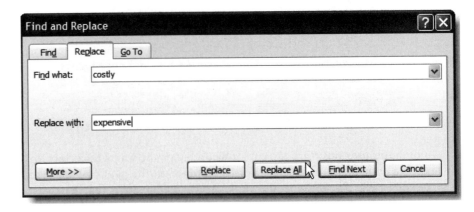

1. Highlight the text that you want to move.

2. Use the cut function to delete the specified portion of text.

3. Position the cursor where you want the material to be placed and then instruct the computer to paste or insert. The text will arrange itself automatically with proper spacing.

COPY

The **copy** function works similarly to cut and paste. With this feature you make a copy of what you want elsewhere and then you paste it in a new location.

DRAG AND DROP

With the **drag-and-drop** feature, you use the mouse to select a small block of text. Then, while pressing the mouse button, you can drag the text to a new location. This function is very handy for moving text short distances within a document.

In addition to the basic editing features, the majority of word processors have a spelling checker, a grammar checker, and a thesaurus.

SPELLING CHECKERS

The spelling checker checks the spelling of the words in your document against those in a dictionary that is stored on the hard disk drive. If a word in the document does not appear in the dictionary, the spelling checker will display the word in question and give you the opportunity to override the query or select an alternative. Using Apple's *Pages* word processor (Figure 6.3), the word *looks* is misspelled; the spelling checker suggests

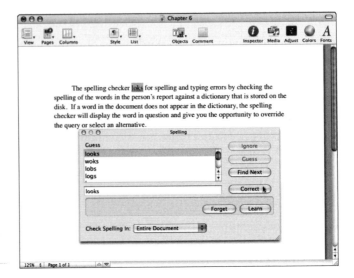

many alternatives and highlights the most likely. You can add any words you wish to the spelling checker's dictionary by pressing the learn button. Once you have added a word, the spelling checker will no longer question that particular spelling. A good spelling checker lets you see the misspelled word in the context of your document. Advanced spelling checkers can correct misspellings automatically the next time they appear.

GRAMMAR CHECKERS

Grammar checkers are built into a word processing program. They help with grammar, style, punctuation, and even spelling errors. The grammar checker identifies problems such as incorrect verb tense, lack of subject–verb agreement, and misuse of specific words.

It will also check for inconsistencies, awkward phrases, clichès, and wordiness. After it identifies the problem, it suggests corrections and provides an online tutorial explaining the grammar rule that applies. Usually, you make the correction with a click of the mouse. You have the option of rewriting the incorrect sentence or leaving it just as it is.

In *Microsoft Word*'s Spelling and Grammar dialog box (Figure 6.4), under the heading *Subject–Verb Agreement* the pertinent part of the writer's document appears. Under *Suggestions* the correction "are" appears. You can click on *Explain* for an explanation of the error. In this case, the user takes the suggestion "are" by clicking on *Change.* If the user had not liked the suggestion, he or she could have clicked on *Ignore Once* or *Ignore Rule.* The *Next Sentence* button lets the writer skip the sentence entirely. Even though there have been advances in recent years, grammar checkers are still in the process of evolving.

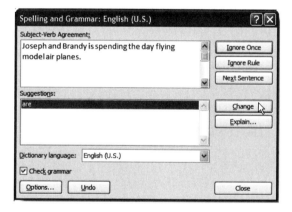

Figure 6.4
Microsoft Word 2007
Grammar Checker
(*Source:* Reprinted with permission from Microsoft Corporation)

THESAURUS

The **thesaurus** has the capacity to generate synonyms for any word that it has in its dictionary. For example, if you want a different word for *peculiar*, *WordPerfect*'s thesaurus lists such words as *curious*, *strange*, and *funny*. Figure 6.5 shows the

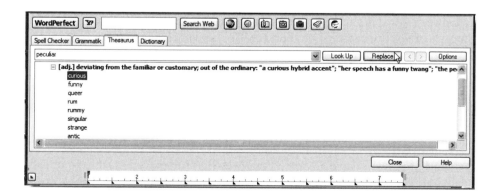

Figure 6.5
WordPerfect X3 Thesaurus
(*Source:* Courtesy Corel Corporation)

WordPerfect thesaurus screen. The user selects the word that he or she wants to use—in this case, *curious*—and clicks *Replace*. The program automatically substitutes the new word.

Standard Formatting Functions

Besides being able to edit your document, you must also be able to format it. Formatting involves making the text appear a certain way on the printed page by adjusting margins, tabs, text justification, header size and font, and line spacing, among other things.

FONT

Font is a term that refers to the appearance of a typed character, including its typeface, its pitch, its point size, and its style. **Typeface** refers to the design of a character, such as Geneva or Palatino. **Pitch** represents the number of characters per inch. **Point size** is the height of a character. **Style** refers to whether a character is Roman, *italicized*, **boldface**, or underlined. Programs vary in the number of fonts that can be used. Figure 6.6 shows examples of different typefaces, pitches, sizes, and styles that can be generated on a computer. Fonts can be printed as bitmap, in a pattern of dots, or as outlines defined by a mathematical formula.

Figure 6.6
Font Choices

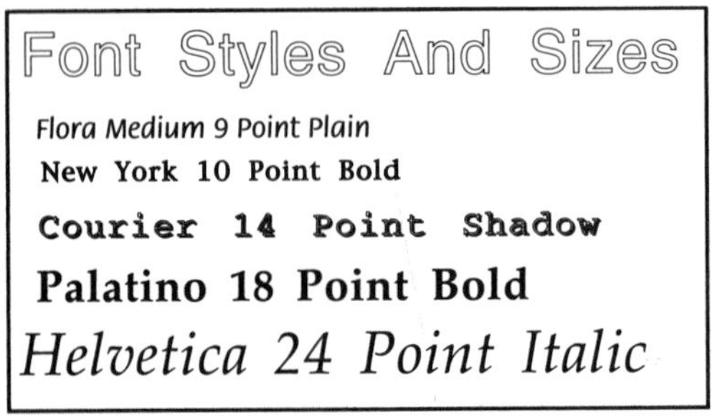

> Font Styles And Sizes
>
> Flora Medium 9 Point Plain
> New York 10 Point Bold
> Courier 14 Point Shadow
> **Palatino 18 Point Bold**
> *Helvetica 24 Point Italic*

JUSTIFICATION

Justification aligns the margins of text. Text can be aligned along the left side or the right side of a page, it can fill the type space to align both left and right, or it can be centered.

In left-justified text (Figure 6.7A), the left margin is aligned and the right margin is uneven. This is the most common type of justification, and word processing programs usually have this as their default. In right-justified text (Figure 6.7B), the right margin is aligned and the left margin is uneven. Full-justified text (Figure 6.7C) is aligned along both margins. The computer achieves this alignment by adding space between words in a line of text to extend it. In center-justified text (Figure 6.7D), all the lines of text are centered on the page. This type of justification is often used to make headings more attractive on a page. Table 6.1, on page 109, summarizes additional standard formatting functions.

Advanced Word Processing Features

Many word processors have advanced features that range from desktop publishing capabilities to graphic organizer functions. Word processing software programs have become so feature laden that they have everything but the kitchen

Figure 6.7
Justification Types

A. Left-Justified Text

Suddenly this giant computer stopped working, and everyone was frantically attempting to discover the source of the problem.   Grace Hopper and her coworkers found the culprit was a dead moth in a relay of the computer. They removed the moth with a tweezer and placed it in the Mark II logbook.

B. Right-Justified Text

Suddenly this giant computer stopped working, and everyone was frantically attempting to discover the source of the problem.   Grace Hopper and her coworkers found the culprit was a dead moth in a relay of the computer. They removed the moth with a tweezer and placed it in the Mark II logbook.

C. Full-Justified Text

Suddenly this giant computer stopped working, and everyone was frantically attempting to discover the source of the problem.   Grace Hopper and her coworkers found the culprit was a dead moth in a relay of the computer. They removed the moth with a tweezer and placed it in the Mark II logbook.

D. Center-Justified Text

Suddenly this giant computer stopped working, and everyone was frantically attempting to discover the source of the problem.   Grace Hopper and her coworkers found the culprit was a dead moth in a relay of the computer. They removed the moth with a tweezer and placed it in the
Mark II logbook.

sink. *Microsoft Word* offers essential desktop publishing features with which students and teachers can create graphics and produce elegant newspapers from scratch. In addition, Microsoft comes with a series of templates that help students produce newsletters, flyers, brochures, and more. This particular word processor can perform many of the functions of a desktop publishing program.

Table 6.1 Additional Standard Formatting Functions

Feature	Description
Margin	The margin is the spacing between the edge of the page and the main text area.
Tabs	Tabs position text precisely within a line in a document or within a column in a table.
Headers and Footers	A header is text that appears at the top margin of each page of manuscript (e.g., a title), and a footer is text that prints in the bottom margin of a page of manuscript (e.g., page numbers).
Line Spacing	Line spacing is the amount of space between lines of text.
Superscripts and Subscripts	Superscripts and subscripts are used in mathematical formulas and as footnote markers. The 8 in 2^8 is a superscript; the 1 in A_1 is a subscript.
Page Numbering	Many word processors offer automatic numbering functions. You can also instruct the computer to start numbering a document with a particular number, for example, page A-1.

Writer's Companion (Visions Technology in Education) is a combination graphic organizer, word processor, and desktop publishing program (Figure 6.8). This program is also an instructional tool that helps students learn how to use it. Students brainstorm, organize, and sequence their work. When they are satisfied, they produce a rough draft. Final drafts can include graphics and sound. If students want to e-mail their stories to others, *Writer's Companion* will automatically create a Web page to facilitate such sharing.

Figure 6.8

Writer's Companion

(*Source:* Reprinted with permission of Visions Technology in Education TM. www.Toolsfor Teachers.com)

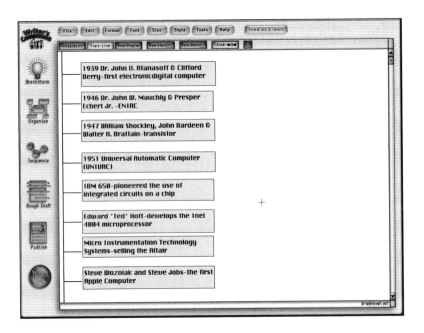

SAVING AND PRINTING

Word processors let you save a document in different file formats. This feature is important if you are exchanging documents with a person who uses different software than you.

A powerful word processor lets you save in a variety of formats such as HTML (Hyper Text Markup Language), PDF (Portable Document Format), and RTF (Rich Text Format). The HTML format lets you create documents that can be placed on the Internet, PDF lets you save documents that can be read by *Adobe Acrobat Reader*, and RTF removes all the formatting so that your document can be read by almost any word processing application. Figure 6.9 shows some of the file formats that are available in Microsoft Word.

Figure 6.9

File Formats in *Microsoft Word 2007*

(*Source:* Microsoft product screenshot reprinted with permission from Microsoft Corporation)

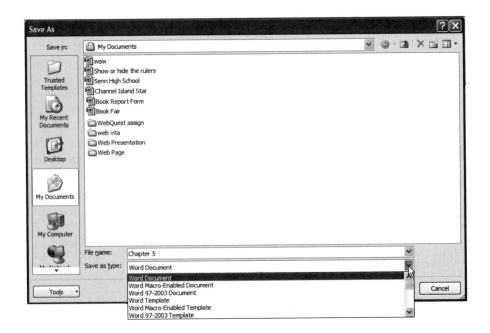

All word processing programs allow you to print documents either in color or in black and white. There are many printing options, ranging from different layouts to different image quality.

Table 6.2 summarizes some of the advanced word processing features that you can find in word processing programs. **You will find a more complete list in a PDF file online at** http://www.wiley.com/college/sharp.

Table 6.2 **Advanced Word Processing Features**

Feature	Description
AutoCorrect	When you type words, the AutoCorrect feature automatically corrects common spelling, typing, and grammatical errors.
AutoFormat	The AutoFormat feature automatically applies formatting to the text. For example, it can convert a Web address to a hyperlink or number a list.
Change tracking	This feature lets you color-code changes you make to a text so you and others can see how you changed it. It also lets you add comments without changing the document.
Collaboration	Collaboration allows users to enter comments in documents online. They can reply to these comments and edit the results.
Charts	With this feature you can create charts and insert them in a document.

Feature	Description
Desktop capabilities	With such capabilities you can resize, rotate, and scale graphic objects. You also can create borders.
Equation editor	With this feature you can generate complex equations using special math symbols:

$$\frac{-b \pm \sqrt{b^2 - 4ac}}{2a}$$

Feature	Description
Graphic organizer	With this feature, you can outline and use symbols and graphics.
Graphic import	Using this feature, you can insert images in different graphic formats such as PICT, GIF, PCX, BMP, or EPS into a document.

(*Source:* Courtesy Vicki Sharp)

Feature	Description
Hyperlinks	You can create hyperlinks that enable a reader of a document to jump to another location in the document or to a Web page. Here is an example: http://www.csun.edu/
Kerning	The word processor adjusts the space between letters.

(continued)

Table 6.2   continued

Feature	Description
Macros	This feature enables you to record a series of keystrokes or menu selections and then allocate to them a key or name combination. For example, you could record a macro that would insert a picture when you press the F1 key.
Mail merge	Mail merge creates a personalized document by inserting information such as a recipient's name and address into a form letter.
Math computations and sorting	You can use this feature to perform simple math calculations on columns of numbers and then sort the columns.
Speech recognition	Using this function, you can speak into the computer and your words will be displayed on the screen as text.
Voice annotation	You can use this feature to add sound comments to a text.
Web page creation	Many word processors help you create Web pages.
Wizards	A wizard leads you through the process of creating a document in a step-by-step fashion.

Evaluation of Word Processing Programs

Word processing programs have so many features that it is difficult for the beginner to tell a good program from an inferior one. It takes time to explore the programs and evaluate them. The computer you are using also limits you. Old computers more than likely will not work with the latest word processing package. For this reason, before you begin your exploration of software, consider your computer's capabilities.

HARDWARE COMPATIBILITY

Check out the computers that are available at your school. For example, do you have old Apple IIes, Macintosh G5s, or IBM compatibles? How much memory do these machines have: 64 MB, 256 MB, or 4 GB of RAM? What is the computer's processor speed? How much storage space does the hard disk drive contain? What other peripherals or external devices are available? Does the school district have a CD-ROM or DVD-ROM player or a scanner? After you are knowledgeable about your hardware and you have examined the different word processing features, you are ready to consider a software program's instructional design.

INSTRUCTIONAL DESIGN AND FEATURES

For the lowest grade levels, a word processor should offer at least the following functions: insert, delete, center, underline, double space, save text, and print. A word processor program should be easy for a student to learn and not require hours of instruction.

Write:OutLoud is a talking word processor that provides auditory feedback for students with or without learning disabilities (see Chapter 13). This word processor is a perfect example of a picture- or icon-based application. *Write:Outloud* displays its functions at the top of the screen (Figure 6.10), which is ideal for beginners

Figure 6.10
Write:Outloud
Icons
(*Source:* Used with permission of Don Johnston Incorporated, 26799 W. Commerce Dr., Volvo, IL 60073. Phone: 800-999-4660, 847-740-0749, Fax: 847-740-7326, Web: www. donjohnston.com, E-mail: info@ donjohnston.com)

Pyramid c1

because it saves them from having to remember functions. For example, to print a document the user chooses the printer icon on the toolbar; to save work he or she chooses the floppy disk icon on the toolbar.

iWork '08 includes a word processing program called *Pages*. This program lets you create documents with an array of Apple-designed templates. A template is a formatted document for a specific use such as an Education Scrapbook (Figure 6.11). The opening dialog box with its list of templates makes it easy for the novice to begin using the program. The program also offers a very useful help function, a spelling checker, a thesaurus, hypermedia functions, and desktop capabilities.

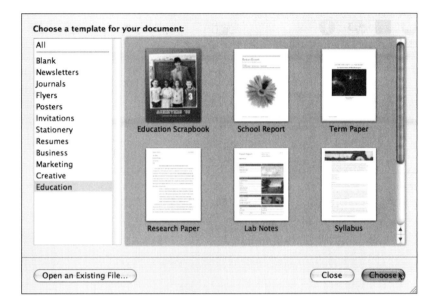

Figure 6.11
Pages Education Templates
(*Source:* Screenshot reprinted with permission from Apple, Inc.)

In your search for a word processor, examine only those with easy-to-remember keys for functions. Find out how the word processor carries out simple functions such as underlining or boldfacing.

In the higher grades, students make considerable use of word processing, so they need a more sophisticated word processor like *WordPerfect* (Corel Corp.). This program includes many advanced features but is simple to use. For example, the program enables a user to click a button to select a specific margin justification (Figure 6.12).

Figure 6.12
Justification Buttons

EASE OF USE

You should make sure that using the word processing program's functions, such as centering, boldfacing, and italicizing, is effortless. Take the program for a test drive and see how much you can learn in an hour. The program's features are immaterial if the program is difficult to learn.

Clicker 5, for grades K–6 (Crick Software, Figure 6.13), is exceptionally easy to use. Most instructions appear on the top of the screen, so teachers do not have to read a large manual. Every step of the way icons suggests the function of each button. For example, users choose the printer button to print a document and the disk button to save a document.

Also, users click words and pictures at the bottom of the screen to help them write. Are there help screens that tell students what to do each step of the way? Is there a tutorial disk or manual that guides users through the program? Is there good online help? The majority of software programs include online help, which you access by clicking help on the menu bar. Can you set up the printer easily and is it ready to print immediately?

Figure 6.13
Clicker 5 (Crick Software)
(*Source:* Crick Software, Inc/Clicker 5™)

Figure 6.13
Clicker 5 (Crick Software)
(*Source:* Crick Software, Inc/Clicker 5™)

Scholastic Keys is a simple interface for elementary students or for students that have learning disabilities. After the school district purchases Microsoft Office suite (Windows) it installs *Scholastic Keys*, which results in *Microsoft Word* becoming *MaxWrite*, *Microsoft PowerPoint* becoming *MaxShow*, and *Microsoft Excel* becoming *MaxCount*. Students can then learn basic operations without being frightened by complicated menus. The buttons are larger and the toolbar is simpler with the addition of new buttons. For example, there is a text reader (Figure 6.14) that lets students read what they write. *Scholastic Keys* comes with an assortment of lessons, activity files, and worksheets.

Figure 6.14
Scholastic Keys: MaxWrite
(for Microsoft Word)
(*Source:* Screenshots from
teacher.Scholastic.com. Copyright © 2008
by Scholastic Inc. Used by permission.)

Most programs also include many safety features to protect you from making an error, such as by mistakenly deleting a document.

SAFETY FEATURES

A program should come with enough safety devices to prevent the user from making errors. It is important to have as many of these safeguards as possible, especially when you are about to save material. These safeguards consist of queries to warn both the novice and advanced user about what they may be on the verge of doing. Many word processing programs try to protect against data loss by automatically saving material intermittently. Other programs remind the user to save. *Microsoft Word 2007* displays the screen in Figure 6.15 when the user is about to quit an application without saving the changes.

Figure 6.15
Microsoft Word 2007 Dialog Box
(*Source:* Microsoft product screenshot reprinted with permission from Microsoft Corporation)

The user then has three options: not to save, to cancel, or to save. Another important safety feature is the **undo** feature, which reverses the last action performed on the document. *Nisus*, *Word*, and *WordPerfect* advanced-level word processing programs feature unlimited **undos**.

CONSUMER VALUE

Software is expensive, and for teachers cost is often a consideration. Consider the free Web-based pack *Google Docs & Spreadsheets*. *Google Docs & Spreadsheets* (http://docs.google.com/) is a free Web-based word processing application (Figure 6.16). You can create documents from scratch or import ones that you previously created. You can choose to collaborate from remote locations with students and update from

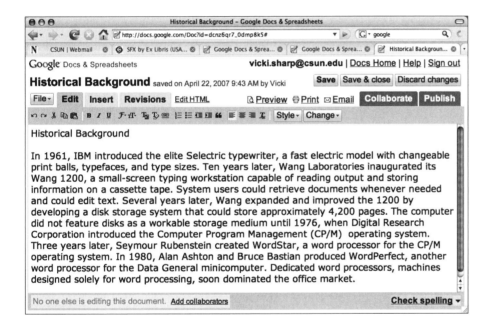

Figure 6.16
Google Docs & Spreadsheets
(*Source:* © 2008 Google™. All rights reserved.)

your own computer. Using this product you can publish a document, edit information, and make changes anytime you wish.

Also consider any **public domain software** package that can be purchased for a minimal price and duplicated, as often as needed, as long as it offers the features you need. There is one catch: The program cannot be sold to anyone. **Shareware** is inexpensive software that is copyrighted but that you can try before you buy. Usually, commercial software is more expensive, but there are exceptions. Even though public domain and shareware is inexpensive, you generally do not receive the same quality of technical support with it that you get from a vendor of commercial packages.

SUPPORT

Support refers to personal as well as written help from the software company. Can you call a technician at the software company to get immediate help or must you sift through a series of messages and wait an unbearable amount of time? Is the technical

For a listing of recommended word processing software programs, visit our online site at http://www.wiley.com/college/sharp.

support knowledgeable and understandable? Is the technical support toll-free or does it require a pay call? Are you charged for the amount of time you are on the telephone with the technician? Is there a yearly fee for unlimited support, and is it reasonable? Is the manual readable, and does it include activities, lesson plans, and an index? Is there a Web site on the Internet that provides support?

Word Processing Program Checklist

As you can see, a teacher looking for a classroom word processing program must weigh many factors. Choosing software for the classroom is a five-step process: (1) determine the hardware compatibility; (2) study the program's features; (3) consider its instructional design; (4) evaluate its ease of use; and (5) measure its cost effectiveness and technical support. Use the Word Processing Program Checklist form on page 117 to guide you through the process.

Integrating a Word Processor into the Classroom

Teachers as well as students can use a word processing program in a variety of ways. Teachers can use it to prepare lesson plans, worksheets, book flyers (Figure 6.17), memos, lab sheets, book report forms, assignment sheets, course syllabi, and other instructional materials. They can create quizzes, tests, and different types of evaluation forms. Furthermore, they can write letters and create weekly newsletters for parents.

Figure 6.17
Word Processing Flyer,
Microsoft Word 2007

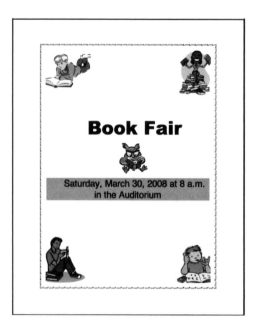

For video tutorials on how to create resumés, flyers, and letters, and for templates and examples, visit our online site at http://www.wiley.com/college/sharp.

Students at all grade levels can use word processing software to create an assortment of projects. In the lower grades, they can create large-font stories, alphabet books, and journals. Students can create classroom reports, outlines, flyers, book reports, and lab reports with tables and graphs. Furthermore, students can create a class newspaper using clip art or create their own letterhead stationery. After their letterhead stationery has been designed, students can use the software to write letters to people in the class, across the country, or around the globe. Finally, they can use the word processor to edit, using grammar and spelling checking and an electronic thesaurus.

WORD PROCESSING PROGRAM CHECKLIST

Directions: Examine the following items and determine which ones you feel are important for your class situation. Place an X on each line for which the software meets your needs.

Product Name _____ **Manufacturer** _____ **Grade Level** _____

Hardware
___ 1. Computer processor speed
___ 2. Computer compatibility
___ 3. CD-ROM or DVD capabilities
___ 4. Monitor resolution
___ 5. Hard disk space required
___ 6. Memory needed
___ 7. Printer compatibility
___ 8. Microphone and/or camera

General Features
___ 1. Cursor control
___ 2. Word wrap
___ 3. Page breaks

Standard Editing Features
___ 1. Cut and paste
___ 2. Copy
___ 3. Drag and drop
___ 4. Find and replace
___ 5. Insert and delete
___ 6. Spelling checker
___ 7. Grammar checker
___ 8. Thesaurus
___ 9. Saving and printing

Standard Formatting Functions
___ 1. Automatic page numbering
___ 2. Font
    ___ a. Typeface
    ___ b. Pitch
    ___ c. Point size
    ___ d. Style
3. Headers and footers
4. Justification
5. Line spacing
6. Margins
7. Superscripts and subscripts
8. Tabs
9. Underlining

Advanced Features
1. AutoCorrect
2. AutoFormating
3. Automatic indexing
4. Change tracking
5. Charting

___ 6. Columns
___ 7. Desktop publishing capabilities
___ 8. Endnotes
___ 9. Equation editor
___ 10. Footnoting
___ 11. Glossary
___ 12. Graphic organizer
___ 13. Hyperlink creation
___ 14. Importing of different graphic file formats
___ 15. Kerning
___ 16. Macros
___ 17. Mail merge
___ 18. Math computations and sorting
___ 19. Outlining
___ 20. Speech recognition
___ 21. Style sheets
___ 22. Table of contents
___ 23. Tables
___ 24. Templates
___ 25. Voice annotation
___ 26. Web page creation
___ 27. Windows
___ 28. Wizards

Safety Features
___ 1. Undo last move(s)
___ 2. Warning questions
___ 3. Automatic save

Ease of Use
___ 1. Help screens
___ 2. Online tutorial
___ 3. Printer setup
___ 4. Talking processor

Support Features
___ 1. Technical support
___ 2. Tutorial material
___ 3. Readable manual
    ___ a. Activities and lesson plans
    ___ b. Tutorial
    ___ c. Index

Consumer Value
___ 1. Cost
___ 2. Free technical support
___ 3. Guarantees

Rating Scale
Rate the word processor by placing a check in the appropriate line.

Excellent_____ Very good_____ Good_____ Fair_____ Poor _____

Comments:

SAMPLE CLASSROOM LESSON PLANS

I. TRAVELING ABROAD

Subject: Social Studies, **Grade(s)** 4 and up

Objective: Students will use the word processor to create a travel brochure like the one shown in Figure 6.18.

Figure 6.18
Travel Brochure Template,
Make It with Office 2007
(*Source:* Microsoft products screenshot. Reprinted with permission from Microsoft Corporation Microsoft Word 2007.)

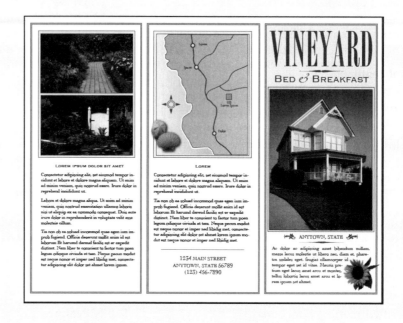

Standards
• National Council for the Social Studies Curriculum Standards 3
• ISTE NETS for Students 1, 3, 4, 5

Materials
You will need a word processing program such as *Microsoft Word* and one or more computers.

Procedures
1. Divide the class into small groups.
2. Explain to students that they will create a travel brochure about a country they have visited or a country that they would like to visit.
3. Instruct students to create their brochures in such a manner that anyone who reads them will want to visit the countries advertised.
4. Ask students to use the Internet or print resources to research the country and collect facts and images.
5. Have groups use a word processor to create their brochures.
6. When all groups are done, discuss how effective each brochure is in publicizing the country chosen.

Variation
The brochure can cover any topic, and students can work independently.

II. NEWSLETTER

Subject: English

Grade(s): 2 and up

Objective: Students will use a word processor to create a newspaper.

Standards
- NCTE English Language Arts Standards 4, 5, 7, 8, 12
- ISTE NETS for Students 1, 2, 3, 4, 5

Materials
You will need a word processing program such as *Writer's Companion*, *Pages*, or *WordPerfect* and one or more computers.

Procedures
1. Divide the class into small groups.
2. Meet with students to discuss what the newspaper will cover.
3. Have students make a list of topics.
4. Ask each group to choose a leader and divide their tasks; one person might write a gossip column, another might handle sports, and another might cover world news, for example.
5. Have students use a word processor to produce the newspaper (see Figure 6.19 for an example).

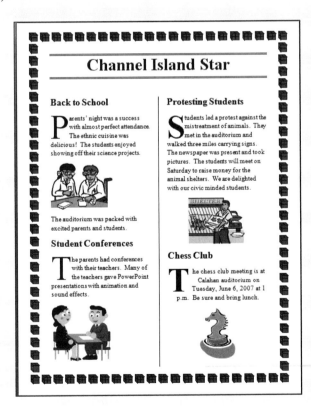

Figure 6.19
Newspaper, *Make It with Office 2007*
(*Source:* Courtesy Visions Technology in Education)

Variation

The newspaper can cover a multitude of topics, from famous historical figures or current political leaders to scientific inventions.

III. WRITING A WACKY STORY

Subject: English

Grade(s): 2 and up

Objective: Students will improve their writing skills and, in the process, use the cut and paste and find and replace functions.

Standards
• NCTE English Language Arts Standards 4, 5, 6, 12
• ISTE NETS for Students 1, 2, 3, 4

Materials
You will need a word processing program such as *Writer's Companion*, *Pages*, or *WordPerfect* and one or more computers.

Procedures

1. Have each student independently create a random sentence for a story file.
2. Instruct each student to write his or her sentence on a piece of paper.
3. Ask students to examine the sentences of two classmates, correcting grammar errors.
4. Next instruct the students to enter, one at a time, their sentences into the computer.
5. When the sentences are entered, have students separate them by a line and number them in the order they are entered.
6. Ask the last student to enter his or her sentence and save the entire file of sentences under a name such as *Story 1*.
7. Go around the room asking students to call out random numbers no higher than the number of sentences that were recorded for *Story 1*.
8. Call up *Story 1* on the computer and record at the top of the screen the random sequence of numbers the students gave.
9. Have the students take turns using the find and replace function to locate the sentences in a random sequence and using the cut and paste function to move the sentences into the order of the random sequence.
10. Print out a copy of the ordered sentences for each student. During independent work time, ask the students to make stories out of their sentences, without changing the order of sentences, by adding sentences or words.
11. Ask students to share their finished stories.

Example
Use the find and replace and cut and paste functions to create a story from the sentences that follow. Arrange the sentences in the following sequence: 1 4 8 2 3 5 6 9 7.

1. Do not judge food on calories alone.
2. The professor was frustrated with the paperwork he had to turn in next week.
3. The student was eagerly awaiting an exciting lecture on computers.
4. The wind blew a bee into the room.
5. "Don't forget to pick up the groceries at the store," said Paul.
6. "Did the emergency rations arrive?" asked Maria.
7. There were many children on the playground.
8. The centerfielder could not catch the ball.
9. The sound came from another room.

Do not judge food on calories alone. This is what the professor was saying as the wind blew a bee into the classroom. I was daydreaming as usual, watching the baseball team. The centerfielder could not catch the ball. The professor banged on the board.

I looked up. He seemed crabby. I think he was frustrated with the paperwork he had to turn in next week. He called on Dewayne. The student was eagerly awaiting an exciting lecture on computers but instead he was invited up to the board to solve a complicated problem. I went back to daydreaming. There was something I was supposed to do after class. Suddenly I remembered. While I was brushing my teeth that morning, my roommate made a grocery list. "Don't forget to pick up the groceries at the store," said Paul as I ran out the door. Then at the bus stop, I ran into my friend Maria, who was heading up an earthquake disaster team. She was talking to someone else on the disaster team. "Did the emergency rations arrive?" asked Maria. As Dewayne tried to solve the problem, I decided I would donate some of my groceries to Maria's earthquake relief efforts. An explosion interrupted my daydreaming. The sound came from another room, the chemistry lab. Dewayne still wasn't finished. I looked back out the window. There were many children on the playground.

IV. UNSCRAMBLE THE STORY

Subject: English

Grade(s): 2 and up

Objective: Students will improve their reading comprehension and learn how to use a word processor's copy and paste function.

Standards
- NCTE English Language Arts Standards 3, 6
- ISTE NETS for Students 1, 6

Materials
You will need a word processing program such as *Writer's Companion*, *Pages*, or *WordPerfect* and one or more computers.

Procedures

1. Choose a story that the students are currently reading.
2. Type the story or part of the story into the computer. You might choose "The Hare and the Tortoise,"[2] one of Aesop's Fables, as follows:

The Hare and the Tortoise

A hare was once boasting about how fast he could run when a tortoise, overhearing him, said, "I'll run you a race." "Done," said the hare and laughed to himself, "but let's get the fox for a judge." The fox consented and the two started. The hare quickly outran the tortoise, and knowing he was far ahead, lay down to take a nap. "I can soon pass the tortoise whenever I awaken." But, unfortunately, the hare overslept. When he awoke, though he ran his best, he found the tortoise was already at the goal. *Slow and steady wins the race.*

3. Save this story under *Hare/Tortoise.*
4. Now use the cut and paste functions on the word processor to scramble the story.

The scrambled Hare and Tortoise story might look like this:

The Scrambled Hare and the Tortoise

The hare quickly outran the tortoise, and knowing he was far ahead, lay down to take a nap. "Done," said the hare and laughed to himself, "but let's get the fox for a judge." *Slow and steady wins the race.* The fox consented and the two started. But, unfortunately, the hare overslept. When he awoke, though he ran his best, he found the tortoise was already at the goal. A hare was once boasting about how fast he could run when a tortoise, overhearing him, said, "I'll run you a race." "I can soon pass the tortoise whenever I awaken."

[2] From *The Children's Treasury,* Paula S. Goepfert, ed. New York: Gallery Books, 1987, p. 229.

5. Save this scrambled fable under *AERH*, which is *Hare* scrambled.

6. Load *AERH* into each student's computer.

7. Ask students to use their word processors to arrange the story correctly.

8. Record each student's score by writing down the time taken to complete the activity and the number of sentences arranged correctly.

Variation

1. Divide the class into two teams, Team A and Team B.

2. Instruct Team A to scramble a story.

3. Instruct Team B to rearrange the story.

4. Determine Team B's score by calculating the time it takes the team to rearrange the story and the number of sentences correct on completion.

5. Then have the teams swap roles.

V. WEB PAGE

Subject: English

Grade(s): 2 and up

Objective: Students will gain practice creating simple Web pages. They will create a Web page similar to the one shown in Figure 6.20.

Figure 6.20
Web Page, *Make It with Office 2007*
(*Source:* Courtesy Visions Technology in Education)

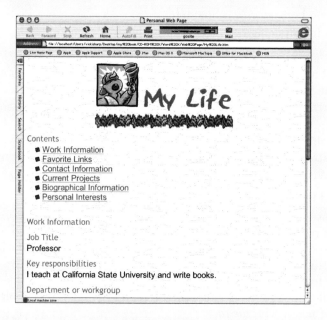

Standards

• NCTE English Language Arts Standards 3, 4, 5, 6, 7, 8, 12
• ISTE NETS for Students 1, 2, 4

Materials

You will need a word processing program such as *Writer's Companion*, *Pages*, or *WordPerfect* and one or more computers.

Procedures

1. Give the class pointers on how to plan and create a Web page.

2. Show different Web page examples.

3. Have students discuss which pages they consider excellent and the reasons for their choices.

4. Ask students to create their own Web pages using the word processor. The Web pages can be on any topic.

SUMMARY

This chapter traced the historical beginnings of word processing and showed how word processing has come a long way from the Wang 1200. We discovered how easy it is for users to change and edit documents with word processors. We became familiar with the basic features of word processing and gained insight into what features to consider when selecting a word processor. The chapter presented a checklist and evaluation scale to facilitate this decision-making process, along with specific ideas on how to incorporate the word processor into the classroom. Five word processing activities covered a range of curriculum areas.

STUDY AND ONLINE RESOURCES

CHAPTER 6 ONLINE RESOURCES

 In the **student section** of the book's online site at **http://www.wiley.com/college/sharp**, you will find templates and examples, video tutorials on creating a letter, flyer, resume, checklists, PDFs, and articles, along with top-rated Web sites, software reviews, and chapter quizzes. Access these resources to learn about technology and integrating it into the classroom.

CHAPTER MASTERY TEST

Lets check for chapter comprehension with a short mastery test. Key terms, Computer Lab, and Suggested Readings and References follow the test.

1. What is word processing and why is it important in education?

2. What are two advantages of using Web-based applications like *Google Docs & Spreadsheets*?

3. Identify and describe five features that are common to all word processors.

4. Discuss three different ways a word processor would be useful in the classroom.

5. Select two standard editing features and justify their use.

6. Explain the concept of line justification as it relates to the computer and give two examples.

7. Discuss the factors involved in selecting a word processor for a school district. The Online Learning Center presents an annotated list of word processing software.

8. Define the following terms: (a) font, (b) copy and paste, (c) justification (d) drag and drop, and (e) find and replace.

9. What safety features should be included in a word processor and why?

10. Evaluate a real or hypothetical word processing software program based on the criteria used in this chapter.

11. Choose three advanced word processing features and explain how you would use them in a high school classroom.

12. If you were buying a word processing program for use in an elementary school, what three features would be essential in your selection and why?

13. Compare two word processors on the basis of their features; then review each one separately.

14. Americans generally use word processing software more than Europeans do. Explain why you think this situation will or will not change.

15. Explain why templates have become a highly popular word processing tool.

KEY TERMS

COMPUTER LAB: Activities for Mastery and Your Portfolio

6.1 Footnotes and Bibliographic Styles Learn how to cite information found on the Internet.

6.2 Create a form letter and then do a mail merge for a small group of students in the class. Watch the Video tutorial online and learn how to do a mail merge.

6.3 Make a certificate for any occasion. Watch the Video tutorial online and learn how create a certificate.

6.4 Create a piece of letterhead stationery. Write another member of the class using the stationery.

Watch the Video tutorial online and learn how write a letter.

6.5 Use a word processing template to prepare a résumé. Watch the Video tutorial online and learn how write a résumé (using templates).

6.6 Create a flyer publicizing a hypothetical product that you want to sell. Watch the Video tutorial online and learn how create a flyer.

6.7 Write a research report with footnotes and bibliography.

SUGGESTED READINGS AND REFERENCES

Bahr, Christine M. "The Effects of Text-Based and Graphics-Based Software Tools on Planning and Organizing of Stories." *Journal of Learning Disabilities* 29, no. 4 (July 1996): 355–370.

Balajthy, E. "Keyboarding, Language Arts, and the Elementary School Child." *Computing Teacher* (February 1988): 40–43.

Bangert-Drowns, Robert L. "The Word Processor as an Instructional Tool: A Meta-analysis of Word Processing in Writing." *Review of Educational Research* 63, issue 1 (Spring 1993): 69–93.

Campbell, George. "Get Their Attention with Voice Attachments." *PC World* 18, no. 3 (March 2000): 265.

Cavanagh, Sean. "On Writing Tests, Computers Slowly Making Mark." *Education Week* 26, issue 23 (February 14, 2007): 10.

Daiute, C. *Writing and Computers.* Reading, Mass.: Addison-Wesley, 1985.

Greenleaf, Cynthia. "Technological Indeterminacy: The Role of Classroom Writing Practices and Pedagogy in Shaping Student Use of the Computer." *Written Communication* 11, no. 11 (January 1, 1994): 85.

Guhlin, Miguel. "The Case for Open Source." *Technology and Learning* 27, no. 7 (February, 2007): 16–21.

Kissell, Joe. "The Google Office." *MacWorld* (August 2007): 60–72.

Langone, John. "The Differential Effects of a Typing Tutor and Microcomputer-Based Word Processing on the Writing Samples of Elementary Students with Behavior Disorders." *Journal of Research on Computing in Education* 29, no. 2 (Winter 1996): 141–158.

MacArthur, Charles A. "Using Technology to Enhance the Writing Processes of Students with Learning Disabilities."*Journal of Learning Disabilities* 29, no. 4 (July 1996): 334–354.

MacArthur, Charles A. "Word Processing with Speech Synthesis and Word Prediction: Effects on the Dialogue Journal Writing of Students with Learning Disabilities." *Learning Disability Quarterly* 21, no. 2 (Spring 1998): 151–166.

McLester, Susan. "Let's Teach Students to Innovate." *Technology and Learning* 25, issue 10 (May 2005): 3.

Milone, Michael N. *Every Teacher's Guide to Word Processing: 101 Classroom Computer Activities for Every Grade.* Englewood Cliffs, N.J.: Prentice Hall, 1985.

Montague, Marjorie, and Fionelle Fonseca. "Using Computers to Improve Story Writing." *Teaching Exceptional Children* 25, no. 4 (Summer 1993): 46–49.

Montgomery, Donna J., and Lori J. Marks. "Using Technology to Build Independence in Writing for Students With Disabilities." *Preventing School Failure* 50, issue 3 (Spring 2006): 33–38.

Pfaffenberger, Bryan. *Webster's New World Dictionary of Computer Terms, 10th ed.* New York: John Wiley & Sons, 2003.

Poftak, Amy, Mark Smith, and K. C. Jones. "Survey Says." *Technology and Learning* 26, issue 3 (October 2005): 5.

Schroeder, Ken. "Raising Writing Skills." *Education Digest* 72, issue 4 (December 2006): 74–75.

Sharp, Vicki. *Make It with Microsoft Office XP (Windows).* Eugene, Ore.: Visions Technology in Education, 2003.

Sharp, Vicki. *Make It with Microsoft Office 2004 (Macintosh).* Eugene, Ore: Visions Technology in Education, 2006.

Sharp, Vicki. *Make It with Microsoft Office 2007 (Windows).* Eugene, Ore.: Visions Technology in Education, 2007.

Sharp, Vicki. *Make It with Microsoft Office 2008 (Macintosh).* Eugene, Ore.: Visions Technology in Education, 2008.

Stone, M. David. "Choose Your Words." *PC Magazine* 19, no. 6 (March 21, 2000): 113.

"Sunburst Introduces Write Brain to Teach Writing to Grades 2–8." *Students Electronic Education Report* 13, issue 13 (July 14, 2006): 4.

Van Leeuwen, Charlene A., and Martha A. Gabriel. "Beginning to Write with Word Processing: Integrating Writing Process and Technology in a Primary Classroom." *Reading Teacher* 60, issue 5 (February 2007): 420–429.

Desktop Publishing

Integrating Desktop Publishing into the Classroom

Desktop publishing is probably the second most popular use of computers in schools next to word processing (Kearsley, Hunter, & Furlong, 1992). In classrooms, students can use desktop software to create a variety of projects such as minibooks, book reports, yearbooks, newsletters, posters, and flyers.

Teachers can use a desktop publishing program to create awards, worksheets, signs, flyers, and posters for classroom display. This chapter discusses how to select a desktop publishing program for the classroom and the general features of a desktop publishing program. A checklist helps you choose the right desktop publishing software, and exercises help you integrate desktop publishing into the classroom.

Using the computer, students and teachers can do the following:

students can

- create a class newspaper,
- design cards for other students,
- design posters and fliers,
- create a banner for the class,
- create a school yearbook
- make a personal resumé, and
- design science experiment sheets.

teachers can

- create a school newspaper,
- create a brochure for the school,
- design an award or certificate,
- create flash cards or vocabulary cards,
- create a layout for the school yearbook, and
- create a letter to the parents.

Word Processing versus Desktop Publishing

Many of the word processing programs we studied in Chapter 6 had desktop publishing capabilities. Users could manipulate text, add graphics to the text, and lay out the text and graphics. These programs included graphic fonts as well as a variety of different type sizes. The distinction between desktop publishing and word processing has certainly become blurred.

Although the majority of word processing programs are capable of performing some desktop publishing functions, the strength of such programs is text manipulation. Word processing programs outshine desktop publishing programs when it comes to checking spelling and grammar, changing margins, performing global replace and find searches, and setting tabs for an entire document. The strength of desktop publishing programs, on the other hand, is graphic design, or the ability to combine text and graphics to communicate effectively. A desktop publishing program gives the user more control over a document's design than does a word processing program. These programs offer more features, tools, and color palettes.

Historical Background

Before the 1400s, few people could read or write, and books were scarce because they had to be handwritten. Around 1450, Johannes Gutenberg revolutionized communication with the invention of **movable type**. Modifying a winemaker's press to

Figure 7.1
Early Printing Press

hold type, he poured hot metal into molds from which he created letters, numbers, and symbols (Figure 7.1).

Gutenberg's printing innovation gave more people the opportunity to read by making books more available. Even though Gutenberg's methods were refined over time, the basic concept behind his press remained unchanged for 400 years.

In the late 1880s, Ottmar Mergenthaler invented the **Linotype machine**, the first successful automated typecasting machine. This mechanical type-composing machine enabled the operator to cast an entire line of type at once by using a keyboard. It was first used to typeset the *New York Tribune* in 1886. A year later, Tolbert Lanston invented the **Monotype machine**, which produced three characters of set type a second and was widely used for books.

The Linotype and Monotype, along with handset type, dominated typesetting until Intertype introduced the first phototypesetting machine in 1950. Phototypesetting used film to reproduce type and images on metal plates that could then be inked for reproduction on paper.

The search for higher typesetting speeds resulted in the development in the mid-1960s of a method that stores characters in electronic digital format. Computer-typesetting equipment generates letterforms as nearly invisible dots. This invention led the way for desktop publishing, a term coined by Paul Brainerd of Aldus Software.

What is Desktop Publishing?

Desktop publishing (DTP) uses the personal computer (in conjunction with specialized software) to combine text and graphics to produce high-quality output on either a laser printer or as a postscript file you can take to a service bureau for high-volume printing. The elements of this multistep process, which involves different types of software and equipment, are as follows (see Figure 7.2):

Figure 7.2
Desktop Publishing Process
(*Source:* All others © 2008 Jupiterimages Corporation)

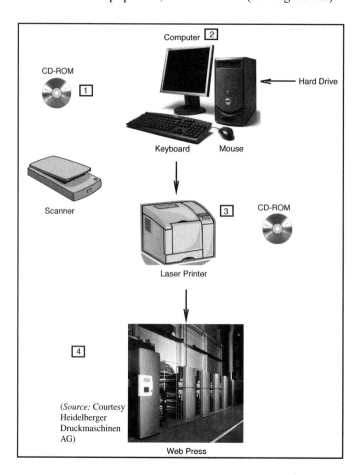

1. Input your material using the keyboard, a scanner, a flash drive, a CD-ROM, or a video digitizer. Also input illustrations from clip art, from a drawing or painting program, or from a screen capture program such as *SnagIt* (TechSmith Corporation).

2. Lay out the text and graphics on the screen, revising and refining the material using the DTP's capabilities.

3. At this point, you have two choices: to print the finished document on a laser printer or, for better quality, to have a service bureau print it on a machine such as the Heidelberg Web press.

4. After obtaining proofs, make further changes and corrections and ready the final copy for printing or instruct the service bureau or printer to do so.

Desktop publishing has become an all-encompassing term. It can refer to 14 Macintosh computers connected to a magazine's editorial and design departments; to a Macintosh user running *Print Shop 2* (MacKiev) to produce a newsletter on an inkjet printer; or to an 8-year-old creating a sign about a lost pet. DTP is no longer the exclusive property of the skilled technician or computer programmer. With a desktop publishing program, you can design a business newsletter, create a banner, or produce a school newspaper.

In the past, each student working on a high school or college newspaper was assigned a different task. Typically, there was a designer, a writer, an illustrator, a typesetter, and a paste-up artist. Now DTP makes it possible for one person to perform all these functions. DTP permits a student to

1. create onscreen layouts,
2. select among different typefaces or fonts,
3. justify text and lay out multiple columns,
4. insert art and text on the same page, and
5. print camera-ready copy.

There are many advantages to preparing student publications this way. DTP offers great flexibility in designing graphics and headlines and gives the user a great deal of control over the final product. DTP is a more versatile, faster, and less expensive way to produce publications than the traditional methods because fewer people need to be involved and fewer revisions are necessary.

As recently as 1985, there were few DTP programs, and the available ones, *PageMaker* (Adobe) and *Ready Set Go* (Manhattan Graphics), were designed only for the Macintosh computer. Today, there are more programs to choose from, and they exist for all computers. The software and hardware that the student needs for DTP range in price from inexpensive to very expensive. If you want to print an informal newsletter, you might use a program such as *Print Shop 2* (MacKiev) or *Microsoft Publisher* and a simple color inkjet printer. You also might use an advanced word processing program with desktop features like *Microsoft Word* or *Pages 2*. If you are responsible for a business presentation, you might use expensive scanning equipment with programs such as *Adobe InDesign*, *Adobe PageMaker*, or *QuarkXPress* (Quark). Although the resolution from a laser printer is not as high as that from a professional Web press, the resulting copy would be exceptional.

Desktop programs differ in degree of complexity, cost, and features. Lets explore some of the basic characteristics of these programs.

Basic Desktop Publishing Features

Although desktop programs differ in their sophistication, all of them offer the ability to (1) do page layout, (2) do word processing, (3) create style sheets and templates, (4) create and manipulate graphics, (5) manipulate the page view, and (6) create Web pages.

PAGE LAYOUT

Page layout is the process of arranging various elements on a page. The process involves setting page margins, selecting page and column width and the number of text columns, and positioning graphics and text.

The most powerful programs, such as *Adobe PageMaker* and *QuarkXPress*, allow the greatest control in page design; however, these programs are sophisticated and come with a steep learning curve. Less powerful programs, such as *Print Shop* and *Microsoft Publisher* (Windows version), offer a wide variety of templates and wizards and require less learning time. *Microsoft Publisher* (Windows version) includes designs for flyers, newsletters, calendars, award certificates, and more (Figure 7.3). Once you select a template design, you can make all kinds of modifications to it with a click of the mouse.

Figure 7.3
Microsoft Publisher 2007
(*Source:* Mircorsoft product screenshot reprinted with permission from Microsoft Corporation)

For example, you can choose among a variety of fonts and colors. This program includes Web sites and e-mail wizards and Design Sets. *Microsoft Publisher* is more complicated than *Print Shop,* but it lacks some of the more sophisticated features of *PageMaker* or *QuarkXPress.*

Word processing programs such as *Microsoft Word*, *WordPerfect*, and *Pages 2* include sufficient desktop capabilities to fulfill the desktop publishing needs of students from age 10 and up. Finally, a program such as *Storybook Weaver Deluxe* (Riverdeep) offers thousands of graphics and sound effects from which students can choose to create a multimedia story. Students can then hear the text in either Spanish or English.

In *PageMaker*, you determine the page size, set the margins, and choose the number of columns and the width of each column. *PageMaker*'s master pages enable you to design a template for a document with measuring rulers and guides to help with the placement of graphics and text on each page. Like the majority of DTP programs, *PageMaker* shows a reduced-size view of a page or page spread so you can see it all at once on screen. Most programs can resize, reshape, and reposition text or graphics, and they all feature automatic page numbering.

The majority of page-layout programs are based on **frames**. Frames are boxes that contain text or graphics. They have resize handles for stretching and resizing. If you want to put text into a document, you may place it on the base page, an immovable frame that covers the entire page. Alternatively, you may draw a frame with the help of a screen ruler. Once the frame is defined, you can import text or graphics into it. You also can stack frames or create captions that overlay illustrations. The desktop publishing program should allow you to create as many frames as you want and put them anywhere on the page, stacking them and adjusting them as necessary. If you link text frames, you can add text to the first one, and it will overflow into other text frames, which is useful for newspaper layouts involving articles that continue from a column on one page to a column on another.

WORD PROCESSING

Word processor power varies among desktop publishing programs, but all DTPs can edit and format text to some degree.

EDITING

The majority of DTP packages enable you to enter text, edit it, and import documents from other programs. The typical word processing functions are *delete*, *insert*, and *copy*. The majority of DTP programs also offer a spelling checker and a thesaurus. High school students require *move*, *search*, and *replace* functions as well.

FORMATTING

Formatting features, such as *type size*, *font*, and *typeface*, determine how a page will look. The more control you have over the text, the more professional looking your document. Many DTP programs enable you to center or align text along uniform margins, and some programs enable you to define the space between letters (kerning), words, and lines to improve the readability and appearance of the document.

STYLE SHEETS AND TEMPLATES

A **style sheet** stores formatting that you can repeat throughout a document. For example, you might design a style sheet that puts page numbers in the right corner, 2 inches from the top of the page. Once you have created the style sheet, all pages in your document will automatically have page numbers in the right corner. On your style sheet, you can set margins, type style, line spacing, headers, footers, and quotation style for your entire document.

Figure 7.4 shows the *QuarkXPress* dialog box defining a style. In this example, the paragraph style's name is *Body Text*, and it uses bold Times New Roman with a 10-point font size (Figure 7.4).

Figure 7.4
QuarkXPress Style Sheets
(*Source:* QuarkXpress Courtesy Quark, Inc.)

To apply this style you would select the text you wanted to apply it to and click on *Body text* in the *Style* dialog box. The style sheet then automatically would be applied to the selected text. It would look like this:

"The longest running-computer crime. Double-entry inventory control at Saxon Industries. A Fortune 500 company that reported profits of $7.1 million and $5.3 million in 1979 and 1980, respectively, it went bankrupt in 1982. A bogus inventory record was maintained by computer by Saxon's Business Products Division. It was used to inflate the company's annual revenues. The double books were kept for thirteen years, and the crime might never have been revealed if the company had been profitable. Saxon was $53 million in the hole when it went under." (Rochester & Gantz, 1983, p. 117)

Quite a few DTP programs feature their own style sheets, and others enable you to import style sheets from other programs. Many DTPs provide **templates**, which are predesigned "molds" into which you can "pour" your text, and some companies enable you to create your own templates. Templates are time-savers because the user does not have to establish styles. The Flyer template in Figure 7.5 is from *Microsoft Publisher 2007* (Windows). This program is packaged with a multitude of templates for different uses.

Figure 7.5
Microsoft Publisher Flyer Template
(*Source:* Microsoft Product screenshot reprinted with permission from Microsoft Corporation)

 For training videos on how to create a newsletter and a certificate, as well as templates and examples, consult **http://www .wiley.com/college/sharp.**

GRAPHICS

Desktop publishing programs enable you to add different types of pictures or graphics to text, either by drawing them or by importing them. Even though graphics can be created in DTP programs, these programs rarely offer full-featured graphic capabilities. Typically, you need to create a graphic in a draw or paint program and then import it into the publishing program.

TOOLS

A desktop program usually features a variety of tools (Figure 7.6) for manipulating text and graphics:

Figure 7.6
QuarkXPress Tools

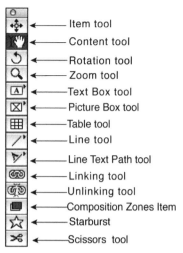

(*Source:* QuarkXpress Courtesy Quark, Inc.)

- The item tool ⊕ moves boxes, items, or lines on a page.

- The content tool 🖑 manipulates the content within a box.

- The rotation tool ↺ rotates an item.

- The zoom tool 🔍 enlarges or reduces the document view.

- The text box tool Ⓐ draws rectangle text boxes that are used to hold text. By clicking on this tool, you have access to other text box tools.

- The picture box tool ⊠ creates a rectangle box. By clicking on this tool, you have access to other picture box tools.

- The table tool ▦ creates tables.

- The line tool ╱ draws lines at any angle.

- The line text path tool ⊻ will create text at any angle. This tool also gives access to other text path tools.

- The linking tool 🔗 connects text boxes, permitting the flow of text from one box to another.

- The unlinking tool breaks the connection between these text boxes.

- The composition tool creates composition zones.

- The starburst tool ☆ draws stars.

- The scissors tool ✂ cuts line segments.

Generally, DTPs feature tools for customizing artwork; reducing, enlarging, rotating, or flipping a drawing; zooming in for detail; and editing graphics, pixel by pixel. With some programs you can trace edges and change perspective, which is useful in producing halo effects around graphics, in outlining type, or even in converting silhouettes to simple outline form. With a DTP, you can crop or trim away part of an image and use it as a separate graphic. You can also repeat or duplicate an image. Figure 7.7 shows the same rose pattern image duplicated in a regular border pattern.

Figure 7.7
Rose Pattern
(*Source:* © 2008 Jupiterimages Corporation)

Make sure your DTP program includes a **text wrap** feature to take care of any graphic overlay problems caused by importing. This feature will wrap lines of text around a graphic without covering it.

PAGE VIEW

After your page layout is completed, you will want to see how it looks before printing out the document. The *majority of programs today* give you a full range of **page view** magnifications.

WEB PAGE CREATION

Programs such as *QuarkXPress* and *Microsoft Publisher* offer Web capabilities. *QuarkXPress* enables you to create Web documents with hyperlinks. These Web documents can then be exported as HTML documents and posted on the Web. They also can be edited in other programs such as *Dreamweaver. Quark* exports Web document pictures in different graphic formats such as JPEG, GIF, or PNG formats. Less difficult programs such as *Microsoft Publisher* feature Web site wizards that help you build Web pages.

Now that you have some idea of what the basic features of a desktop publishing program are, let us explore how to use a desktop publishing program.

Learning to Use a Desktop Publishing Program

This section gives an overview of how a desktop publishing program operates. It should not serve as a substitute for a program's operation manual. For illustrative purposes, we will use *Microsoft Publisher*, a good middle-school desktop program that offers many more advanced features than *Print Shop*, a DTP program for grades 2 and above. We consider how *Microsoft Publisher* creates a layout, adds text and graphics, and produces a printout.

When you open *Microsoft Publisher* you are asked to select the type of publication from a list. You can create a document from scratch or you can use a template to speed up the procedure. In Figure 7.8, the *Newsletters* publication type has been selected. You next select a newsletter design, in this case Arrows, and click "Create".

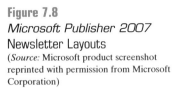

Figure 7.8
Microsoft Publisher 2007
Newsletter Layouts
(*Source:* Microsoft product screenshot reprinted with permission from Microsoft Corporation)

The dialog box now changes and at the left side of the screen there are different options for the newsletter design (Figure 7.9), ranging from page options to font schemes.

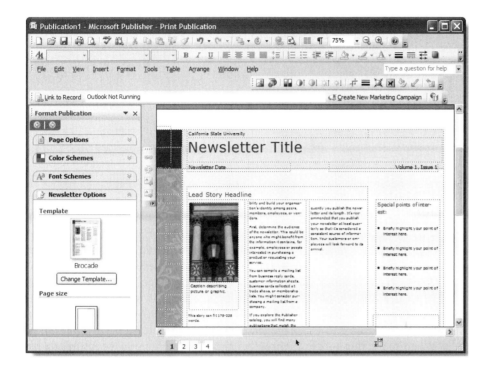

Figure 7.9
Microsoft Publisher
Newsletter Options
(*Source:* Microsoft product screenshot reprinted with permission from Microsoft Corporation)

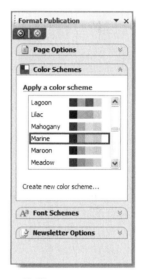

Figure 7.10
Microsoft Publisher 2007
Color Schemes
(*Source:* Microsoft product screenshot reprinted with permission from Microsoft Corporation)

If you decide to change the colors in your newsletter, you must select the color schemes option. In Figure 7.10, the Marine color scheme has been selected. If you want, you can experiment with different color schemes. While creating your newsletter, you also can change the margins, column size, borders, and page numbers style.

When you are ready to write text or import text and pictures into the document, you need to decide whether to use the program's word processing functions or to do your word processing in another program and then import the text into *Publisher*.

You may want to add graphics to illustrate a story; this usually means defining spaces or frames for the graphics. In *Microsoft Publisher*, you insert the picture you select from the Clip Gallery or from a separate file, you scan or import from a digital camera, or that you import from another program. The picture then appears with eight frame handles around it (Figure 7.11).

You can use the handles to resize it, move it, rotate it, or turn it sideways. *Microsoft Publisher*'s Clip Gallery features hundreds of pictures covering a range of subjects; you also can import pictures from other clip art collections or pictures that you created with paint programs (this particular program includes painting and graphics tools of its own).

As you experiment with layout and importing of art, you frequently need to view the entire page. Activate the page preview function to display the document in a reduced size that fits onscreen, as shown in Figure 7.12. Many DTP programs include a zoom feature that enables you to see a closeup of small sections of the document.

The last step is to print the document either on an inkjet or a laser printer. The laser printer produces a very professional-quality copy, but this output does not approach the resolution of that produced by a Web press.

Figure 7.11
Microsoft Publisher 2007
Picture Frame with Handles

Figure 7.12

Microsoft Publisher 2007
Page Preview Function
(*Source:* Microsoft product screenshot reprinted with permission from Microsoft Corporation)

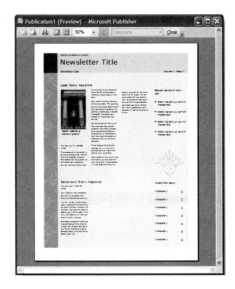

As you can see, using a program like *Microsoft Publisher* is not difficult. This program is appropriate for junior high and high school students. *Microsoft Publisher* is less expensive and does not have all the features of a professional program such as *QuarkXPress*, which is more suitable for serious high school and college students. *QuarkXPress* is a more sophisticated program with which you have to make more decisions that are not as clearly defined. For example, when you open the program, the tool palette appears and you have to know to use the file menu to choose a new project. When the dialog box in Figure 7.13 appears, you have to be knowledgeable enough to make choices about such items as number of columns, gutter width, and page size.

Figure 7.13

QuarkXPress™ Dialog Box
(*Source:* QuarkXpress Courtesy Quark, Inc.)

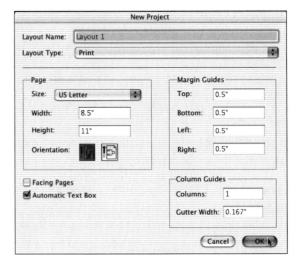

You then import text and graphics into your blank document. After you are finished creating your document, you can view it in different ways such as a thumbnail sketch, at 50 percent of actual size, at 200 percent of actual size, or in a presized window (Figure 7.14).

Although using a DTP program seems like a straightforward process, compatibility problems between programs will often arise. Some programs are much easier to use than others and import graphics easily, and others offer more flexibility and painting and drawing tools but are more difficult to use.

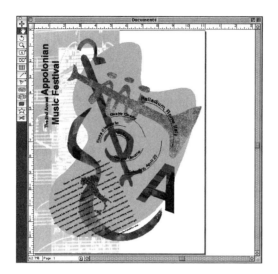

Figure 7.14
QuarkXPress™ Preview
(*Source:* QuarkXpress Courtesy Quark, Inc.)

How to Choose a Good Desktop Publishing Program

Many desktop publishing packages are on the market today, and they come with every imaginable feature. Among these are DTP programs that lend themselves easily to classroom use, such as *Storybook Weaver Deluxe*, *Print Shop* (Windows), *EasyBook Deluxe* (Sunburst), and *Microsoft Publisher* (Windows version).

To choose a DTP program for the classroom, (1) examine the program hardware compatibility; (2) consider the program's general features; (3) study the program's instructional design; (4) investigate how easy it is to use the package; (5) evaluate the program's cost effectiveness; and (6) check out the program's technical support.

HARDWARE COMPATIBILITY

Find out what computers are available at your school and whether they are Windows-based PCs or Macintoshes. Are these computers new and running the latest systems, or are they dinosaurs that are limited in the software they can run? How much memory does each machine have: 64 MB, 4 GB, or more? How large are their hard drives: 80 GB or 250 GB? What are the computers' processing speeds? What type of backup storage is available: a 750 MB Zip drive, a 2.2 GB ORB removable media drive, or something else? What other equipment is available: video digitizers, printers, multipage monitors, modems, CD-recordable drives or DVD-recordable drives, or scanners?

GENERAL FEATURES

Next, consider the features of each program. How many columns can you create for a document? (*PageMaker* creates 20 columns, *Print Shop 2* has a 3-column layout.) Is the program a what-you-see-is-what-you-get (WYSIWYG) program? Can you enlarge or shrink the graphics you import? If you make a mistake, can you easily change it? When you load a program into the computer, what is displayed on the screen?

Is there an untitled document with tools or an endless series of screens? How difficult is it to change the fonts and italicize or boldface the text? How many fonts are included and can you mix type and font styles and sizes anywhere on the page? How easy is it to insert art in the document? What graphic formats does the program handle? What graphics tools are supplied to change the artwork that was imported or created? How extensive are the word processing features? Does the program have a find and replace feature; the ability to copy, cut, and paste text; and a spelling checker and thesaurus? There are myriad features to consider, but the most important question to ask is, which features are necessary? In choosing a computer for the elementary school child, the goal should be to find a product that produces pleasant results. The high school student or novice requires more features and more versatility.

INSTRUCTIONAL DESIGN

A desktop publishing program design should be straightforward. Programs with a picture bar displayed are ideal for beginners who do not then have to memorize the different functions. *Print Shop 2* (MacKiev), for grades 2 and above, features such a toolbar (Figure 7.15).

It clearly displays the choices that are available in this program. Picture bars make it easy for any novice to change the font, add a picture, or use the printer. The advantages of programs such as *Print Shop 2* and *Microsoft Publisher 2007* are the flexibility of their design and the many options available for the beginning user.

In looking at instructional design, you should ask the following questions: Is it a simple matter to make changes? Can you easily delete, add, or insert text? How fast is the general performance? (A program that is very slow can waste time—an annoyance if you are in a hurry to complete a job. For example, *Newsroom*, one of the first DTP programs for the elementary school, was a slow and cumbersome program.) How quickly can you change fonts, font style, line spacing or leading, and paragraph justification? What flexibility does the program have in printing a newspaper? How easy is it to access the program functions? (Programs such as *Microsoft Publisher 2007* feature keyboard shortcuts for many of their functions, so it is not necessary to use their pull-down menus.)

EASE OF USE

The program must be easy to learn and must use simple English commands. Ask the following questions: Can a student in approximately 60 minutes learn to use this program? Do help screens inform users what to do each step of the way, and are they easily accessible? Is there a menu bar or tabs across the screen so users do not have to memorize the different functions? Does a tutorial disk or manual take students through the program? How difficult is it to figure out how to print a document? Can the printer be set up quickly? Is the program tedious to use because of too many help prompts and safety questions? Is there an automatic save feature?

CONSUMER VALUE

Cost has to be a major consideration in choosing a program for the classroom. *Print Shop* can be purchased for around $49.00, whereas programs such as *PageMaker* and *QuarkXPress*, even with academic pricing, cost hundreds of dollars. To determine a program's value, ask the following questions: Does the program include templates and graphic art? (*Print Shop* and *Microsoft Publisher 2007* provide templates and art, which makes these programs better value for the money.) Are on-site licenses, lab packs, or networked versions available? Software companies, at a special price, offer on-site licenses so that you can freely copy the software for in-house use. Other manufacturers distribute lab packs that enable you to purchase software at a reduced price. Finally, many manufacturers offer networked versions of the software so that a set of software can be shared among many computers.

SUPPORT

Is the documentation accompanying the program helpful or bulky and unreadable? Can you call someone to get immediate help on the telephone, or must you wade through a series of recorded directions and wait an unbearable amount of time? (Many software companies now tell you how many customers are in "line" before you and how long the wait is. When the wait is too long, some manufacturers ask you to leave your number and promise to call you back.) Are these technical support

Figure 7.15
Print Shop Toolbar
(*Source:* Courtesy Software MacKiev)

people knowledgeable and understandable? Do you have to pay a yearly fee or a fee per incident to get technical support? Is customer support available toll free or must you pay long-distance rates? Does a tutorial accompany the software package? Is the tutorial in manual form, is it on disk, or does it come both ways? (Some manufacturers provide both to simplify learning of their programs.) Is the manual readable and does it feature activities, lesson plans, and an index? How easy is it to get a refund or a new disk if the disk is defective? Is it easy to get an update to bug-riddled software?

Desktop Publishing Program Checklist

 Recommended Software For a listing of recommended desktop publishing software, go to the Online Learning Center.

Before selecting a desktop publishing program, consider the pupils' needs in the classroom. Determine what features meet these needs. Next, examine one of these programs using the sample checklist and evaluation-rating instrument on page 138. After using this checklist a couple of times, you should be able to make a more informed decision when selecting software.

Integrating Desktop Publishing into the Classroom

Teachers and students can use desktop publishing programs to produce a multitude of projects. Teachers can create worksheets, signs, flyers, business cards (Figure 7.16), posters, or other graphic-based materials to display in the class.

They can create a class newsletter to send home to parents. In addition, teachers can make brochures to promote extracurricular activities at the school. Students can use desktop publishing software to create minibooks, book reports, yearbooks, product advertisements, newsletters, posters, and flyers.

DESKTOP PUBLISHING PROGRAMS FOR THE CLASSROOM

Lets quickly review a few desktop publishing programs in terms of age-level suitability. *Storybook Weaver Deluxe* and *Kid Works Deluxe* are early-grade programs with desktop publishing features. *Storybook Weaver Deluxe* enables children to design and publish their own illustrated books. Children can choose from hundreds of graphics to illustrate their books. With *Kid Works Deluxe*, a child can create stories with graphics. These programs have very limited word processing and picture handling features, but they are superior programs for the primary grades because of their low learning curve.

Print Shop is more advanced and suitable for the middle grades because of their better picture handling and increased word processing capabilities. Although these programs offer improved features, they are by no means fully functioning desktop publishing programs. With *Print Shop*, students can make banners, certificates, greeting cards, newsletters, brochures, postcards, and more. Students can incorporate headers and footers into documents and edit their work using a spelling checker and thesaurus. When students graduate from this type of program, they might try programs such as *Microsoft Publisher 2007*, which fill a void by providing additional drawing tools and word processing and page-layout features that are useful for the junior high school and high school student.

Finally, at the advanced high school, college, and adult level, professional programs such as *Adobe PageMaker* and *QuarkXPress* offer a multitude of features, file-handling capabilities, and flexibility. They are very expensive, but academic versions exist for these products.

DESIGN AND LAYOUT TIPS

When you look at a well-designed page you do not notice the separate elements but instead view the page as a whole. On this type of page the text and graphics are arranged attractively. In order to design this type of document you have to be

Figure 7.16
Print Shop, Business Card
(*Source:* Courtesy Software MacKiev)

DESKTOP PUBLISHING CHECKLIST

Directions: Examine the following items and determine which ones you feel are important for your class situation. Place an **X** on each line for which the software meets your needs.

Product Name_____ **Manufacturer**_____ **Grade Level**_____

Hardware
___ 1. Computer processor speed
___ 2. Computer compatibility
___ 3. Monitor resolution
___ 4. Hard disk space required
___ 5. Memory needed
___ 6. Printer compatibility

Features
___ 1. Comprehensive undo
___ 2. Page size selection
___ 3. Adjustable column size
___ 4. Page preview
___ 5. Graphics
   ___ a. Ruler guides
   ___ b. Resize, position, crop
   ___ c. Flip, rotate, invert
   ___ d. Graphic importing
   ___ e. File formats (EPS, PICT, GIF, JPEG, etc.)
___ 6. Wraparound graphics
___ 7. Word processing
   ___ a. Insert and delete
   ___ b. Find and replace
   ___ c. Cut and paste
   ___ d. Spelling checker
   ___ e. Thesaurus
   ___ f. Tabs
   ___ g. Automatic pagination
   ___ h. Hyphenation
___ 8. Typesetting
   ___ a. Variety of type sizes
   ___ b. Different type styles
   ___ c. Variety of fonts
   ___ d. Kerning (spacing between letters)

___ e. Margin setting
___ 9. Drawing/painting tools

Design
___ 1. Speed of execution
___ 2. Ease of graphics insertion
___ 3. Simple saving function
___ 4. Easy printing procedure
___ 5. Number of columns possible
___ 6. Type of page layout
___ 7. Method of graphic importing
___ 8. Formatting within program

Ease of Use
___ 1. Onscreen help
___ 2. Tutorial disk
___ 3. Easy printer setup
___ 4. Minimal learning time
___ 5. Automatic save

Consumer Value
___ 1. Cost
___ 2. Templates
___ 3. Clip art included
___ 4. Lab pack
___ 5. Networked version
___ 6. On-site license

Support Features
___ 1. Technical
___ 2. Tutorial material
___ 3. Readable manual
   ___ a. Activities
   ___ b. Lesson plans
   ___ c. Index
___ Money-back guarantee

Rating Scale

Rate the DTP software by placing a check in the appropriate line.

Excellent_____ Very good _____ Good _____ Fair _____ Poor _____

Comments:

cognizant of certain principles governing space, color (light and dark), and lines. A successful layout is the result of choices about balance, alignment, proximity, contrast, repetition, and white space. Is there a difference between headlines and subheadlines? Do narrow columns feature smaller type? Did you limit your use of white text on black, using it only to emphasize a letter or a word? If you boxed your text, did you make sure you had large enough margins around the words so that they did not appear crowded? Did you restrict your use of fancy or unusual type to headlines only?

What follow are design guidelines for desktop publishing projects:

Design Guidelines

1. Spend time planning and collecting the items that will be included in your project.
2. Make a sketch or a rough layout.
3. Review what will be communicated. Who is the audience? What approach will be best for communicating the message? Be flexible and willing to experiment.
4. Look for consistency on each page of the document and check for balance of design.
5. Add interest when it is needed.
6. Organize a page around a dominant visual.
7. Pay close attention to borders and margins.
8. Provide a dramatic graphic for the front page.
9. Use forceful headlines to organize the writing.
10. Add emphasis to the work. For example, use a large type size to emphasize important ideas when needed. When necessary, vary the type style by using boldface or italics.
11. Be careful not to clutter the page with too many elements. At the same time, use a variety of items to avoid boring the audience.
12. Do not use too many typefaces because it detracts from the general feeling of the writing.
13. Select typefaces that are easy to read, such as Times. Avoid typefaces such as Techno.
14. Make type large enough so that any student can read it.
15. Use white space to focus attention on areas that contain information.
16. Make the design fit the content of the document.
17. Make sure the information is easy to find and not buried. Have it flow from the upper left corner to the right.
18. Balance related columns and facing pages. Make sure that facing pages and columns are aligned within approximately one or two lines of each other.
19. Make the size of the components on the page match the size of surrounding components.
20. Face artwork into the text.
21. Check the work thoroughly before printing out copies. Look at a printout to detect where finishing touches are needed.
22. When possible, place titles below illustrations and guide the reader with headings.
23. Do not overuse pictures and elaborate graphics. Remember, they are to convey information but not distract the reader.
24. Avoid excessive underlining, lines composed of leftover single words, unequal spacing, and cramped logos.

The books and articles in the suggested readings will provide more information about design.

SAMPLE CLASSROOM LESSON PLANS

I. NEWSLETTER DESIGN

Subject: English

Grade(s): 4 and up

Objectives: Students will learn some preliminary organizational skills and produce a simple picture with a few lines of text.

Standards
- NCTE English Language Arts Standards 4, 5, 6, 12
- ISTE NETS for Students 1, 3

Materials
You will need a desktop publishing program such as *Microsoft Publisher* and one or more computers.

Procedures
1. Ask students to bring newsletters, newspapers, and magazines to class. Distribute these items around the class.
2. Divide the class into groups of five and have each group clip text and pictures from the newspapers and magazines.
3. Next, instruct each group to choose a picture and a line or two of text and put them together to communicate a message. Students might choose a headline from an article, a graphic from an advertisement, and a line of text from an article, for example.
4. Now have each group use the desktop publishing program to translate its paste-up representation into print. Students will have to make some substitutions depending on the graphics available with their desktop publishing program.
5. End the process by having each group display its final design and discuss it with the entire class.

II. STUDENT STORIES

Subject: English

Grade(s): 4 and up

Objective: Students will learn some preliminary DTP skills.

Standards
- NCTE English Language Arts Standards 4, 5, 6
- ISTE NETS for Students 1, 3

Materials
You will need a desktop publishing program such as *Microsoft Publisher* and one or more computers.

Procedures
1. Ask each student in the class to write a story.
2. Discuss each story with the student and, as a class, make recommendations on how to improve it.
3. Have the students use their scissors to revise their stories.
4. Next, instruct each student to use the DTP program to enter his or her story into the computer.

5. Print out copies of each child's story for the entire class.
6. Divide the class into groups and have each group read and discuss the stories.

III. MATH STORIES

Subject: Math—Problem Solving

Grade(s): 2–6

Objective: Students will learn how to write math word problems using their DTP program.

Standards
• National Council of Teachers of Mathematics Standards 1, 2, 6
• ISTE NETS for Students 6

Materials
You will need a desktop publishing program such as *Microsoft Publisher* and one or more computers.

Procedures
1. Distribute a math story similar to the one shown in Figure 7.17.

Figure 7.17
Math Story
(*Source:* © 2008 Jupiterimages Corporation)

2. Ask the students to read and solve the word problems found in the story.
3. Next, ask students to write their own stories and related word problems.
4. After the students have finished writing their story problems, they should take turns entering these stories into the computer.
5. Have the students lay out and illustrate their stories with clip art, scanned images, or their own art created in a drawing program.
6. Use the printed stories as a math test for class.

IV. SCIENCE EXPERIMENTS

Subject: Science

Grade(s): 5 and above

Objective: Students will design their own science lab sheet and experiment.

Standards

- National Science Education Standards A1, A2
- ISTE NETS for Students 1, 3, 5, 6

Materials

You will need a desktop publishing program such as *Microsoft Publisher* and one or more computers.

Procedures

1. Help the students design individual experiments related to an overall classroom science topic.
2. Show students some sample lab sheets similar to the one in Figure 7.18.

Figure 7.18
Lab Sheet
(*Source:* Microsoft product screenshot reprinted with permission from Microsoft Corporation)

3. Ask students to use the DTP to design lab report forms for their experiments.
4. Have students conduct their experiments using their own lab reports. After the experiments, discuss how the students could modify their reports for the next experiment.

V. HISTORICAL FIGURES

Subject: History

Grade(s): 5 and up

Objective: Students will create professional-looking stationery. In the process, they will learn how to write a grammatically correct letter and at the same time learn something about a historical figure.

Standards

- National Council for the Social Studies Curriculum Standards IIB and IVD
- ISTE NETS for Students 1, 3, 5

Materials

Students should have access to a desktop publishing program and clip art.

Procedures

1. Bring to class sample letterhead stationery such as that shown in Figure 7.19. If the desktop publishing program you are using includes letterhead templates, show these templates to the class.

Figure 7.19
Letterhead Stationery
(*Source:* Microsoft product screenshot reprinted with permission from Microsoft Corporation)

California State University
18111 Nordhoff Street
Northridge, California 91330

California State University

2. Ask each student to design his or her own stationery.
3. Discuss the results in class.
4. Next, have each student write a letter as a historical figure such as Abraham Lincoln or Clara Barton. When the students write this letter, they must talk about some of the problems the individual is facing.
5. Next, have the students choose appropriate pictures to illustrate their letters. Talk about the importance of visual appeal and pictures that correlate with the time period.
6. The students should then check their work for grammar and spelling errors and historical accuracy.
7. Discuss the letters in class.

VI. NEWSLETTER PRODUCTION

Subject: English

Grade(s): 5 and up

Objective: Students will produce a newsletter for the class using word processing, page layout, and graphics programs.

Standards
- NCTE English Language Arts Standards 4, 5, 6, 7
- ISTE NETS for Students 1, 3, 5
- National Council for the Social Studies Curriculum Standards VIA and VIC

Materials
Students should have access to a desktop publishing and graphics program.

Procedures

1. Bring to class sample newspapers and newsletters and distribute them to everyone.

2. Divide the students into work groups and assign each group a different writing task. For example, one group might write a news article on the presidential election, another group might write an editorial on a controversial issue such as abortion, and a third group might be responsible for a gossip column or movie reviews. Discuss with the students the process followed by journalists. Instruct them to determine who, what, why, where, and when in their reporting.

3. Have each work group write and revise its story.

4. Next, have the students write headlines and choose the pictures they want to use to illustrate their articles. Talk about the importance of visual appeal. Discuss how to be bold with headlines and how to place pictures effectively. The students should plan their placement of articles early in the process. Check their work for grammar and spelling errors. Use the sample from *Print Shop* in Figure 7.20 as a model.

Figure 7.20
Sample from *Print Shop 2*
(*Source:* Courtesy Software MacKiev)

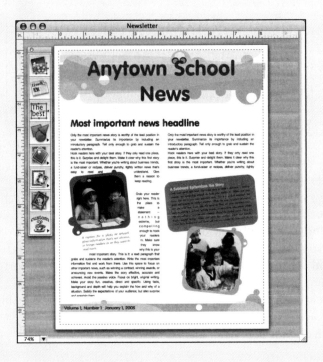

5. Ask students to use the DTP program to enter their articles for the paper into the computer. Make sure students view the entire document repeatedly to check its visual appeal.

6. After everyone is satisfied with the product, print out a copy. For later editions of the paper, rotate the tasks of the different groups in the class.

ADDITIONAL ACTIVITIES

The list of DTP activities is almost endless. Students can write historical, autobiographical, art, sports, or science newsletters. Find out where your students' interests are and capitalize on those interests. They can design awards, flyers, progress reports, questionnaires, and outlines for book reports. A sample award sheet created with *Microsoft Publisher* is shown in Figure 7.21.

Figure 7.21
Microsoft, Sample Award Sheet
(*Source:* Microsoft product screenshot reprinted with permission from Microsoft Corporation)

SUMMARY

The computer has changed the steps involved in publishing a newsletter, magazine, or book. What was done mechanically is now handled electronically. Desktop publishing has altered the way school newspapers, business newsletters, and advertisements are produced.

This chapter traced the historical beginnings of desktop publishing. In the process, we considered the merits of desktop publishing. We discovered how easy it is for a user to produce a newsletter or lab report with one of these programs. We became familiar with the basic features of desktop publishing and gained insight into what features to consider when selecting a program. A checklist and evaluation scale presented in this chapter facilitates this decision-making process. The chapter also offered specific ideas on how to incorporate DTPs into the classroom. We considered six DTP activities that cover a range of curriculum areas.

STUDY AND ONLINE RESOURCES

CHAPTER 7 ONLINE RESOURCES

In the **student section** of the book's online site at **http://www.wiley.com/college/sharp**, you will find templates and examples, PDFs, and articles, along with top-rated Web sites, software reviews, and chapter quizzes. Watch the video tutorial online at **http://www.wiley.com/college/sharp** to learn how to create a newsletter and a certificate. Access these resources to learn about technology and integrating it into the classroom.

CHAPTER MASTERY TEST

Let us check for chapter comprehension with a short mastery test. Key terms, Computer Lab, and Suggested Readings and References follow the test.

1. What is desktop publishing? Explain its importance in education.

2. Explain the difference between a word processing program and a desktop publishing program.

3. Name and describe three features of a desktop publishing program.

4. Discuss a few general rules to follow when creating a newsletter or advertisement using desktop publishing software.

5. What five DTP features are critical in producing a school publication? Explain why.

6. Discuss three uses of DTP programs in the classroom.

7. Does DTP software make the traditional methods of producing newsletters and books obsolete? Justify your answer.

8. What is a layout? Briefly discuss why it is important to take considerable time when creating a layout.

9. Explain in general terms the way a newsletter might be produced with a DTP program.

10. Briefly trace the history of DTP from inception to the present.

11. What are some of the software, hardware, and design requirements of a typical DTP program?

KEY TERMS

Desktop publishing (DTP) p. 126
Frames p. 128
Linotype machine p. 126

Monotype machine p. 126
Movable type p. 125

Page layout p. 128
Page view p. 132
Style sheet p. 129

Templates p. 130
Text wrap p. 132

COMPUTER LAB: Activities for Mastery and Your Portfolio

7.1 Make a small-book for a specified reading level.

7.2 Create a Newsletter about your class to hand out at parent night or send home on the first day of school. Watch the Video tutorial online and learn how create a Newsletter.

7.3 Create templates for transparency masters, student worksheets, signs, newsletters, flashcards, and more. Watch the Video tutorial online and learn how to use the templates.

7.4 Develop a lesson plan using a DTP program.

7.5 Describe one DTP activity and show how a teacher can use it in a classroom situation.

7.6 Examine two DTP programs and compare their strengths and weaknesses.

7.7 Learn more about DTP by interviewing someone who uses a program. Have the individual demonstrate three or four features of the program. Identify any feature that is too complicated and then discuss some way of reducing the difficulty.

7.8 Read two articles about one DTP program and then use the program. Next, prepare a report that might persuade a school district to buy this program. In the presentation, discuss the benefits of using a DTP program.

SUGGESTED READINGS AND REFERENCES

Bear, Jacci, Howard. Desktop Publishing Lesson Plans: Use Desktop Publishing to Teach Any Subject. http://desktoppub .about.com/od/lessonplans/a/lessonplans.htm

Fraser, Bruce. "Print Publishing Secrets." *Macworld* 19, issue 1 (January 2002): 74–76.

Krause, Jim. *Layout Index: Brochure, Web Design, Poster, Flyer, Advertising, Page Layout, Newsletter, Stationery.* Boston: North Light Books, 2003.

Lake, Susan, and Karen Bean. *Digital Desktop Publishing, The Business of Technology* (with CD-ROM). Oklahoma City, Southwestern Educational, 2007.

Lindroth, Linda. "How To. . . Create Exciting Brochures." *Teaching PreK–8* 35, issue 5 (February 2005): 23–24.

Lumgair, Christopher. *Teach Yourself Desktop Publishing.* New York: McGraw-Hill/Contemporary Books, 2001.

Niemeyer, Kevin. *Introduction to Desktop Publishing with Digital Graphics, Student Edition.* Boston: Glencoe/McGraw, 2007.

Reid, Goldsborough. "Looking Good in Print." *Information Today* 23, issue 4 (April 2006): 37–38.

Rochester, Jack B., and John Gantz. *The Naked Computer.* New York: William Morrow & Co., 1983.

Sharp, Vicki. *Make It with Microsoft Office 2004 (Macintosh).* Eugene, Ore.: Visions Technology in Education, 2005.

Sharp, Vicki. *Make It with Microsoft Office 2007 (Windows).* Eugene, Ore.: Visions Technology in Education, 2007.

Sharp, Vicki. *Make It with Microsoft Office 2008 (Macintosh).* Eugene, Ore.: Visions Technology in Education, 2008.

Williams, Robin. *The Non-Designer's Design Book, 2nd ed.* San Francisco: Peachpit Press, 2003.

Williams, Robin. *The Non-Designer's Type Book, 2nd ed.* Berkeley, Calif.: Peachpit Press, 2005.

Databases

Integrating Databases into the Classroom

Teachers can use a database to prepare classroom materials, locate instructional resources, search for information while doing research, locate student records, and send personalized letters to parents. Students can use a database to engage in higher-level thinking, develop research skills, and manage information. This chapter examines how to select a database program for the classroom and consider the general features of a database program. A checklist has been designed to help you choose the right database software. Furthermore, exercises help you integrate the database into the classroom.

Using the computer, students and teachers can do the following:

students can

- design an opinion survey database,
- create a dictionary of spelling words,
- construct a database of presidents of the United States,
- create a database of planets, animal groups, and rocks and minerals,
- develop research skills by using a database to search for information, and
- create a database of world events.

teachers can

- create a parent address/phone list,
- create a mail merge document for letters sent home,
- create a classroom inventory,
- create a weekly progress report,
- design a database for classroom management with students' reading levels, discipline problems or health problems, and schedules, among other things.

objectives

Upon completing this chapter, you will be able to do the following:

1 Explain what a database is and name its basic components.

2 Describe the basic features of a database.

3 Evaluate database software according to standard criteria.

4 Create and utilize a repertoire of database activities for the classroom.

5 Explain three methods of organizing data within a database.

6 Describe three different types of databases.

What is a Database?

We are constantly bombarded with information in the workplace, at home, or at school. John Naisbitt, in his book *Megatrends*, writes, "We are drowning in information but starved for knowledge" (1982, p. 24). Since teachers cannot possibly retain all this information in memory, it is imperative that they develop skills in finding and interpreting data. Students also must master skills of organizing, retrieving, manipulating, and evaluating available information.

A **database** is a collection of information organized according to some structure or purpose. An all-encompassing term, *database* describes anything from an address book, recipe box, dictionary, or file cabinet to a set of computerized data files with sophisticated data relationships. To understand what a database is, you must be familiar with three terms: file, record, and field:

• *File:* A file is a collection of information on some subject. For example, a class studying birds may place all its information on this topic in a file labeled *birds*.

• *Record:* A record contains the information about one entry in a file. In our example of birds, a record would be information about a particular bird, such as a *hummingbird*.

• *Field:* Within a record there exist fields or spaces for specific information. The fields set aside for a hummingbird might include *beak type*, *scientific name*, *habitat*, and *migration patterns*.

The file cabinet, or database, in Figure 8.1 contains files that store information in a systematic way. A counselor using this file cabinet at Clayton College might take a stack of files from the student information drawer. She searches through the files for the senior class file. This file contains a number of records, including John Doe's record. She scans the record for John Doe's telephone number.

Figure 8.1
How a Database Works

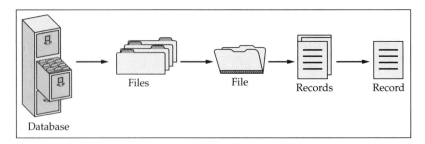

The record is organized into five fields, or categories of information (Figure 8.2): name, address, phone number, birth date, and Social Security number. She gets John's phone number from the phone field.

Figure 8.2
Record

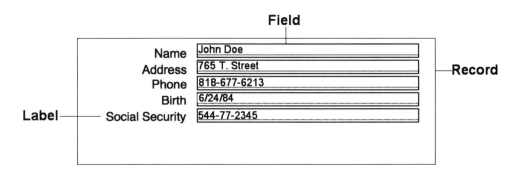

In an electronic database, the information is similarly stored but on a disk. After the teacher designs the format or template, the record is saved. Figure 8.3 shows seven individual student records in *FileMaker Pro.*

Figure 8.3
Sample Database FileMaker Pro
(*Source:* © 1994–2008 FileMaker, Inc. All rights reserved. Use with permission. FileMaker is a trademark of FileMaker, Inc., registered in the U.S. and other countries.)

Name	Address	Phone	Birth	Social Security
Adams, James	343 Elm Street	201-798-3409	6/26/84	244-34-9876
Bart, Bill	845 St. Dennis	805-657-4566	8/4/83	899-22-5679
Clinton, George	478 Dayton Street	213-488-6745	2/45/84	733-44-3467
Devlin, John	966 Bennett Street	314-677-9723	3/4/81	343-33-9876
Doe, John	765 T. Street	818-677-6213	6/24/84	544-77-2345
Elliott, Vicki	786 Nordhoff Street	314-485-2400	8/27/83	567-66-2356
Smith, Tom	467 Chasen	310-988-4545	2/22/85	844-55-3478

Advantages of an Electronic Database

A computerized database has many advantages over a file cabinet. Every database has a method of organization that enables a person to retrieve information using some keyword. For example, the database in Figure 8.3 arranges the last name alphabetically. The problem with the non-electronic listing of this information is it cannot easily be modified; after too many changes, the sheets of paper become unreadable and need retyping. This is not the case with an electronic database, in which the information is stored on disk.

The computer database also minimizes data redundancy; that is, the same information is available in different files. When a clerk searches through a file cabinet, he has to use his fingers to locate key files, which can take a long time. The electronic database user can generate reports, retrieve files, sort data in a variety of ways, edit, and print information with more flexibility and at faster speeds than can the file clerk. Furthermore, electronic files cannot easily be misplaced, and data can be shared easily among individuals. In addition, a user can execute a file search with incomplete information. With only the first half of a name and a brief description, for example, the police can use a database to search for a suspect. The only disadvantages to using a database are the time and effort expended in learning how to use it and the need to convert existing written files into the electronic format.

Computerized databases are used daily in government, occupational, and professional agencies. Teachers and students can choose among virtually thousands of repositories of information, such as Educational Resources Information Clearinghouse (ERIC), for their research work. ERIC, the primary database for teachers, is the basic indexing and abstracting source for information about education. For example, a student searching for *problem solving* in *primary math* would input these keywords to locate abstracts from recent papers on this topic.

Whenever there is a large amount of information to be managed, there is a need for **database management system** software. This software controls the storage and organization of data in a database.

How a Database Works

We will use *FileMaker Pro* as an example of how an electronic database operates, but this discussion should not substitute for *FileMaker Pro*'s documentation. Imagine that a teacher needs to keep track of the software she has accumulated haphazardly in a closet. The teacher wants to create a database to make order of this chaos. This particular database consists of one file simply labeled *Software*, which represents the software collection. The teacher must first determine the number of fields for the record. She designs a record based on library referencing techniques that includes five fields: Title, Subject, Company, Copies, and Grade Level. In Figure 8.4 the first field the teacher creates is a *Title*.

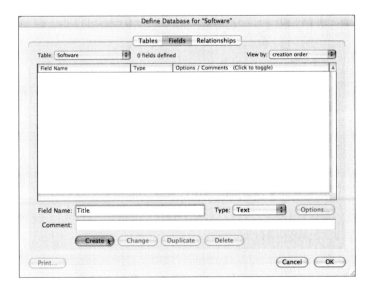

Figure 8.4
Selecting a Field
(*Source:* © 1994–2008 FileMaker, Inc. All rights reserved. Use with permission. FileMaker is a trademark of FileMaker, Inc., registered in the U.S. and other countries.)

After she designs the format, or template, the record is automatically saved. Her record is shown in Figure 8.5.

Figure 8.5

Sample Record

(*Source:* © 1994–2008 FileMaker, Inc. All rights reserved. Use with permission. FileMaker is a trademark of FileMaker, Inc., registered in the U.S. and other countries.)

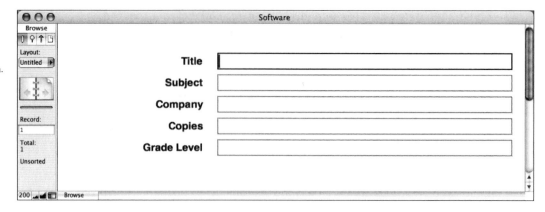

The next step is to enter the record data for each piece of software in the closet. A completed software file record is shown in Figure 8.6. The field *Title* has the entry *Pixie*, the field *Subject* has *Art*, and the field *Company* has *Tech4Learning*. As the teacher enters the information, she has the option of adding or changing it. When one record is completed, she generates another. The teacher continues filling in records until she decides to stop or reaches the storage capacity of the particular database file program.

Figure 8.6

Software File Record

(*Source:* © 1994–2008 FileMaker, Inc. All rights reserved. Use with permission. FileMaker is a trademark of FileMaker, Inc., registered in the U.S. and other countries.)

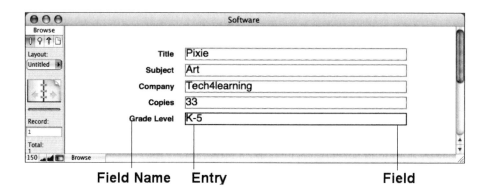

When the task is finished, she has a database file that lists 10 records for the software file (Figure 8.7).

Figure 8.7

Records from Software File

(*Source:* © 1994–2008 FileMaker, Inc. All rights reserved. Use with permission. FileMaker is a trademark of FileMaker, Inc., registered in the U.S. and other countries.)

Title	Subject	Company	Copies	Grade Level
Clicker 5	Multimedia Tool	Crick	21	Primary
Crossword	Worksheet Generator	Visions Technology	20	All
Inspiration	Concept Mapping	Inspiration	30	4-Adult
Inspire Data	Spreadsheet	Inspiration	9	4-12
Pages 2	Desktop Publishing	Apple Company	20	4-Adult
Pixie	Art	Tech4learning	33	K-5
PowerPoint	Presentation	Microsoft	12	4-Adult
Squibs (In Space:	Science	Ignite	25	4-6
The Print Shop	Desktop Publishing	Mackiev	8	4-Adult
Type to Learn 3	Typing	Sunburst	10	3-Adult

Now that the database is completed, the teacher can use it.

RETRIEVING INFORMATION

One of the major tasks of any database is to retrieve information. This can be accomplished in a variety of ways:

1. You can retrieve an entire file by listing this file on the screen or printing it out.

2. You can retrieve only a few field headings, such as *Title* and *Subject* (Figure 8.8).

3. You can use a field to search for one record in the database. For example, you might type *Clicker 5* in the *Title* field. Figure 8.9 shows this retrieved record.

4. You can retrieve a record using more than one criterion, such as the company name and the grade level, by using **Boolean operators**.[1] For example, in this next search, the teacher uses the Boolean operator *and* to search for software that meets two criteria: (1) is a desktop publishing program and (2) has more than eight copies available. The result of this search (Figure 8.10) generates one program: *Pages 2*. The Boolean operator *or* enables the teacher to find records that meet the requirements of either criterion. In this instance, either a desktop publishing program or software with more than eight copies available is acceptable.

5. You can search for a record with **data strings**. There are times when the database user wants to search for a record and is not sure how to find it. For

---

[1]In arithmetic, the primary operations are *add*, *subtract*, *multiply*, and *divide*, but in Boolean logic, the primary operations are *and*, *or*, and *not*.

instance, suppose the teacher cannot remember the name of a publisher but recalls that it begins with *Sun.* A data string is a subset of the characters within a field. *Sun* and *burst* are data strings for the publisher *Sunburst.* To find Sunburst, the teacher need only type *Sun* as the field name to distinguish the choice from information in other records. This type of search is often called a **wildcard search.** The search usually uses symbols to represent any value. For example, an asterisk (*) will act as a wildcard character, and the word *Sun** will return documents with the words *Sunburst, Sunfield,* or *Sunland,* depending on what publishers are in the database. This type of wildcard use is the most common and is known as *right-hand truncation.*

SORTING INFORMATION

The other important function of a database program is sorting, the ability to arrange the records in a file so that the values in a field appear in alphabetical, numerical, or chronological order. Any field can be sorted, and sorting is done by field type. If the field has characters in it, it is sorted alphabetically, A to Z or Z to A. If the field is numeric, it is sorted lowest to highest or highest to lowest. Finally, a user can sort a field chronologically by date or time.

Types of Databases

Database software programs employ different methods of data organization. These include hierarchical, network, *HyperCard* (Apple), free form or encyclopedia, relational, and flat-file databases.

HIERARCHICAL DATABASES

The **hierarchical database** was one of the first methods of database organization developed for the computer. This database stores information in a top-to-bottom organization. Data are accessed sequentially through this database. In other words, you start at the top and proceed through the hierarchical levels. The database organizes data into a series, with the most general grouping first and the subgroups next. Each subgroup branches downward and can link only to the parent group. For example, a professor who wants to access a student's record must move first through the university, then the college, and then the departmental data before accessing the record of the particular student. There are two disadvantages to such a database. First, you cannot easily locate records in different sections or subgroups of the database. In the example just given, if you wanted to access another student's record, you would have to start all over again by moving first to the university level; there are no shortcuts. This method can be inefficient and time-consuming. Second, the hierarchical database requires a complete restructuring each time the user adds a new field. On the positive side, once the data are set up, searching is fast and efficient because you do not have to search through all the records; you just search through specific groups.

NETWORK DATABASES

The **network database** works the same as a hierarchical database except that it permits a record to belong to more than one main group. This database is superior to the hierarchical database because it allows the user access to multiple data sets. Data can be accessed with speed and ease through different types of sources. However, networked databases still require every relationship to be predefined, and the addition of any new field requires a complete redefinition of the database.

FREE-FORM DATABASE

A **free-form** or **encyclopedia database** enables the user to access data without specifying data type or data size. In this type of database, the user does not search for data in a field but instead uses a keyword or keywords. The software then searches all its text entries for matches. The advantage of an encyclopedia database is that a user who forgets the exact title of an article can find the article with only a single relevant word. Many of the Internet search engines use keyword searches. The main application of the free-form database is the online encyclopedia. For example, Grolier Online (Scholastic Library Publishing) includes seven encyclopedia databases including Grolier Multimedia Encyclopedia. This online site has two different environments, one created for older students and adults and the other for younger students. The user types in a relevant word such as "George Washington," and then is able to click on an article about George Washington (Figure 8.11).

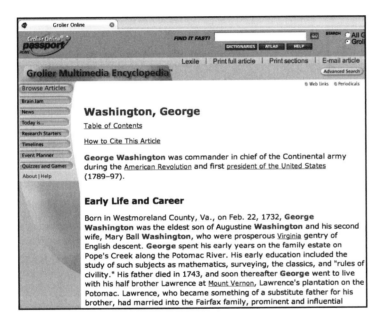

The encyclopedia database maintains a large collection of information that is subject oriented. For example, an education database may group files according to different issues in education. You can then search by categories. Many of these databases are collections of data from other large free-form databases, giving users access to vast amounts of information. Typically these databases include such topics as news, microcomputer information, magazine articles, and medical information. *News* would enable you to access current news articles, newspapers, and information from news wire services. *Microcomputer information* would contain data from popular computing magazines. *Magazine articles* would enable you to access thousands of periodicals that focus on specialized areas such as medicine, education, and business. *Medical information* would give you access to medical journals.

HYPERCARD DATABASES

HyperCard, an early multimedia program, played an important role in changing the way databases are used in education. *HyperCard* was the first program to integrate data organization with graphics. Using *HyperCard,* teachers and students created individual cards or screens of data with both text and graphics. They linked these cards to produce a stack, or group of cards. The *HyperCard* stack was equivalent to a database. We explore other programs of this nature such as *MediaBlender* (Tech4Learning) and *eZediaMX* (eZedia, Inc.) in Chapter 11.

RELATIONAL DATABASES

A **relational database** enables the user to work with more than one file at a time. It helps eliminate data redundancy. For example, a department chair might need several different files, such as test scores and transcript data, for a particular student. If each of these files is a separate electronic file, the chair would have to duplicate information for each file to make it understandable. The relational database removes this problem by linking separate files or even entire databases through a common key field such as the student's Social Security number. In relational databases, changes made in one file are automatically reflected in the other files of the record. The product *dBase* (dataBased Intelligence, Inc.) is a classic example of this type of database. This database is very useful for the administration of elementary, high school, and college records. However, the majority of classroom teachers have little need for this type of database software.

FLAT-FILE DATABASES

Classroom teachers want a simple, straightforward way of entering their data, and the **flat-file database** fulfills this requirement. It works with only one data file at a time, and offers no linking to other data files. This database does not permit multiple access to data files or advanced questioning techniques. There is variation among flat-file databases, but generally they do not allow merging with other application programs.

In the past, the administrative office of a school district was the only place in the district that needed a database; the office was where student records, personnel files, and school resources were kept. Recently, however, classroom teachers are using computerized databases to keep track of students' progress and to store anecdotal comments on individual students. Furthermore, students are using prepared databases such as the *Britannica Ultimate Reference Suite*, which contains thousands of articles and online links. *Microsoft Encarta Premium* includes reference tools with an interactive world atlas (Figure 8.12), thesaurus, and dictionary. This database provides users with a vast amount of geographic, historic, and demographic information.

Figure 8.12
Encarta World Atlas
(*Source:* Microsoft product screen shot reprinted with permission from Microsoft Corporation)

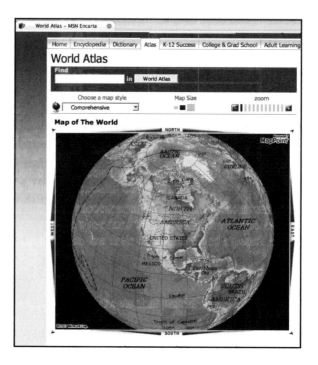

There is a powerful search tool, along with Internet links to thousands of sites and geographic articles covering most important events.

The database is the perfect tool for teaching higher-level critical thinking skills, such as the ability to hypothesize, draw inferences, and use Boolean logic. Imagine that students in a class are instructed to search a hypothetical database for the names of students who took Dr. Smith's computer class. After the students develop a strategy, they perform the search and find out who the students are. The teacher then asks them to hypothesize how many female students received As in the computer class. This time their strategy is more complex, as they are looking for names of people who meet two criteria: (1) students who are female and (2) students who received an A. Following this search, the students are asked to draw inferences about the results of the search and conduct further searches to see if there is any correlation among other items.

Besides helping with higher-level thinking, a database can help students learn content material in any of the curriculum areas. Many databases on the Internet cover specific academic areas. An excellent federal government site is *Digital Classroom* (http://www.archives.gov/education/). If students understand how to manipulate a database, they can gain deeper insight into any field of study; they can find patterns, draw relationships, and identify trends.

Today, students can use database files that they create themselves or files prepared by teachers or software houses. It is often more beneficial for students to enter their research into a design created by their teacher. The mastery of databases takes longer than the mastery of word processing because, to learn databases, students need a good deal of hands-on experience and varied types of assignments.

The manuals supplied with databases include instructions on how to manipulate data, student worksheets, and suggested activities. Although schoolchildren cannot understand the logic behind database programs, they can understand some essential concepts such as record, field, and search. Nevertheless, it may be wise to save the complex searching for the junior high school students.

How to Choose a Database for the Classroom

There are many questions to ask when choosing a database program. For example, you will want to know how limited the program is in its ability to search. Can you easily add or change the data in the files? If there is a prepared database with the product, is the content proper for students? Is the information accurate? What is the quality of the documentation? How easy is the program to use? Let us examine these factors more closely for the purpose of understanding how to make more informed decisions.

The database packages on the market today offer every imaginable feature, some more appropriate for classroom use than others. Examples of stand-alone programs that are appropriate for education are *FileMaker Pro* and *Bentō* (FileMaker, Inc.) and *Microsoft Access. Access* a program often used in high schools is sold as a part of the *Microsoft Office Suite.* The *integrated program* offers other capabilities such as e-mail/Internet tools, calendar, word processing, and spreadsheet creation. Two examples of this type of database are *Microsoft Works*, and *AppleWorks (not upgraded).* Generally, these classroom-appropriate databases come with fewer features and are easier to use than programs such as *dBase.*

To choose a database program for the classroom you must consider six factors: (1) hardware compatibility, (2) general features, (3) instructional design, (4) ease of use, (5) consumer value, and (6) support.

HARDWARE COMPATIBILITY

Check out the computer that your school is using. Is it an old Apple IIe, a Sony with a Pentium IV chip, or a Macintosh with a G5 chip? How much memory does it have: 64K, 4 GB, or more? (Some database programs need a huge amount of computer memory.) How large are their hard drives: 80 GB or 1 TB? What type of backup storage is available? What printers will work with this database program?

GENERAL FEATURES

The most common functions provided by database programs are (1) sorting data, (2) changing or updating data, (3) searching for specific information, and (4) deleting and adding.

Sorting.   **Sorting** is the ability to arrange the records in different ways. Programs should enable you to name the field type easily and do the sort quickly. At the very least, the program should perform the following: (1) an alphabetical sort from A to Z or Z to A, in any appropriate character field; (2) a numeric sort from lowest to highest and highest to lowest, in any numeric field; and (3) a chronological sort from earlier to later. No matter what program you choose, you should be able to sort to the screen and the printer.

Changing and Updating.   Every database can update and change a file. The questions that must be asked are the following: How difficult is it to accomplish this task? Is it easy to find the record and change it? How hard is it to add a record to the file, and is it a drawn-out procedure?

Searching or Retrieving.   Database programs vary in the type of search criteria used to find forms in a file. For instance, there may be exact matches, partial matches, numeric matches, and numeric range matches. In an exact match, the program looks for the forms that exactly match the search criteria. An exact match for Florence Singer is Florence Singer or FLORENCE SINGER. Mrs. Florence Singer; Singer, Florence; and FlorenceSinger are not matches.

All database programs have exact matches, and many database programs have partial matches. You would use a partial match when unsure of how the information was entered into the database or when interested in locating different records with the same information. For instance, you might be able to find Florence Singer's file by just typing in *Florence* or *Singer*. Or, you would use a partial match to find the records containing the names of students with computer experience.

The more advanced the database, the more exotic the features. *FileMaker Pro* (FileMaker Publishing Corporation), an advanced program for Windows and Macintosh, does quite a few numeric searches. This program enables you to look for items less than, greater than, or equal to a given number. If you want to find the records for all children who were born later than 1982, you would enter Year: >1982. This program also has a numeric range match feature that enables you to search for numbers within a certain range. For instance, you might search for dates within the range of 1988 to 2007.

The database program should let you search using multiple criteria as well. For instance, you might want to search for the names of students eligible to take your advanced computer course. You would use two criteria: (1) students who are in 11th grade and (2) students who have computer experience. At the end of your search, the computer would generate the names of students who fit these qualifications.

Deleting and Adding.   The database program should enable you to add information to or delete it from a record or field with minimum trouble. When you add a new field to one record, you want the new field to be added to all the records. The ideal program has a way to lock files so they will not be accidentally erased.

Printing.   Your program should allow you to print a neat report. The instructions for this task should be easy to follow, and the printout should show the data fields that you select for the report.

ADVANCED FEATURES

Some programs enable you to design the way the data will be displayed. Some perform mathematical calculations on data. Database programs do not perform the complex functions of a spreadsheet, but they will total simple columns of numbers or compute student averages. Most database programs show the final list or report on the screen before it is printed. With *FileMaker Pro, Microsoft Works* (Windows only), *FoxPro* (Microsoft), and *Microsoft Access*, you can select fields for different records and display them on the screen all at once. Some programs enable you to publish their database on the Web, and other programs enable you to store a picture with each record. The advanced student can merge data from a database document with a word processing document to produce a customized letter or report. With the **mail merge** function, the computer will automatically place a name, address, and grade from the database into the word processing document's form letter. To produce a mail merge document, start by writing a basic form letter, the general text you want to send each person on your mailing list. In this letter do not include the name or address of the recipient or grades because these items will be inserted automatically from a mailing list. In their place insert placeholders, or merge fields, that tell your word processor where to put the items.

Next, click on a mail merge tool. Select the list you want to merge, and the word processor will print one personalized letter for each record received from your mailing list.

FLEXIBILITY

The key to the success of database programs is their flexibility. How easy is it to make changes, and how easy is it to add a field or add information to a field in the database program? When you do, do you lose the information that already exists in the field? Does the database program make you start again when you want to make changes? What is the search speed of the program? What flexibility is there in printing a report? Can you be selective in printing certain columns or are you forced to print all the items as shown on the screen? What is the limit of the database? With *FileMaker Pro* you theoretically can have 256 million fields over the lifetime of a file, and a file size of 8 terabytes. Is there a size limitation for the information in each field? *FileMaker Pro* allows 1 billion characters per page or field. Database programs vary in the kinds of searches they are capable of accomplishing—what type of searches do you require? Can you conduct Boolean searches? Does the searching technique fit the skills you are emphasizing in the classroom?

 For database video tutorials, as well as templates and examples, consult the online site at **http://www.wiley.com/college/sharp.**

EASE OF USE

A major concern in buying a database program is how easy the program is to learn. Its features are immaterial if it is difficult to comprehend. A database program should require minimum learning time. The program that displays a menu bar at the top of the screen is ideal for beginners because users do not have to memorize the different functions. The *Microsoft Access* database has easy-to-use tabs and *FileMaker Pro* has a useful collection of templates (Figure 8.13) that help you use the product quickly. The templates can be modified easily to suit your own needs. Just add or modify fields, layouts, or text when necessary.

Before buying a program ask some questions: Can you learn in a reasonable amount of time to use this program? Is there a tutorial disk that takes the user through the program? (*Microsoft Access* uses simple English commands and offers online help to teach you the program step-by-step.) Do help screens tell the user what to do each step of the way? Can you access these help screens whenever you need them? Are there menu bars across the screens so users do not have to memorize the different functions? Is the printer setup easy, and can you be ready to print immediately? Are there too many help prompts and safety questions?

CONSUMER VALUE

Because software is expensive, cost is a major consideration. Since public domain software costs very little, it is a natural alternative to commercial software. For example, free software can be obtained in California through the California State

Figure 8.13
FileMaker Pro Template
(*Source:* © 1994–2008 FileMaker, Inc.
All rights reserved. Use with permission.
FileMaker is a trademark of FileMaker,
Inc., registered in the U.S. and other
countries.)

Department of Education. Commercial software is more expensive, but many programs are worth the cost. Many software companies sell one disk that you can use to load the software on all your computers. Other companies offer an inexpensive on-site license that enables you to make as many copies as you need. Some companies offer lab packs of a large quantity of software at a reduced price. Other companies offer free Web-based database applications like *Zoho Creator* (http://www.zoho .com/) (Figure 8.14). You can create database documents from scratch using a template or import ones that you previously created. You can choose to collaborate from remote locations with students and update from your own computer. Using this product, you can publish a document, edit information, and make changes anytime you wish.

Figure 8.14
Zoho Creator
(*Source:* Courtesy Zoho)

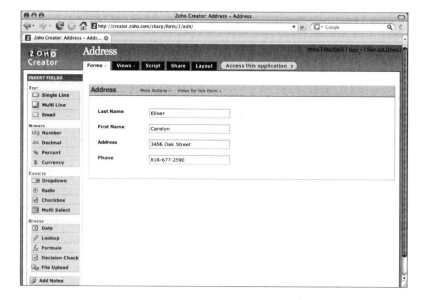

SUPPORT

Support may be the thing that stands between a good program and your ability to use it. Can you call someone on the telephone at the software company and get immediate help, or must you wade through a series of messages and wait an unbearable amount of time? (As mentioned previously, many publishing houses will tell you how many customers are in line before you and how long you must wait.) Is the technical support available toll free? (Many companies are charging a fee for technical support.) Is the technical help knowledgeable and understandable? Does the software package offer tutorial lessons to help the beginner learn the program? Is the manual readable and does it have an index? Does the program feature templates or computer-based files? Do the software producers offer data files for various content areas?

Before selecting the software, decide which features are important for your particular class. Next, examine one of these programs using the sample checklist and evaluation rating instrument in the Database Program Checklist form on page 160.

Integrating the Database into the Classroom

Teachers can use databases to help locate instructional material and to meet students' needs, among many other things. For example, a teacher may categorize the books and resources in the classroom in a database. The teacher then can easily search this database for instructional material to motivate the class. The teacher might create a database to store student information such as birthdays, reading levels, special medication, learning problems, students' favorite hobbies, and people with authorization to pick up a student from school. The teacher could use an address database to personalize letters to parents.

Students can use databases for a multitude of classroom tasks. In language arts students might use a database to write book reports. For data fields, the students would include *Title*, *Author*, *Type of Book*, *Setting*, *Main Character*, and *Summary*. After the books are catalogued, students might search for books that meet their interests. A synonyms database could help students write poetry. Other language arts ideas for database files are diaries, famous quotes, funny stories, legal terms, novelists, and parts of speech.

Social studies is the perfect curriculum area to use databases. Students might create databases on countries, states, or famous people such as Albert Einstein, U.S. presidents, African-American politicians, and inventors and their inventions. There are all sorts of "Who Am I?" games that can be executed in the classroom (see the lesson plan activities at the end of the chapter).

In science, databases may be created for animal groups (birds, insects, snakes), plant groups (flowers, vegetables, trees), and rocks and minerals. Furthermore, students might create databases for food groups, calories, nutrients, amphibians, animal behavior, chemical compounds, chemical elements, fish, gems, geological formations, planets, poisons, and antidotes.

In the arts, students might use databases on artists, classical music, famous works of art, musical instruments, and popular music. Students might add pictures to any database to make it easier for the visual learner.

Teacher Practice Activities

The following exercises can be used in conjunction with any database. If a computer lab is not available, just follow this section to get an idea of what kinds of activities can be used in the classroom. The first exercise is a step-by-step introduction to a database program.

Database Checklist

Directions: Examine the following items and determine which ones you feel are important for your class situation. Place an X on each line for which the software meets your needs.

Product Name_____ Manufacturer_____ Grade Level_____

Hardware

____ 1. Computer processor speed
____ 2. Computer compatibility
____ 3. Hard disk space required
____ 4. Memory needed
____ 5. Printer compatibility

Features

____ 1. Selection of field types
____ 2. Sorting
    ____ a. Alphabetic
    ____ b. Numeric
    ____ c. Chronological
    ____ d. Reverse order
    ____ e. To screen and printer
____ 3. Changing and updating
____ 4. Searching
    ____ a. Alphabetic
    ____ b. Numeric
    ____ c. And–or
    ____ d. Using multiple criteria
____ 5. Deleting and adding fields
____ 6. Printing
____ 7. Calculation
____ 8. Mail merge
____ 9. Copy and paste
____ 10. Capacity to generate reports
____ 11. Publishing your database on the Web

Flexibility

____ 1. Speed of search
____ 2. Ease of changing fields

____ 3. Ease of adding new fields
____ 4. Size requirements
    ____ a. Field size
    ____ b. Characters per field
    ____ c. Number of records in a file
____ 5. Display versus printing
    ____ a. Can display selected fields
    ____ b. Selective printing

Ease of Use

____ 1. Onscreen help
____ 2. Tutorial disk
____ 3. Easy printer setup
____ 4. Warning question
____ 5. Automatic save

Consumer Value

____ 1. Cost
____ 2. Templates
____ 3. Clip art included
____ 4. Lab packs
____ 5. Networked version
____ 6. On-site license

Support Features

____ 1. Technical
____ 2. Tutorial material
____ 3. Readable manual
    ____ a. Activities
    ____ b. Lesson plans
    ____ c. Index

Rating Scale

Rate the database software by placing a check in the appropriate line.

Excellent_____Very good _____Good _____ Fair _____ Poor _____

Comments:

DATABASE 1

1. Open your database program.

2. From the main menu, select the option that creates a file and gives the file a name, such as *Class*.

3. Type in the following field names: *Teacher*, *Students*, *Room*, *Grade*, and *Gender*. Correct any mistakes made.

4. Using the add-a-record function, type the information shown in Table 8.1 for each record.

Table 8.1 **Practice Data**

Teacher	Students	Room	Grade	Gender
Smith	23	21	K	Male
Adams	16	14	4	Female
Gramacy	17	25	3	Female
Witham	33	29	1	Female
Youngblood	21	24	K	Male

5. Add another record to the list: *Teacher*, Sharp; *Students*, 20; *Room*, 12; *Grade*, 3; and *Gender*, Female.

6. Change the name *Smith* to *Small* and his room number from *21* to *24* and the name *Adams* to *Allen* and the number of students she has from *16* to *28*.

7. Next, delete the *Gramacy* record.

8. Alphabetize the list of records A to Z in the *Teacher* name field. The list should now look like the one shown in Table 8.2

Table 8.2 **Revised Data**

Teacher	Students	Room	Grade	Gender
Allen	28	14	4	Female
Sharp	20	12	3	Female
Small	23	24	K	Male
Witham	33	29	1	Female
Youngblood	21	24	K	Male

9. Print out the results.

10. Next, numerically sort the field *Grade* from highest to lowest.

11. Search for the following records:

a. Youngblood (type the name *Youngblood* in the *Teacher* field);

b. Allen; and

c. the kindergarten records (type *K* in the field *Grade*).

The program should find *Small* and *Youngblood*. The database shows the records that match the specifications you type. If there is no record, the program usually displays a 0. You also get a 0 if you spell the record name differently from the way it was spelled in the original entry in the database.

12. Search for records using two criteria: (a) teachers who are male and (b) teachers who have exactly 21 students. Type *21* for the *Students* field and *Male* for the *Gender* field. For this search, there is only one record: *Youngblood.*

13. Find the male kindergarten teachers' records. Type *K* for the *Grade* and *Male* for *Gender.* In this case, there are two teachers who fit these criteria: *Small* and *Youngblood.*

14. If the database program has a greater than (>) or less than (<) feature, find the following records:

a. all the teachers who have a class size greater than 20;

b. the male teachers who have 23 or more students; and

c. the female teachers who have 18 or more students.

DATABASE 2

For practice, create another database. Type in the following field names: *Student, Gender, Hair color,* and *Birth date.*

1. Using the add function, type the information shown in Table 8.3 for each record.

Table 8.3 **Student Data Sheet**

Pupil	Gender	Hair Color	Birth Date
Smith, Joan	Female	Brown	1985
Lorenzo, Max	Male	Black	1984
Chen, Mark	Male	Black	1983
Sharp, David	Male	Brown	1980
Schainker, Nancy	Female	Red	1982
Edwards, Bobbie	Female	Blond	1978
Lopez, Mary	Female	Black	1986
Jefferson, LeMar	Male	Black	1981
Jung, Nicky	Female	Red	1980

2. Change the field name *Pupil* to *Student.*

3. Next, change David Sharp's birth date to 1984, Nicky Jung's description to *Male* with *Black* hair, and Bobbie Edwards's *Hair color* to *Red.*

4. Add the following file: *Student,* Lee, Bessie; *Hair color,* Brown; *Gender,* Female; *Birth date,* 1985.

5. Alphabetize the list A to Z in the *Student* field and print out the list.

6. Find the following files:

a. David Sharp;

b. all students who are female;

c. students who have red hair;

d. students born after 1982;

e. students born before 1983; and

f. all students who are female and have red hair.

SAMPLE CLASSROOM LESSON PLANS

I. PLANETS

Subject: Science

Grade(s): 5–12

Objective: Students will use a database program to create a scientific database like the one in Table 8.4.

Table 8.4 Planet Data

Planet	Diameter (millions)	Distance from Sun (millions of miles)	Satellites	Rings	Atmosphere	Rotation Around the Sun	Rotation on its Own Axis
Earth	7,926.2	92.9	1	0	Water (70%), air, and solid	365.2 days	23 hrs, 56 min, 4 sec
Jupiter	88,736	483.88	16	1	Colored dust, hydrogen, helium, methane, water, and ammonia	12 Earth years	9 hrs, 55 min
Mars	4,194	141.71	2	0	Carbon dioxide (95%)	687 Earth years	24 hrs, 37 min, 23 sec
Mercury	3,032.4	36	0	0	Helium (95%) and hydrogen	88 Earth years	59 days
Neptune	30,775	2,796.46	8	4	Hydrogen, helium, methane, and ammonia	165 Earth years	16 hrs, 7 min
Pluto	1,423	3,666	1	?	Methane	248 Earth years	6 days, 9 hrs, 18 min
Saturn	74,978	887.14	19	1,000	Hydrogen and helium	29.5 Earth years	10 hrs, 40 min, 24 sec
Uranus	32,193	1,783.98	17	11	Hydrogen, helium, and methane	84 Earth years	17 hrs
Venus	7,519	67.24	0	0	Carbon dioxide (95%), nitrogen sulfuric acid, other elements	225 Earth days	243 Earth days

Standards

- National Science Education Standards A1, A2, C3, D1, D2
- ISTE NETS for Students 1, 3, 4, 5

Materials

You will need a database program such as *Microsoft Access* or *FileMaker Pro* and one or more computers.

Procedures

1. Divide the class into small groups.
2. Ask each group of students to create a scientific database. Give them a list of topics from which to choose, such as *planets*, *dinosaurs*, and *presidents*.
3. Have the students research their topics using books or the Internet.
4. Instruct each group to create cards that look like the one in Figure 8.15.

Figure 8.15
Microsoft Access,
Planets Database
(*Source:* Courtesy Visions
Technology in Education)

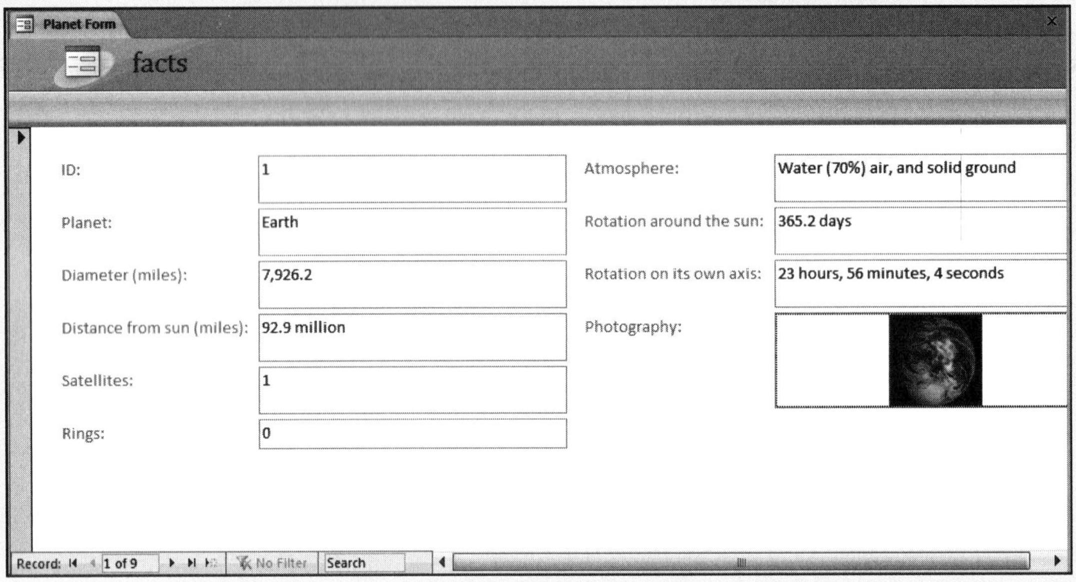

5. Each group should make up a list of 10 questions for their database.
6. After the databases are created, have the groups exchange questions and databases.
7. Give the class a time limit to find answers to their 10 questions.

II. DOING A BOOK REPORT

Subject: Language Arts

Grade(s): 2–6

Objectives: Students will create a database book report file, learn to sort alphabetically, and read a book.

Standards
• NCTE English Language Arts Standards 2, 3, 5, 6
• ISTE NETS for Students 1, 3, 5, 6

Materials

You will need the Book Report Form, a database program (*FileMaker Pro*, *Microsoft Access*, *Microsoft Works*, etc.), and one or more computers.

Procedures

1. Have each student read a book.
2. After the reading assignment is finished, have each student complete the Book Report Form (shown in Table 8.5).

Table 8.5 Book Report Form

Student's name _____

1. Author:

2. Title:

3. Type of book:

4. Setting:

5. Main character of the story:

6. Summary of the story:

---

3. Instruct students to input their information under each field name on the same data file disk. This activity requires a database program that has a *Comment* field. If the database program does not have this feature, eliminate this field name.

4. After this task has been completed, have the students do the following:

a. Search for books they might like to read, using the search function.

b. Print out a list of all the books in the database.

c. Sort the database alphabetically by title and print out the list.

d. Sort the database file alphabetically by author and print out the list.

e. Find out how many students read baseball stories or biographies by using the find function of the database program.

III. FINDING OUT ABOUT DINOSAURS

Subject: Science

Grade(s): 5–8

Objectives: Students will create a dinosaur database, learn about dinosaurs, sort alphabetically, practice using Boolean operators, and sort by number.

Standards

• National Science Education Standards A1, A2, C1, C3

• ISTE NETS for Students 1, 3, 4, 5, 6

Materials

You will need the Dinosaur Database Form, a database program (*FileMaker Pro*, *Microsoft Works*, etc.), and one computer or more.

Procedures

1. Have each student read about a dinosaur.

2. After the reading assignment is completed, have each student fill out the Dinosaur Database Form shown in Table 8.6.

Table 8.6 Dinosaur Database Form

Name	Habitat	Food	Feet	Armored

3. Instruct each student to enter his or her information on the same data file disk. Table 8.7 shows a sample Dinosaur Database Form that has been completed.

Table 8.7 Completed Dinosaur Database Form

Name	Habitat	Food	Feet	Armored
Ankylosaurus	Land	Plants	4	Yes
Tryannosaurus	Land	Meat	2	No
Brachiosaurus	Water-Swamp	Plants	4	No
Apatosaurus	Water-Swamp	Plants	4	No
Corythosaurus	Water-Swamp	Plants	2	No
Diplodocus	Water-Swamp	Plants	4	No
Iguanodon	Land	Plants	2	No
Protoceratops	Land	Plants	4	Yes
Stegosaurus	Land	Plants	4	Yes
Coelophysis	Land	Meat	2	No

4. After this task has been completed, have the students do the following:

a. Sort the file by the number of feet in the field, highest to lowest.

b. Using the Boolean operator *and*, find out if there are any two-legged plant eaters and any four-legged meat eaters.

c. Sort alphabetically by name and print out the list.

Variation

Have students add fields such as *Weight*, *Height*, and *Nickname* and sort the fields by (1) length (lowest to highest), (2) weight, and (3) characteristics.

IV. STATE SHEET

Subject: Social Studies

Grade(s): 3–8

Objectives: Students will create a geographical data file for each state, learn geographical information about each state, sort the data alphabetically, and search using the Boolean operators *and* and *or*.

Standards

• National Council for the Social Studies Curriculum Standards 3, 5
• ISTE NETS for Students 1, 3, 4, 5

Materials

You will need the State Geographical Sheet, a database program (*FileMaker Pro*, *Microsoft Access*, *Microsoft Works*, etc.), and one or more computers.

Procedures

1. Have each student in the class choose a state to research.

2. Have the students use reference books or the Internet to complete the State Geographical Sheet shown in Table 8.8.

Table 8.8 State Geographical Sheet

Field Name	Data
1. Location (Midwest, Northeast, etc.)	
2. Size (square miles)	
3. Natural resources	
4. Climate	
5. Terrain (desert, mountains, etc.)	

3. Have the students enter the proper information under each field name on the data file disk.

4. After this task has been completed, have the students independently use the search function to answer *Who am I?* questions such as those shown in Table 8.9.

Table 8.9 Who Am I? Questions

1. I am a small state.
2. I am known for my mountains.
3. I have red clover flowers

V. STATES

Subject: Social Studies

Grade(s): 4–12

Objectives: Students will create a state data file, learn statistical information about the United States, sort alphabetically, and search using the Boolean operators *and* and *or.*

Standards
- National Council for the Social Studies Curriculum Standards 3, 5
- ISTE NETS for Students 1, 3, 4, 5

Materials
You will need the State Data Sheet, a database program (*FileMaker Pro, Microsoft Works, Microsoft Access,* etc.), and one computer or more.

Procedures

1. Have each student in the class choose a state to research.

2. Have the students use encyclopedias or the Internet to complete the State Data Sheet shown in Table 8.10.

Table 8.10 State Geographical Sheet

Field Name	Data
1. Capital	
2. Population	
3. Number of representatives in Congress	
4. Year of statehood	

3. Have the students enter the proper information under each field name on the same data file disk.

4. After this task has been completed, have the students independently use the search function to carry out the following tasks:

a. Search for the states that have populations over 2 million.

b. Find the last state that was added to the United States.

c. Sort the records according to population from lowest to highest.

d. Sort the records alphabetically by the name of the state and print out a list.

e. Sort the states by population and print out a list.

5. Next, divide the class into two teams and collect each team's State Data Sheet.

6. Read aloud one of the State Data Sheets without revealing the name of the state.

7. Ask Team One to try to figure out what state the data sheet describes.

8. Ask Team Two to check Team One's answer by using the computer. If Team One has answered correctly, it scores a point.

9. Read another data sheet.

10. Ask Team Two to try to identify the state and Team One to check Team Two's answer.

The first team to reach 10 points wins.

VI. MUSIC

Subject: Arts

Grade(s): 3–12

Objectives: Students will learn how to create a database by cataloging their own music CD collection or the school's CD collection and they will find information using certain criteria.

Standards
• ISTE NETS for Students 1, 2, 3, 5

Materials
You will need a database program (*FileMaker Pro*, *Microsoft Works*, etc.) and one or more computers.

Procedures

1. Ask the class to decide which fields they are going to use to create their database. For example, they could use *Artist*, *Title*, *Description*, and *Style* of music.

2. Have the students create their own database using their CD collection at home or at school.

3. After the databases are created, have the students do the following:

a. Find their favorite performer.

b. Find the CDs that are rock and roll.

c. Find female vocalists only.

d. Find male vocalists only.

4. Next, have each student share his or her database with another member of the class.

ADDITIONAL SUGGESTIONS

Julie M. Reitinger, Webster University, School of Education, Educational Technology (2007) uses an online database to teach her students everything from language arts to math. She said, "There are several online that are excellent including one on nutritional content in foods, an American Presidents database, and a "Time Capsule" database (http://www.dmarie.com/timecap/) (Figure 8.16). What I have found to be great about using databases in curriculum instruction is that you can create a single worksheet that asks the same questions for all students but the students are assigned different main topics such as John Adams or George Washington. I love the Time Capsule database because I use it as a math worksheet. For example, I have them choose any date in history, then go to the Web site and find out how much a loaf of bread costs and a gallon of gas or the price of a house. Then I ask them to use the information on hourly wage to determine how much their mortgage payment might be or how many gallons of gas they can buy and compare it to today's prices. The learning objective is math calculations such as multiplication, division, percentages, etc."

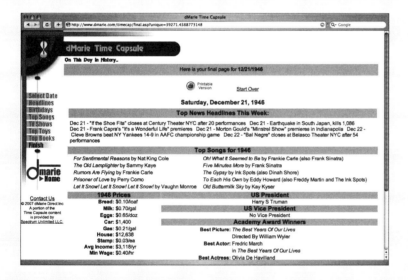

Figure 8.16
Time Capsule
(*Source:* Reprinted by permission Mark Burggraf. http://www.dmarie.com/timecap/)

SUMMARY

The database is an effective manager of information and a powerful tool for learning in the classroom. With a database, students can look for relationships among data, test hypotheses, and draw conclusions. This chapter discussed the merits of an electronic database and its basic features.

We examined a database checklist evaluation form and learned how to introduce the database to the class. Classroom activities covered a range of curriculum areas. Be sure to review the annotated list of award-winning database software in the Online Learning Center.

STUDY AND ONLINE RESOURCES

CHAPTER 8 ONLINE RESOURCES

 In the **student section** of the book's online site at **http://www.wiley.com/college/sharp**, you will find templates and examples, PDFs, and articles, along with top-rated database lesson plan Web sites, software reviews, and chapter quizzes. Watch the video tutorial online at **http://www.wiley.com/college/sharp** to learn how to create a mail merge, simple queries and use the Report Wizard. Access these resources to learn about technology and integrating it into the classroom.

CHAPTER MASTERY TEST

Lets check for chapter comprehension with a short mastery test. Key Terms, Computer Lab, and Suggested Readings and References follow the test.

1. What is a database and how can it be used in the classroom?

2. Define the following: *file*, *record*, and *field*.

3. Name and describe two ways of sorting data.

4. What differentiates a file cabinet from a database?

5. What are three ways you would use a database to help your teaching?

6. Discuss the factors involved in selecting a database for a school district.

7. Name and describe three ways of searching for a file.

8. When should a student use a wildcard search?

9. Explain three methods of organizing data within a database.

10. What is a relational database?

11. Name two common functions of a database.

12. What is a free-form database?

KEY TERMS

Boolean operators p. 151

Database p. 147

Database management system p. 149

Data strings p. 151

Encyclopedia database p. 153

Field p. 147

File p. 147

Flat-file database p. 154

Free-form database p. 153

Hierarchical database p. 152

HyperCard database p. 153

Mail merge p. 157

Network database p. 152

Record p. 147

Relational database p. 154

Sorting p. 156

Wildcard search p. 152

 COMPUTER LAB: Activities for Mastery and Your Portfolio

8.1 Create a database of parent information. Run reports, make queries, print address labels, and more. Watch the video tutorial online and learn how to create simple queries and use the report wizard.

8.2 Create a database of information on cultural, scientific, and civic institutions in your area that might make for interesting field trips or that might send educators to your school.

8.3 Create a database of information about the books in your classroom library.

8.4 Create a database file on famous composers.

8.5 Examine three database programs and compare their different features.

8.6 Choose a grade level and create a database activity for it.

SUGGESTED READINGS AND REFERENCES

Bergen, Doris. "Differentiating Curriculum with Technology-Enhanced Class Projects. Technology in the Classroom." *Childhood Education* 78, no. 2 (Winter 2001–2002): 117–118.

Braun Jr., Joseph A. "Ten Ways to Integrate Technology into Middle School Social Studies." *Clearing House* 72, no. 6 (July 1999): 345–351.

Bromann, Jennifer. "Use the News: Promoting Newspapers in the Library." *Library Media Connection* 23, issue 2 (October 2004): 45.

Caughlin, Janet. *Access Workshop for Teachers*. New York: Scholastic Books, 2002.

"Electronic Databases." *Media and Methods* 36, no. 4 (March/April 2000): 39.

Gaither, Herman. "Students First. *Technology and Learning* 26, issue 2 (September 2005): 30.

Gerber, D. Timothy, and David M. Reineke. "Simple Database Construction Using Local Sources of Data." *American Biology Teacher* 67, issue 3 (March 2005): 150–155.

Holzberg, Carol S. "Going Ga-Ga for Google." *Technology and Learning* 27, issue 1 (August 2006): 40.

Jones, Pamela S. "Teaching Students About Locating Resources @ Your Library." *Library Media Connection* 25, issue 5 (February 2007): 36–37.

LaBare, Kelly M., and R. Lawrence Klotz. "Using Online Databases to Teach Ecological Concepts." *American Biology Teacher* 62, no. 2 (February 2000): 124–128.

Levetan, Janice. "Apples and Oranges and Lemons?" *Online Elementary Periodical Indices Library Talk* 12, no. 4 (September/October 1999): 38.

Lindroth, Linda. "Blue Ribbon Technology. *Teaching PreK–8* 37, issue 3 (November/December 2007): 22–24.

Naisbitt, J. *Megatrends*. New York: Warner, 1982.

Oppel, Andrew. *Databases Demystified*. Boston: McGraw-Hill Osborne Media, 2004.

Priore Jr., Charles F., and John L. Giannini. "Integrating Bibliographic Software, Database Searching, and Molecular Modeling in an Introductory Biology Course." *Journal of College Science Teaching* 36, issue 5 (March/April 2007): 21–23.

Reaves, Treva. "Language Arts/Science/Math/Art: ZOOming into Animals." *School Library Media Activities Monthly* 23, issue 8 (April 2007): 16–18.

Schrock, Kathy. "Scouting the Web for Science Resources." *Library Media Connection* 25, issue 1 (August/September 2006): 16–17.

Sharp, Vicki. *Make It with Office 2007*. Eugene, Ore.: Visions Technology in Education, 2007.

Sharp, Vicki. *Make It with Office 2008*. Eugene, Ore.: Visions Technology in Education, 2008.

Street, Chris. "Tech Talk for Social Studies Teachers." *Social Studies* 96, issue 6 (November/December, 2005): 271–273.

Troutner, Joanne. "Best New Software." *Teacher Librarian* 33, issue 5 (June 2006): 29.

Spreadsheets and Integrated Programs

Integrating Spreadsheets into the Classroom

An electronic spreadsheet is faster and more flexible than the traditional methods of numerical calculation and data prediction. Teachers can use a spreadsheet as a grade book or for classroom budgets, attendance charts, surveys, and checklists. Students can use a spreadsheet to create time lines, game boards, or graphs and to keep track of classroom experiments. This chapter discusses the general features of a spreadsheet program and how to select one for the classroom, as well as provides exercises for integrating the spreadsheet into the classroom. A checklist has been designed to help you choose the right spreadsheet software. In addition, we discuss integrated software programs and software suites.

objectives

Upon completing this chapter, you will be able to do the following:

1 Define spreadsheet, integrated software, software suite, cell, windowing, macro, and logical functions.

2 Describe the basic features and functions of spreadsheets and integrated programs.

3 Evaluate different spreadsheet software programs based on standard criteria.

4 Utilize and create a repertoire of spreadsheet activities for the classroom.

5 Visit our online site and explore relevant Internet sites, tutorials, tips, and discussion forums.

Using the computer, students and teachers can do the following:

students can

- track results of science experiments,
- find area and perimeter,
- create time lines and charts,
- keep track of their own grades,
- plan a budget
- calculate data and store equations and numbers,
- analyze statistics for team sports.

teachers can

- calculate and enter student grades,
- create charts and graphs,
- create lesson planners,
- construct game boards,
- create seating charts,
- create inventories.
- develop rubrics, and
- set up schedules.

What is a Spreadsheet?

Yearly, people across the United States prepare their income tax forms. College students often request government loans, and families determine their budgets and predict their annual expenses. The businessperson keeps a record of transactions to determine profits and liabilities, and the scientist performs mathematical calculations on experimental data. A teacher enters pupils' test scores and assignments, performs calculations, and makes inferences about the numerical data. To accomplish their various tasks, these people use worksheets or electronic spreadsheets. A **spreadsheet** is "a graphical representation of an accountant's worksheet, replete with rows and columns for recording labels (headings and subheadings) and values" (Pfaffenberger, 2000).

Historical Overview

The spreadsheet is one of the earliest applications of the microcomputer. In the early 1970s, it was primarily hackers and hobbyists who used the microcomputer. This all changed when Dan Bricklin, a Harvard student, and Robert Frankston, an

MIT student, combined efforts to create the first spreadsheet, *VisiCalc*, introduced in 1979. *VisiCalc*, primarily designed for microcomputers, had a small grid size and limited features. Because the Apple Computer was the only computer that could run *VisiCalc*, it became the first computer to be accepted by business users. *VisiCalc* served as a prototype for many other programs, such as *LogicCalc* and *Plannercalc*, designed for microcomputers. Within a decade, spreadsheets improved vastly, offering more features (such as the ability to create graphic displays), faster execution speeds, and a larger grid size.

In 1982, *Lotus 1-2-3* (Lotus Development) initiated a new generation and became the leading spreadsheet. It was the first integrated spreadsheet, meaning that it combined several different programs so that information could be presented in different formats. Later versions of spreadsheets had extended capabilities: a communication component, expanded spreadsheet size, and word processing. The word processor feature enabled the user easily to explain the figures presented in the spreadsheet, and the communication component enabled computers to communicate with each other over telephone lines.

Components of a Spreadsheet

Every electronic spreadsheet is organized in a similar manner with two axes: rows and columns. Figure 9.1 shows *Microsoft Excel*'s blank spreadsheet (Windows version). The letters across the top are used to identify the columns, and the numbers along the side identify the rows.[1]

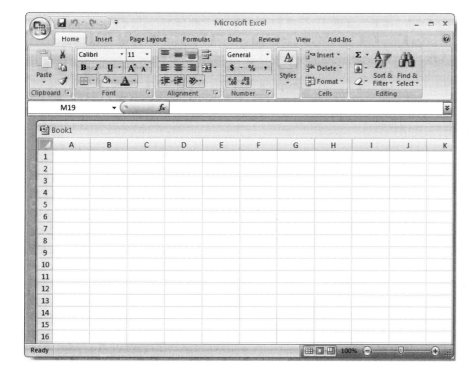

Figure 9.1
Microsoft Excel 2007
Spreadsheet
(*Source:* Microsoft product screenshot reprinted with permission from Microsoft Corporation)

The intersection of each row and column forms a box, called a **cell**. A cell is identified by its column letter and row number. For example, in Figure 9.2, cell A1 is in

[1] Spreadsheets can differ in the system used to label rows and columns.

the top left corner, and cell B1 is one cell to the right. To locate cell D4, you would count over to column D and then count down four cells to row 4. You would select cell D4 by clicking the cursor in its box. When selected, a cell shows a heavy border, and its name appears in the indicator box above the A label.

Figure 9.2
Microsoft Excel 2007
Spreadsheet Cells
(*Source:* Microsoft product screenshot reprinted with permission from Microsoft Corporation)

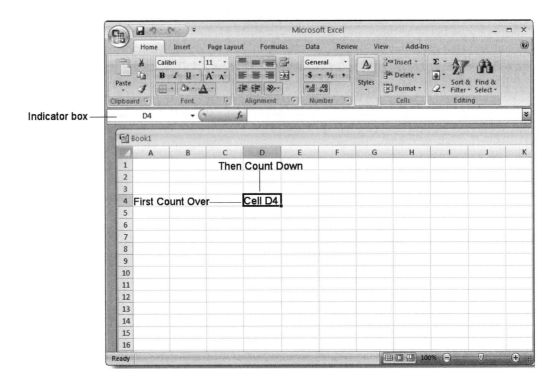

Three types of information can be entered into any single cell: number, text, or formula. The ability to enter formulas onto the spreadsheet makes it a powerful tool for business, science, and education.

How a Spreadsheet Operates

For illustrative purposes, lets use *Microsoft Excel 2007* (Windows version) and a grade book example, a popular educational use of the spreadsheet.

To use a manual spreadsheet for grade records, you would enter the students' names and their test scores. Imagine there are nine students and three test scores (Figure 9.3).

Figure 9.3
Teacher's Grade Roster

Name	Test 1	Test 2	Test 3	Total	Average
1. Adams, Jayne	78	86	88	252	84
2. Bannon, John	95	88	85	268	89
3. Bentley, David	91	93	93	277	92
4. Brown, Melissa	77	67	77	221	74
5. Fink, Karen	95	94	96	285	95
6. Johnson, Alex	83	58	83	250	83
7. Kelly, Jim	77	78	74	209	70
8. Romero, Scott	87	84	96	261	87
9. Schainker, Holly	88	98	88	274	91

Next, using paper, pencil, and a calculator, you would add Jayne Adams's scores, obtaining a total of 252. You would record the answer in the Total column and then divide this total by 3 for an average of 84. You would continue this manual procedure for each subsequent student. If you made an error or changed a score, you would have to recalculate everything.

An *electronic* spreadsheet offers many advantages over a manual one. When you open *Microsoft Excel*, you see a blank spreadsheet (see Figure 9.1). You enter the headings *Name*, *Test 1*, *Test 2*, *Test 3*, and *Average*.[2] Then you type the nine pupils' names, last name first, and their respective test scores. While entering this information, you can easily make changes, corrections, deletions, or additions. You also can use the sort function to alphabetize automatically the list of students by last name. When you are finished, your screen resembles the one in Figure 9.4.

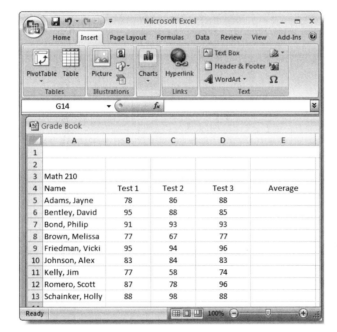

Figure 9.4
Microsoft Excel 2007
Gradebook Roster
(*Source:* Microsoft product screenshot reprinted with permission from Microsoft Corporation)

The beauty of any spreadsheet is that each cell serves as an individual calculator that performs computations quickly and accurately. For example, to determine each student's average score, select cell E5 and type, in *Microsoft Excel*'s formula tool bar, =(B5+C5+D5)/3. The spreadsheet calculates the mean for numbers 78, 86, and 88 and records the answer, 84, instantaneously in cell E5. (The equal sign that begins the formula (B5+C5+D5)/3 tells the computer to compute an average from cell B5 to D5; see Figure 9.5.)

To calculate the averages for the remaining pupils, you would not have to rewrite the formula, since every spreadsheet has a way of copying the original formula. In *Microsoft Excel 2007*, you could use the fill handle to select cells E5 through E13 by dragging the small box in the bottom right corner of the dark border surrounding cell E5 (see Figure 9.5). The rest of the students' averages would

Fill Handle ⌐

---

[2] It is unnecessary to create a Total column in this electronic spreadsheet, as the program keeps track of totals for averaging purposes.

Figure 9.5

Excel 2007 Gradebook
Roster with Average
(*Source:* Microsoft product
screenshot reprinted with
permission from Microsoft
Corporation)

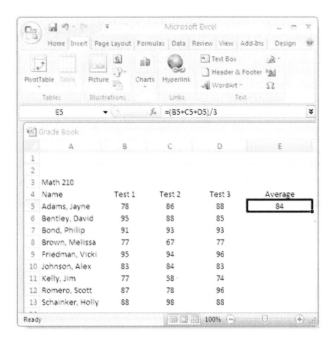

automatically be displayed in the appropriate cells, as shown in the highlighted cells
in column E of Figure 9.6.

Figure 9.6

Microsoft Excel 2007
Completed Roster
(*Source:* Microsoft product
screenshot reprinted with permission
from Microsoft Corporation)

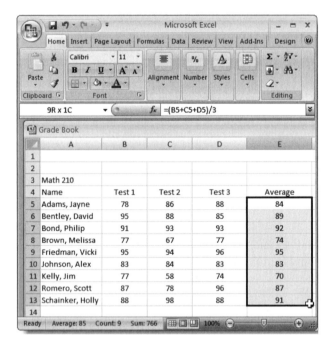

For a gradebook tuto-
rial using Excel, visit
our online site at
http://www.wiley.com/college/sharp.

Microsoft Excel features more than 233 functions, or shortcuts, that save you
from typing in formulas. A **function** is a built-in software routine that performs a
task in the program. To apply the average function to the cell, on the ribbon click on
the *Formulas tab* and then click on the *Insert Function* button. From the dialog
box choose the function you want (Figure 9.7).

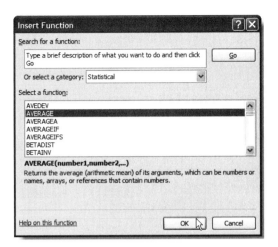

Figure 9.7
Microsoft Excel 2007
Average Function
(*Source:* Microsoft product
screenshot reprinted with
permission from Microsoft
Corporation)

Every spreadsheet has its own collection of built-in functions, ranging from *sum* to *average* to *sine*. These functions make the use and application of formulas quick and easy. Generally, the more built-in or predetermined functions the more versatile the spreadsheet. *InspireData* (Inspiration), a cross between a spreadsheet, database, and presentation program for grades 4–12, has only a few functions compared to a programs like Excel.

Why Use an Electronic Spreadsheet?

There are many reasons for a teacher to choose a computerized spreadsheet over a manual worksheet. The electronic spreadsheet is faster and more flexible than the traditional methods of numerical calculation and data prediction, permitting you to change the information on the screen as often as you want. A noncomputerized spreadsheet with a matrix of more than 25 rows and columns is cumbersome, whereas a computerized spreadsheet with a matrix of thousands of data entries performs instant calculations. Furthermore, on a computerized spreadsheet you can access any number instantaneously, simply by pressing a key or two. Another major feature of a spreadsheet is its ability to recalculate; that is, when you change the number in a cell, the spreadsheet automatically recalculates the other values. The recalculation feature of an electronic spreadsheet enables you to employ **what-if analysis** strategies, which are used to answer questions such as "What would happen if Elena scored a 90 on this exam instead of a 60?" Another question commonly asked by students is "What grade will I achieve in the course if I earn an 80 on the final exam?" Homeowners might ask, "If the interest rate drops from 8 to 5 percent, what will my mortgage payments be?" As a spreadsheet user, you would only have to enter the score or rate to see the effects or answers immediately.

There are still more advantages to the electronic spreadsheet. It enables you to display and print the output in many visually appealing ways. Also, as long as you enter the formula correctly, your data will be accurate. Spreadsheets have the invaluable copy function, with which you effortlessly repeat a formula once it has been defined. Clearly, the electronic spreadsheet has enormous advantage over a manual spreadsheet in terms of saving time and increasing productivity.

Basic Features of a Spreadsheet

Table 9.1 lists some of the basic features of a spreadsheet.

Table 9.1 Basic Features of a Spreadsheet

Feature	Description
Attached Notes	Enables you to attach notes to cells, much as you would attach sticky notes to your written work.
Cell Names	Lets you label the cells with words like *Profit*. You can then use the name *Profit* in any formula that refers to this range.
Copying Command	Copies the contents of a group of cells from one column to the cells in another, replicating formulas, values, and labels.
Date and Time Function	Automatically calculates how many days have elapsed between two dates in spreadsheet cells.
Editing	You should be able to insert and delete rows and columns. You should be able to widen or narrow the spreadsheet's columns.
Formatting	Enables you to align numbers and text labels or apply different fonts and type styles.
Graphing	Generates bar or pie graphs based on data entered. The more advanced spreadsheets can generate dozens of different types of charts and feature all sorts of design options.
Memory	A spreadsheet that has a running indicator of the memory available.
Online Help	Online help allows you to get help from the computer while using the program.
Predetermined Functions	Predetermined functions are ready-made formulas that enable you to solve problems quickly.
Protected and Hidden Cells	Spreadsheets have built-in safeguards to protect a group of cells from being altered or erased. In addition, some spreadsheets allow you to take confidential information and hide it from view, even blocking it out in your printed reports.
Sorting	Data is arranged alphabetically and numerically.
Templates	A simple spreadsheet that contains no data but comes with selected functions for certain cells.

Advanced Features of a Spreadsheet

The more powerful spreadsheets can link with other spreadsheets so they can perform complex calculations. Linking spreadsheets allows you to get information from one spreadsheet and pull it directly into your current sheet (this complicated feature is not meant for novices).

LOGICAL FUNCTIONS

Powerful spreadsheets include logical functions that evaluate whether a statement is true or false. For example, imagine a teacher created a grade book spreadsheet with four exam grades and an average score for each student. He now wants to invite into honors math only those students who received averages of 97 or above. Since the first average is in cell F4, he would enter a formula in G4 and repeat this formula for every student's score. With the spreadsheet program *Lotus 1-2-3*, this formula would read as follows: @If(F4>96,100,0).

The formula makes a 100 represent the honors class and a 0 represent the standard class. When the spreadsheet does its calculation, it checks to see whether the value entered (F4) is greater than 96, and if it is, the spreadsheet will print the first option (100) in cell G4. If the average in F4 is lower than 96, the spreadsheet will print the second option (0) in G4. All the students with 100s meet the requirements for honors class.

DATABASE CAPABILITIES

Many spreadsheet programs come with database capabilities. With such capabilities, you can sort a set of rows numerically or alphabetically and choose items that match particular criteria. *Lotus 1-2-3* has database capabilities, but these functions are not comparable to those of a database program; what they offer is a spreadsheet approach to database functions.

WINDOWS

When you work on a large spreadsheet, you cannot see the whole spreadsheet on the screen but must use the cursor to scroll among sections. If you need to compare figures on different screens, it is helpful to be able to split the screen into two or three sections, each windowing a different part of the work, so that you can see your current location in the spreadsheet, see the effect your work has on cells in different locations, and easily compare figures from different sections. If the spreadsheet does not have a split-screen option, it may come with the ability to set fixed titles. A fixed title option enables you to keep designated rows and columns permanently on the screen, even as you scroll through sections.

DESKTOP PUBLISHING TOOLS

Many spreadsheets feature desktop publishing tools that enable you to shade boxes, vary fonts, add pictures and logos, and print sideways. (Generally, printing is limited to 80 columns, or 136 if you use compressed type.)

INTERNET CAPABILITIES

The most advanced spreadsheets offer special fonts, multiple dimensions, sound, and add-on software. These spreadsheets have Internet capabilities that enable you to save your data to a Web site by converting the worksheet to HTML format (see Chapter 4). When you save the worksheet this way, you can see it in your Web browser. In addition, many spreadsheet programs enable you to add **hyperlinks** to your worksheet. This means that when you click on specific text or graphics you are sent to a specific Web page, a file on your disk, or a file on a local network.

MACROS

Advanced spreadsheets offer macros, which are a group of routines or commands combined into one or two keystrokes. You can play these routines back at the touch of a key or two. This is how it works. First, you determine what key(s) you want to use, such as key F12. Then, you decide what the key will generate; for instance, F12 could generate a name, address, and telephone number. Finally, you program the macro so that, when F12 is pressed, it automatically enters the name, address, and telephone number in the chosen cell. Some macros execute their commands to a certain point, wait for the input, and then continue with the command execution.

How to Select a Spreadsheet for the Classroom

Spreadsheets were originally designed for adults, but a handful of programs are suitable for the classroom. *Cruncher 2.0* is for grades 3 and up, InspireData (Inspirations) grades 4–12, and high schools utilize *Microsoft Works, Numbers*

(Apple), *Lotus 1-2-3*, *Microsoft Excel 2007* (Windows), *Microsoft Excel 2008* (Macintosh), or *Quattro Pro* (Corel).

Choosing spreadsheet software for the classroom is a six-step process: (1) determine the hardware compatibility; (2) study the program's features; (3) test how easy it is to use the program; (4) examine the program's built-in functions; (5) investigate the program's consumer value; and (6) check out the technical support.

HARDWARE COMPATIBILITY

You need to determine what computers are available in the school: old Apple IIGs, Windows-based machines, or Macintosh G5s? How much memory do these machines have? Is there enough memory to accommodate the spreadsheets the students are using?

GENERAL FEATURES

Determine how the labeling is done on the spreadsheet. Can you easily center the labels or move them to the left or right? How does the spreadsheet handle decimal points and dollar signs? If you make a mistake, can you effortlessly modify the cell or cells? Can the width of the columns be adjusted easily? Can you protect the cells from being erased accidentally? Can you hide certain cells and not print them out? How does the spreadsheet show negative values? How many predetermined functions does the spreadsheet have? Does it have a date and time function? Can you easily calculate how many days have passed between two dates entered in the spreadsheet? Does the spreadsheet include macros? Can you generate bar or pie graphs? How does the spreadsheet indicate the amount of memory it has left? Does the spreadsheet have windows so that you can split the screen into two or three sections, each displaying a different part of the work? Can you link this spreadsheet with other spreadsheets or arrange the information in the spreadsheet alphabetically or numerically? Does the spreadsheet have enough columns and rows to meet the classroom needs? What special functions do the students need to use in the class? For example, when students use the spreadsheet, is it to calculate sums, averages, or standard deviations?

EASE OF USE

The spreadsheet is much more difficult to use than a database program because it involves working with numbers and formulas. Therefore, it is imperative that you choose a spreadsheet program that gives online help that can be accessed quickly. *Cruncher 2.0* fits these criteria with a step-by-step tutorial and online help. Figure 9.8 shows a screen from this tutorial. *InspireData*, a simple interface, is a combination

Figure 9.8
Cruncher 2.0

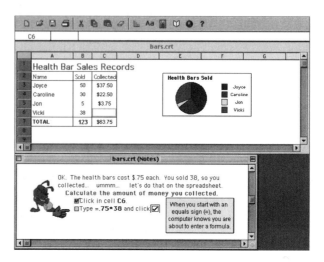

database/spreadsheet and presentation program. The program is packaged with over 50 curriculum-based examples and templates (Figure 9.9).

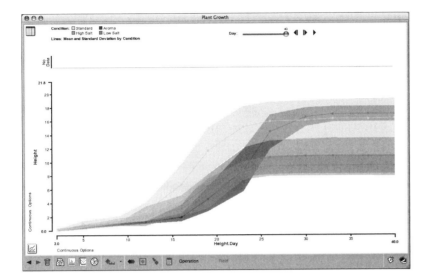

Figure 9.9
InspireData
(*Source:* © 2008 Inspiration Software(R), Inc. Use with permission.)

Scholastic Keys is a simple interface for elementary students or students that have learning disabilities. After the school district purchases Microsoft Office Suite (Windows) it installs *Scholastic Keys*, which results in *Microsoft Excel* becoming *MaxCount*. The students can then learn basic operations without being frightened by complicated menus. The buttons are larger and the toolbar is simpler with the addition of new buttons. For example, there is text reader (Figure 9.10) that lets students read what they write. *Scholastic Keys* comes with an assortment of lessons, activity files, and worksheets.

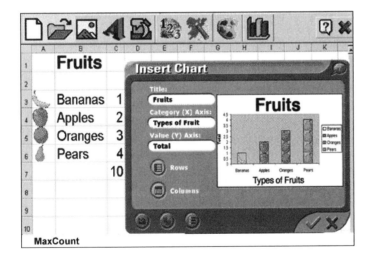

Figure 9.10
Scholastic Keys: MaxCount (for Microsoft Excel).
(*Source:* Screenshots from teacher.Scholastic.com. Copyright © 2008 by Scholastic. Inc. used by permission.)

When considering ease of use, ask these questions: How fast can you edit the cells and enter the data? Can you smoothly delete and insert rows or columns? Is it hard to copy formulas from one row to another? How do you move the cursor from one cell to another?

CONSUMER VALUE

Software is expensive, and for teachers cost is often a consideration. Consider the free Web-based pack *Google Docs & Spreadsheets. Google Docs* (http://docs .google.com/) is a word processing application (see Chapter 6) and *Spreadsheets* is a spreadsheet application (Figure 9.11). You can create documents from scratch or import ones that you previously created.

Figure 9.11
*Google Docs
& Spreadsheets*
Spreadsheet
(*Source:* Courtesy Google,
Inc.)

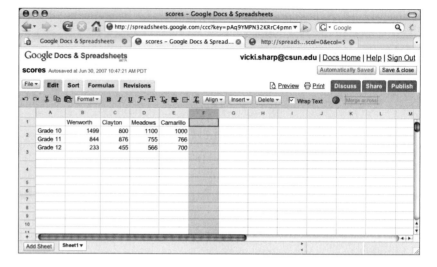

Cruncher 2.0 costs under $100, but *Microsoft Excel* sells for more than $250. Some software companies offer onsite licenses so that you can freely make copies of the software for in-house use. Other manufacturers distribute lab packs that enable you to purchase multiple copies of software at a reduced price.

SUPPORT

A software company's willingness to support its product is an extremely important factor. Can you call someone on the telephone at the company and get immediate help? Do you have to spend excessive time waiting on the phone? Is the technical support toll free or are you charged by the minute? Do you have to pay a yearly fee to receive any type of assistance? Is the technical expert knowledgeable and understandable? Does the software package come with a tutorial? Is the manual readable? Does it come with an index? Does the program have templates? Before selecting the software, decide which features are important for your particular class. Use the checklist on page 183 when selecting a spreadsheet.

Integrating a Spreadsheet into the Classroom

The spreadsheet can be used as a grade book or for classroom budgets, attendance charts, lesson plans, surveys, seating charts, rubric development, checklists, or displaying test scores graphically (Figure 9.12). The spreadsheet is not only a management tool; it is also a tool for learning in the classroom. Spreadsheets can be used to supplement instruction in a variety of curriculum areas.

Figure 9.12
*Make It with Office
2007* Graph
(*Source:* Courtesy Visions
Technology in Education)

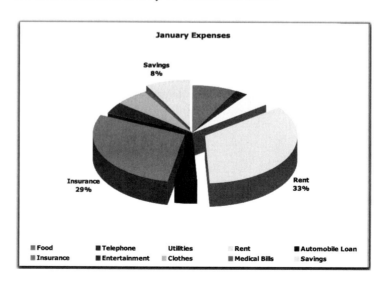

Spreadsheet Checklist

Directions: Examine the following items and determine which ones you feel are important for your class situation. Place an X on each line for which the software meets your needs.

Product Name_____ **Manufacturer**_____ **Grade Level**_____

Hardware

___ 1. Computer processor speed

___ 2. Computer compatibility

___ 3. Hard disk space required

___ 4. Memory needed

___ 5. Printer compatibility

Features

___ 1. Protected cells

___ 2. Hidden cells

___ 3. Sorting

    ___ a. Alphabetical

    ___ b. Numerical

___ 4. Windowing

___ 5. Macros

___ 6. Formulas

___ 7. Logical operators

___ 8. Fixed titles

___ 9. Transfer to word processing

___ 10. Link to other spreadsheets

___ 11. Integration with database

___ 12. Name ranges

___ 13. Graphing

___ 14. Flexibility of printing

___ 15. Manual recalculation

___ 16. Sound

___ 17. Internet capabilities

___ 18. Deleting and adding columns

___ 19. Changing column width

___ 20. Copying labels and formulas

___ 21. Formatting of cells

___ 22. Erasure

___ 23. Date and time

___ 24. Memory tracking

Ease of Use

___ 1. Onscreen help

___ 2. Tutorial disk

___ 3. Quick printer setup

___ 4. Easy editing of cells

___ 5. Simple command names

___ 6. Quick cell movement

___ 7. Warning questions

Consumer Value

___ 1. Cost

___ 2. On-site license

___ 3. Lab packs

___ 4. Networked version

Support Features

___ 1. Technical

___ 2. Tutorial material

___ 3. Readable manual

___ 4. Templates

Rating Scale

Rate the spreadsheet program by placing a check in the appropriate line.

Excellent_____ Very good _____ Good _____ Fair _____ Poor _____

Comments:

The teacher can use a spreadsheet as a study aid for history, for physics experiments, and for accounting problems. Teachers can improve learning by using spreadsheets to demonstrate numerical concepts such as percentages, multiplication, and the difference between electoral votes and popular votes. Using the spreadsheet, teachers can generate graphs to illustrate abstract concepts. Teachers can have the class keep track of a stock portfolio's performance with a spreadsheet. The spreadsheet can aid teachers in preparing class materials or completing calculations.

Students can use the spreadsheet to create time lines, game boards, and graphs or to solve problems, keep track of classroom experiments, explore mathematical relationships, and delve into social studies or scientific investigations. Students can test various hypotheses and conduct what-if analyses. They can calculate averages and standard deviations for statistics problems and even keep track of their grades. They can also create their own what-if questions to see what scores they need to raise their grades. They can use a spreadsheet to determine how much water and money are wasted by a dripping faucet. Furthermore, they can calculate the travel time between cities by different means of transportation or they can explore relationships in the chemical periodic chart. They can convert Fahrenheit to Celsius temperatures, compare characteristics of the major groups of vertebrates or invertebrates, and compare the climates of several countries. Students can learn about the weather and use the spreadsheet to store data about such items as temperature, precipitation, and barometer readings. They can use a spreadsheet for comparison shopping, calculating the expense of keeping a pet, calorie counting, calculating income tax returns, figuring baseball statistics, and creating a budget (Figure 9.13). They can keep track of money from fundraising activities such as magazine drives. Teachers can use the spreadsheet to perform activities that range from statistics management to energy consumption calculation to simple science experiments.

For a list of recommended spreadsheet software, downloadable templates and examples, and Web sites, visit our online site at http://www.wiley.com/college/sharp.

Figure 9.13
Make It with Office 2007
Budget
(*Source:* Microsoft product screenshot reprinted with permission from Microsoft Corporation)

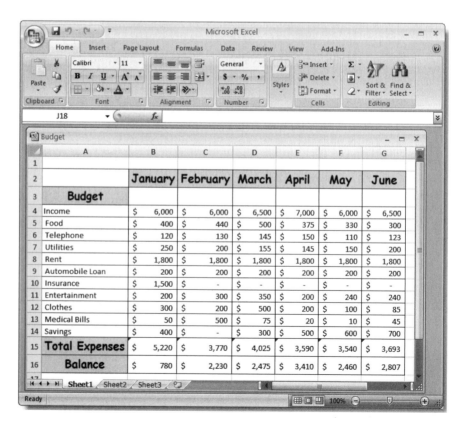

Teacher Practice Activity

The following exercises are meant to be used in conjunction with any spreadsheet. If a computer lab is not available, simply read through this section to get an idea of how you would set up a spreadsheet. The first exercise introduces you step-by-step to a spreadsheet program.

1. Open the spreadsheet program.

2. Create a new file and give it the name *Grade Book*.

3. Begin by entering labels across the first row of the spreadsheet. Starting at cell B1, type the following labels: *Exam 1, Exam 2, Exam 3, Exam 4, Exam 5*. Place the label *Exam 1* in cell B1, *Exam 2* in C1, *Exam 3* in D1, *Exam 4* in E1, and *Exam 5* in F1. Leaving cells A1 and A2 empty, put the label *Pupils* in cell A3. These labels will describe the contents of the cells. The spreadsheet should look similar to the one in Figure 9.14, which is in *Microsoft Excel*.

	A	B	C	D	E	F
1		EXAM 1	EXAM 2	EXAM 3	EXAM 4	EXAM 5
2						
3	PUPILS					
4						

Figure 9.14
Microsoft Excel Spreadsheet
(*Source:* Microsoft product screenshot reprinted with permission from Microsoft Corporation)

4. Starting at A5, enter the pupils' last names: A5, *Smith*; A6, *Sharp*; A7, *Garcia*; A8, *Raj*; A9, *Friedman*; A10, *Washington*; A11, *Reilly*; A12, *Hughes*; A13, *Sherrin*; and A14, *Jones*.

5. Using the sort or arrange function, alphabetize the names and align each name on the left side of the cell.

6. Now enter the data in the grade book. Enter Friedman's Exam 1 score as *89* in cell B5, his Exam 2 score as *46* in cell C5, Exam 3 as *69* in D5, Exam 4 as *74* in cell E5, and Exam 5 as *35* in cell F5. Now continue entering the exam scores for the remaining students; the spreadsheet should look like the one in Figure 9.15.

	A	B	C	D	E	F
1		EXAM 1	EXAM 2	EXAM 3	EXAM 4	EXAM 5
2						
3	PUPILS					
4						
5	FRIEDMAN	89	46	69	74	35
6	GARCIA	45	23	75	75	34
7	HUGHES	89	43	67	67	34
8	JONES	99	45	75	75	40
9	RAJ	98	50	73	73	39
10	REILLY	56	50	67	67	32
11	SHARP	98	45	72	71	39
12	SHERRIN	78	46	73	72	34
13	SMITH	99	45	74	74	40
14	WASHINGTON	87	45	72	72	34
15						

Figure 9.15
Microsoft Excel Spreadsheet with Grades
(*Source:* Microsoft product screenshot reprinted with permission from Microsoft Corporation)

7. Next, type the label *AVERAGE* in cell G1. You want to enter a formula to calculate the average score for Friedman's five exams. Begin by putting the cursor on cell G5 and type the formula; for instance, for *Microsoft Excel*, the formula is = (B5+C5+D5+E5+F5)/5. After you enter the formula, the average (62.6) should appear instantly in cell G5.

8. Next, use the copy or fill function to calculate the averages for the remaining students (Figure 9.16).

9. Learn how to save the data on the formatted disk and print them out for inspection.

	A	G
1		AVERAGE
2		
3	PUPILS	
4		
5	FRIEDMAN	62.6
6	GARCIA	50.4
7	HUGHES	60
8	JONES	66.8
9	RAJ	66.6
10	REILLY	54.4
11	SHARP	65
12	SHERRIN	60.6
13	SMITH	66.4
14	WASHINGTON	62
15		

Figure 9.16
Calculating Averages in *Microsoft Excel*

SAMPLE CLASSROOM LESSON PLANS

I. SPEED AND DISTANCE

Subject: Math/Science

Grade(s): 5 and up

Objectives: Students will learn about speed and how to use a spreadsheet to do simple calculations.

Standards

• National Council of Teachers of Math Standards 1, 2, 6, 9

• National Science Education Standards A1, A2

• ISTE NETS for Students 1, 3

Materials

You will need a spreadsheet program such as *InspireData*, *Excel*, *Cruncher 2.0*, or *Quattro Pro*.

Procedures

1. Discuss how fast an automobile can travel and the relationships among distance, miles, and time.

2. Have the students create a spreadsheet similar to the one in Figure 9.17.

Figure 9.17
Microsoft Excel Speed Spreadsheet
(*Source:* Microsoft product screenshot reprinted with permission from Microsoft Corporation)

	A	B	C
1	RATE	TIME	DISTANCE
2	25	0.5	
3	30	1	
4	35	2	
5	40	2	
6	45	3	
7	50	3	
8	55	4	
9	60	5	
10	65	6	
11	70	7	

3. Next, pose the following question: What is the distance covered when traveling so many hours at a given speed?

4. Have the students type a formula in cell C2 that multiplies cell A2 by cell B2. Then copy this formula for cells C3 to C11.

5. After the students have accomplished this, have them examine the results and determine the answers to questions that you and they pose. If there are not enough computers, let the students use their calculators and a pencil and paper to complete this task.

Variations

You can generate other spreadsheets that would enable students to answer the following questions:

1. How much time does it take to travel a specified number of miles at a certain speed?

2. At what speed must you travel to go 300 miles in 5 hours?

II. EXPENSE TRACKING

Subject: Math

Grade(s): 5 and up

Objective: Students will use a spreadsheet to keep track of expenses.

Standards
- National Council of Teachers of Math Standards 1, 2, 6, 9
- ISTE NETS for Students 1, 3

Materials

You will need a spreadsheet program such as *Numbers*, *Excel*, *Cruncher 2.0*, or *Quattro Pro*.

Procedures

1. Discuss the following problem with the students: The $10 Computer Club is having a fundraiser to buy software for its club. The cost of the software is $700, and the club members expect to sell three raffle tickets apiece. They are selling these tickets for $3 each. Figure 9.18 shows how many tickets each student in the club sells.

	A	B	C	D	E	F	G	H	I
1	$10 CLUB			DAYS OF THE WEEK					AVERAGE
2		1	2	3	4	5	6	7	
3									
4	Adams	6	4	6	2	3	4	5	
5	Barrett	5	4	4	5	0	0	3	
6	Devlin	5	2	6	2	6	1	2	
7	Johnson	2	1	4	4	2	1	3	
8	Mason	3	0	0	0	10	0	2	
9	Garcia	1	2	3	4	3	2	1	
10	Youngblood	2	3	4	5	5	7	8	
11	Sands	1	3	2	5	0	4	3	

10 club   —   Ready   100%

Figure 9.18
Ticket Sales Spreadsheet
(*Source:* Microsoft product screenshot reprinted with permission from Microsoft Corporation)

2. Have each student create the same spreadsheet and then finish the data by calculating the average for each student.

3. Tell the students to use the logical function to determine how many club members sold six or more tickets on a daily basis. Was the $10 Computer Club able to buy its software?

Variation

1. Change the totals in the spreadsheet for any two students not selling at least three raffle tickets daily to three raffle tickets and record the value the spreadsheet recalculates.

2. Have the students compute the averages again for the raffle ticket price raised to $5.

III. FAMILY AND CONSUMER EDUCATION

Subjects: Home Economics and Math

Grade(s): 7 and up

Objective: Students will use a spreadsheet to keep track of their expenditures for 6 months.

Standards
- National Council of Teachers of Math Standards 1, 2, 6, 9
- ISTE NETS for Students 1, 3, 6

Materials

You will need a spreadsheet program such as *Numbers, Excel, Cruncher 2.0,* or *Quattro Pro.*

Procedures

1. Have each student record in a spreadsheet expenditures for the 10 items shown in Figure 9.19 during a 6-month period.

Figure 9.19
Expenditures Spreadsheet
(*Source:* Microsoft product screenshot reprinted with permission from Microsoft Corporation)

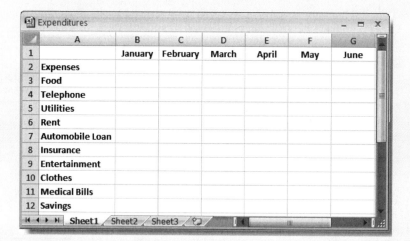

2. Have students use the sum formula to total each column.
3. Ask them to add an additional column to keep track of 6-month totals.
4. Change values in the completed spreadsheet so that the students can answer what-if questions such as "If I cut down on my entertainment, how much more can I save a year?"

Variation

From the savings row, create a spreadsheet that shows how much an initial deposit of $200 would grow at different interest rates and at different intervals of time.

IV. THE PENDULUM

Subjects: Science and Math

Grade(s): 5 and up

Objectives: Students will practice predicting, changing variables, and estimating and learn how to use a formula in a spreadsheet.

Standards
- National Council of Teachers of Math Standards 1, 2, 3, 4, 6, 9
- National Science Education Standards A1, A2, B1, B2
- ISTE NETS for Students 1, 3, 4, 5, 6

Materials
You will need string, thumbtacks, weights, and a spreadsheet program like *InspireData*, *Excel*, *Cruncher 2.0*, *Numbers*, or *Quattro Pro*.

Procedures
1. Before beginning, make sure students understand how the pendulum works.
2. Have each student experiment with different weights, lengths, and amplitude values. The objective is to determine what affects the pendulum's period. A period is simply the time it takes the pendulum to swing from point A to point B and then back to point A again.
3. Ask each student to create a table like the one in Table 9.2.

Table 9.2 Pendulum Investigations

Length	Weight	Amplitude	Period

4. Have students use a formula to figure each period for the pendulum.

V. THE ELECTION

Subjects: Social Studies and Math

Grade(s): 4 and up

Objectives: Students will learn about elections and in the process how to use a spreadsheet to add and figure percentages.

Standards
- National Council of Teachers of Math Standards 1, 6, 8
- National Council for the Social Studies Curriculum Standards 3, 6
- ISTE NETS for Students 1, 3, 4

Materials
The students will have to make voting booths and have access to a spreadsheet program such as *Excel* or *Cruncher 2.0*. They will need ballots and tallies for each voting booth.

Procedures
1. Before beginning, make sure students understand the election process.
2. Have the students nominate candidates for president of the room or school.
3. Conduct an election with voting booths.
4. Have students create a spreadsheet similar to the one in Figure 9.20.
5. Have students write the candidates' names and tally the votes.
6. Have students enter the number of valid ballots that were cast.
7. Have students use the sum function to calculate the total number of valid ballots.

8. Have students use the percent function to calculate the percentage of the total vote that each candidate received.

9. Pose questions such as the following: Was the election close? What percentage of the total votes did my candidate earn? How many votes were there all together?

VI. ACID RAIN

Subject: Science and Math

Grades(s): 7–12

Objectives: Students will learn about acid rain and in the process evaluate data and develop research skills.

Standards
• National Council of Teachers of Math Standards 1, 2, 4, 10
• National Science Education Standards A1, A2, B3, D1, D3
• ISTE NETS for Students 2, 3, 4, 5, 6

Materials
The student will need an Internet connection, a browser such as Internet Explorer, and a spreadsheet program such as *Microsoft Office Excel*.

Procedure

1. Students should use their Internet browser to go to a site on acid rain. For example, the U.S. Environmental Protection Agency site at http://www.epa.gov/acidrain/.

2. Students will then read about acid rain.

3. Next, students need to collect data for pH levels of rainwater for their state at http://nadp.sws.uiuc.edu/sites/ntnmap.asp? (the National Atmospheric Deposition).

4. At this Web site they should record the latitude, ph level, and longitude on their Excel spreadsheet.

5. Finally, they should answer questions like the following:

a. What causes acid rain?

b. How does your state compare to "normal" rainwater pH?

c. Do you see any trends for your state?

d. Who contributes the most to acid rain in your particular state?

e. How can you prevent acid rain?

f. How do you measure acid rain?

Modified from Microsoft at http://www.microsoft.com/education/acidrain.mspx

Integrated Programs

Previously, we discussed three popular applications of the computer: the word processor, the database, and the spreadsheet. Each application was dedicated to a separate task: The word processor created and edited documents, the database organized information, and the spreadsheet worked with numerical data.

Once you are comfortable with these individual programs, you may require software that allows for the free interchange of data among programs. For example, you may need to take budget information stored in the spreadsheet and transfer it to a letter that you are writing on the word processor. Stand-alone programs are generally not capable of communicating with other applications. There are many aspects of programming that limit the ability of these programs to address one another, and one important limitation is the differences among their command structures. For example, a *Cruncher 2.0* spreadsheet cannot electronically transfer information into an *AppleWorks* word processor because of their different commands.

The **integrated program**, on the other hand, includes in its most common configuration a word processor, a database, and a spreadsheet that can communicate with one another. *Lotus 1-2-3* was one of the first programs to offer as a part of its design a database with some graphics capabilities. After the success of *Lotus 1-2-3*, many programs followed its example such as *SuperCalc 3*, *Microsoft Works*, and *AppleWorks* (not upgraded) (Figure 9.21). These programs expanded and offered more applications such as painting, drawing, Internet, and presentation.

Figure 9.21
AppleWorks Starter Screen
(*Source:* Screenshot reprinted with permission from Apple, Inc.)

The applications of an integrated program share a similar command structure. Because of this similarity of command structure across the various applications, the program is easy to learn. Since each module is a component of one program, data are transferred seamlessly. You can effortlessly combine tables with text, for example. Finally, integrated programs cost much less than the total price of several stand-alone programs. Nevertheless, some integrated programs have disadvantages. They typically need more memory, and the applications usually offer fewer functions than comparable stand-alone programs.

ALTERNATIVES TO INTEGRATED PROGRAMS

Some alternatives to integrated programs exist:

1. You can use the stand-alone program as it is and cut and paste between applications when necessary. If you are fortunate, your stand-alone program may come with all the database or word processing capabilities that you require, even if they are limited.

2. You can retype your data into the separate applications. This sounds like a reasonable alternative, but it requires much typing and opens your data to errors. Also, anytime you change a number in one application, you will have to remember to change it in the other applications.

3. You can file share, which permits access to the files of the other programs. Because there is little standardization among the files of programs, these files cannot be directly read. If you want to read them, you need a special translator program like *MacLink Plus* (DataViz) for the Macintosh or *Conversions Plus* (DataViz) for

Windows. These translator programs enable you to input a file of one type, make it conform to the file structure of another type, and then output this transformed file.

Unfortunately, these translator programs are not available for all software programs, and sometimes in the process of transforming the data the formatting may be lost. If you do not need to transfer data among applications, a basic stand-alone application that fits your computer needs should suffice. However, if you are going to need to transfer information from one application to another, you should buy an integrated software package or perhaps try a software suite.

In the 1990s software companies started a new trend with the introduction of software suites. A **software suite** is a package of individual programs designed to work together to share data easily and quickly. A suite consists of stand-alone applications that are otherwise sold individually. Each application works together through special links that create a mock integration. Four popular examples of suites are *Corel WordPerfect Office*, *Microsoft Office 2007* (Windows), *Microsoft Office 2008* (Macintosh), *Microsoft Works*, and *Lotus SmartSuite*. A suite costs less than the total of the individual stand-alone applications and offers more features. For example, *Corel WordPerfect Suite* includes *WordPerfect* (word processing), *Quattro Pro* (spreadsheet), *Corel Presentations*, and *Paradox* (database), as well as hundreds of templates, hundreds of fonts, and thousands of clip art images. You can install the entire suite or only the programs that you want.

There are many similarities between an integrated package and a suite. Both enable you to run many programs at once, and they are designed to work together. An integrated program and a suite feature a **clipboard**, a place to store text, graphics, audio, and video clips. You use this clipboard to move data among the programs of the suite or integrated program applications. You copy the data to the clipboard and then paste it into the other applications. Both integrated programs and suites enable you to write more sophisticated reports and papers because they give you access to a variety of programs.

The main difference between a software suite and an integrated program is that the suite's components are full-featured programs and not limited versions. These applications usually started as independent programs that were popular before being combined in a suite. In most cases, a suite is very economical, because software vendors use it to induce people to buy their products. It serves as a marketing strategy for preventing the user from switching to a new product.

On the negative side, the various components in a suite do not work as smoothly as the applications on an integrated program. There are very high hardware requirements to run a suite. The hard disk space, the memory, and the speed of the computer should all be taken into consideration. A suite like *Microsoft Office 2007* requires more than 2 gigabytes of hard disk space. This would not be a problem for modern computers, but old relics that are often found in poorer elementary schools might have some problems. It is preferable to have a more powerful computer to take full advantage of the programs' capabilities. Mastering a suite is definitely harder than mastering an integrated program. Expect to spend considerable time and effort if you want to learn more than just the basics.

When you scrutinize an integrated program or suite you are concerned with the same features as you would be when considering separate applications. You should consider the same questions: How rapidly does the database sort? How much time is needed to load a file? How quickly does the spreadsheet calculate? How many columns and rows can you create using the spreadsheet document? Does the word processor have a thesaurus or grammar checker? You should find out how quickly and easily each module in the integrated package or software suite shares data.

SUMMARY

The electronic spreadsheet, which consists of a matrix of rows and columns intersecting at cells, was developed to handle complicated and tedious calculations. In this chapter, we became familiar with the basic features of a spreadsheet and discussed which features to consider when buying a spreadsheet program for the classroom.

We also explored activities for introducing the spreadsheet to students.

In addition, we examined the integrated software package, a group of programs that freely exchange data with each other. In their most common configuration today, these integrated programs include a word processor, database, spreadsheet, Internet module, drawing module, and graphics module. Additionally, we discussed the software suite, a bundling of linked stand-alone programs.

STUDY AND ONLINE RESOURCES

CHAPTER 9 ONLINE RESOURCES

In the **student section** of the book's online site at **http://www.wiley.com/college/sharp**, you will find templates and examples, video tutorials, PDF, Podcasts, articles, Web sites, software reviews, and chapter quizzes. Watch video tutorials online at **http://www.wiley.com/college/sharp** and learn how to create a grade book, sort a list, and create a graph. Access these resources to learn about technology and integrating it into the classroom.

CHAPTER MASTERY TEST

Lets check for chapter comprehension with a short mastery test. Key Terms, Computer Lab, and Suggested Readings and References follow the test.

1. What is a spreadsheet?

2. Give an example of each of the following terms: (a) macro, (b) cell, (c) logical functions, (d) predefined functions, (e) windows.

3. What is the advantage of being able to copy a formula in a spreadsheet?

4. Choose two important features of a spreadsheet and show how they can be utilized in the classroom.

5. Discuss the factors involved in selecting a spreadsheet for a school district.

6. Explain the advantage of a spreadsheet over a calculator.

7. Give an example of a situation in which an integrated software program has an advantage over a stand-alone program.

8. Describe the advantage of using what-if analysis with a spreadsheet. Name some applications in which this type of comparison would be important.

9. Explain and suggest reasons for the popularity of software suites.

10. If you were buying an integrated program, what are some features you would look at before buying?

KEY TERMS

Cell p. 173
Clipboard p. 192
Function p. 175
Hyperlinks p. 179
Integrated program p. 191

Logical functions p. 178
Macros p. 179
Predetermined functions p. 178
Software suite p. 192

Spreadsheet p. 172
What-if analysis p. 177

COMPUTER LAB: Activities for Mastery and Your Portfolio

9.1 Create a Classroom Budget Planner and chart expenses for art materials, bulletin boards, holiday decorations, and so on. Watch the Video tutorial online and learn how to create a graph.

9.2 Create a grade book and keep track of student grades in all subjects. Watch the Video tutorial online and learn how to create a grade book and sort a list.

9.3 Create a day planner and keep track of daily class schedules, assembly times, prep periods, and so on.

9.4 Develop a spreadsheet activity for the classroom.

9.5 Create a spreadsheet similar to the grade book example given in this chapter, but for this example have 12 students take three exams and a final. Calculate the final exam as 40 percent of the grade and the other three exams as 20 percent each. Watch the Video tutorial online and learn how to create a grade book and sort a list.

9.6 Prepare a review comparing three spreadsheets.

9.7 Use a spreadsheet to compare the expenses with a devised budget.

9.8 Outline in a lesson plan format three different ways a spreadsheet would be useful in the classroom.

9.9 Prepare a report on integrated programs, comparing their strengths and weaknesses.

9.10 List the different ways an integrated program would be useful in the school district office.

SUGGESTED READINGS AND REFERENCES

Abramovich, Sergei, and Peter Brouwer. "Revealing Hidden Mathematics Curriculum to Pre-Teachers Using Technology: The Case of Partitions." *International Journal of Mathematical Education in Science and Technology* 34, issue 1 (January 2003): 81–95.

Ageel, M. I. "Spreadsheets as a Simulation Tool for Solving Probability Problems." *Teaching Statistics* 24, issue 2 (Summer 2002): 51–55.

Beaudrie, Brian; Boschmans, Barbara. "Infusing Technology into Mathematics Lessons." *Media and Methods* 41, issue 1 (August 2004): 10.

Beigie, Darin. "Investigating Limits in Number Patterns." *Mathematics Teaching in the Middle School* 7, issue 8 (April 2002): 438–443.

Bourgeois, Michelle. "The Cruncher 2.0." *T.H.E. Journal* 27, no. 1 (August 1999): 52.

Brown, Graeme. "Spread It on Thick." *Times Educational Supplement,* issue 4478 (April 26, 2003): 26–28.

Brown, J. M. "Spreadsheets in the Classroom." *Computing Teacher* 14, no. 3 (1987): 8–12.

Burns, Mary. "Beyond Show and Tell: Using Spreadsheets to Solve Problems" *Learning and Leading with Technology* 31, no. 2 (2003): 22–27.

DeMarco, Neil. "Numbers Tell Their Own Story." *Times Higher Education Supplement,* issue 1536 (May 3, 2002): 10–12.

Donovan, II, John E. "Using the Dynamic Power of Microsoft Excel to stand on the Shoulders of GIANTS." *Mathematics Teacher* 99, issue 5 (December 2005/January 2006): 334–339.

Drier, Hollylynne Stohl. "Teaching and Learning Mathematics with Interactive Spreadsheets." *School Science and Mathematics* 101, no. 4 (April 2001): 170–179.

Horton, Robert M., and William H. Leonard. "Mathematical Modeling in Science." *Science Teacher* 72, issue 5 (Summer 2005): 40–45.

Jones, Keith. "Using Spreadsheets in the Teaching and Learning of Mathematics: A research bibliography." *Micro Math* 21, issue 1 (Spring 2005): 30–31.

Kissell, Joe. " The Google Office." *MacWorld* (August 2007): 60–72.

Lannin, John K. "Generalization and Justification: The Challenge of Introducing Algebraic Reasoning Through Patterning Activities." *Mathematical Thinking and Learning* 7, issue 3 (2005): 231–258.

Lesser, Lawrence M. "Exploring the Birthday Problem with Spreadsheets." *Mathematics Teacher* 92, no. 5 (May 1999): 407.

Luehrmann, Arthur. "Spreadsheets: More Than Just Finance." *Computing Teacher* 13 (1986): 24–28.

Manouchehri, Azita. "Exploring Number Structures with Spreadsheets." *Learning and Leading with Technology* 24, no. 8 (May 1997): 32–36.

Percival, Rob. "Maths." *Times Educational Supplement*, issue 4718 (January 5, 2007): 51.

Pfaffenberger, Bryan. *Webster's New World Computer User's Dictionary, 8th ed.* New York: Macmillan, 2000.

Ray, Beverly. "PDAs in the Classroom: Integration Strategies for K–12 Educators." *International Journal of Educational Technology* 3, no. 1 (November, 2002).

Richgels, Glen. "Teaching Math: Spreadsheets & Graphing Programs." *Media and Methods* 41, issue 6 (May/June 2005): 4–5.

Riley, Kyle. "Using Spreadsheets to Estimate the Volatility of Stock Prices." *Mathematics and Computer Education* 36, no. 3 (Fall 2002): 240–246.

Scahill, Marilyn P. "Mathematics: How Much?" *School Library Media Activities Monthly* 22, issue 8 (April 2006): 11–13.

Sharp, Vicki. *Make It with Microsoft Office 2007 (Windows).* Eugene, Ore.: Visions Technology in Education, 2007.

Sharp, Vicki. *Make It with Microsoft Office 2008 (Macintosh).* Eugene, Ore.: Visions Technology in Education, 2008.

Smith-Gratto, Karen, and Marcy A. Blackburn. "The Computer as a Scientific Tool: Integrating Spreadsheets into the Elementary Science Curriculum." *Computers in the Schools* 13, no. 1–2 (1997): 125–131.

Van Horn, Royal. "Web Applications and Google." *Phi Delta Kappan* 88, issue 10 (June 2007): 727–792.

Varrati, Richard. "Multimedia Projects for Technology-Rich Classrooms." *Media and Methods* 42, issue 1 (September/October 2005): 6–7.

Wagner, Judson E. "Using Spreadsheets to Assess Learning." *Physics Teacher* 45, issue 1 (January 2007): 34–37.

Walkenbach, John. "Surprise, Surprise! Excel Can Handle Fractions." *PC World* 18, no. 5 (May 2000): 254.

Warner, C. Bruce, and Anita M. Meehan. "Microsoft Excel as a Tool for Teaching Basic Statistics." *Teaching of Psychology* 28, no. 4 (August 2001): 295–298.

Digital Photography and Newer Technologies

Integrating Digital Photography and New Technologies into the Classroom

Everywhere you travel people are taking pictures with their digital cameras. No place is out of bounds for these amateur photographers. You see them at school events, on buses, at amusement parks, on cable cars, at disasters, and on hiking trails. They are motivated by a desire for an instant record of their adventures. Teachers and students have embraced this technology by sharing their digital images, printing them, and sending them over the Internet. This has led to image-sharing sites like Flickr [www.flickr.com]. The Web is also responsible for the emergencies of different and unique technologies. In this chapter we cover emerging learning technologies such as blogs, Podcasting, Wikis, and social bookmarking.

Using the computer, students and teachers can do the following:

students can

- create a digital portfolio,
- make a Podcast,
- engage in blogging,
- participate in social bookmarking, and
- design a Wikis.

teachers can

- Post podcasts online,
- Create a student Web site with pictures,
- Communicate by blogs, and
- Work on collaborative projects.

Introduction

According to the Photo Marketing Association (2007), for the past two years digital cameras have outsold film cameras. We are in the middle of a revolution where sales of digital cameras are in the millions. We have come a long way from 1991 when Kodak released the first digital camera, the Nikon F-3 with its Kodak 1.3 megapixel sensor. It was three short years that teachers saw the first consumer digital camera, the Apple QuickTake 100 (co-produced with Kodak). The camera was expensive, selling for about $749, and it stored between 8 and 32 images depending on the resolution that was set. Since that time other camera manufacturers have introduced a multitude of cameras and the digital camera market has exploded.

What is a Digital Camera?

Allan Freedman (2008) states that a digital camera is "A still camera that records images in digital form. Unlike traditional film cameras that record a light image on film (analog), digital cameras record discrete numbers for storage on a flash memory card or optical disk. As with all digital devices, there is a fixed, maximum resolution and number of colors that can be represented. Images are transferred to the computer with a USB cable, a memory card, or wireless. Digital video cameras also use FireWire." **(Chapter 11 has a section that covers digital video cameras.)**

Figure 10.1 shows the various components of the digital process.

Figure 10.1
The Digital
Process

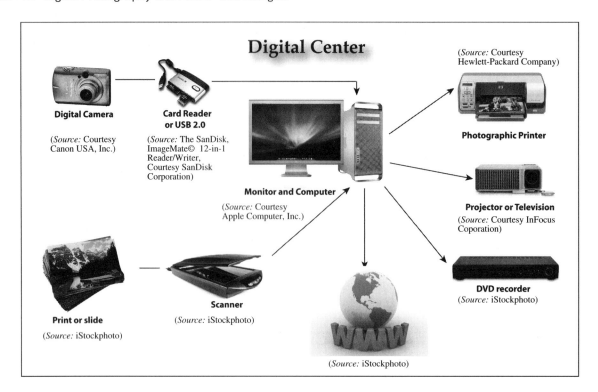

1. The digital camera inputs images and then transfers the images through a USB port or card reader to the computer. You can also take a print or slide and scan it into the computer, making it a digital image.

2. Once these images are in the computer you can edit them using a photo-editing program such as *Adobe Photoshop Elements*.

3. Next, you can save these pictures to your desired storage media (e.g., a hard drive or DVD).

4. You can print the pictures out using a photographic printer or you can share them using a projector or television, the World Wide Web, e-mail, a DVD recorder, or a VCR tape machine.

Advantages and Disadvantages of Digital Photography

The advantages of a digital camera over a film camera are numerous. Everyone wants instant gratification. When you use a digital camera you see the pictures you took right away, and delete the ones you do not want. You do not need to develop these pictures, because they stay on your hard disk, DVD, or memory card. You can also take hundreds of pictures and not worry about changing film rolls every 24 or 36 shots. You never have to buy a roll of film again. This is not the case with a film camera because you cannot reuse film. When you buy film you are dependent on a processing lab to develop these pictures.

The digital camera also lets you edit the digital pictures on the computer and make the changes you want. You have complete control of the process. You don't have to worry about negatives getting scratched because you can put your pictures on a CD.

With all these advantages there are still some disadvantages. Digital cameras are more expensive and more delicate than film cameras. There is also a higher cost per print because of the equipment required. At the very least you should have a photo printer and editing software. Unfortunately, when you use a digital camera you do not see as much detail or shadow in your pictures as with film. Shutter delay is a factor on less expensive digital cameras. In addition, digital cameras usually have poor low-light focusing and quickly drain your battery. Finally, film is still higher quality than the digital camera's image. However, in the next few years digital camera technology will equal film.

How to Choose a Digital Camera

Every three months a new batch of digital cameras appears in stores. They come in all sizes, shapes, weights, and features.

TYPES OF DIGITAL CAMERAS

Digital cameras are generally classified as subcompact, compact, and single lens reflex (SLR). The subcompact camera is smaller than the compact camera and usually can fit in a shirt pocket. The compact and subcompact cameras weigh less than SLR cameras but they have fewer features. You cannot add lenses to the compact and subcompact cameras. However, these cameras are easier to travel with and take into the classroom. They are usually automatic point-and-shoot cameras.

The SLR cameras have interchangeable lenses, cost more, offer more features, have longer battery life, and can save images similar to a film negative in a RAW file format. The three types of cameras are pictured in Figure 10.2.

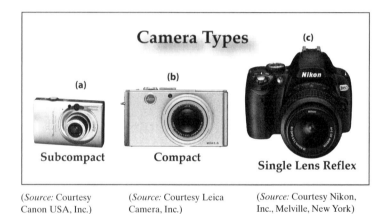

(*Source:* Courtesy Canon USA, Inc.)   (*Source:* Courtesy Leica Camera, Inc.)   (*Source:* Courtesy Nikon, Inc., Melville, New York)

Figure 10.2
(a) Subcompact,
(b) Compact,
(c) Single Lens Reflex

Trying to choose between these cameras can be a daunting task. You not only have to decide on the type of camera you want to buy but features such as megapixels, LCD size, price, and power source. First, consider the camera's *image quality*. The more expensive cameras have the higher image quality. One factor that determines image quality is pixel density or pixel depth. A pixel is "generally, the smallest addressable unit on a display screen or bitmapped image" (Freedman, 2008). If you use the zoom feature on your editing program you can see a digital picture's pixels (Figure 10. 3). Digital cameras are calculated in megapixels or millions. For example, 6 megapixels is equal to 6 million pixels.

Figure 10.3
Pixels

Megapixels

The question you may want to ask is how many megapixels should my camera have. Lately there has been a megapixel war and every six months the camera manufacturers raise the pixel level. The best way to decide how many megapixels you need is to consider the final destination of your images. Are these images being used solely for Web publications or will they be turned into printed posters? If these pictures are being used for Web publications, you can buy any camera and reduce its resolution and not worry. However, if they will be cropped and blown up to poster print size you have to be more concerned about pixels. Following is a rough guide for determining the amount of megapixels you will need to print your photos at 300 dpi print. For the majority of teachers 5 megapixels produce excellent quality pictures for classroom use.

Guide for a 300 DPI Print Size

Destination	Megapixels
Web site or email	1 or 2
3 x 5 and 4 x 6 prints	2
5 x 7	5
8 x 10	6
11 x 14	14
13 x 20	23 MP

However, megapixels alone does not determine print quality. There are other factors such as optical quality of the lens, sensor size, and the design of the camera.

LENS QUALITY

The optical quality of your camera lens is very important in determining the quality of your picture. Since you can't test every camera your best source of information is reading books, photography magazines, and viewing photography-expert Web sites such as Digital Photography Review http://www.dpreview.com/, Digital Camera Resource Page http://www.dcresource.com, and Steve's Digicams http://www.steves-digicams.com/. These Web sites give lengthy reviews, discussing lens quality and rating the cameras on items such as the camera's sensor, internal processing capability, etc. A few of the better-known camera manufacturers are Canon, Nikon, Sony, Leica, and Fuji.

Liquid Crystal Displays and Viewfinders

The majority of digital cameras have liquid crystal display (LCD) screens. The LCD screen lets you see 100 percent of your picture before you take it and preview the picture after you take it. These screens are different in size and pixels. In many cases they have coatings or glass that reduces glare. There are two problems with LCD displays: (1) If you use this display frequently it drains the camera's battery, and (2) if there is bright sunlight it is difficult and sometimes impossible to view your subject. You either have to shade the LCD with your hand or buy a LCD lens shade. The Leica C-LUX 2 lets you increase the brightness of your LCD screen.

An optical viewfinder is a little window that sits on the camera's body, usually above the camera's lens, and lets you see 97–100 percent of the picture. The picture is not the same because you are not seeing exactly what the lens is seeing. However, it is useful because unlike the LCD screen there is no battery drain and you can use this viewfinder on sunny days. With an optical viewfinder you can estimate the depth of field, and you also can see who will be entering your frame.

Most viewfinders are optical viewfinders, but some cameras come with electronic viewfinders, which are more difficult to view, but display more information than the optical viewfinder.

Memory Cards

Without a place to store pictures your digital camera would be a useless device. Digital cameras usually store their images on memory cards or internal memory inside the camera. Memory cards come in an assortment of sizes and shapes and are removable. A few of the different types of cards are CompactFlash Types I and II, Memory Stick (Sony digicams) MultiMedia cards, and the most common Secure Digital cards. Some of these cards are only meant for specific cameras so you have to be careful when you buy a card. Figure 10.4 shows a few of the different types of memory cards that are available.

Figure 10.4
Memory Cards
(*Source:* Hugh Threlfall/Alamy)

Unfortunately, the majority of digital cameras you buy today have memory cards that do not store enough images on them to be useful. Depending on the megapixels of your camera, buy a large enough card to store at least 200 images. It is better to buy a 2-gigabyte card than a bunch of little cards. Consider the speed of the memory card. The higher the speed rating the faster the digital camera writes the images to the card. However, not all cameras will take advantage of a high-speed card, so check with the camera manufacturer.

Optical versus Digital Zoom

The optical zoom is the actual resolution of your lens whereas the digital zoom is an interpolated resolution that is computed by software. Therefore, a 12 optical zoom is superior to a 12 digital zoom. Do not buy too powerful a zoom, because the greater your magnification the greater the possibility of image degradation.

Power Supply

Batteries are either a standard AA battery or a rechargeable lithium-ion battery. If your camera comes with a rechargeable battery it will take time to recharge it so bring another one with you. If your camera takes AA batteries they can be purchased anywhere that you travel.

Formats

Digital cameras have three types of formats: Joint Photographic Experts Group (JPEG), Tagged Image File Format (TIFF), and Raw. Most entry-level cameras use JPEG, which is easy to use. This format gives you different compression options. Compression encodes the data so it takes less storage space. The less compression you use the larger the file size and the better the quality of the picture.

TIFF is useful for print materials, posters, manuscripts, etc. TIFF retains all the details of your picture and lets you store images with greater color depth, but has a large file size. You need a large memory card to shoot TIFF.

The more expensive digital cameras will let you shoot in a "Raw" format. This format has a large file size but it lets you save specific information about each pixel. It is the unadulterated data as captured on the camera chip. The Raw format can differ, depending on the camera that you use. If you are a new user, Raw format could be a problem to use and finding support could be difficult.

Cost, Weight, Price, and Feel

Price varies so it is important to check discount stores and online. Weight is an important concern for most people, especially when you are walking great distances. Another concern is the feel of your camera. Does it feel good in your hands? Are the controls easy to reach? What about the camera's interface? Remember the old adage, try before you buy.

Photography Software

Many cameras come with a CD that contains software that lets you edit and organize photos on your computer. This is sufficient for basic tasks, but you will eventually want to use other programs for advanced functions. Look first at your computer's programs. Apple offers *iPhoto* (Figure 10.5) with its Macintosh X and Microsoft offers *Microsoft Photo Gallery* with its Vista operating system.

Figure 10.5
iPhoto 8
(*Source:* Screenshot reprinted with permission from Apple, Inc.)

These programs offer basic functions such as remove red eye, crop, flip, and rotate pictures. *Apple's iPhoto* offers more features than Photo Gallery such as calendars, Web pages, and photo books. There are also free programs offered online such as *Picasa* (picasa.google.com), *IrfanView* (www.infranview.com), and *Snapfire 1.0* (www.corel.com). The previous programs are great for organizing and editing pictures. However, if you need more advanced features you probably will need a commercial package such as *Adobe Photoshop Elements* (Figure 10.6), *Adobe Photoshop*, *ACDSee Photo*, *Corel Snapfire 1.10*, or *Roxio Easy Media Creator Suite* (Roxio).

Figure 10.6
Photoshop Elements
(Source: Screenshot reprinted with permission from Apple, Inc.)

(Microsoft has discontinued its Image Suite products.) These programs fix damaged pictures and have tools that will let you work picture elements independently.

Table 10.1 summarizes additional digital camera features.

Tabel 10.1 More Digital Camera Features

Feature	Explanation
Image Stabilizer	Controls for camera shake. It is important for tiny cameras and ones that have a zoom of 3x or more.
Movie Mode	Lets compact and subcompact cameras record video. You can now put that family video on YouTube.
Interchangeable Lens	Only applies to the digital single lens reflex camera.
Shutter Lag	The delay that you experience when you take your first shot.
Next Shot Delay	Refers to the delay for your follow-up shot.
Flash Range	The distance the camera illuminates the subject. Most digital cameras have a built-in flash with a range of 10-16 feet.
Manual Options	Lets you adjust the camera's settings.
Wide Angle Imaging	The ability to take wide-angle shots.
Face Detection	Identifies faces and makes them the main focus.
Self-timer	Presses the shutter when you are unable to do it.
Red Eye	Eliminated by using this feature.

As you can see, a teacher looking for a classroom digital camera must decide which factors are important to him or her. What will the camera use be in the classroom? Is the camera for class trips, newspaper publications, or maybe a Web site? How cost-effective is the camera? What about technical support? Use the Digital Camera Checklist form on page 202 that follows to guide you through the process.

Digital Cameras in the Classroom

Today, teachers and students are using digital cameras throughout the curriculum. They are using digital images in science for data collection, in language arts for digital storytelling, in mathematics for problem solving, and in social science for

Digital Camera Checklist

Directions: Examine the following items and determine which ones you feel are important for your class situation. Place an X on each line for which the camera meets your needs.

Camera Model_____ **Manufacturer**_____ **Store**_____

Computer Hardware

____ 1. System requirements_____

____ 2. Computer compatibility

____ 3. Hard disk space

____ 4. Printer compatibility

Type of Camera

____ 1. Subcompact

____ 2. Compact

____ 3. Single lens reflex

Features

____ 1. Number of megapixels _____

____ 2. Memory card type

   ___ a. CF—CompactFlash Type I and II

   ___ b. MS—Memory Stick (Sony)

   ___ c. MMC—MultiMedia Card

   ___ d. SD—Secure Digital (most common)

   ___ e. Other _____

____ 3. Optical zoom

____ 4. Digital zoom

____ 5. Image formats

   ___ a. JPEG

   ___ b. TIFF

   ___ c. Raw

   ___ d. Other

____ Other

____ 6. Battery type_____

____ 7. Red-eye reduction

____ 8. Included software_____

____ 9. Movie mode

____ 10. Lens quality

____ 11. Face detection

____ 12. Liquid crystal displays (LCD)

   ___ a. Size

   ___ b. Pixels_____

____ 13. Manual flash_____

____ 14. Focusing range_____

   ___ a. Wide angle_____

   ___ b. Telephoto_____

   ___ c. Manual focusing

____ 15. Viewfinder_____

____ 16. Weight_____

____ 17. Camera feel_____

____ 18. Image stabilizer_____

____ 19. Shutter lag_____

____ 20. Next shot delay_____

____ 21. Flash range_____

____ 22. Manual options_____

____ 23. Self-timer

Ease of Use

____ 1. Help screens

____ 2. Online tutorial

Support Features

____ 1. Technical support

____ 2. Tutorial material

____ 3. Readable manual

Consumer Value

____ 1. Cost

____ 2. Free technical support

____ 3. Guarantees

Rating Scale

Rate the digital camera by placing a check in the appropriate line.

Excellent_____ Very good _____ Good _____ Fair _____ Poor _____

Comments:

primary digital sources. Students can post pictures on the Internet or e-mail them to fellow students. Students can paste images into their applications. For example, they can insert images into programs such as *Word* and *Excel*. They can use applications such as *Photoshop Elements* to edit and manipulate these images. They can put mountains where there are no mountains, create a red sky where there is none (Figure 10.7), get rid of red eye, crop, and rotate. They can do family history photos, photo essays, famous person time lines, zoo trip photos, and book reports.

Figure 10.7
Bob Sachs, Storm Clouds
(*Source:* Courtesy of Bob Sachs, http://bobsachs.com)

Teachers can do visual seating charts and identification cards, and a visual roll book. They can create a teacher portfolio, or show historic monuments and do photo flashcards. A teacher might create a presentation that teaches a foreign language or a training module on how to use a digital camera. They may even want to create a digital photo album (Figure 10.8) for an open house. For such an onscreen presentation, each student's photo would appear with music, text, and dazzling effects. The list is endless and that is why digital photography has become such a popular phenomena.

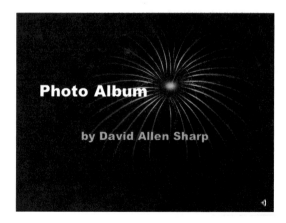

Figure 10.8
Digital Photo Album
(*Source:* Courtesy Visions Technology in Education)

You can spruce up your classroom laboratory sessions with the following fun activity. I give the class a picture and have the students modify it to my specifications; for example, a picture of my son who thinks he is a punk rocker (Figure 10.9).

Using *Photoshop Elements*, the class removed David's beard and earrings, fixed his slightly closed eye, changed his complexion, and gave him a better haircut. After a digital picture is modified to your liking, you can then incorporate it into a multimedia presentation into a classroom newspaper or written report. You

Figure 10.9
Before and After
(*Source:* Photo by Vicki
Sharp; Photoshop
changes by Tim Yost)

can do a photographic scavenger hunt with the students by preparing a checklist for them and giving them a fixed time to find the appropriate pictures using their cameras.

Emerging Web Technologies

Because of the Internet we are awash in terms such as blogs, Podcasting, Wikis, and social bookmarking. If Rip Van Winkle were to wake up right now he would think we are not of this world.

BLOG (WEBLOG)

We**BLOGS** are usually referred to as *blogs*. A blog is an online text entry written by one student or a group of contributing students. Blogs range from personal diaries and newsletters to strong personal opinions by individuals on different topics. In 1999 to create a Blog you needed to be able to program using HTML. Today, companies such as Blogger and *Live Journal* offer free blog publishing. Blogger (http://www .blogger.com) is free, but students must register with an e-mail address. During the registration process they name their site, they work from online templates, and then write whatever they want (Figure 10.10). Whenever a student logs on, a window appears to

Figure 10.10
Three steps for creating a blog
(*Source:* © 2008 Jupiterimages
Corporation)

CREATING A BLOG

❑ Setup the account
❑ Give your blog a name
❑ Choose a template

which the user can add a journal entry. When the student is done, the entry is posted and can be viewed at the site. A blog is a very motivating activity encouraging students to write, experiment with new ideas, and expand their horizons. Students can use their blog as a response journal, to share comments and feedback with other students. They can use it as a public forum for discussing issues with a community of students as well as a private place to write down their ideas. Faculty can use these blogs to increase course dialogue, express opinions, and help students with course requirements.

PODCAST

"[iPOD broadCAST] is an audio broadcast that has been converted to an MP3 file or other audio file format for playback in a digital music player or computer" (Freedman, 2008). The term *Podcast* originated from Apple's music player, the iPod. Podcasts are usually vocal but often they contain music. These audio broadcasts are posted and distributed online. A Podcast allows you to publish your own radio program on the Internet, ranging from politics to personal logs. In many instances a Podcast is a regularly produced television series like *Meet the Press* (http://www.msnbc.msn.com/id/3032608/) or *Washington Week* (http://www.pbs.org/weta/washingtonweek/rss/index.html). These television programs have the audio portion of their show online. Any individual who has a computer, MP3 player, cell phone, or handheld device like a Palm Pilot can click and download or subscribe to these Podcasts. To listen to a Podcast on the computer you need software that will play these media files such as *iTunes* or *Windows Media Player*.

Podcasts can be produced quite inexpensively if you have a computer, microphone, and recording and editing software such as *Audacity* or *GarageBand*. The audio software lets you export audio as an MP3 file, the format that is needed for a Podcast. Finally, you need a way to publish your Podcast: create a Web page with links to audio files. People that are interested in your Podcast can then download these audio files. The more professional way to publish a Podcast is with a **r**eal **s**imple **sy**ndication (RSS) feed.[1] Any interested person can then subscribe to your Podcast and when you have a new show it will automatically download to the subscriber's computer. A few Podcast directories are *Yahoo! Podcasts*, *Apple iTunes Podcasts*, *Podcast.net*, and *Podcast Alley*. Podcasts take careful planning and thoughtful construction. Table 10.2 gives you some suggestions.

Table 10.2 Podcast Preparatory List

1. Check out other professional Podcasts.
2. Plan what you'll say for each episode.
3. Create an outline.
4. Use variety to keep your episodes interesting for the user.
5. If the show is a half-hour show, each particular segment should be roughly 5 minutes.
6. Record an introduction, which describes who you are and what topic you will cover. For example, you might what to do a Podcast on how to create a PowerPoint slide show.
7. Record a few informative segments. For example, "How to animate your PowerPoint presentation" and "How to add sound to your PowerPoint presentation"
8. Record a short exit ("outro") to end your Podcast. If you have music at the beginning, replay it at the end.
9. Spice up your Podcast by adding music and pictures.

Integrating the Podcast into the Classroom. Podcasts are very beneficial for the classroom. Teachers and students can create them for a variety of purposes. Podcasts range in quality from the absurd to the informative. Teachers can record

---

[1]"A syndication format that was developed by Netscape in 1999 and became very popular for aggregating updates to blogs and the news sites" (Freedman, 2008).

their lectures and students can download them. Many universities have Podcasts of professors' lectures online for students to download. Students can create their own Podcasts on topics ranging from the Civil War to an analysis of Beethoven's Seventh symphony. The following chart shows a few ways that Podcasts can be used in the classroom.

Interviews	Lectures
Student presentations	Language lessons
Scientific research studies	Speeches
Current events summary	Storytelling
Instructions for tasks	Guest lectures
Daily homework assignments	Audio tour of museum

To learn more about Podcasting, visit our online site at **http://www.wiley.com/college/sharp**. You can see a video tutorial on how to create a Podcast as well as numerous Web sites and Podcasts. In the Podcast folder you will find the latest trial versions of Peak LE and SoundSoap 2. Produced by BIAS, these products are a must for anyone creating Podcasts **http://www.bias-inc.com/**.

Video Podcasts are now becoming popular. These Podcasts deliver their video content online. Podcasting has a promising future.

Sound Editing.   While creating your Podcast, accidents happen because nothing really comes out the way you want it. You might find breathing noises you do not want or segments that are too long and need to be edited. It is for this very reason you need a sound-editing program such as *GarageBand* (Apple), *Audacity* (Open Source), or *Bias Peak Le* (Bias). *Audacity* is free open-source software that lets you record and edit sounds for the Mac OS X, Microsoft Windows, and other operating systems. It is a work that is in progress and better for the more advanced users. *GarageBand* (Apple) is a beginner program that easily lets you create and edit your Podcasts. *Bias Peak Le* (Figure 10.11) has an easy interface with all sorts of advanced features and presets.

Figure 10.11
Bias Peak Le
(*Source:* Courtesy Bias)

These programs let you cut, copy, and paste audio segments from and to the audio file. You can also apply sound effects such as echoes and fade in and out to an audio file. You can also record new sounds through a microphone. This is important when you are making a Podcast. In addition, Bias software produces *Soap 2* (Figure 10.12), a simple-to-use program that removes unwanted noise from your digital audio and video files. Using a one-step Learn Noise button, it eliminates everything from clicks to rumbles. It not only removes digital audio, but also digital video. (See Chapter 11 for information about compression and music file formats.)

Figure 10.12
SoundSoap 2
(*Source:* Courtesy Bias)

WIKIS

A Wiki is a Web site where individuals can view, edit, and add information. Ward Cunningham, presently at Microsoft Corporation, coined the term, which means "quick" in Hawaiian. An example of a well-known Wiki is Wikipedia, a free online encyclopedia (http://en.wikipedia.org/wiki/Wiki). Wikipedia is written by volunteers and can be edited by anyone that is using the World Wide Web. People writing and editing Wikipedia do not have to use their real names. Unfortunately, there is the possibility that the information is inaccurate and individuals can maliciously delete information or vandalize the site. The site's creators are attempting to rid themselves of these individuals.

Larry Sanger, a co-founder of Wikipedia, decided to build an online encyclopedia that was more authoritative called Citizendium (http://en.citizendium.org/wiki /Main_Page) (Figure 10.13). This encyclopedia also uses volunteers, but tries to avoid Wikipedia's inaccuracies by having experts approve the articles that are submitted and having contributors use their real names.

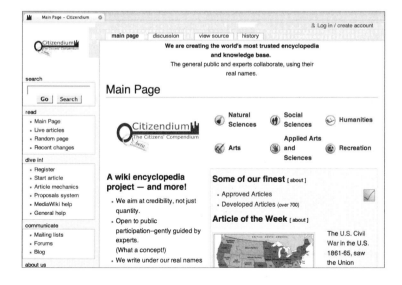

Figure 10.13
Citizendium

A Wiki can contain sounds, movies, and pictures. There are quite a few "Wiki" tools for creating these sites, for example, www.editme.com and www.swiki.net. Wikis are being used in higher education for student collaborative projects, brainstorming, debate, digital stories, multimedia presentations, and electronic portfolios. Teachers are using Wikis for meeting notes, agendas, journal articles, and textbook editing.

COLLABORATIVE EDITING

Using Collaborative Editing tools, a group of individuals can simultaneously edit a document and watch in real time as people make changes to this document. This procedure depends on a conscientious and skilled group of editors. For example, a college instructor might put a document on the Internet and have students access it and make changes to this document. Collaborative editing is especially useful in distance-learning situations.

SOCIAL NETWORKING

According to the National School Boards Association (2007), 96% of students using the computer online use some form of social networking. Social Networking is a Web site that lets individuals of similar interests spend time together. They communicate with each other by voice, video conferencing, instant messaging, and blogs. In many instances they contact each other in person. This virtual community talks about every-thing from politics to sex. For the 2008 Democratic Primary, senator Barack Obama used social networking to raise money, to form a community of devoted volunteers, and to spread his ideas. Popular examples of social networking sites are: *MySpace* (www.myspace.com), *Facebook* (www.facebook.com), *TagWorld* (www.tagged.com), and Twitter (twitter.com). *MySpace* offers a network of friends, personal profiles, pho-tos, groups, blogs, and music. *Facebook* originally targeted college students. This serv-ice now connects people of similar interests through photos, notes, and by posting videos; *TagWorld* has tools for creating personalized Web pages and emphasizes tag teams for teen with similar interest. *Twitter* informs your friends about your daily schedule. In addition, it lets you update a blog from a cellphone, send text-based mes-sages to friends, do instant messaging, and e-mail. In 2008, Hitwise, a leading intelli-gence service monitoring anonymously millions of United States Internet users (http://www.hitwise.com/press-center/hitwiseHS2004/social-networking-visits-april .php) announced the top 5 social Networking websites visited (Figure 10.14).

Figure 10.14
Top 5 social networking websites.

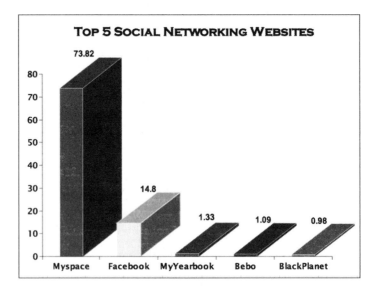

Social Networking popularity is growing and with this growth problems have arisen. Because you are collecting personal information there are privacy issues. Users of these sites share information with their friends and it is too easy for this informa-tion to fall into the hands of complete strangers, the press, authorities, and the public at large. Also sexually explicit information has been displayed on these sites, as well as assaults have occurred when people arrange to meet personally. Teachers should discuss the kinds of problems that can happen and try to educate their students. They should tell their students not to give personal information out on their Web pages.

SOCIAL BOOKMARKING

Social bookmarks let individuals take their favorite bookmarks and download them to a site such as *del.icio.us* (http://del.icio.us). At this site the individual can store and rank the bookmarks. Users of this site are able to see how many other people have bookmarked identical pages. Social bookmarking is useful for sharing bookmarks, as well as doing research. Table 10.3 displays some other emerging technologies. Visit our online site for a write-up of these technologies.

Table 10.3 **Other Emerging Technologies**

Technology	Description
Mapping Mashups	Use an Internet service such as Google to put together map information from more than one source. For example, *Map the Candidates* mashup (MapTheCandidates.com) lets you track the U.S. presidential candidates' campaign trails across the country. Teachers can create their own tours and maps.
Google Jockeying	When a presenter gives a lecture and an individual presents, a jockey, using a search engine like Google, searches for ideas or Internet terms that the presenter discusses. These searches are then shown during the presentation.
Google Earth	Has aerial/satellite images and interactive maps of the United States.
Screencasting	When a video recording is made of a computer screen. Screencasting is really a video Podcast.
Virtual Meetings	Real-time encounters that take place on the Internet using audio, video, and chat tools.

SAMPLE CLASSROOM LESSON PLANS

I. RECORDING YOUR TRAVELS

Subject: English

Grade(s): 3–12

Objective: Use the digital camera to create a photo journal (Figure 10.15).

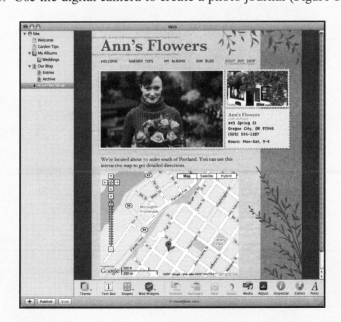

Figure 10.15
iPhoto Digital Journal
(*Source:* Courtesy Apple Computer, Inc.)

Standards

• National Council of Teachers of English 1, 2, 3, 4, 5
• ISTE NETS for Students 1, 2 3, 4, 5, 6

Materials

You will need a digital camera to take pictures, an editing program such as *Photoshop Elements* or *Photoshop*, a printer, and an application such as *Microsoft Word* or *iPhoto*.

Procedures

1. Give students tips on taking a good photo. Tips may include: (a) be sure to catch detail, (b) take unusual shots, and (c) keep things simple.
2. Divide the class into small groups.
3. Give the students practice in taking pictures and critiquing their work.
4. Tell each group of students to visit an interesting place and take pictures.
5. Students should next edit their pictures in *Photoshop Elements*.
6. Have students insert their pictures into a word processing document or a program like *iPhoto* and then write about each photo.
7. When all groups are finished, talk about how effective each journal handles its subject matter.

Variation

The photo journal can cover any topic, and students can work independently and post their projects on the Web or e-mail them to different people.

II. LEARNING WORDS

Subject: English

Grade(s): 2–6

Objective: Use the digital camera to take pictures of different vocabulary words (Figure 10.16).

Figure 10.16
Flowers
(*Source:* Courtesy Vicki Sharp)

2007 Vicki Sharp Photography

Standards

• National Council of Teachers of English 1, 2, 3, 4, 5
• ISTE NETS for Students 1, 2 3, 4, 5, 6

Materials

You will need a digital camera to take pictures, a computer, a printer, and a word processing application such as *Microsoft Word*.

Procedures

1. Give your class a vocabulary list.
2. Divide the class into small groups.
3. Tell the class to use their digital cameras to illustrate each word on the vocabulary list by taking pictures with their digital cameras.
4. When students find a word they cannot illustrate, tell them to use the word's first letter.
5. After the students have taken pictures, have them put them in a word processing document and label each picture.
6. Have the students print the vocabulary words and pictures.
7. Place the resulting projects on the bulletin board.
8. When all groups are finished, talk about how effective the groups were in matching the pictures with the words.

Variation

Younger students could illustrate the letters of the alphabet by taking pictures. For example, for the letter "a" they could take a picture of an apple.

III. HISTORICAL PODCAST

Subject: Social Studies

Grade(s): 4–12

Objective: Create a Podcast about a famous historical figure.

Standards

- National Council for Social Studies, II, VI, X
- National Council of Teachers of English 1, 2, 3, 4, 5
- ISTE NETS for Students 1, 2, 3, 4, 5, 6

Materials

You will need a computer, microphone, and audio editing software such as *Audacity*, *Bias Peak LE*, or *GarageBand*.

Procedures

1. Use Table 10.2 to give students an introduction to Podcasting.
2. Have the students examine good Podcasts such as *Meet the Press* or (http://www .msnbc.msn.com/id/3032608/) or *Washington Week* (http://www.pbs.org/weta/ washingtonweek/rss/index.html).
3. Divide the class into small groups.
4. Have each group pick an important historical figure for their Podcast.
5. Using the Internet, have each group research their topic.
6. Students should brainstorm and come up with unique ways of handling Podcasts. For example, they could add introductory music and pictures.
7. Students should create an outline before they begin recording and write out a script.
8. Have the students record their Podcasts and share them with their classmates.

Variation

Students can work independently and post their projects on the Web or e-mail them to different people.

IV. MUSIC PODCAST

Subject: Music

Grade(s): 4–12

Objective: Create a Podcast about a famous composer.

Standards
- National Council of Teachers of English 1, 2, 3, 4, 5
- ISTE NETS for Students 1, 2, 3, 4, 5, 6

Materials

You will need a computer, microphone, and audio editing software such as *Audacity*, *Bias Peak LE*, or *GarageBand*.

Procedures

1. Use Table 10.2 to give students an introduction to Podcasting.
2. Divide the class into small groups.
3. Have each group pick an important composer for their Podcast.
4. Using the Internet, have each group research their topic and download some of their chosen composer's music. (You must be careful of copyright laws.)
5. Students should use samples of this music by using an editing program.
6. Students should brainstorm and create an outline before they begin recording and write out a script.
7. Have the students record their Podcasts and share them with their classmates.

Variation

Students can work independently and post their projects on the Web or e-mail them to friends.

V. MY BLOG

Subject: Language Arts and Science

Grade(s): 4–12

Objective: Create a blog on a scientific topic.

Standards
- National Science Education Standards, F1
- National Council of Teachers of English 1, 2, 3, 4, 5
- ISTE NETS for Students 1, 2, 3, 4, 5, 6

Materials

You will need access to the Internet.

Procedures

1. Have the students sign up with a blog host. This host will give them a Web address, ready-made templates, and tools for updating their blog.
2. Have the students look for sample blogs. Have them type the word *blog* followed by a few search terms into Google.

3. Have each student decide on a scientific experiment they want to do in class or at home. For example, they may want to see the effect of Coke on a penny, the life cycle of a butterfly, or grow plants in different types of environments.

4. Have the students do their experiment.

5. They should observe the results of their experiment everyday. They should then blog observations daily.

6. The class should then share their blogs and discuss them in class.

Variation

Students can work in groups. High school students will have more difficult topics and will use a science laboratory.

SUMMARY

We explored digital photography and how easy it is to integrate this technology into the classroom. We saw the advantages of seeing your picture right away, deleting pictures you do not like, and not having to deal with film. We examined disadvantages such as loss of shadow and expense. We found out how to choose the right digital camera. In addition, we also looked at emerging technology such as blogs, Podcasting, Wikis, collaborative editing, social networking, and social bookmarking.

STUDY AND ONLINE RESOURCES

CHAPTER 10 ONLINE RESOURCES

 In the **student section** of the book's online site at **http://www.wiley.com/college/sharp**, you will find templates and examples, video tutorials, PDF, Podcasts, checklists, articles, Web sites, software reviews, and chapter quizzes. Access these resources to learn about technology and integrating it into the classroom. Watch the video tutorials online at **http://www.wiley.com/college/sharp** to learn how to create a Podcast.

CHAPTER MASTERY TEST

Lets check for chapter comprehension with a short mastery test. Key terms, Computer Lab, and Suggested Readings and References follow the test.

1. What is digital photography?

2. What are the advantages of a digital camera over a film camera?

3. Examine some ways in which you can integrate digital photography into the classroom.

4. When purchasing a digital camera for your school, discuss what three factors to consider before making your purchase.

5. Explain how you can use a blog as a motivating activity.

6. What is Podcasting? Give two examples of how it can be an important tool for classroom learning.

7. What are some preparatory steps you must take before recording a Podcast?

8. Define the terms blog, social networking, and social bookmarking.

9. What is collaborative editing and how is it being used in the schools?

10. What are some of the ways students can protect themselves from the problems associated with social networking?

11. Why would anyone want to use a Wiki? What is a major problem with this tool?

12. Give an example of how a blog and social networking can be used in a classroom setting.

KEY TERMS

Blog (Weblog) p. 204
**Collaborative
   editing** p. 208
Digital camera p. 195
Google Earth p. 209
Google jockeying p. 209

**Image
   stabilization** p. 201
**Liquid crystal
   display** p. 198
Mapping mashup p. 209
Megapixels p. 197

Memory cards p. 198
Podcast p. 205
Screencasting p. 209
**Social
   bookmarking** p. 209
Social networking p. 208

Sound editing p. 206
Virtual meetings p. 209
Wikis p. 207

 COMPUTER LAB: Activities for Mastery and Your Portfolio

10.1 Create a Classroom Yearbook. Have the students take pictures of each other and then write about each other.

10.2 Have the students edit a sound clip. They should delete unwanted sections, raise and decrease the sound clip's volume, and add another sound to it.

10.3 Create a Blog. Have students keep track of their daily activities by posting an article on their blog.

10.4 Create a Podcast. Create a Podcast for the classroom. Watch the Video tutorial online and learn how to do a Podcast.

10.5 Compare and contrast three digital cameras.

10.6 Prepare a report comparing three sound editing programs and their strengths and weaknesses.

10.7 Use the checklist in the chapter to choose a digital camera. Justify the choice.

10.8 Produce an outline for a Podcast that you might want to create.

10.9 Prepare a report on Wikis, giving examples and evaluating them.

10.10 Use a photo editing program, such as *Photoshop Elements*, to edit a sample file of pictures located online at www.wiley.com/college/sharp.

SUGGESTED READINGS AND REFERENCES

Abrams, Arnie. *Learn Digital Photography in a Day*. Eugene, Ore.: Visions Technology in Education, 2006.

Baker, Michael, and Chuck Favata. "Do Social Networking Applications Have a Place in the Classroom?" *Learning & Leading with Technology* 34, no. 4 (December/January 2006–07): 8–17.

Blogs and Education. http://www.techlearning.com/story/showArticle.php?articleID=18400984

Boss, Suzie, and Jane Krauss. "Power of the Mashup." *Learning & Leading with Technology* 35, no. 1 (August 2007): 12–17.

Branzburg, Jeffrey. "How to Make Your Voice Heard!" *Technology & Learning* 27, no. 3 (October 2006): 32–34.

Bull, Glen, Gina Bull, and Sara Kajder. "Writing with Weblogs (Reinventing Student Journals)." *Learning & Leading with Technology* 31, no. 1 (September 2003): 32–35.

Bull, Glen, and Lynn Bell. *Teaching with Digital Images*. Eugene, Ore.: ISTE Publications, 2005.

Farivar, Cyrus. "Create a Video Podcast." *MacWorld* (April 2006): 78–79.

Freedman, A. *The Computer Desktop Encyclopedia*. New York: American Management Association, 2008, http://www.computerlanguage.com/techweb.html.

Honan, Mathew. The Podcast Listener's Guide. *Macworld* 24, issue 2 (February 2007): 82–83.

Janowski, Davis D. "A Truly Social Bookmarking Site." *MacWorld* (May 9): 2007 42.

Kelby, Scott. *The Digital Photography Book*. Berkeley, Calif.: PeachPit, Press 2006.

Kelby, Scott The Digital Photography Book Volume 2, Peach Pit, 2008.

Levy, Steven. "Facebook Grows Up." *Newsweek* (August 27, 2007): 41–46.

McLeod, Scott. "Professors Who Blog. *Technology & Learning* 27, no. 10 (May 2007): 50.

McLester, Susan. "Technology Literacy and the MySpace Generation." *Technology & Learning* 27, no. 8 (March 2007): 16–22.

Morgan, Russell. "Business Blogging." *PC Magazine* (March 6, 2007): 97.

National School Boards Association, http://www.nsba.org/site/docs/41400/41340.pdf, 2007.

O'Hanlon, Charlene. "If You Can't Beat'em Join'em." *T.H.E Journal* (August 2007): 39–44.

Photo Marketing Association, http://pmai.org/index.cfm/ci_id/1198/la_id/1.htm, 2007.

Salpeter, J. (2005). "Telling Tales with Technology." *Technology & Learning* 25, no. 7, p. 18, 20, 22, 24. http://www.techlearning.com/shared/printableArticle.jhtml?articleID=60300276

Schmit, Dan. "KidCast Podcasting in the Classroom." Bloomington, Ill.: FTC Publishing, 2006.

Tait, Matthew. "Be Your Own Broadcaster." *PC Magazine* (August 22, 2006): 87–88.

Trinkle, Catherine. Wikis Are for You! *School Library Media Activities Monthly* 23, issue 6 (February 2007): 31–32.

Troutner, Joanne. "Best Sites for Educational Podcasts." *Teacher Librarian* 34, issue 3 (February 2007): 43–44.

Villano, Matt. "Social Revolution." *Campus Technology* (January 2007): 40–45.

Yang, Jonathan. *The Rough Guide to Blogging.* New York: Penguin Books, 2006.

"Your Next Digital Camera." *Consumer Reports* (July, 27, 2007): 26–39.

Williams, Robin, and John Tollett. *Podcasting and Blogging with GarageBand and iWeb.* Berkeley, Calif.: PeachPit Press, 2007.

Multimedia and Video Technology

Integrating Multimedia and Video Technology into the Classroom

Students learn more when they are involved in the learning process. This involvement increases as more of the senses are used in acquiring information. Multimedia provides an interactive, multisensory learning experience, which motivates the learner and improves the quality of learning. This chapter provides suggestions on how to integrate movies into your multimedia presentations. In addition, we cover other Web 2.0 emerging technologies such as video blogs, YouTube, Second Life, and digital storytelling.

Using the computer, students and teachers can do the following:

students can

- create a video blog,
- make a movie,
- join and use Second Life,
- create a digital story, and
- write biographies of famous leaders and show them on the Internet.

teachers can

- post a video blog online,
- make a movie about Van Gogh,
- present lectures, online,
- prepare a Web page tutorial, and
- create a presentation on the human body using a presentation program.

objectives

Upon completing this chapter, you will be able to do the following:

1 Define multimedia.

2 Identify several major contributors to the field of hypermedia.

3 Discuss some of the issues surrounding hypermedia.

4 Describe the basic features of a video camera.

5 Discuss the video camera and how it can be used to create multimedia presentations.

6 Be familiar with emerging technology such as video blogs, YouTube, Second Life, and digital storytelling.

7 Describe QuickTime, morphing, warping, and virtual reality.

What is Multimedia?

We are bombarded with the term "multimedia" everywhere we travel: on television, at the shopping mall, in newspapers, and in educational circles. What does this ubiquitous and elusive term really imply? Is it just a catchword tossed about, or does it have a specific meaning? In general and in this textbook, multimedia refers to communication of more than one media type, such as that involving text, audio, graphics, animation, and full-motion video.

Multimedia is not a new concept. For years, teachers have made presentations using different kinds of media. Traditionally, they have used slides, movies, cassette players, and overhead projectors to enrich lessons. Now, however, teachers may employ personal computer and hard disk storage to combine these different media sources in their teaching. Computers offer input and output devices, such as CD-ROM, DVD-ROM, and stereo sound.

Historical Perspective

In the professional literature, words closely related to multimedia are *hypertext* and *hypermedia*. Hypertext originated more than 50 years ago. Vannevar Bush, an electrical engineer and Franklin Delano Roosevelt's first director of the Office of Scientific Research and Development, is given credit for first proposing the idea of a hypothetical machine, predating computers, that would mimic the mind's associative process. In 1945, Bush described a workstation called a memex that imitated the linking and retrieval functions of the human mind. Influenced by Bush's associative linking and browsing concepts, Douglas Engelbard conducted research at the Stanford Research Institute in 1960 that led to several significant inventions, including the mouse, and the concept of a "viewing filter" (Fiderio, 1988).

These developments were important, but it was Ted Nelson who took the critical step in the development of multimedia. Around 1965, he coined the term "hypertext," meaning nonsequential writing, and he developed the writing environment called Xanadu that enables a user to create electronic documents and interconnect them with other text information.

Hypertext and Hypermedia

In hypertext, text, images, sound, and actions are linked together in nonsequential associations so the user can browse through related topics in any order. At the center of this system is linking. No document or bit of information exists alone; each document contains links to other related documents (Figure 11.1).

An example of hypertext is a computer glossary from which a user can select a word and retrieve its definition. This definition is linked to other words, and the user can move from it to other, related terms.

Hypermedia is nearly synonymous with hypertext; it emphasizes the nontextual components of hypertext. Hypermedia uses the computer to input, manipulate, and output graphics, sound, text, and video as part of a system. The different forms of information are linked together so that the user can move from one to another. When a teacher uses hypermedia, the computer directs the action of devices such as a video camera, digital camera, videodisc player, CD-ROM or DVD-ROM player, tape recorder, VCR, scanner, or musical keyboard. Figure 11.2 shows an example of a typical hypermedia workstation.

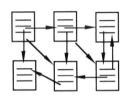

Figure 11.1
The Nonlinearity of Hypertext

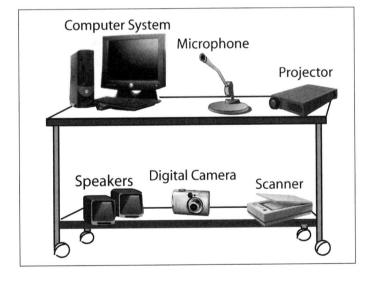

Figure 11.2
Using Technologies in the Classroom—Hypermedia Workstation
(*Source:* Computer Courtesy Dell. All other © 2008 Jupiterimages, Inc.)

A computer and a monitor are the basic equipment necessary for a hypermedia presentation, with the computer acting as a controller and the monitor displaying images. Depending on the sophistication of their equipment, teachers can add a variety of devices and software programs to enhance hypermedia creation.

For example, they can use the digital camera to take pictures and the video camera to film a scene while the DVD records a television program. The scanner adds graphics or text and the projector displays the results on a screen.

FlexCam-iCam
(*Source:* Courtesy Ken-A-Vision)

Students creating presentations for biology can use a FlexCam-iCam (SEO Enterprises) camera to project images from a microscope to a television or computer.

Teachers can also use programs such as *CorelDraw*, *Frames* (Tech4Learning), or *Kid Pix Deluxe 3X* (MacKieve) to enhance artwork; a musical keyboard to provide customized musical accompaniment; and a laser printer to produce high-quality images. Hypermedia components range from sound-enhanced documents that will play on any computer to PowerPoint presentations that include sound, animation, and color.

Hypermedia Authoring Tools

Hypermedia authoring tools prepare students for the information-intensive society of the future in which hypermedia publishing may eliminate publishing as we know it.

HYPERCARD AND HYPERSTUDIO

In 1987 Bill Atkinson at Apple Computer created *HyperCard*, one of the first implementations of hypermedia. *HyperCard* (Figure 11.3) was an authoring tool that enables users to organize information, browse through it, and retrieve it. Information was stored in the form of onscreen cards (rectangular boxes on the screen) that contained text, graphics, sound, and animation. These cards also included buttons with which the user could navigate through the cards and perform actions such as playing video and accessing Web sites.

Figure 11.3
HyperCard Elements
(*Source:* Screenshot reprinted with permission from Apple, Inc.)

Many other authoring tools followed. However, it wasn't until Roger Wagner produced *HyperStudio* for the Apple IIGS that hypermedia took a giant leap forward. *HyperStudio*, like *HyperCard*, displayed its information in the form of cards. It was simple to use and did not require programming. *HyperStudio* was very popular for years but almost vanished from sight when it was sold. Currently Roger Wagner, the original creator of *HyperStudio* and Software MacKiev, an education software publisher, have a new version of *HyperStudio* called *HyperStudio 5* for Macintosh and Windows users (Figure 11.4). This program adds more than 200 new features such as Podcasting support and advanced graphics effects.

POWERPOINT

PowerPoint (Microsoft), a presentation tool for all age levels, enables users to turn ideas into powerful presentations. *PowerPoint*, unlike *HyperStudio*, displays its information in the form of slides in that contain text, graphics, sound, and animation. By examining two *PowerPoint* (Microsoft) slides in Figures 11.5–11.6 closely, you will gain an understanding of what is involved in working with this presentation tool.

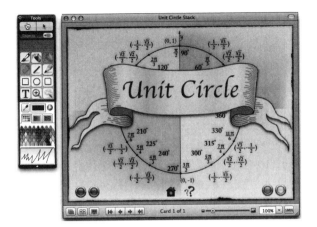

Figure 11.4
HyperStudio ® 5
(*Source:* Courtesy Software MacKiev)

Slide 1 (Figure 11.5) is the title screen with text, sound, two spirals that play video movies, and a button. The text, spirals, and button are all animated, appearing on screen one by one. When the button in the bottom right corner is pressed, the next slide is shown.

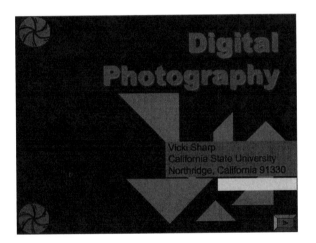

Figure 11.5
PowerPoint Slide 1
(*Source:* Courtesy Visions Technology in Education)

Slide 2 (Figure 11.6) shows the major factors to consider when buying a digital camera. The slide contains text, bullets, sound, and animation. When the slide comes on the screen, a voice reads the text. Each bullet point is made with the teacher's mouse click. The left arrow button takes users back to Slide 1, and the right arrow button plays a sound clip and then takes users to Slide 3.

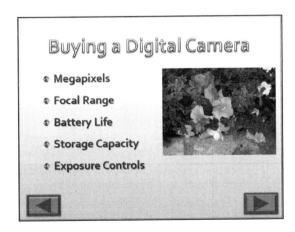

Figure 11.6
PowerPoint Slide 2
(*Source:* Courtesy Visions Technology in Education)

As you can see, PowerPoint is a versatile product, and the kinds of slide shows a teacher and student can create are endless. From this example, you can envision the amount of time, effort, and creativity involved in creating a presentation.

KEYNOTE

Keynote, released in 2003, is an easy-to-use presentation program for Apple computers. Using this program you can create compelling presentations, with charts and tables (Figure 11.7). The program features layered graphical elements and fantastic transitions. *Keynote* supports most file types and comes with professionally designed images and themes.

Figure 11.7
Keynote Pie Chart
(*Source:* Screenshot Reprinted with permission from Apple, Inc.)

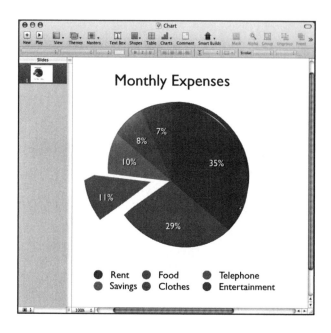

Finally, *Google Presentations*, included in Google "Docs," is a free presentation program that lets users collaborate on presentations and share them in real time. In addition to these programs, are many others including *Create Together* (Bytes of Learning), *EZedia MX* (eZedia), *Kid Pix Deluxe 3X* (MacKiev), and *Media Blender, VideoBlender,* and *Pixie* (Tech4Learning).

For a listing of recommended multimedia software, visit our online site at http://www.wiley.com/college/sharp. The Podcast folder contains a Podcast by Melinda Kolk, the co-owner of Tech4Learning (http://www.tech4learning.com/). Also in the folder is a trial version of Pixie. Tech4Learning, Inc. (phone 877-834-5453) is an educational technology company that has creativity products for K-12 education.

Classroom Suggestions for Using Hypermedia

Students and teachers have a rich selection of software and hardware to choose from when developing first-class hypermedia presentations. Students can write and illustrate stories that combine text with graphics. They can create their own book reports, interactive wildlife books, research presentations, tours, historical portraits, travelogues, animal reports, world events chronologies, and even school yearbooks (Figure 11.8). Students can create science presentations on a variety of different topics including chemistry, plants, animals, and rockets. In the process of developing these presentations, students could learn to use the program's drawing tools to create illustrations. With a program such as *PowerPoint* or *Keynote,* students can even create organizational charts and *Jeopardy*[TM]-like games.

Figure 11.8
Yearbook
(*Source:* Courtesy Visions Technology
in Education)

Teachers can generate slide shows on a range of topics from Beethoven to cell mitosis—all accompanied by music, sound effects, and digitized human voices. Using video cameras, teachers can prepare interesting film clips of field trips or school events. A presentation can be combined with computer graphics, photographs, animation, sound, and music.

A teacher could create a slide show to enable students to browse through the permanent collection of the National Gallery of Art in Washington, D.C. He or she could import color images of the different works of art from the gallery onto the slides and record a narration about each painting. Students in his or her class could move through the gallery at their leisure, clicking buttons to move on to new paintings or to return to ones they had already seen. A teacher might create a presentation that teaches a foreign language or a training module (Figure 11.9) on how to use a digital camera. A teacher may even want to create a digital photo album for an open house. For such an onscreen presentation, each student's photo would appear with music, text, and dazzling effects.

Figure 11.9
PowerPoint Training Module
(*Source:* Courtesy Visions Technology
in Education)

Guidelines for Creating a Multimedia Presentation

To plan a good presentation or multimedia stack, it is useful to follow these guidelines:

1. Consider your teaching objectives. What should users learn? What will they do?

2. Plan ahead. Do a sketch or rough layout of the slides or cards in your stack. Review what is to be communicated. Who is the audience? What approach will best express your message? You should be willing to experiment and be flexible.

3. Look for consistency on each card or slide and check for balance of design. Add interest when it is feasible and organize a card or slide around a dominant visual image.

4. Look at the format of your cards or slides. Pay close attention to borders and margins. Provide a dramatic graphic for the title card.

5. Add emphasis to the work. For example, use a large font size to call attention to important ideas. When needed, vary the type style by using boldface or italics. Use blank spaces to make designs stand out. Highlight the objects on the page with artwork, but do not overdo it. Help the reader's eyes focus on a particular part of a card or slide.

6. Do not use too many fonts because that detracts from the general message a card is communicating.

7. Use color wisely. Avoid clashing colors; work with complementary ones instead.

8. If you are only working in black and white, try to avoid too much white space. If this is unavoidable, surround the area with gray or black space.

9. Check your work thoroughly before showing or printing out copies of your work. Use the Computer Multimedia Checklist form to help you evaluate your multimedia projects.

10. Do not put too much on your slides; they will then look crowded and distracting.

11. Have students or other intended audience members preview your work. Watch their reactions. Do they learn what you intended? Are they able to navigate your stack successfully? (See Comedian Don McMillan's Video, "How Not to Use PowerPoint" at http://www.youtube.com/watch?v=HLpjrHzgSRM.) What follows is a Computer Multimedia Project Checklist.

Computer Multimedia Project Checklist

Directions: Examine the following items and determine which ones you feel are important for your class situation. Place an X on each line for which the project meets the criteria.

Title _____ **Date** _____ **Subject Area** _____

Grade Level _____ **Length** _____ **Audience** _____

Objectives_____ **Prior Knowledge** _____

Contents

___ 1. Is current

___ 2. Is accurate

___ 3. Is clear and concise

___ 4. Matches curriculum

___ 5. Has no bias or objectionable language

___ 6. Has clear directions

___ 7. Contents include graphics, text, sound, and visuals

Graphics, Sound, and Visuals

___ 1. Each slide has text and graphics appropriate to the content.

___ 2. Buttons on each card work appropriately.

___ 3. Graphics and sounds are not distracting

___ 4. Screens are neither cluttered nor barren.

___ 5. Special effects are used appropriately.

___ 6. Buttons and sounds associated with buttons are appropriate.

Fonts

___ 1. There are not too many fonts or type sizes.

___ 2. Font shadowing and outlining are not overdone.

___ 3. Type is large enough for reading when projected.

Rating Scale

Rate the multimedia presentation by placing a check on the appropriate line.

Excellent _____ Very good _____ Good _____ Fair _____ Poor _____

Comments:

Multimedia Software

As evidenced by the software catalogs, almost every software program incorporates some form of multimedia. In fact, just about every program mentioned in this book has some multimedia elements. Let's examine two of these programs to discover what makes them particularly useful in a classroom setting.

INSPIRATION

Multimedia visual mapping programs such as *Inspiration* for students in grades 5 and up and *Kidspiration* (Inspiration Software) for students in grades K–5 are perfect for planning a multimedia presentation, creating stories, organizing information, developing understanding of concepts, and expressing and sharing ideas. Figure 11.10 is a book analysis of *The Outsiders* by S. E. Hinton created with *Inspiration*. Through the the process of creating this diagram, the student gathers all the information needed to write an in-depth book report. At the same time the student is creating this visual map, he or she is simultaneously creating an outline, which will aid in the writing process. This outline can be transferred to *Microsoft Word* or *AppleWorks*. Using this program across curriculum lines, students can brainstorm, create concept maps, make graphic organizers, design storyboards, generate cause-and-effect diagrams, and prepare outlines.

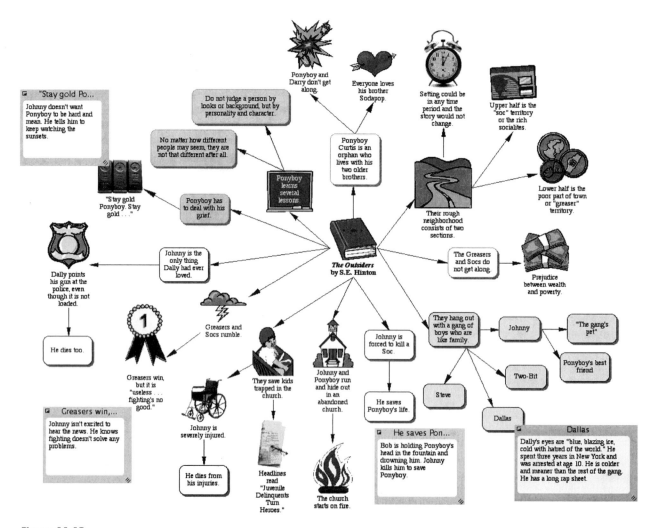

Figure 11.10
Inspiration Book Analysis of *The Outsiders*
(*Source:* Diagram created in Inspiration® by Inspiration Software®, Inc.)

Kidspiration (Inspiration Software), used for grades K–5, lets students combine pictures, text, and spoken words into a document. When this is occurring they are developing language skills and organizing their writing for reports.

SQUIBS

Squibs science DVDs (Ignite! Learning) (http://www.squibs.com/) are a collection of animated videos for younger students to learn life, physical science, and earth concepts. Nine discs range from looking inside cells to atom, elements, and chemistry. The discs contain 3- to 4-minute video clips, or Squibs, that enrich the science curriculum. What makes these discs (Figure 11.11) unique is they are full of humor, music, and motivate students to learn difficult concepts.

Figure 11.11
Squibs
(*Source:* Copyright 2005, Property of Ignite! Learning)

You can see that current educational programs have come a very long way from the static drill-and-practice texts of the 1970s. These new programs push technology to new heights with their multimedia features and their lifelike animations.

Video Cameras in the Classroom

Because of the sophistication of these multimedia software programs, we are now seeing students and teachers using digital cameras (Chapter 10) as well as video cameras in the classroom. They are inserting photographs as well as video clips in their presentations. Using a video camera, students and teachers can gain practice in writing movie scripts, creating their own personal movies, editing these movies, and showing them in class.

WHAT IS A VIDEO CAMERA?

A video camera is "a camera that takes continuous pictures and generates a signal for display or recording" (Freedman, 2008). Video cameras were originally destined for television work and they required the use of two pieces of equipment: a video camera and a VCR. These cameras were very large and bulky and used primarily in the television industry. As technology improved, video cameras became smaller and more portable. In 1983 Sony released the first video camcorder (CAMera reCORDER) a combination videocassette recorder and video camera. Shortly afterward, JVC (Figure 11.12) released a camera using VHS-C format tape. Even

Figure 11.12
JVC's First VHS-C Camcorder
(*Source:* Courtesy JVC Company of
America)

though these cameras were expensive, they were useful for capturing birthdays and anniversaries. In the last 20 years video camera technology has become more miniaturized and much easier to use in the classroom.

DIGITAL VIDEO CAMERA TECHNOLOGY

Using a digital video camera and a computer, you can transform your classroom into a movie studio, producing educational movies that have transitions, background music, narrations, scrolling titles, and more. The way a digital video camera works (Figure 11.13) is similar to the digital camera (Chapter 10).

Figure 11.13
Digital Video
Process

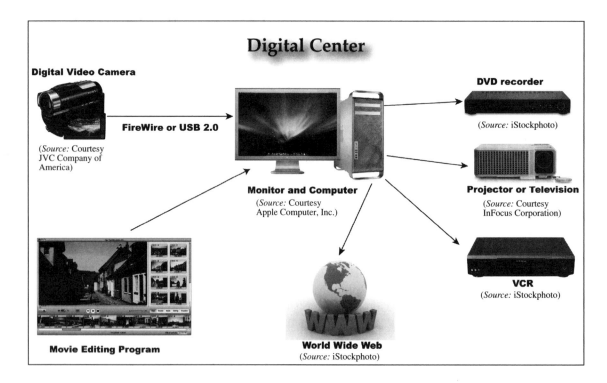

1. You use the video camera to capture the images then transfer these images to the computer connected by a USB cable, a FireWire connection, or a card reader.

2. Once on the computer's hard drive, you can use movie-editing software such as *Movie Maker* (Microsoft) to edit the video.

3. You can then preview these video clips on a projector or television.

4. Finally, you save the results to the media of your choice, for example, a VHS tape or DVD-R to be played later and send the video to a friend by email or post it on your Web Page.

How to Choose a Video Camera

Like the still camera the video camera should have a quality lens. A video camera needs image stabilization, preferably an optical stabilizer, to control for camera shake (see Chapter 10).

In a classroom the feel of the camera is very important. Features become unimportant if your camera is hard to hold. The camera should not be heavy, the controls should be accessible, and it should be easy for the student to use. Cost is an important factor and because of the changing nature of the video camera it is unwise to spend too much money.

Format is a major concern. What type of tape or disc does the camera use to record? Does the camera record in analog or digital? Analog formats are quickly disappearing and will eventually only be for history buffs. These formats include VHS, VH-C, Super-VHS-C, and Hi8. They are cheaper cameras but the video quality is not as good as the digital formats. A few of the more popular digital formats are listed in Table 11.1.

Table 11.1   Digital Formats

Format	Description
MiniDV	Uses small cassettes about the size of the 2007 iPod shuffle, excellent images, and has a shorter recording time than other formats.
MicroMV	Uses smaller tapes than MiniDVs and are manufactured by Sony; not compatible with many video-editing programs.
Digital8	Uses Hi8 tape or 8mm tape and has shorter recording time than most formats.
DVD-RAM	Records on a 3-inch disc in MPEG-2 format. This type of camera has problems playing on most DVD players.
DVD-R/DVD+R	Records in MPEG-2 format; discs can be played on most DVD players. You can record on this media once so it is better to buy an erasable disc such as DVD-RW or DVD+RW/.
Hard Drive	Uses its internal hard drive to store video. Can record a long time, about 14 hours, but once you fill the hard drive you have to find a computer to transfer information.
Hybrid Drive	Uses hard drive and DVD or hard drive and SD (Secure Digital) card.

The CCD (charged coupled device) converts light into electrical signals similar to film. A CCD that has a higher resolution is capable of capturing more graphic detail and a sharper recording. If you can afford it you should choose a model that has three separate coupled devices (3CCD).

Also look at optical zoom, which offers the best quality. Remember digital zoom enlarges the picture and lessens quality. Look at your camera's outputs. All cameras have the standard video outputs that connect to a TV or VCR. However, camcorders vary in their connections to the PC. It is better to have a camera with a FireWire connection because its speed and quality is better. Having a remote helps you operate the camcorder from a distance—allowing you to be in your picture. Having a LCD that is integrated into the system lets you have instant playback. You can then use onscreen menus to change options. Find out how good the camcorder shoots in low light or darkness. Some models record in high definition; they have outstanding detail and quality, but are expensive.

The majority of digital cameras capture movies as well as still images. In most cases the quality of the still picture is not that good, but you don't have to take two cameras with you. Many cameras come with basic editing for sequencing the soundtrack and film and dubbing. Finally, you should have a viewfinder. Most inexpensive models have a black-and-white viewfinder. The more expensive models have color options. As you learned in Chapter 10 the viewfinder saves on battery usage and you do not have to use your LCD screen as much. What follows is a checklist for video cameras.

Digital Video Camera Checklist

Directions: Examine the following items and determine which ones you feel are important for your class situation. Place an X on each line for which the camera meets your needs.

Camera Model _____ **Manufacturer** _____ **Store** _____

Camera Format
___ 1. MiniDV
___ 2. Digital8
___ 3. DVD-R/DVD+R
___ 4. Hard drive
___ 5. Hybrid drive
___ 6. MicroMV
___ 7. Digital8
___ 8. Other

Features
___ 1. CCD resolution_____
___ 2. Optical zoom
___ 3. Digital zoom
___ 4. Lens quality
___ 5. Battery type_____
___ 6. Battery life (minutes)_____
___ 7. Included software_____
___ 8. Still mode
___ 9. Remote
___ 10. Liquid crystal display (LCD)
    ___ a. Size
    ___ b. Pixels_____
___ 11. Focusing range_____

___ 12. Output
    ___ a. FireWire
    ___ b. USB
    ___ c. Other
___ 13. Fully automatic
___ 14. Manual controls
___ 15. Shutter speed_____
___ 16. Viewfinder_____
___ 17. Weight_____
___ 18. Camera feel_____
___ 19. Image stabilizer_____
___ 20. Shutter lag_____

Ease of Use
___ 1. Help screens
___ 2. Online tutorial

Support Features
___ 1. Technical support
___ 2. Tutorial material
___ 3. Readable manual

Consumer Value
___ 1. Cost
___ 2. Free technical support
___ 3. Guarantees

Rating Scale

Rate the video camera by placing a check on the appropriate line.

Excellent _____ Very good _____ Good _____ Fair _____ Poor _____

Comments:

Video Editing Technology

Video editing involves integrating multimedia elements such as text, video, and audio into a presentation and then changing these elements to improve the presentation. Video editing includes cutting out unnecessary parts of an audio or video, recording dialogue, adding video and audio transitions such as fades, and creating a more finished product. *Adobe Premiere* is a full-featured video-editing package that is daunting for the beginner. Apple's *iMovie '08* and *Unlead Video Studio* (Corel) are easy-to-use video-editing programs that are more appropriate for the classroom. Apple's *iMovie '08* (Figure 11.14) is a relatively simple-to-use digital video-editing software program that works on Macintosh computers. *iMovie '08* uses a storyboard interface where the user orders and reorders video clips by dragging and dropping. This program easily shares videos to YouTube, a Web page, iTunes, iPod, .Mac-Web-Gallery, and iPhone. Ulead's *Video Studio 11*, a Windows program, uses a time-line interface where the student lays out video clips chronologically. This product has a movie wizard to simplify the process of editing.

Figure 11.14
iMovie '08
(*Source:* Screenshot reprinted with permission from Apple, Inc.)

Movies in the Classroom

Students and teachers are excited about writing scripts and working together to make movies in the classroom. Individuals with special needs enjoy making movies and it seems to boost self-esteem and allows them to be creative.

Teachers can bring their lessons to life by using teacher-created movies. They can create video tutorials to explain concepts. Teachers can make movies about fractions and create tutorials on algebra. They can also create a commentary on an important social issue.

Students can record trips to the zoo, the aquarium, and places like Washington, D.C., and Africa. They can do science experiments and record each stage of the experiment. Students can produce video reports to demonstrate concepts. After the students' movies are created, they can e-mail these movies or post them on the Web.

Feeding into this technology are many other multimedia technologies. YouTube has inspired everyone to want to publish these movies; video blogs and digital story-telling has kept this excitement alive.

YouTube

YouTube (www.youtube.com) is a popular video-sharing site that lets individuals post videos online. YouTube is a free site, but those that want to post video have to register online. The videos range from the very professional to the amateur. A recent nationally televised 2008 Presidential debate sponsored by CNN and YouTube had the candidates respond to questions from people appearing on home-made videos. These questions ranged from the war in Iraq to same-sex marriage (Barabak & Finnegan, 2007). If you look at YouTube's Science and Technology videos you will find some interesting examples, such as "Numb3rs Math for Beginners" and "The Math Education: An Inconvenient Truth." Two other examples of engaging YouTube videos are Sugar in a Soda Can http://www.youtube.com/watch?v=F10EyGwd57M) and Dr. Dennis Denenberg speaks about George Washington http://www.youtube.com/watch?v=7Nl7I9x6K7Q0).Use the site's search engine to find the videos you want.

YouTube is great practice for those who want to be directors of music videos or filmmakers. It is a perfect outlet for creative students to test skills and get feedback from other individuals. The content is not necessarily education oriented, but this site encourages students to experiment with creating content, viewing videos critically, and understanding subject matter.

A safer venue for K-12 teachers and students is TeacherTube (http://www.teachertube.com/). This online community covers the major curriculum areas featuring hundreds of free instructional videos designed for students to view in order to learn a concept or skill.

Video Blog

A video blog, referred to as a vlog, is a blog that contains video. These clips are produced using webcams or digital video cameras. Students or teachers can use inexpensive or free video-editing software to edit their projects. They can then transfer these clips, which are usually 1–3 minutes long, to a portable video player such as an iPod. This gives teachers the chance to record lectures and post them online for student viewing. Students can use their video segments in electronic portfolios, for personal expression, and for class presentations.

Digital Storytelling

Digital storytelling is a new technology that gives students the opportunity to be a famous director like Steven Spielberg. Students first write their own story. Next, they combine sound, images, audio, and video to create a short movie (usually 1–4 minutes long) that can be viewed on the Internet. These digital stories range from personal narratives to historical events. In the process of creating a digital story, the student develops skills in analyzing Internet content, doing research, and writing content for different audiences. In addition, they improve their communication skills and learn to use multimedia software. They also have the opportunity to publish their work on the Internet. Using digital storytelling, teachers can enhance their lessons or units and motivate students. Teachers can give students experience in researching different topics and expressing a point of view. For examples of some digital stories, check out the BBC site at http://www.bbc.co.uk/wales/digitalstorytelling. At this site people present digital stories around the United Kingdom that reflect their traditions and culture. The College of Education at the University of Houston has a wonderful site explaining digital storytelling and giving examples (http://www.coe.uh.edu/digital-storytelling/introduction.htm).

To create a digital story you need software to edit and manipulate images, a microphone, a recording device, a camera to take pictures or video. There are a variety of tools that support digital storytelling. The more advanced and expensive applications are *Macromedia Flash* and *Adobe Premiere*. The tools that are more commonly found in the classroom are shown in Table 11.2.

Table 11.2   Digital Storytelling Programs

Program	Description	Platform
Apple iLife	Create a story with pictures, audio, and video clips.	Apple only
Adobe PhotoShop Elements	Edit and modify images and text used in the digital story.	Apple/Windows
Microsoft Photo Story 3	Create digital stories using audio and pictures.	Windows only
Windows Movie Maker	Create digital stories from video clips and audio.	Windows only
Audacity (Free)	Record and edit digital audio.	Windows/Apple
GarageBand	Record and edit digital audio.	Apple only

Video and Sound Players

Apple was the first to integrate motion video into its operating system through *QuickTime*. (The Windows options are presently called Audio—Video Interleaved [AVI] and QuickTime for Windows.) *QuickTime* is a video and sound player used to display miniature motion picture sequences in a screen window. A *QuickTime* file can contain all kinds of digital media. Any application that is compatible with *QuickTime* can play video, sound, and animation within its program. *QuickTime* is also used on the

Web to provide Web pages with animation and video. *QuickTime* users also can create, edit, publish, and view multimedia content. With *QuickTime*, students and teachers can create and edit their own movies and incorporate them in *PowerPoint* or *Keynote* presentations. No special hardware is required to play *QuickTime* videos. The *QuickTime* movies that are viewed are usually in Moving Picture Experts Group (MPEG-3) file format. MPEG-3 is a compression technology that eliminates 50–95 percent of file size.

QuickTime VR, an extension of *QuickTime*, enables the user to view and create videos in 3-D space. Videos are created from renderings or multiple still shots taken from all sides. The images are then fastened together into one continuous file. Thus, viewers are able to see around an object in 360 degrees, with seamless pan-and-zoom abilities. In addition, viewers are able to interact with the videos. Students may be able to use *QuickTime VR* to create walk-through presentations of their schools or sites of interest.

Morphing and Warping Technology

Morphing programs animate a picture sequence by gradually blending one image into another. An example of morphing is the shape-shifting security guard in the movie *Star Trek: Deep Space Nine* or the evil terminator in *Terminator 2: Judgment Day*. I used *Morph*, a program by Gryphon, to morph a picture of my son, David, at 5 years old into a picture of him at 10 years old. This 5-second video clip shows his transformation over the 5-year period. Figure 11.15 shows four still pictures from

Figure 11.15
Morph 2.5 Gryphon Software
(*Source:* Author's Photo, Altered using Morph 2.5, Gryphon Software)

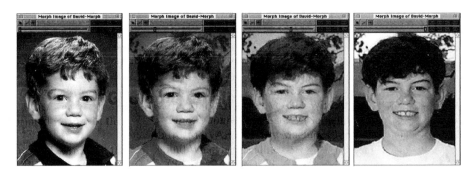

this transition. The morphing software accomplishes the smooth transformation by matching a series of central points set in the beginning image to points in the ending image. In my short film, I selected the nose in the first image as a central point to be matched to the location of the nose in the last image. I kept adding these central points until the important features such as the mouth, eyes, ears, and head shape were charted. When the points are established, the morphing software sends the dots that are charted in the beginning image to their final location in the ending image, blending their shapes and colors. The more points you add in morphing, the smoother the transition from one figure to the other.

Warping is a completely different type of special effect from morphing. In warping, the key points of one image are used to create an effect that does not involve the blending of two images. By adjusting these main points, you push the selected points of the original image into a different shape. The final image is stretched so as to look completely different from the original one. For example, a rounded human face could be stretched into a narrow face, with pointed jaw and bulging eyes. In the movie *The Mask*, warping was used to stretch Jim Carrey's face whenever he put on the mask. The Mona Lisa's face in Figure 11.16 is warped using *Kai's Power Goo* (Corel). With this program, the user can create liquid images and manipulate them by smearing, smudging, stretching, and fusing them.

You can superimpose these images and blend parts of one image with another to create a third image. As motivational devices, morphing and warping have some practical classroom applications.

Figure 11.16
Kai's Power Goo Warping
(*Source:* Author's Photo, altered using
Kai's Power Goo, Metacreations
Corporation)

Students can experiment with different images and then copy and paste them to illustrate a story or report. They can create a morphed movie or warped picture for a hypermedia presentation. For example, students might show cell division or plant growth by morphing different pictures together. They might morph pictures of their parents to create new offspring or pictures of themselves and their grandparents to see how they might age.

Virtual Reality

Virtual reality (VR) is a three-dimensional, interactive simulation. Participants in a computer-generated VR environment can manipulate what they see around them. In VR, users are electronically immersed in a simulated environment, in which they use their sight, hearing, and touch in all three dimensions to manipulate that environment. Participants wear headgear in which computer-generated images are sent to small screens placed before their eyes and to headphones in their ears. The headgear permits users to block out all actual stimuli to concentrate solely on the simulated stimuli. Participants also wear gloves or bodysuits equipped with sensors that communicate changes in body position to the computer, which then communicates the changes to the headgear (Figure 11.17).

Figure 11.17
Virtual Reality
(*Source:* Photo by Kathie Koenig-Simon
http://www.mel.nist.gov/galleryph/simvis/
pages/imersdsk.htm)

Imagine that you are entering a simulation of the Tate Gallery. You look into one of the exhibit rooms. All around you are paintings and sculptures. As you turn your head, the screens in your headgear adjust to show you what you would be seeing in the actual gallery. If you walk forward, the screens will change again to simulate your movement. As you approach the security guard to ask her a question, her voice becomes louder and louder in your headphones. When you raise your hand to point at one of the paintings, you see a simulated hand on your headgear screen. When you pick up one of the sculptures to examine it from different angles, the screen shows your hands and the different views of the sculpture, and your head-phones transmit the angry voice of the security guard.

Virtual reality has found its way into research labs, businesses, the dentist's office, the military, building design, and video arcade games. In some video games, you direct the action of the game with the movements of your own body, wearing headgear, gloves, and a bodysuit.

In education, virtual reality technology will enable students to interact more fully with information being presented in all subject areas. Students with physical disabilities could benefit from VR by immersing themselves in different environments in which they have full abilities. Students and teachers could conduct experiments and experience situations that otherwise might be too costly or dangerous. Imagine networking an educational virtual reality system worldwide in real time. It would be a wonderful way to foster positive interaction among people of different cultures. Consider the usefulness of a virtual reality tour of London. Or your students could don helmets and fly the first spaceship to the moon or enter the human bloodstream to look at the heart.

In a physical education class, students could use a simulation to practice pitching to an all-star batter. In a science class, they could explore the laws of physics in a virtual world by testing how changes in gravitational forces affect virtual objects. In a language arts class, students could visit a virtual Mark Twain who could talk to them about his books and even answer students' questions. A student violinist might even practice with the world's finest virtual orchestra and receive individualized tutoring. These are but a few of the options that will be available to educators in the near future. The biggest impediment to this advancement in technology is cost. Still, a future with virtual reality holds much promise for educators. Second Life is just the beginning of a movement to explore this virtual world.

SECOND LIFE

In 2003, Linden Labs developed a Web-based 3-D virtual world called Second Life. What was exciting about this site was that members (Figure 11.18) created the majority of *Second Life*'s content using animation, sound tools, and graphics.

Figure 11.18
Second Life Web Site
(*Source:* Second Life is a trademark of Linden Research, Inc. Certain materials have been reproduced with permission of Linden Research, Inc. Copyright © 2001–2008 Linden Research, Inc. All rights reserved)

This virtual world lets users develop personal figures called avatars (Figure 11.19) or alter egos that could talk, walk, fly, visit the library, ride in vehicles, and buy and sell virtual products for real money. Second Life even has it own currency called Linden dollars (L$) that could be exchanged for U.S. dollars.

Currently, universities and colleges purchase virtual islands in Second Life where they can restrict the users to their faculty and students. In this virtual world students interact with each other. Professors at major universities such as Harvard University, New York University, Vassar College, and Rice University use Second Life for lectures and online projects. Students from ages 13–17 use a teen Second Life version. Librarians are also active users of Second Life. The International Society for Technology in Education's (ISTE) Second Life site is a place where educators contact each other, learn about current educational practices, collaborate, and engage in online learning (http://www.iste.org/Content/NavigationMenu/ Membership/Member_Networking/ISTE_Second_Life.htm).

When students become comfortable using Second Life, they find it fun to interact with their fellow avatars as they learn. Because of this student interaction, they no longer feel as isolated as when they participate in regular online courses. Unfortunately, as with any open society, Second Life is prone to problems ranging from pornography to legal issues. Even if Second Life does not endure, there will certainly be other virtual world communities that will succeed.

Figure 11.19
Second Life Avatar
(*Source:* Second Life is a trademark of Linden Research, Inc. Certain materials have been reproduced with permission of Linden Research, Inc. Copyright © 2001–2008 Linden Research, Inc. All rights reserved)

SAMPLE CLASSROOM LESSON PLANS

I. ORGANIZING YOUR THOUGHTS

Subject: Language Arts

Grade(s): 2 and up

Objective
Students will learn how to map their lives visually using a software program such as *Kidspiration* or *Inspiration* (Figure 11.20).

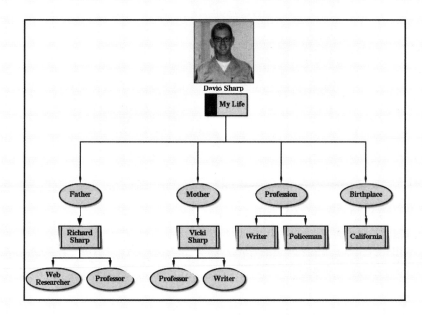

Figure 11.20
Inspiration Life Map
(*Source:* Diagram created in Inspiration(R) by Inspiration Software(R), Inc. Photo by Vicki Sharp.)

Standards
- NCTE English Language Arts Standards 1, 4, 5, 6, 12
- ISTE NETS for Students 1, 2, 3, 4, 5

Materials
You will need a program that does graphic organizing such as *Kidspiration* or *Inspiration* and one or more computers.

Procedures

1. Have the students write about themselves, their friends, their families, and their future goals.
2. Ask the students to take digital pictures of themselves and then use the scanner to scan pictures they already have, and bring in clip art for their autobiographies.
3. Have the students work in teams to experiment with *Kidspiration* or *Inspiration*.
4. Next, ask each student to use *Kidspiration* or *Inspiration* to create a visual map of his or her life.

Variation
Have the students write about what they will be doing 10 years from now. They can take digital pictures of themselves and change them to make themselves appear older.

II. ANIMAL RESEARCH

Subject: Science

Grade(s): 4 and up

Objectives
Students will learn how to work with a software program such as *HyperStudio*, *PowerPoint* (Figure 11.21), *MediaBlender* (Tech4Learning), *Keynote*, or *MP Express* and create a presentation in some subject area.

Figure 11.21
Evangelina A. Luna,
PowerPoint

Standards
- National Science Education Standards A1, A2, C1
- ISTE NETS for Students 1, 2, 3, 4, 5

Materials
You will need a multimedia program such as *HyperStudio*, *PowerPoint*, *MediaBlender*, or *Keynote*.

Procedures

1. Divide the students into small groups.
2. Have each group choose an animal to read about and research.

3. Ask the students to go on the Internet to find information about this animal. They can copy pictures of their animal and download sounds.

4. Have the students plan their stacks together.

5. Have the students in each group write a description of the animal and about where it lives, its enemies, its reproduction, its eating habits, and its prospect for survival in the future.

6. Finally, tell the students to create their slides or stacks and then have them share their presentations with the class.

III. TRAVELING TO ANOTHER COUNTRY

Subjects: Social Studies and Language Arts

Grade(s):   4 and up

Objective
Students will use a software program such as *HyperStudio*, *MediaBlender*, *PowerPoint*, *Keynote*, *MP Express*, or *Kid Pix Deluxe 3X* to create a presentation about a country they would like to visit.

Standards
• National Council for the Social Studies Curriculum Standards 1, 3
• NCTE English Language Arts Standards 1, 4, 5, 6, 8, 12
• ISTE NETS for Students 1, 2, 3, 4, 5, 6

Materials
You will need a multimedia program such as *HyperStudio*, *PowerPoint*, or *Keynote* and a word processing program such as *Microsoft Word* and access to the Internet.

Procedures

1. Divide the students into small groups.

2. Have each group choose a country it would like to visit.

3. Have the students work in groups to research this country, finding out about the country's climate, people, money, language, and famous sites. They can go on the Internet or use books from the library for their research.

4. After this task is completed, have students create an itinerary for their country.

5. Ask students to use the Internet to find out the cost of hotels and airline tickets.

6. Next, have students plan their slides together, collecting pictures of their country and downloading sounds and movies.

7. Have students use a multimedia software program such as *PowerPoint* to create their presentations.

8. When the presentations are finished, ask students to show their presentations to the class.

Variation
The students could use a word processing program such as *Microsoft Word* to produce brochures.

IV. MATH CONCEPTS

Subject: Math

Grade(s):   2–8

Objective

Students will use a software program such as *HyperStudio*, *PowerPoint*, *eZediaMX*, *MediaBlender*, or *Kid Pix Deluxe 3X* to create a presentation that illustrates mathematical terms such as fractions and percent.

Standards

- National Council of Teachers of Math 8, 9, 10
- ISTE NETS for Students 1, 2, 3, 4

Materials

You will need a multimedia program such as *HyperStudio*, *PowerPoint*, *MediaBlender*, or *Keynote*.

Procedures

1. Divide the students into small groups.
2. Have each group devise a definition for each mathematical term.
3. Ask students to plan their presentation together, collecting pictures and downloading sounds.
4. Have students use a multimedia software program such as *PowerPoint* to create their slides.
5. When the slides are finished, ask students to share their presentations with the class.

V. FAMOUS GENERALS

Subject: Social Studies

Grade(s): 4 and up

Objective

Students will use a software program such as *HyperStudio*, *PowerPoint*, *MediaBlender*, *eZediaMX*, *MP Express*, or *Kid Pix Deluxe 3X* to create slides about famous generals of the Civil War.

Standards

- National Council for the Social Studies Curriculum Standards 1, 2, 3
- ISTE NETS for Students 1, 2, 3, 4, 5

Materials

You will need a multimedia program such as *HyperStudio*, *PowerPoint*, or *Keynote* and a word processing program such as *Microsoft Word* and access to the Internet.

Procedures

1. Divide the students into small groups.
2. Have each group choose a general.
3. Have the students work in groups to research the general, finding out about his life. They can go on the Internet or use books from the library or a multimedia encyclopedia to do their research.
4. After this task is completed, have the students create an outline.
5. Next, ask students to plan their presentation together, collecting pictures and downloading sounds and movies.
6. Have students use a multimedia software program such as *eZediaMX* to create their presentations.
7. When the presentations are finished, ask students to present their work to the class.

SUMMARY

Hypermedia uses the computer to input, manipulate, and output graphics, sound, text, and audio in the presentation of information. In this chapter, we learned how hypermedia authoring tools such as *PowerPoint* and *Keynote* operate and how they may be used as tools for instruction. We examined two unique multimedia programs, special effects that are available for the classroom, and some suggested activities for multimedia software. We examined a checklist for evaluating a multimedia presentation, and considered some guidelines for creating a presentation. This chapter provided suggestions on how to use movies and other technologies such as video blogs, YouTube, Second Life, and digital storytelling.

STUDY AND ONLINE RESOURCES

CHAPTER 11 STUDY AND ONLINE RESOURCES

 In the **student section** of the book's online site at **http://www.wiley.com/college/sharp**, you will find templates and examples, video tutorials, PDFs, Podcasts, checklists, articles, Web sites, software reviews, and chapter quizzes. Watch video tutorials online at **http://www.wiley.com/college/sharp** and learn how to create a slide show, photo album, and Web page. Access these resources to learn about technology and integrating it into the classroom.

CHAPTER MASTERY TEST

Lets check for chapter comprehension with a short mastery test. Key Terms, Computer Lab, and Suggested Readings and References follow the test.

1. What is hypermedia?

2. What are two advantages of using your own authoring tool for a hypermedia presentation?

3. In preparing your multimedia presentation for class, name two mistakes that you want to avoid.

4. If you were to evaluate a multimedia presentation, what criteria would you use and why?

5. Define virtual reality and discuss some of its implications.

6. Explain how morphing and warping work.

7. When purchasing a video camera for your school, what factors should you consider before making the purchase?

8. Explain how digital storytelling can be used in the classroom.

9. YouTube was recently used in a presidential debate. What are some advantages and disadvantages of using this service in this manner?

10. Define the term video blog. Explain how this technology can be used in the classroom.

11. What is Second Life? How is it being used at the universities?

12. How would you use a video camera in your classroom?

KEY TERMS

COMPUTER LAB: Activities for Mastery and Your Portfolio

11.1 Make a photo album for the classroom. Watch the Video tutorial online and learn how to do create a photo album.

11.2 Using the checklist included in the text, evaluate a sample multimedia program or application for possible use in the classroom.

11.3 Learn a hypermedia application (such as PowerPoint or MediaBlender) and write a short report describing its strengths and weaknesses. Watch the video tutorial online and learn how to create a PowerPoint presentation.

11.4 Explain a mathematical concept by generating your own slide show, using software such as *Kid Pix Deluxe 3*.

11.5 Record an interview on some important topic. Write a script using the speaker's words and add your own synchronized sound effects. Using one of the hypermedia authoring tools, create a presentation from this interview.

11.6 Record an interesting event or trip with a video camera and combine this with animation, speech, and music, using one or more of the software programs discussed in this chapter.

SUGGESTED READINGS AND REFERENCES

Adam, Anna, and Helen Mowers. "YouTube Comes to the Classroom." *School Library Journal* 53, issue 1 (January 2007): 22.

Azevedo, Roger. "Using Hypermedia as a Metacognitive Tool for Enhancing Student Learning?: The Role of Self-Regulated Learning." *Educational Psychologist* 40, issue 4 (Fall 2005): 199–209.

Banaszewski, T. "Digital Storytelling Finds Its Place in the Classroom." *Multimedia Schools* 9, no. 1 (2002): 32–35, http://www.infotoday.com/MMSchools/jan02/banaszewski.htm.

Barabak, Mark Z., and Michael Finnegan. "YouTube Debate Brings Questioners into Picture." *Los Angels Times*, (January, 2007), p. A12.

Barrett, H. "Storytelling in Higher Education: A Theory of Reflection on Practice to Support Deep Learning." *Technology and Teacher Education Annual.* Charlottesville, VA: Association for the Advancement of Computing in Education, 2005, pp. 1878–1883.

Branzburg, Jeffrey. "Ready for Your Close Up." *Technology & Learning* 27, no. 6 (January 2007): 26–27, http://electronicportfolios.com/portfolios/Kean.pdf

Buckleitner, Warren. "Classrooms Without Walls." *Instructor* 110, no. 2 (September 2000): 91.

Bull, G., & S. Kajder. "Digital Storytelling in the Language Arts Classroom." Learning & *Leading with Technology* 32, no. 4 (2004): 46–49, http://cs2.cust.educ.ubc.ca/csed/400/csed_readings/display%2024.pdf.

Carr, Tracy, and Asha K. Jitendra. "Using Hypermedia and Multimedia to Promote Project-Based Learning of At-Risk High School Students." *Intervention in School and Clinic* 36, no. 1 (September 2000): 40.

Chen, S. "A Cogitive Model for Non-linear Learning in Hypermedia Programmes." *British Journal of Educational Technology*, 33, Issue 4 (September 2002): 449–460.

Dell, Kristina. "Second Life's Real-World Problems." *Time* (August 20, 2007): 49–50.

Fiderio, Janet. "Grand Vision." *Byte* 13, no. 10 (October 1, 1988): 237–242.

Foster, Andrea L. "Harvard to Offer Law Course in 'Virtual World'." *Chronicle of Higher Education* 53, issue 3 (September 8, 2006): 38.

Freedman, Alan. *Computer Desktop Encyclopedia.* Point Pleasant, Pa.: The Computer Language Company, 2008.

Gibson, William. *Neuromancer.* New York: Ace Books, 1984.

Green, Tim, and Abbie H. Brown. "Multimedia Projects in the Classroom: A Guide to Development and Evaluation." *MultiMedia Schools* 9, no. 4 (September 2002): 20–24.

Lagorio, Christine. "Pepperdine in a Treehouse." *New York Times* (January 7, 2007), Section 4A, p. 7.

Madian, Jon. "Multimedia—Why and Why Not?" *Leading and Learning* 22, no. 7 (2003): 16.

Marchionini, G. "Hypermedia and Learning: Freedom and Chaos." *Educational Technology* 28, no. 11 (1988): 8–12.

Mayer, Richard E. "Multimedia Aids to Problem-Solving Transfer." *International Journal of Educational Research* 31, no. 7 (1999): 611–623.

Miller, Joe. "Second Life: The Future of the OS." *InfoWorld* 29, issue 5 (January 29, 2007): 16.

Moreno, Roxana, and Richard E. Mayer. "Learning Science in Virtual Reality Multimedia Environments: Role of Methods and Media." *Journal of Educational Psychology* 94, no. 3 (September 2002): 598–610.

Oliver, Kevin, and Michael J. Hannafin. "Student Management of Web-Based Hypermedia Resources During Open-Ended Problem Solving." *Journal of Educational Research* 94, no. 2 (December 2000): 75–92.

Packer Randall, and Ken Jordan, editors. *Multimedia: From Wagner to Virtual Reality.* New York: Norton, 2001.

Papo, William. "Integration of Educational Media in Higher Education Large Classes." *Educational Media International* 38, issue 2/3 (June/September, 2001): 95–99.

Rapoza, Jim. "Will the Web 2.0 Bubble Burst?" *eWeek* 24, no. 26 (August 13, 2007): 54.

Rehbein, Lucio, Enrique Hinostroza, Miguel Ripoll, and IsabelAlister. "Students' Learning through Hypermedia." *Perceptual and Motor Skills* 95, issue 3 (December 2002): 795.

Roblyer, M.D., J. Edwards, and Mary Anne Havriluk. *Integrating Educational Technology into Teaching.* Upper Saddle River, NJ: Prentice Hall, 1997.

Shapiro, Amy M. "Promoting Active Learning: The Role of System Structure in Learning from Hypertext." *Human-Computer Interaction* 13, No. 1 (1998): 1–35.

Sharp, Vicki. *HyperStudio 3.2 in an Hour (Windows and Macintosh Version)*. Eugene, Ore.: ISTE, 1999.

Sharp, Vicki. *Make It with Inspiration*. Eugene, Ore.: Visions Technology in Education, 2006.

Sharp, Vicki. *Make It with Office, 97, 2000, XP, 2003, 2007 (Windows Version), 98, 2001, X, 2004 and 2008 (Macintosh Version)*. Eugene, Ore.: Visions Technology in Education, 2008.

Sharp, Vicki. *Make It with PowerPoint 2004 (Windows/Macintosh Version)*. Eugene, Ore.: Visions Technology in Education, 2004.

Song, Chiann-Ru. "Literature Review for Hypermedia Study from an Individual Learning Differences Perspective." *British Journal of Educational Technology* 33, issue 4 (September 2002): 435.

Wei-Fan Cheng, and Francis Dwyer. "Hypermedia Research: Present and Future." *International Journal of Instructional Media* 30, issue 2 (2003): 143–148.

Selecting Software and Integrating It into the Classroom

Integrating Software into the Classroom

Math software such as the classic *Quarter Mile* can help a student improve his or her computational skills. Students can use the computer as an instructional tool to aid them in learning math, language arts, and other curriculum areas. This chapter discusses computer-assisted instruction and computer-managed instruction. We examine criteria for selecting software for the classroom and learn different ways of using educational software in the school.

Furthermore, the chapter presents examples of lesson plans that can be used in a variety of situations. Online the reader will review Internet sites containing a rich assortment of lesson plan content, software reviews, shareware, educational resources, and links to software publishers and reviews.

Using the computer, students and teachers can do the following:

objectives

Upon completing this chapter, you will be able to do the following:

1 Differentiate between computer-assisted instruction and computer-managed instruction.

2 Define these software terms: public domain, shareware, open-source, drill and practice, problem solving, tutorial, simulation, and instructional games.

3 Name and discuss the criteria for selecting quality software.

4 Evaluate a piece of software based on standard criteria.

5 Create a plan for organizing a software library.

6 Identify useful lesson plans and Internet sites.

students can

- search the Internet for different kinds of software,
- try Open Source software,
- evaluate different software using a checklist,
- use a software library organizational plan.

teachers can

- create a software checklist,
- define terms such as shareware, public domain,
- show students quality software based on selected criteria,
- find lesson plans and instructional material,
- create a software organizational plan.

Computer-Assisted Instruction

In previous chapters, we considered the computer as a productivity tool in the classroom—its uses as a word processor, database, spreadsheet, and desktop publisher. This chapter focuses on the computer as an instructional tool, or as a tutor.

The computer has many purposes in the classroom, and it can be utilized to help a student in all areas of the curriculum. **Computer-assisted instruction (CAI)** refers to the use of the computer as a tool to facilitate and improve instruction. CAI programs use tutorials, drill and practice, simulation, instructional games, and problem-solving approaches to present topics, and they test students' understanding. These programs enable students to progress at their own pace, assisting them in learning the material. The subject matter taught through CAI can range from basic math facts to more complex concepts in math, history, science, social studies, and language arts.

Historical Background

In 1950, MIT scientists designed a flight simulator program for combat pilots, the first example of CAI. Nine years later, IBM developed its CAI technology for elementary schools, and Florida State University offered CAI courses in statistics and physics.

About the same time, John Kemeny and Thomas Kurtz at Dartmouth College created **Beginner's All-Purpose Symbolic Instruction Code (BASIC)**, which provided a programming language for devising CAI programs.

In the early 1960s, CAI programs ran on large mainframe computers and were primarily used in reading and mathematics instruction. Computer programmers also produced simulation programs, modeled after real-life situations. Unfortunately, most of this early software was tedious, long on theory and short on imagination, and lacking in motivating sound and graphics.

The invention of the microcomputer led to the development of improved instructional software and, indirectly, to the resurgence of interest in classroom computer use because of public demand and the competition among companies. Software companies employed teams of educators to enhance their products, and textbook publishers were involved in producing software. For years educational software programs like *Millie's Math House*, *Math Blaster*, and *Reader Rabbit* were popular in the classroom.

Since 2000, the situation changed and big software companies gobbled up little ones and software sales decreased. The emphasis in education was now on immediate achievement results with frequent testing to see that educational standards were being met. The No Child Left Behind Act became the rally cry. For software companies to be eligible for federal money, they had to show through research studies that their software programs were valuable. School funding was also reduced and there was less emphasis on computer software programs in the classroom. Web-based programs started to dominate and open-source programs like *Goggle Docs* (Chapter 6) came into their own. "Open source refers to software that is distributed with its source code so that end user organizations and vendors can modify it for their own purposes" (Freedman, 2008). As for the educational programs that were created in the past, many have been updated and are sold today. In the pages that follow, I will include Web-based programs and open-source programs along with software packages old and new.

 To learn more about software, visit our online site at http://www.wiley.com/college/sharp. Dr. Warren Buckleitner, who is an expert on software and technology, imparts his wisdom on educational software programs. He is editor of Children's Technology Review (http://www.childrenssoftware.com/. Also refer to (www.littleclickers .com/) for a list of Websites for elementary school children.

Types of CAI

Computer-assisted instruction facilitates student learning through various methods. CAI can provide the student with practice in problem solving in math; it can also serve as a tutorial in history and provide further drill and practice in English. Let us look at the different types of CAI: (1) tutorial, (2) simulation, (3) drill and practice, (4) problem solving, and (5) instructional games.

TUTORIAL PROGRAMS

A **tutorial**'s job is to tutor by interactive means—in other words, by having a dialogue with the student. The tutorial presents information, asks questions, and makes decisions based on the student's responses. Like a good teacher, the computer decides whether to move on to new material, review past information, or provide remediation. The computer can serve as the teacher's assistant by helping the learner with special needs or the student who has missed school because of illness, for example. The computer tutorial is very efficient, because it gives individual attention to the student who needs it (Figure 12.1). In addition, the student using this software can progress at his or her own pace. A good tutorial is interesting and easy to follow; it enhances learning with sound and graphics. It has sound educational objectives, is able to regulate the instructional pace, and provides tests to measure the student's progress.

CAI tutorials are based on the principles of programmed learning: The student responds to each bit of information presented by answering questions about the material and then gets immediate feedback on each response. Each tutorial lesson

Figure 12.1

Teacher Helping Student Use
a Math Tutorial

(*Source:* Courtesy Vicki Sharp)

has a series of frames. Each frame poses a question to the student. If the student answers correctly, the next frame appears on the screen. Educators disagree about the arrangement of these frames. Some educators are proponents of the linear tutorial, and others prefer the branching tutorial. The **linear tutorial** presents the student with a series of frames that supply new information or reinforce the information learned in previous frames. The student has to respond to every frame in the exact order presented, and there is no deviation from this presentation, but the student does have the freedom to work through the material at his or her own speed. The **branching tutorial** offers more flexibility in the way the material is covered. The computer decides what material to present to each student. The pupil's responses to the questions determine whether the computer will review the previous material or skip to more advanced work.

There are many tutorial programs, spanning the gamut of software. Kaplan offers a series of online prep courses for the SAT, PSAT, ACT, AP, and CLEP tests. Kaplan's online preparation includes practice, in-depth review, motivation, remedial lessons according to the student's needs, and test strategies. Kaplan also has an SAT CD version.

Encore Software produces *Math Advantage 2008*. The program covers math subjects that range from basic math to trigonometry (Figure 12.2). It features animated examples, narrated text, quizzes, games, and a problem generator with which a user can get unlimited practice with problem sets within each subject area. Encore also publishes *Elementary Advantage*, *Middle School Advantage*, and *High School Advantage*. These programs are comprehensive core curriculum educational suites that help students in subject areas that range from math to world history.

Figure 12.2

Math Advantage 2008,
Trigonometry
(*Source:* Advantage is a trademark of
Encore Software, Inc.)

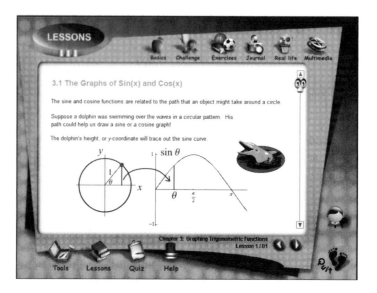

SIMULATION PROGRAMS

In **simulation** programs, students can experience real-life situations without having to risk the consequences of failure. For laboratory simulations, students can experiment with dangerous chemicals on the computer screen, for example, and not be in danger from the actual chemicals. There is no expensive lab equipment to buy, and students can observe the results without waiting a long time. Moreover, students can repeat experiments easily and as often as they wish. Many educators feel that well-designed simulation software affords students the opportunity to learn in more realistic situations than can otherwise be set up in a classroom.

A classic example of a simulation program is *The Oregon Trail*, where students try to survive various conditions and hardships as they travel along the Oregon Trail. They make significant decisions about resting, hunting, crossing rivers, and avoiding starvation, exposure, and death. (*Oregon Trail* is produced by Riverdeep and owned by Houghton Mifflin.) *The Digital Frog* (Digital Frog International) (http://www.digitalfrog.com/) (Figure 12.3) is an award-winning interactive frog dissection program that covers the major systems in a frog's body in depth. Students perform a complete frog dissection with their "digital scalpel." They learn which cuts to make and if they make a mistake they can easily correct it. There are full-screen videos and over 70 anatomy screens.

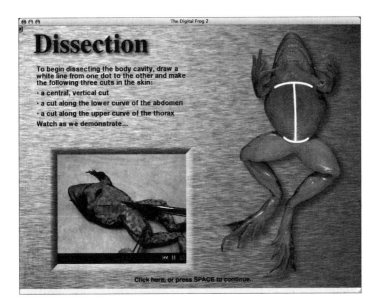

Figure 12.3
Digital Frog 2
(*Source:* Courtesy Digital Frog International, Inc.)

DRILL-AND-PRACTICE PROGRAMS

In 1963, Patrick Suppes and Richard Atkinson produced **drill-and-practice software** on a mainframe computer. The computer screen displayed a problem, the student responded, and the computer provided immediate feedback. The learner stayed with the problems until reaching a certain level of proficiency and then moved on to a more difficult level. With the arrival of the microcomputer in the 1970s, this drill-and-practice software began to be produced widely in all subject areas. It was so popular that 75 percent of the educational software developed at this time was drill and practice. In the 1980s, many educators argued that drill-and-practice software was being overused. They believed that the computer should be used to encourage higher-level thinking and not as an electronic workbook. Today's drill-and-practice programs are more sophisticated, offer greater capabilities, and are accepted in the schools. Most educators see the value of a good individualized drill-and-practice program; this software frees the students and the teachers to do more creative work in the classroom. Many of these programs serve as diagnostic tools, giving the teacher relevant data on how well the students are doing and what they need to work on. The programs also provide immediate feedback for students, allowing them to progress at their own speed and motivating them to continue.

Drill-and-practice software differs from tutorial software in a key way: It helps students remember and utilize skills they have previously been taught, whereas a tutorial teaches new material. Students must be familiar with certain concepts prior to working with drill-and-practice programs in order to understand the contents.

The typical drill-and-practice program design includes four steps: (1) the computer screen presents the student with questions to respond to or problems to solve; (2) the student responds; (3) the computer informs the student whether the answer is correct; and (4) if the student is right, he or she is given another problem to solve, but if the student responds with a wrong answer, he or she is corrected by the computer. Figure 12.4 illustrates the four steps.

Figure 12.4
Drill-and-Practice Program Steps

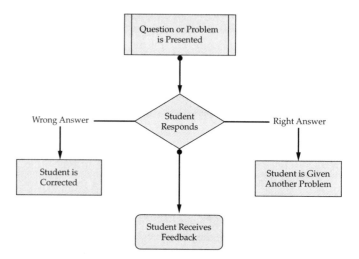

The computer program can handle incorrect responses in several different ways. The computer display might tell students to try the problem again. If they keep giving the wrong answer, the computer gives the right answer and then proceeds to the next problem. The computer might ignore all keys pressed except the right one or even beep when students try to type another response. It might display the answer that should have been typed. It might give students a hint when they respond incorrectly and a better hint if they miss the answer again. After three or four hints, it shows the right answer. Finally, it might give students additional information to help them respond to a question. This type of drill-and-practice program is similar to a tutorial program.

Many drill-and-practice programs motivate students with their ingenious use of graphics and sound. Some programs are games in which players are rewarded points for the correct answers. An example of an addictive drill-and-practice program is *Know Your USA* (Edware Interactive Learning), a geography program that helps students learn more about the United States. They learn about its regions, states, major cities, rivers, mountains, and more. This program has interactive maps, timed quizzes, exams, and games. For example, there is a Quickfire quiz (Figure 12.5) where a capital is named, in this example Illinois, and the student must choose the right answer. The company also has titles covering the world, Europe, and Ireland.

PROBLEM-SOLVING PROGRAMS

Problem-solving skills are necessary in a complex world, and a good way to develop these skills is to use problem-solving programs. Teachers like this type of software because it teaches students to test hypotheses and take notes. Similar to simulation programs, problem-solving programs can easily be used with only one computer and as many as 30 students. The whole class can be involved in critical thinking and making inferences. The critical thinking needed for problem solving can be practiced in

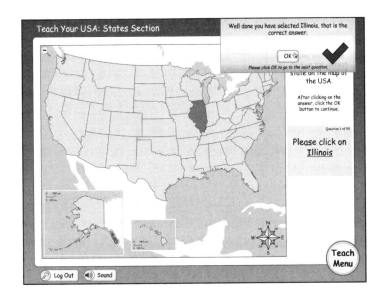

Figure 12.5
Know Your USA
(*Source:* Know Your USA Copyright ©
Luke M. Curley t/a EdWare)

any content area. Problem-solving programs emphasize cooperation and are suitable for small groups or individual students. This type of software gives students more freedom to explore than does drill-and-practice software.

A variety of computer programs focus on higher-level thinking. Riverdeep (now Houghton Mifflin) produces the revised *Thinkin' Things® Collection*, the *Zoombinis Logical Journey* series, and the Carmen series.

BrainWare Safari 2.0 (Figure 12.6), introduced by Learning Enhancement Corporation (LEC), focuses on developing a student's mental capacity and is created for students ages 6–12. It is designed to work on different cognitive skills such as pattern recognition, memory, and thinking. For example, in Bear Shuffle, students arrange cards in the proper order while Tree-Tic-Tac-Toe focuses on students playing Tic-Tac-Toe at increasing levels of difficulty. The activities all have a jungle theme and have animated characters that mature as the student progresses through the program. Also, as the student runs the program, his or her data is recorded and automatically saved. Students have a choice of reading or listening to instructions.

Figure 12.6
BrainWare Safari 2.0
(*Source:* Learning Enhancement
Corporation)

GAME PROGRAMS

Game programs for the computer usually involve fantasy situations with some sort of competition. Game programs are classified as either entertainment or educational software.

Educational programs have specific learning objectives, with the game serving as a motivational device, whereas the major goal of the entertainment programs is amusement. Educational software offers a range of learning outcomes; entertainment software has little academic value except in teaching game strategy.

Most CAI programs use a game format that ranges from drill and practice to logic. For example, the revised *Dr. Seuss Green Eggs and Ham* for Macintosh (Software MacKiev) is an early reading program where students can listen and watch Dr. Seuss's classic book come alive. Each interactive page has talking characters and fun sound effects. The student clicks on the different items in a scene and get animated surprises. There are three games the student can play. Figure 12.7 is a picture of the rhyming game.

Figure 12.7
Green Eggs and Ham
(*Source:* Courtesy Software MacKiev)

Software MacKiev also has revised Dr. Seuss's *ABC* and Dr. Seuss's *Cat and the Hat*.

Crazy Machines 1.5 (Viva Media) is an educational game program for students from grade 3 to adult. Using this program they attempt to solve over 200 brainteasers. For example, a student might be given a puzzle to knock over a domino, which is sitting amidst a set of balls, ramps, or bellows. The user is usually given a tool to begin the puzzle, such as a metal ball that will roll in a certain manner. The students then use other tools to solve the puzzle that range from bottle rockets to funky toasters to programmable robots. When the player turns the game on they are able to see the results of their work. To proceed to the next level they must try to solve more complex puzzles. Students can also create their own unique designs and have others solve their puzzles. They can experiment with electricity, air pressure, gears, robots, a physics engine, explosives, and more in a virtual lab (Figure 12.8).

Figure 12.8
Crazy Machines
(*Source:* © viva media, LLC)

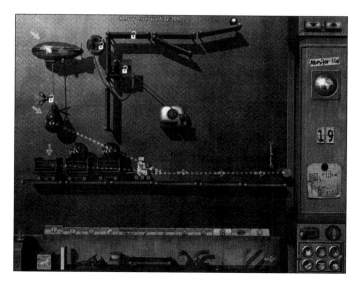

Because computer games are very popular, many educators think that CAI programs should be designed in a game-like format. A good educational game involves the active physical and mental participation of the players. Graphics, fast motion, and sound effects are used to enhance the program, not to detract from its educational value.

Most CAI programs incorporate more than one type of software in their design. For example, a program that is a tutorial may have a drill-and-practice element, and a simulation may have a game as an integral part of its program. Now that we have looked at the different types of CAI, lets look at some of the educational software programs that are available for grades K–12.

Subject-Area Software

There are thousands of quality educational software programs. These programs are typically designed for specific areas of the curriculum.

MATHEMATICS PROGRAMS

The research literature offers no apparent agreement on how best to use computer software for improving math skills or for developing higher-order thinking. In 2000, the National Council for Teachers of Mathematics (NCTM) published its extensive standards for using technology. See the NCTM site for information on these standards at http://www.nctm.org/standards/. Even with these standards, teachers must decide how to use math software according to their own classroom needs.

They might choose a program called *Math Pathways* (Sunburst). This program consists of six programs covering math content from grades 6 to 12. It is standard based and has interactive content. *Math Pathways* has videos, real-world examples, animations, a visual dictionary, interactive experiments, tests and assessments, and virtual reality to demonstrate math concepts. Students use this self-paced tool (Figure 12.9) to explore, gain important concepts, and learn necessary computational skills.

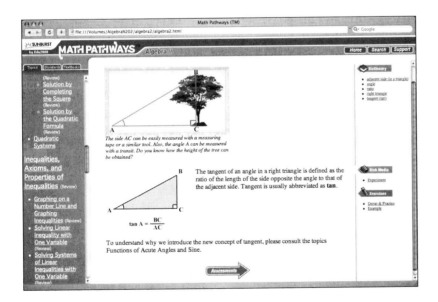

Figure 12.9
Math Pathways Algebra II
(*Source:* Courtesy Digital Xpert, Inc.)

Pet Vet 3D Animal Hospital (Figure 12.10) and *Pet Vet Wild Animal Hospital* (Viva Media) let students run their own animal hospital. In the process they earn money by diagnosing animals and finding out what is wrong. They receive money for treating their patients and helping them recover. They can then use the money earned to improve the hospital's buildings or expand them. For example, students can buy a building or build a rabbit hutch. Students can then earn money when people visit the building to see their animals.

Figure 12.10

Pet Vet 3D Animal Hospital
(*Source:* © Viva Media, LLC)

As business improves the user can hire additional help. They go shopping and pick up food for pets, toys, and supplies. These exciting programs have three levels with 3D graphics and animation.

SCIENCE PROGRAMS

In many elementary schools, science programs are limited to requiring memorization of textbook facts; teachers have not had the time or money to collect the necessary materials for exciting hands-on science lessons. Furthermore, the breadth of a science class has depended on a teacher's interests and specific areas of expertise. Because of their general lack of knowledge in science, some teachers have ignored many science topics, and most elementary students have received very little science education. Experimentation has occurred primarily in the high school science lab, an experience usually reserved for college-bound students.

The computer has begun to change this unfortunate situation. The science investigation skills of classifying, synthesizing, analyzing, and summarizing data are skills that the computer is designed to reinforce. The computer cannot replace the actual science laboratory, but it can simulate complex, expensive, and dangerous experiments, saving time and money. Because there is a renewed interest in science education, more schools are incorporating the computer into the science curriculum, and science software is flourishing. There are good science tutorials that are readily available, especially at the upper elementary, high school, and college levels.

At the high school or college level, science programs that help students learn biology, chemistry, and physics are *BioTutor* ® Excalibur, *Physics Tutor* ® Excalibur (Figure 12.11), and *ChemTutor* ® Excalibur (Interactive Learning, Inc.). These

Figure 12.11

PhysicsTutor ® Excalibur
(*Source:* Courtesy Interactive Learning, Inc.)

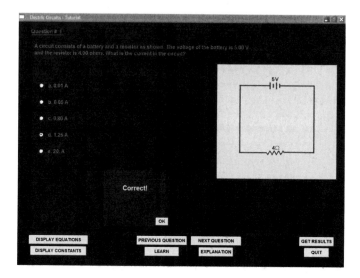

programs cover the full curriculum for a first or second course in these subjects. While working on these tutorials, the students are given immediate feedback at each step. These programs also provide the user with a calculator to answer the tutorial questions that are presented.

The *Learn About* science series (Sunburst) for elementary students provides simple tutorials that teach about plants, dinosaurs, weather, animals, and the human body.

SOCIAL STUDIES PROGRAMS

Social studies software excels at presenting current and historical events that foster class discussion and student decision making. Using **application software**, students can integrate other information into the social studies program. Students can use word processors to write about any subject, spreadsheet and graphics programs to analyze statistical data and to display pertinent information, and database programs to retrieve data and analyze information. For example, students using the Macintosh social studies program *3D Weather Globe & Atlas* (Software MacKiev) (Figure 12.12) can access detailed maps and comprehensive statistics and information. Students can use the software to form patterns and see relationships. *3D Weather Globe & Atlas* gives you real-time 3D animation based on the actual weather and comes with historic journeys such as Magellan's voyage. The program is a good way to teach geography, astronomy, and history. Teachers can also use programs such as *TimeLiner* (Tom Snyder Productions) to create time lines for any subject (see Chapter 14).

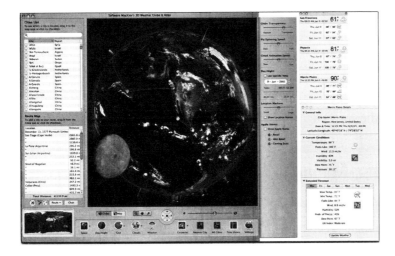

Figure 12.12
3D Weather Globe & Atlas
(*Source:* Courtesy Software MacKiev)

LANGUAGE ARTS AND READING PROGRAMS

Because of the multitude of good language arts programs, it is often easier to integrate language arts programs into the curriculum than any other types of programs. Refer to the Online Learning Center for an annotated listing of helpful programs. Language arts programs are subdivided into many categories: writing, spelling, grammar, reading (including reference tools), and more.

Reading programs range from elementary phonics instruction and basic comprehension to literature analysis. Two programs that help students master basic phonics concepts are *3D Froggy Phonics* (Ingenuity Works) and *Stickybear Reading Room Deluxe* (Optimum Resources). Optimum Resources has an excellent high school comprehension series for grades 9–12. The topics for the high school series include history, cars, fashion, and famous people.

There are lecture series like Great Courses (The Teaching Company) and writing programs such as WriteBrain (Sunburst).

Great Courses (http://www.thegreatcourses.com) lets students listen to audio courses or view DVDs from top-rated professors. Professors are chosen from leading college and universities such as Stanford and Georgetown. There are over 200 courses and the topics range from business and economics to social sciences.

Designed for grades 2–12, *WriteBrain* (Figure 12.13) is a Web-based writing program. Students work through the entire writing process including brainstorming, organizing, drafting, editing, assessing, and revising. This simple-to-use research-based program has 170 lessons with writing prompts and is tied to state standards.

Figure 12.13
WriteBrain
(*Source:* Courtesy Digital Xpert, Inc.)

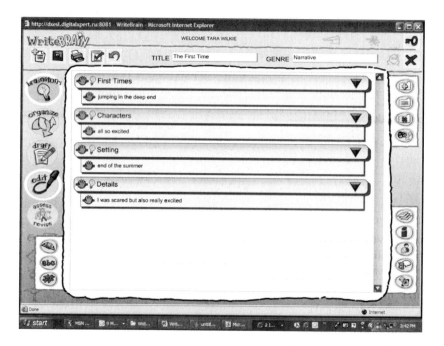

There are test-specific programs such as *Kaplan's SAT & PSAT ACT* (Encore Software), and there are reference tools such as *Encarta Reference Library Educator Edition* (Microsoft) and *World Book (Software MacKiev).*

Computer-Managed Instruction

In this section, we examine **computer-managed instruction (CMI).** CMI differs from CAI in that it focuses on the needs of the teacher, helping him or her manage the learning of students. The computer in CMI manages instruction; keeps track of student test scores, attendance records, and schedules; and offers diagnostic-perspective instruction in all curriculum areas. CMI makes the teaching environment more organized and productive, enabling the teacher to individualize instruction. It directs students so that they can proceed at their own pace, and it supervises instruction by assigning certain books and tapes at the right times. When students finish their work, the computer tests them and gives further assignments. The computer grades the tests and records scores so that the teacher can see and evaluate students' progress. CMI is based on the underlying concept that all children can learn if they proceed at their own pace and are given the proper instructions and materials. CMI can be a comprehensive program for one or more areas of the curriculum. Many computer-managed instruction programs are based on a pretest, diagnosis, prescription, instruction, and posttest. At the beginning of most CMI programs, the student takes a pretest on the computer.

If the computer survey indicates an area of need, the student is given the appropriate test to pinpoint the area of weakness. If questions are missed on this exam, a prescription is given. If the student fails again, he or she must see the teacher. The teacher can customize the program, omitting tests for individuals in the class. The teacher can also select remediation assignments and decide when the testing ends. The instructor can call up records, class lists, tests, and status reports on individuals and can generate class reports, group reports, and graph reports.

CMI is incorporated into the latest CAI. For example, Sunburst's *Math Pathways* (grades 6–12) and *Key Skills for Language Arts* (Figure 12.14) and *Key Skills for Math* (grades K–6) features a teacher management tool that enables the teacher to customize students' experience and track their performance and progress. This system has 160 animated activities, and they are correlated to state standards. *PowerSchool* (Apple) is an example of an online program where teachers, students, and parents can track student progress.

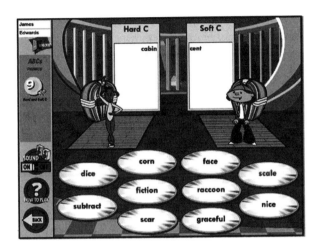

Figure 12.14
Key Skills for Language Arts
(*Source:* Copyright Sunburst Technology Corporation)

Computer-managed instruction increased in popularity as a result of the No Child Left Behind Law signed by President George W. Bush in 2002. This law emphasized accountability and testing. The law's purpose was to close the achievement disparity between disadvantaged students and their peers by proposing stronger accountability, local control, teaching methods that have worked, and more options for parents (http://www.nochildleftbehind.gov/).

Integrated Learning Systems

Integrated learning systems (ILS) (Figure 12.15) are a combination of computer-managed instruction and computer-assisted instruction. Software companies call ILS a one-package educational software solution to teachers' problems because it generates diagnostic data and instruction based on this data, monitors students' performance, and makes changes in instruction when needed. In most cases, software

Figure 12.15
Student Using an Integrated Learning System
(*Source:* Courtesy Vicki Sharp)

companies offer this instruction online through the Internet. ILS usually requires its own file server (computer) to store the different types of software (tutorial, drill and practice, etc.) and the individualized instruction software that keeps track of students' progress.

Curriculum Advantage (www.classworks.com) developed open learning systems that combine software with management tools and integration help. *Classworks* covers English and language arts, reading, and math for grades for K–12 and science for grades K–6 (Figure 12.16). Its new science module will soon cover the middle grades.

Figure 12.16
Classworks Science
(*Source:* Curriculum Advantage, Inc.)

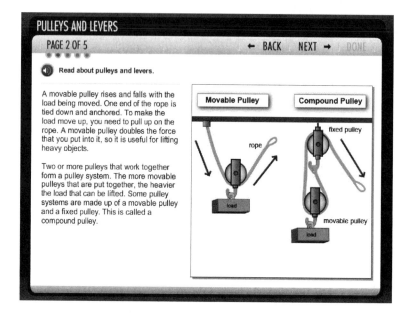

This open learning system helps the teacher test, evaluate student progress, and prescribe work. The teacher views a record of students' progress and is able to customize lessons with placement, assessment, and instruction tailored to students' needs (Figure 12.17). In addition, the teacher can effortlessly change lesson plans and learning levels.

Figure 12.17
Classworks Assessment
(*Source:* Curriculum Advantage, Inc.)

Completed Unit Detail

Unit Name	Unit Completed	Unit Score	%	Total Unit Time On Task
Exploring Literary Elements	6/5/2007	9 / 10	90 %	00:07:55
Exploring Mood	6/5/2007	9 / 10	90 %	00:07:32
Using Hyperbole	6/6/2007	10 / 10	100 %	00:05:23
Using Details to Compare and Contrast	6/6/2007	9 / 10	90 %	00:10:20
Identifying Point of View	6/6/2007	8 / 10	80 %	00:54:59
Exploring Using a Dictionary	6/7/2007	10 / 10	100 %	00:47:43
Using Context Clues	6/7/2007	8 / 10	80 %	00:20:22
Analyzing Nonfiction	6/7/2007	9 / 10	90 %	00:43:00
Exploring Alliteration, End Rhyme, and Onomatopoeia	6/7/2007	9 / 10	90 %	00:28:34
Verb Tense	6/8/2007	1 / 10	10 %	00:56:20
Exploring Using a Thesaurus	6/11/2007	9 / 10	90 %	00:22:01
Reading Comprehension - Research Reading	6/11/2007	7 / 10	70 %	00:28:37
Colons	6/11/2007	7 / 10	70 %	00:58:44
Unnecessary Commas	6/12/2007	7 / 10	70 %	00:23:51
Exploring Capitalization	6/12/2007	10 / 10	100 %	00:09:21
Comma 1	6/12/2007	2 / 10	20 %	00:39:58
Comma 2	6/12/2007	3 / 10	30 %	01:03:50
Exploring Verb Tenses	6/13/2007	5 / 10	50 %	00:17:27
Pronouns and Antecedents	6/13/2007	4 / 10	40 %	00:33:31
Pronoun Case	6/14/2007	5 / 10	50 %	01:26:08
Using Irregular Verbs	6/14/2007	7 / 10	70 %	00:15:21
Punctuating Quotations	6/14/2007	6 / 10	60 %	00:56:08
Exploring Analogies	6/14/2007	4 / 10	40 %	00:23:45
Sentence Fragments	6/15/2007	5 / 10	50 %	00:32:54
Run-on Sentences	6/15/2007	9 / 10	90 %	01:02:43
Subject-Verb Agreement 1	6/15/2007	10 / 10	100 %	00:50:05
		182 / 260	70 %	15:06:32

Public Domain Software, Freeware, Shareware. and Open Source

Most software programs discussed in this book are commercial. Commercial programs can be expensive, especially in multiple copies. Fortunately, there is an alternative to commercial software: public domain software.

Public domain software can legally be copied and shared with other users with no restrictions on use. Public domain is not copyrighted, and its authors choose not to seek formal rights or royalties. The quality of this software varies considerably. There are very useful public domain programs, but you have to choose carefully and wisely; professional programmers and teachers write these programs in their free time.

Freeware is like public domain software because the user obtains it without a charge. However, the company that developed the software retains the ownership. Because they own the product, they have the option of releasing a new version and charging a fee. When this happens, the program is no longer freeware but becomes a commercial software package.

Shareware is software that is distributed on a trial basis through Web sites, bulletin boards, online services, mail-order vendors, and user groups. Users try the program to see if it fits their needs. In most cases the program has a 30-day trial period, and some of the program's functions are disabled. If, after looking over the software, the parties involved wish to use the product, they must register with the owner of the product and pay a fee. In return for the fee, the user usually gets documentation, technical support, and free updates. There are tens of thousands of shareware programs; some are terrific, others mediocre. Two excellent sites for shareware software are *Tucows* at http:// www.tucows.com/ and *CNET Shareware.com* at http://shareware.cnet.com.

Most **open-source software** is written for anyone to use, change, and send to other individuals. This software is distributed with its source code. The majority of open-source software has no charge and is developed by a group of volunteers. Two examples of open-source software are *Goggle Docs*, which is free, and *Linux*, where there is a small fee. For a more complete definition, visit http://www.opensource .org/docs/osd.

Software Selection: A General Guide

In prior chapters, we examined different application software such as word processing and desktop publishing programs and learned how to evaluate these programs by using appropriate criteria. Now we look at some general principles that apply to evaluating any software program. Choosing good software is an eight-step process: (1) specify the software needs of your population; (2) locate the software; (3) research hardware compatibility; (4) examine the program's contents; (5) look at instructional design; (6) check out how easy the program is to learn; (7) evaluate the program in terms of consumer value; and (8) investigate the technical support and cost.

IDENTIFY THE SOFTWARE NEEDS OF YOUR POPULATION

To make a wise decision, it is essential to know the learning/curriculum objectives that you wish to accomplish. After you have determined what these objectives are, you can better determine the software needs of your population. Ask the following questions: What type of program will best meet these objectives? Does the class need a math drill-and-practice program to reinforce some math skills? Does the group need a tutorial program to learn something new? What is the grade and ability level of the software program?

How sophisticated should this software be? For example, should the program be a simple desktop publishing program for a school newsletter or a heavy-duty desktop publishing program for a professional publication? After making these decisions, list the features the classroom requires. If you are teaching first grade, you might want a word processor that produces a nice assortment of large fonts. If you are working with high school students, you might want a sophisticated word processor that has an outliner.

LOCATING SOFTWARE

The major sources of software information are journals, indexes, educational organizations, magazines, software house catalogs, and the Internet. A fast way to locate software is through catalogs such as *Learning Services, Educational Resources, Software Express,* and *CCV Software.* These catalogs include program descriptions and often tell you the names of the company's best-selling programs. The companies operate via mail order and offer discounted prices. Professional journals and periodicals in the field publish numerous reviews. For example, *Arithmetic Teacher* publishes reviews on math software, and the *Journal of Learning Disabilities* prints occasional reviews of software for students with learning disabilities. Other magazines such as *T.H.E. Journal, Technology and Learning, Learning and Leading with Technology,* and the *Journal of Special Education* review software. On the Internet there are sites that focus on reviewing software such as the *Educational Software Preview Guide (ESPG) Consortium* (http://ed.fnal.gov/espg) The host, Fermi National Accelerator Laboratory, Education Office, represents computer education organizations throughout North America. *Children's Technology Review* (http://childrenssoftware.com/) has over 8,000 rated reviews dating back to 1985. The editor of this publication is Dr. Warren Buckleitner, a distinguished reviewer and writer. In addition, SuperKids (http://www.superkids.com) and *Technology and Learning* (http://techlearning.com) also review software online.

Regardless of the source you use, you should read several reviews of a software program to get different perspectives. Often there is disagreement among reviewers on what constitutes "good" software because every reviewer has a priority. For example, Reviewer A may feel that ease of use is the most important factor, but Reviewer B might be concerned with features. Also, look at advertisements for new products. You can see what new products are available just by scanning magazine ads or asking the manufacturers to send a more detailed list. You might want to call the manufacturer of the product directly to find out about some of the features. Software developers such as Sunburst send preview copies if you guarantee their safe return. Many software publishers let you download demonstration copies of their software from the Internet or order a demonstration CD by telephone. After a trial period of 30 or 60 days users have a good idea if they want to buy the program.

There are other sources for previewing software; university software libraries, state departments of education, and software clearinghouses. And always keep in mind any computer enthusiast acquaintance or friend who may have used a product. *Microsoft Word* may be a hot-selling program, but by talking to a friend who is actually using it, you might learn it is not right for your particular situation. Computer user groups recommend good software, demonstrate it at their meetings, and answer questions. At the very least, these groups put you in touch with people who have the software, and they generally keep abreast of new developments in the field.

After you have properly researched different types of software, you will be ready to visit the computer store or go online to examine the software package. Make sure the store is reputable and reliable, and ask about its policy on defective disks and returns. When examining a program, check the version number to be sure it is not an old version that has been languishing in the store. Make sure the version is compatible with the computer that you are using. For example, your old Pentium II processor may not run your chosen program, which may require a computer having at the minimum a Pentium IV processor. Also, inspect the package to see if it is a teacher's version or a consumer version. The consumer edition may be less expensive, but it usually does not come with a backup disk or an activity book.

HARDWARE COMPATIBILITY

Ask the following questions: Do the computers at the school have enough memory to run most programs? The more memory the computer has the better it is for running programs. How many gigabytes is the hard drive? What type of backup storage do the machines have? Do they have old Zip drives or high-speed FireWire hard drives? How fast is the CD-ROM or DVD-ROM drive? Is it a CD-rewritable drive or a DVD-rewriteable drive? Does the software program you want to buy need more RAM to run faster and more efficiently? Is it a networkable program? What are the video-RAM requirements? What equipment is necessary? Does the program require a digital camera or a microphone? What type of printer does the program support?

PROGRAM CONTENT

First, ask these questions: What are the objectives of this program? Do these objectives match my curriculum objectives? Are these objectives clearly stated? Does the program meet these objectives? Many programs are not logically organized and lack a theoretical base. (The objectives do not have to be seen on the computer screen.) However, they should be found in the documentation that accompanies this software package. Next, ask these questions: How appropriate is the program for the students? What knowledge or skills must a student possess to utilize this software program? Are the graphics and skills required reasonable for this grade level? (Be careful not to buy a program that is too easy or hard for the class.) Is the vocabulary appropriate for the grade level? (Many publishers supply readability scores that can serve as a benchmark.) How accurate is the material presented in the program? Is the program free of unnecessary computer jargon, and are the spelling and grammar correct? If it is a historical program, are the data accurate? How much time is needed to run the program? What about the program's transmitted values? Is the program free from prejudices or stereotypes? Is the program violent in nature? Is the program sensitive to moral issues? Does the program insult or talk down to the user?

INSTRUCTIONAL DESIGN

Many important factors relate to program design. These include learner control, reinforcement, sequencing, flexibility, and appearance.

Learner Control.   Who controls the software program, the student or the computer? Can the student move back and forth in the lesson easily? Can the student quickly return to the previous frame? Can the student escape to the menu whenever he or she wants? Can the student control the speed of the program? Does the program move the academically advanced students forward to more difficult problems, or does the level of difficulty remain the same? (It is important to be able to use the program at more than one ability level.) How easy is it for the student to exit the program or to restart an activity?

Reinforcement.   How are the students reinforced? The reinforcement should be delivered in a positive way. The software should be encouraging and not degrading. There should be little reinforcement for inappropriate responses. Some programs have reinforcement for wrong answers that is more rewarding than the reinforcement for right answers. Does the program vary the reinforcement? Is the feedback active, passive, or interactive? (A student receives passive feedback when the program simply states that the answer is wrong or right. The student receives active feedback when animation appears on the screen such as a rabbit doing a jig.)

Sequencing.   Is the instructional sequence appropriate? Does it start from the simple idea and move to the complex?

Flexibility.   You should be able to adapt the program for small and large groups. You also should be able to modify the program to meet the individual needs of the students in the classroom. For example, *Quarter Mile* (Barnum Software) enables you to change the type of problems that appear in each session. Does the program provide a record of the student's progress?

Program Appearance.   Does the program have colorful graphics, animation, and sound? Does the sound motivate the students or does it interfere with their learning? Are the graphics distracting or helpful? How is the screen laid out? Is it crowded or well organized? Is the full power of the computer being used? Are there too many instructions on the screen?

EASE OF USE

Is the program easy to learn? Can the student immediately load the program and use it? Does the program use simple English commands? Can the student access a help screen whenever it is needed? Does a tutorial disk or manual take the user through the program? Is the printer easy to set? Can the student answer a few questions and then be ready to print immediately? Are there help prompts and safety questions? Is there an automatic save feature? What happens when the student hits a wrong key? Must the student reload the program or does the software crash? Does the program have error messages so that the student can correct problems? Are the directions clear and concise? Can the student follow the directions on the screen without going to the documentation that accompanies the software? Are the instructions brief and to the point?

CONSUMER VALUE

Cost is a concern because some software can run into the thousands of dollars. You have to decide whether that $395 word processor is really better than the $50 one. Are all the features found in that $395 package worth the cost? (Find out if a discount house or mail-order firm carries the software at a considerable savings; see Appendix B for a list of recommended mail-order sources.) Is the software protected? Do you have to type in a serial number or find a code word in the manual or use the original disk to install? For a reduction in software price per computer, you can order lab packs, a networkable version of the software, or a site license. **Lab packs** are multiple copies of a program with one set of documentation. **Networkable software** can run over a network without a reduction in performance. You simply install the program on a single file server at one school site with a varying number of computers connected. If you buy a **site license**, the teacher at a site can make a number of copies of the software from the original.

SUPPORT

How good is the technical support? Can you call someone immediately to get help, or must you wait forever on the telephone? Is the technical support knowledgeable and understandable? Do you have to make five or six menu choices and then get a recorded message that sends you online? Is the telephone call toll free or is it a long-distance call? Does the company charge by the minute for technical help? Is there a tutorial with the software package? Is the tutorial on a disk or in book form? (Many manufacturers provide both to simplify learning their program.) Is the manual readable, with activities and lesson plans? (The documentation should be written for the target audience.) Is this publisher reputable? Will the company still be in business when you are having trouble with the software product? If you happen to get a defective disk, will the publisher replace it? Shopping for software is an involved process. Use the Software Program Checklist on page 259 to evaluate software.

Even if software purchased meets high standards, it can have its intent subverted when used. Purchasing software is not the only consideration; teachers must be given instruction and help in incorporating it into the classroom.

Software Program Checklist

Directions: Examine the following items and determine which ones you feel are important for your class situation. Place an X on each line for which the software meets your needs.

Product Name_____ Manufacturer_____Grade Level_____

Subject Area_____ Skill Level_____

Program Type
___ 1. Drill and practice
___ 2. Tutorial
___ 3. Simulation
___ 4. Educational game
___ 5. Problem solving
___ 6. Teacher management
___ 7. Other _____

Hardware Compatibility
___ 1. Memory needed
___ 2. Computer compatibility
___ 3. Printer compatibility
___ 4. Hard disk space
___ 5. CD-ROM drive speed
___ 6. DVD drive speed
___ 7. Peripherals
___ 8. Other _____

Program Content
___ 1. Objectives met
___ 2. Vocabulary appropriate
___ 3. Material accurate
___ 4. Free of bias or stereotype
___ 5. Motivational
___ 6. Grade-appropriate skills
___ 7. Content current

Instructional Design
___ 1. Learner control
    ___ a. Speed control
    ___ b. Program movement
___ 2. Reinforcement
___ 3. Sequencing

___ 4. Flexibility
___ 5. Appearance
    ___ a. No distracting sound/visuals
    ___ b. Animation/sound/graphics
    ___ c. Uncluttered screen
    ___ d. Material clearly presented
    ___ e. Product reliability

Ease of Use
___ 1. Easy program installation
___ 2. Simple screen directions
___ 3. Onscreen help
___ 4. Tutorial manual—hard copy
___ 5. Easy printer setup
___ 6. Student can use without help
___ 7. Students can review directions on demand

Consumer Value
___ 1. Cost
___ 2. Extra programs
___ 3. Lab packs
___ 4. Network versions
___ 5. Site licenses

Support
1. Free technical help
2. Toll-free number
3. Readable manual
   a. Activities
   b. Lesson plans
   c. Tutorial
   d. Index
4. Money-back guarantee
5. Defective disk policy

Rating Scale

Rate the software program by placing a check in the appropriate line.

Excellent_____ Very good _____ Good _____ Fair _____ Poor _____

Comments:

Guidelines for Setting up a Software Library

Once you have the software, the most important job still remains ahead. Every teacher needs guidelines on how to organize a software collection. What follows is one approach to software organization:

1. Consult your school librarian for information on cataloging and advice on time-saving techniques.

2. Choose the location for the collection wisely. It could be a classroom, library, or media center. The more central the library location the easier it is to access.

3. Use a database software program to keep a record of the software. Alphabetize the software by title, subject, type, age, and so on, and simultaneously make an annotated listing of the software.

4. Catalog the software. There is no standardized procedure, but one of the simplest and most effective ways is to color-code the software and documentation by subject area. For example, math software might be labeled with blue stickers or kept in blue folders. If you have a large software collection, use the Dewey Decimal System and the Sears List of Subject Headings.

5. Decide how the software is to be stored. Will you use hanging file folders, file cabinets, stands, or plastic containers?

6. Protect the collection. Make security arrangements and store disks, CD-ROMs, and DVD-ROMs vertically in containers. Protect these discs from dust, dirt, and strong magnetic fields.

7. Separate the computer discs from the documentation and serial numbers for security reasons.

8. Devise a set of rules for software use. For example, forbid food or drinks in any of the computer labs. Not only can food and drink cause damage to the computer, but they also can entice ants. Be sure to place software in their designated containers.

9. Create a policy and procedures manual that handles the following issues:

a. Who is responsible for this collection?

b. What procedures will be used to evaluate, select, and catalog this software?

c. How will the software be checked out?

d. How will a teacher verify that the software is workable?

e. How will the teacher report technical problems?

Organizing and maintaining a software library is a monumental task that requires someone to be in charge of it on a full-time basis. After this library is established, schools can benefit by devising a review procedure so that a continually growing library of software reviews can be developed and made available to all teachers.

SAMPLE CLASSROOM LESSON PLANS

I. MATH FOR THE REAL WORLD

Subject: Math

Grade(s): 6–8

Objective

Students will improve their math skills by using a math simulation program such as *Pet Vet 3D Animal Hospital* (Viva Media), *or Hot Dog Stand Top Dog* (Sunburst).

Standards

- National Council of Teachers of Math 1, 6, 8, 9
- ISTE NETS for Students 1, 3, 6

Materials

You will need a program such as *Hot Dog Stand Top Dog* or *Pet Vet 3D Animal Hospital.*

Procedures

1. Using a math simulation program, work through a problem with the whole class.

2. Next, divide the class into four or five small groups.

3. Ask each group to elect a leader, keyboarder, and recorder.

4. Have each group take a turn on the computer to see how much money it can earn.

5. At the end of the day, ask each group to discuss how well it did. Also, have group members establish a goal for the next day or session.

6. Ask students to keep a written record of their activities and progress.

7. Have groups rotate roles.

8. Move among the groups, asking questions and helping when appropriate.

II. ANIMAL BOOK

Subject: Science

Grade(s): 1–3

Objective

Students will use a product such as *EasyBook Deluxe* (Sunburst) or *Kreative Komix* (Visions Technology in Education) to create an electronic book.

Standards

- National Science Education Standards A1, A2, C1, C2, C3
- ISTE NETS for Students 1, 2, 3, 4, 5

Materials

You will need a book-making program such as *EasyBook Deluxe* or *Kreative Komix.*

Procedures

1. Explain how to use the software program.

2. Have the students use books or the Internet to study a subject such as plants or dinosaurs.

3. Have students create books about what they have learned.

4. When the students have completed the assignment, have them share their electronic books with the class.

III. WRITING AN ARTICLE

Subject: Social Studies and Language Arts

Grade(s): 4 and up

Objective

Students will use an electronic encyclopedia such as *World Book* or *Encarta* to create articles for a newspaper.

Standards

- National Council for the Social Studies Curriculum Standards 1, 3
- NCTE English Language Arts Standards 1, 3, 4, 5, 6, 7, 8, 12
- ISTE NETS for Students 1, 2, 3, 4, 5

Materials

You will need access to the Internet, an electronic encyclopedia such as *World Book* or *Encarta*, and a publishing program such as *Microsoft Publisher*.

Procedures

1. Divide the class into small groups.

2. Have each member of the group determine what famous person he or she wants to research. For example, a student might choose Abraham Lincoln or Harriet Tubman.

3. Have each student use an electronic encyclopedia to research the chosen person and write an article about the time in which this person lived.

4. Have the group then create a newspaper with articles using a publishing program such as *Microsoft Publisher*.

5. At the end of the assignment, have the groups come together and share newspapers.

IV. MY STORY

Subject: Language Arts

Grade(s): 2 and up

Objective

Students will use a multimedia story-writing program such as *Kreative Komix* (Visions Technology in Education) to create a book report.

Standards

- NCTE English Language Arts Standards 1, 4, 5, 6, 12
- ISTE NETS for Students 1, 2, 3

Materials

You will need a writing program such as *Kreative Komix* or *Microsoft Publisher* and one or more computers.

Procedures

1. Have students read a book and then talk about the elements that shape the story.

2. Next, ask students to write down a summary of the events.

3. Show the students how to use the software to insert text and graphics.

4. Have students print hard copies of their reports and present them in class.

5. As a class, discuss the reports and offer suggestions for change.

SUMMARY

The computer has many invaluable uses in all areas of the curriculum. Computer-assisted instruction (CAI) software uses the computer as a tool to improve instruction, provides the student with practice in problem solving, serves as a tutor, and supplies drill and practice. Computer-managed instruction (CMI) assists the teacher in managing learning. We considered eight criteria to apply when choosing software. We examined a software evaluation form (checklist) to aid in software selection. We considered guidelines for setting up a software library. On the Online Learning Center is a comprehensive and annotated list of award-winning programs.

STUDY AND ONLINE RESOURCES

CHAPTER 12 ONLINE RESOURCES

 In the **student section** of the book's online site at **http://www.wiley.com/college/sharp**, you will find PDFs, checklists, articles, Web sites, software reviews, and chapter quizzes. Access these resources to learn about technology and integrating it into the classroom.

CHAPTER MASTERY TEST

Let us check for chapter comprehension with a short mastery test. Key Terms, Computer Lab, and Suggested Readings and References follow the test.

1. Name two advantages of using drill-and-practice software to learn mathematics.

2. Suggest two ways social studies software can be used to teach U.S. history.

3. Should the teacher use language arts software to improve writing skills? Give reasons to support your position.

4. What methods can a teacher use to improve problem-solving skills on the computer?

5. Explain how students might use the computer in gathering, organizing, and displaying social studies information. Include two titles of exemplary software.

6. What are the advantages of using computer math manipulatives over traditional math manipulatives?

7. What is the most critical step in the evaluation of software? Explain its importance.

8. Discuss three criteria that a teacher should consider when choosing software for the classroom.

9. What is the main difference between *shareware, open-source,* and *public domain software*?

10. Why is feedback a crucial element to consider when evaluating software?

11. Should the student or the computer control the direction of a program? Explain.

12. What is the major difference between a drill-and-practice program and a tutorial program?

13. Define *simulation program* and give an example.

14. Can a problem-solving program also be a simulation program? Explain in detail.

15. Give the paradigm for the typical drill-and-practice program design.

16. What is the major difference between computer-managed instruction and computer-assisted instruction?

17. What are important considerations for setting up a software library?

KEY TERMS

Application software p. 251

Beginner's All-Purpose Symbolic Instruction Code (BASIC) p. 243

Branching tutorial p. 244

Computer-assisted instruction (CAI) p. 242

Computer-managed instruction (CMI) p. 252

Drill-and-practice software p. 245

Freeware p. 255

Integrated learning systems (ILS) p. 253

Lab packs p. 258

Linear tutorial p. 244

Networkable software p. 258

Open source software p. 255

Public domain software p. 255

Shareware p. 255

Simulation p. 245

Site license p. 258

Tutorial p. 243

COMPUTER LAB: Activities for Mastery and Your Portfolio

12.1 Use one of several applications to create an interactive time line to use in your classroom.

12.2 Use this activity with your students to create genre signs for the classroom library.

12.3 Use the activity with your students to create a database of books they have read.

12.4 Benjamin Franklin recorded the water temperature every day in his journeys across the Atlantic and discovered the Gulf Stream. Recreate Franklin's efforts.

12.5 Review a software program using the guidelines that were given in this chapter.

12.6 The software evaluation form that was used in this chapter was of a general nature. Develop a software checklist for a drill-and-practice software program in the area of math or science.

12.7 Using the Recommended Software found on the Online Learning Center or a software directory, locate several math software packages for an eighth-grade class. Make a list.

12.8 Find a published review on a software program in the school's collection. Test out the product to determine the validity of the review. Write your own review.

12.9 Visit a school that uses computers and a variety of computer programs. Write a brief report on the criteria used by the school in selecting its software.

12.10 Discuss the problems inherent in language arts software given the existing curriculum. Research the topic to support your discussion. Watch the Video tutorial online and learn how to conduct an Internet search.

SUGGESTED READINGS AND REFERENCES

Baker, Elizabeth. "Integrating Literacy and Technology: Making a Match Between Software and Classroom." *Reading and Writing Quarterly* 19, issue 2 (April 2003): 193–198.

Bourzac, Katherine. "The Trouble with Software." *Technology Review* 110, issue 1 (January 2007): 88.

Buckleitner, Warren, editor. *Children's Technology Revue.* Reviews over 8,000 programs online. http://www .childrenssoftware.com. A monthly printed version of the journal is also available.

Buckleitner, Warren. "Having Some Fun and Learning at the Same Time." *New York Times* (April 19, 2007), p. C8.

Buckleitner, Warren, editor. "Top 100 School Programs." *Children's Technology Review* (September 5, 2007): 1–29.

Carter, Carolyn M., and Lyle R. Smith. "Does the Use of Learning Logic in Algebra I Make a Difference in Algebra II?" *Journal of Research on Technology in Education* 34, no. 2 (Winter 2001–2002): 157–161.

Craig, Roland. "Open-Source Software." *School Arts* 106, issue 9 (May/June 2007): 34.

Educational Software Preview Guide (ESPG) Consortium hosted by Fermi National Accelerator Laboratory, Education Office, is an open access online searchable directory. http://ed.fnal.gov/espg.

Estep, S., W. McInerney, and E. Vockell. "An Investigation of the Relationship beween Integrated Learning Systems and Academic Achievement." *Journal of Educational Technology Systems* 28, no. 1 (1999–2000): 5–19.

Evans, Arnold. "Look, no hands. . . ." *Times Educational Supplement* (March 10, 2006): Special section 4, p. 6.

Freedman, Alan. *Computer Desktop Encyclopedia.* Point Pleasant, Pa: The Computer Language Company, 2008.

Goyne, June S., Sharon K. McDonough, and Dara D. Padgett. "Practical Guidelines for Evaluating Educational Software." *Clearing House* 73, no. 6 (July/August 2000): 345.

Hoffman, Tony. "The Best Free Software for 2007." *PC Magazine* (February 20, 2007): 61–72.

Kafai, Yasmin B., Megan L. Franke, and Dan S. Battery. "Educational Software Reviews under Investigation." *Education, Communication and Information* 2, issue 213 (December 2002): 163–181.

Karre, MaryAnn. "Pet Vet 3D: Wild Animal Hospital." *School Library Journal* 53, issue 9 (September 2007): 78.

Karre, MaryAnn. "Crazy Machines 1.5: More Gizmos, Gadgets and Whatchemacallits." *School Library Journal* 53, issue 9 (September 2007): 78.

Kassner, Kirk. "One Computer Can Deliver Whole-Class Instruction." *Music Educators Journal* 86, no. 6 (May 2000): 34.

Kim, S., M. Yoon, S.-M. Whang, B. Tversky, and J.B. Morrison, "The Effect of Animation on Comprehension and Interest." *Journal of Computer Assisted Learning* 23, issue 3 (June 2007): 260–270.

Lindroth, Linda. "Hot Websites." *Teaching Journal PreK–34*, issue 4 (May 2007): 28–30.

Ostergard, Maren. "Morton Subotnick's Playing Music." *School Library Journal* 53, issue 9 (September 2007): 78.

Paterson, Wendy A., Julie Jacobs Henry, Karen O'Quin, Maria Ceprano, and Elfreda V. Blue. "Investigating the Effectiveness of an Integrated Learning System on Early Emergent Readers." *Reading Research Quarterly* 38, issue 2 (April–June 2003): 172–175.

Riegler, Ben. "Comic Book Creator." *School Library Journal* 53, issue 9 (September 2007): 77–78.

Roblyer, M. D., Jack Edwards, and Mary Anne Havriluk. *Integrating Educational Technology into Teaching.* Upper Saddle River, N.J.: Merrill-Prentice Hall, 2003.

"Six Strategies for Raising a Scientist." *Software Revue* 8, no. 4 (2000): 12–16.

Technology in Special Education: Assistive Technology

Introduction

Technology can help students with disabilities realize their potential. The computer can help such students achieve equal access to the general education curriculum. This chapter provides guidelines on how the teacher can help students accomplish these educational goals. We examine examples of hardware devices that make it easier for students with disabilities to function successfully in regular classroom settings. We also explore some ways in which the classroom teacher can use computer software to help these students learn. Furthermore, the chapter presents examples of lesson plans that can be used in a variety of situations and Internet sites containing a rich assortment of content.

Using the computer, students and teachers can do the following:

students can

- learn about hardware devices for students with disabilities,
- try software programs that are available for students with disabilities,
- evaluate different software using a checklist,
- search for useful Internet sites,
- create your own glossary of terms.

teachers can

- devise a hardware checklist,
- define terms such as Universal Design for Learning,
- show students quality software based on selected criteria,
- find lesson plans and instructional material,
- show quality Internet sites on special education.

objectives

Upon completing this chapter, you will be able to do the following:

1 Describe three hardware devices that can be used by individuals with disabilities to increase access and function.

2 Name three software programs that are available for individuals with disabilities

3 Define universal design for learning and give an example.

4 Discuss some of the problems and issues involved in special education.

5 Utilize (or adapt) activities to increase integration of students with special needs in the classroom.

6 List some Internet sites on special education that range from lesson plans to organizations. (Visit our online site.)

Students with Disabilities

All students display different physical characteristics: Some are tall, others short; some are thin, others heavy; some wear glasses, others do not. Students also differ in learning ability. Some students differ from the average to such an extent that specialized education or adapted programs are necessary to meet their needs. The term **exceptional children** refers to students who have physical disabilities or sensory impairment, students who have behavior and/or learning problems, or students who are gifted or have special talents (Heward, 2005).

The major disability categories recognized by the school districts are learning disabilities, deaf/hearing impairments, speech or language impairments, visual impairments, other health impairments, orthopedic impairments, mental retardation, emotional disturbance, autism, and traumatic brain injury (Smith, Polloway, Patlon, & Dowdy, 2003). We will only cover some of these categories.

LEARNING DISABILITIES

According to the Twenty-Fifth Annual Report to Congress on the Implementation of the Individuals with Disabilities Education Act (2005), the largest number of students that receive special services are those with learning disabilities.

As defined by the U.S. Department of Education, a learning disability is "a disorder in one or more of the basic psychological processes involved in understanding or using spoken or written language, which may appear as an impaired ability to listen, think, speak, read, write, spell, or do mathematical calculations."

For students with learning disabilities, there is a wide assortment of assisted technology products that can help them improve their skills. For example, when students have difficulty reading, they can use programs such as the *Start-to-Finish Books*, *Trudy's Time and Place House* (Riverdeep), *Stickbear Phonics* (Optimum Resources), *Simon Sounds It Out* (Don Johnston), *Edmark Reading Program Series* (Riverdeep), and *The Sound Reading CD-Teens, 20's and Beyond* (Sound Reading Solutions.) These programs enable students to hear whole passages that are highlighted or to click on individual words. The programs feature comprehension checks, voice, and corrective feedback to help the student. The words and sounds are pronounced and accompanied by colorful pictures. In many of the programs, students can record words and listen for evaluation. In Figure 13.1 the children at CHIME Charter School are using these programs.

Figure 13.1
CHIME Charter School, Woodland Hills—Inclusive Setting

An area that causes students problems is writing. Using organizers with speech capabilities such as *Kidspiration* and *Inspiration* (Inspiration, Inc.) and word processors with organizers such as *Draft: Builder* (Don Johnston) and *Writer's Companion* (Visions Technology in Education) help students outline and organize their writing. Talking word processors such as *Write:Outloud* (Don Johnston) and *Kurzweil 3000* (Kurzweil Educational Systems) help students self-correct, set level of speech feedback, and spell check. In addition, these programs enable the student to adjust how the screen looks. This is an important consideration because, with fewer items on the screen, students can more easily focus on their writing. *Dragon Naturally Speaking* (ScanSoft) enables students to dictate their compositions.

Many students with learning disabilities have trouble with telling time, counting coins, and making change. They can use talking calculators such as *Programming Concepts* and *Coin-U-Lator* (Figure 13.2) that teach students coin counting. In addition, they can use software programs such as *Edmark Telling Time* (Riverdeep), *Making Change* (Attainment), and *IntelliMathics* (Intellitools) for problem solving. These programs generate word or number problems and come with full auditory support.

In our discussion thus far we have talked about hardware and software devices that help students with learning disabilities do their academic work. But there is an obvious free option found in our very own computers. Today, computer makers incorporate computer accessibility options into their operating systems.

The location of this feature is dependent on the operating system of your computer. For the Mac OS (Figure 13.3) universal access setting, this feature is found in the *System Preferences*, whereas for Windows Vista, this feature is found in the *Ease of Access Control Panel* (Figure 13.4).

Figure 13.2
Coin-U-Lator
(*Source:* Reprinted with permission of PCI Educational Publishing)

Figure 13.3
Macintosh Leopard
(*Source:* Screenshot reprinted with permission from Apple, Inc.)

The computer includes options for the mouse and input devices other than the keyboard, and there are also display, sound, and speech options.

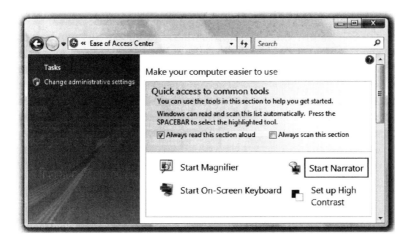

Figure 13.4
Windows Vista
(*Source:* Microsoft product screenshot reprinted with permission from Microsoft Corporation)

STUDENTS WITH VISION IMPAIRMENTS OR BLINDNESS

For the student with visual impairment, a standard monitor that can display large type enables the student to read three lines at a time. Most computers come with the option to switch from black text on a white background to white text on a black background or to change it to grayscale; these features can enhance the visibility of what is on the screen. In addition, a standard zoom feature or advanced screen magnification programs such as *ZoomText* (Windows; Ai Squared) can enhance readability.

Usually, this type of student will be able to use a standard keyboard, but some students may do better with large keytop labels. Standard printers can print out in large size to improve readability. A Braille embosser can print material from the computer in Braille.

Speech Synthesis.   Optical character recognition software can convert printed documents into an electronic format, which can then be read aloud with a speech synthesizer. Many products today use speech synthesis, or computer-generated speech. For example, automobile computers audibly remind drivers to shut the door or fill the gas tank. Speech synthesis is very helpful for students who are visually impaired.

However, students with disabilities are no longer trapped in front of the computer screen to use speech synthesis. Programs such as NextUp.com's *Text Aloud* save files in MP3 or WAV formats. Students can then download their files to an MP3 player or personal digital assistant with sound capabilities.

Screen reading programs such as IBM's *Home Page Reader* make the Internet more accessible to visually impaired students. *Home Page Reader* enables the student to access the Web quickly and easily by requesting a specific URL. Working in conjunction with IBM *ViaVoice Outloud* text-to-speech synthesizer, the program reads the contents of the Web site. Text–speech products such as the *CAST eReader* (Cast Products) read content from word processors, the Internet, and scanned and typed text. Using a simple interface, the student has no trouble navigating and manipulating Web page elements or reading e-mail.

Students with vision impairments or blindness can also use speech synthesis technology to read books and access Braille services online. A free text-to-speech application, *Natural Reader*, is available at http://www.naturalreader.com/. This application reads anything that you view on the monitor.

Voice Recognition. **Voice recognition software** enables users to communicate with the computer through a microphone. The computer then follows their instructions by pulling down a menu or typing text. Everyone's computer fantasy is to be able to dictate a command to the computer through a microphone and have the computer execute the command on the screen. For years, starship captains have been talking to their computers on TV. In the real world, this technology has still not been perfected.

Voice recognition software works by converting the spoken word into binary patterns that are computer recognizable; essentially, it understands human speech. You can enter data or issue simple commands through the system simply by speaking. *Dragon Naturally Speaking* (ScanSoft) is a speech-recognition product that enables users to talk at a natural pace; their words appear on the screen spelled correctly.

Visually impaired students as well as students who cannot type or use handheld devices can benefit from such software. They can create documents, browse the Web, e-mail, and navigate the desktop. Eventually, voice recognition may relegate the mouse and keyboard to the storage bin. As voice recognition systems improve, the visually impaired will attain complete accuracy in their documents when they dictate to the computer.

Adaptive Devices for the Blind. Blind students can use Braille printers, a standard keyboard with Braille key labels, or a **refreshable Braille display** (Sighted Electronics) (Figure 13.5). A refreshable Braille display can be added to a computer system to translate text on the screen into Braille. The Braillex EL 40 S Desktop is a small desktop device that has an easy access bar you can use while you read from any location on the display. It is ergonomically designed and it works with major screen readers.

Figure 13.5
Braillex EL 40 S Desktop
(*Source:* Abledata, http://www.abledata.com/)

STUDENTS WITH HEARING AND SPEECH IMPAIRMENTS

For the student who is deaf or hard of hearing, visual output on the screen replaces sound. The standard flash option can be selected to alert a user when a sound occurs. For example, instead of emitting audible beeps, the monitor blinks. Software programs for the hard of hearing should have captions for spoken elements. People with hearing impairments can learn to speak by matching words displayed on a screen with the sound waves for each word. Because of the growth of the Internet more hearing-impaired individuals use online mail programs instead of specially designed telephones for the deaf (TTY). Currently, Web caption editors, such as *MAGpie* (National Center for Accessible Media), can write video captions in different formats.

STUDENTS WITH HEALTH PROBLEMS

Students who are hospitalized or at home can have easy access to their teachers through the Internet. Using a video camera, they can talk to and see their teachers. They can thus feel some personal connection to the teacher and ask questions that trouble them. The beauty of this arrangement is that the teacher can give the student an automatic response.

With video conferencing, students also can talk and see their fellow classmates and thus feel some personal connection with the classroom environment. Using the Internet, they can send e-mail and get instant messages and access an unlimited library. In the privacy of their house or hospital room, they can view online videos on pertinent topics, research reports, or visit online museums.

These are but a few of the ways that the computer can help the student with disabilities communicate.

Adaptive Technology

The computer has become a natural tool to help the special education student access a general education curriculum. The computer can help the student by acting as a tutor. It can help the student more easily express his or her ideas to the outside world. Using the computer, the student with disabilities is often motivated to spend more time working on an instructional assignment and doing well in school. The computer is very patient and private, so the student is not embarrassed to try or to fail. Students can enjoy the control they can exert over the rate at which they learn; such students often have the experience of having little control over their learning environment.

Special education students receive recognition from the outside world when they achieve something on the computer. Furthermore, the computer increases such students' chances of expressing themselves musically or in words. Students with disabilities who received instruction on computers when they were young can shine when using a computer. They can model skills for other students, boosting their own self-esteem.

The computer can speak for those who cannot speak and generate text for those who cannot move their arms. It can help those with low vision by magnifying text. It can read to the blind and help them communicate more easily. Students who are hearing impaired can easily communicate via e-mail and can participate in chat rooms.

For the student with disabilities to get the full benefits of the computer, certain modifications may be needed for the hardware or software. More than 50 million Americans have some type of disability, necessitating some adaptation of hardware or software for them to use computer technology (Freedman, Martin, & Schoeni, 2004).

Adaptive or assistive technology devices are defined as "any item, piece of equipment, or product system, whether acquired commercially or off the shelf, modified, or customized, that increases, maintains, or improves functional capabilities of individuals with disabilities" (Technology-Related Assistance for Individuals with Disabilities Act). For a list of adaptive or assistive technologies, see the University of Toronto's Adaptive Technology Resource Centre (ATRC) at http://www.atrc.utoronto.ca/.

The distinction between assistive or adaptive technologies and conventional technologies is blurring as more products are being designed for use by a greater number of individuals. A touch screen can be used as an alternative to the mouse by people with disabilities as well as by those without disabilities. For example, touch screens are often used in information booths at airports, in voting machines, and in amusement parks. Eventually, voice recognition may become the most common form of input for everyone, and the keyboard may disappear (Alliance for Technology Access, 2004).

KEYBOARD MODIFICATIONS

The keyboard can be redesigned to meet the user's needs. There are many possibilities, such as an alternative keyboard with greater space between the keys, a simplified arrangement, a keyboard with larger keys, left- and right-handed keyboards, or an onscreen keyboard. Disabling the repeat key helps students with less fine-muscle control; this way, users get one keystroke per character no matter how long the key is held down. For a user with difficulty pressing two keys simultaneously, the keyboard can be designed so that it has **sticky keys**—that is, certain keys that lock in place—allowing the student with a disability to use combination keystrokes without having to press keys simultaneously. A power strip can enable a user to turn on the computer equipment by pressing a single switch as opposed to three or four.

If modifying the keyboard does not work for the student, **keyboard emulators** (onscreen keyboards) may be used. An emulator presents a choice to the student in the form of a whole sentence, phrase, or character; the student then makes a selection with one movement. If a mouse is too difficult to use, a joystick can be used to control speed and direction. Emulators can be used to generate a sequence of keystrokes that can be recalled as sentences or words.

Many students who have disabilities cannot use a traditional input device such as a standard mouse, trackball, or keyboard. For these students, the computer industry has developed alternative devices such as a foot-controlled mouse, touch screens, onscreen keyboards, alternative keyboards, switches, touch tablets, voice-controlled devices, and word prediction software systems.

DISCOVER SWITCH

The **discover switch** is a talking computer switch for the classroom that attaches to the keyboard. With this switch, the computer user can do everything another user could do with a standard keyboard and mouse. A keyboard is displayed on the computer screen to provide choices for writing, using the mouse, or clicking the graphics in multimedia programs such as *Dr. Seuss* (MacKiev). The choices are highlighted automatically, and students then press a switch to make their choice (Figure 13.6). In addition, the onscreen keyboard can speak words, phrases, and even sentences, offering nonspeaking students a way to communicate.

Figure 13.6
Discover Switch
(*Source:* Madentec Limited of Alberta Canada. Used with permission. www. madentec.com)

INTELLIKEYS KEYBOARD

IntelliKeys (IntelliTools) is for people with a wide range of disabilities who require a keyboard (Figure 13.7) with a changing face. The keyboard is compatible with Macintoshes or PC-compatible machines. *IntelliKeys* is packaged with six standard overlays including a setup overlay. Teachers or students can use these overlays with any software or word processing program with keyboard input. Teachers can also create their own custom overlays. Each standard overlay has a bar code that *IntelliKeys* recognizes. Students who use switches can choose from two built-in programmable switch jacks.

Also available are talking keyboards for the classroom, such as *Discover:Board* (Madentec). The student presses *Discover:Board* keys for sounds and speech while doing work. Using this keyboard, the student can receive speech feedback with programs such as *Co:Writer* or *Kid Pix*, as well as with the Internet and online services. It can be used with pictures, text, or just letters.

Figure 13.7
IntelliKeys from Chime School, California.

TOUCH SCREEN

The **touch screen** (Figure 13.8) is a pointing device on which users place their fingers to enter data or make selections. The software program for the touch-screen displays different options on the screen in a graphic button format. For example, in a multiple-choice exam, the student would touch the button for his or her selected answer, and the screen would change in response.

The touch screen offers a real advantage to students with disabilities because it is a fast and natural way to enter data, to make selections, and to issue commands. Despite these wonderful benefits, a touch screen is not useful for inputting large amounts of data or for pointing to a single character. Moreover, it is fatiguing to use for a long period of time, and the screen quickly gets finger marked. Lessons created on one variety of touch screen may not work on another because of software incompatibility.

Figure 13.8
Touch-Screen Panel
(*Source:* © 2008 Jupiterimages, Inc.)

PERSONAL SCANNING PENS

Scanning pens help people with learning disabilities. Two very popular ones are QuickLink Pen (Figure 13.9) and Reading Pen II (Figure 13.10), both produced by Wizcom Technologies. QuickLink Pen scans, stores, and sends text. Using this pen, students take notes and scan printed text, printed Internet links, charts, tables, books, and magazines. The students can then transfer this information to their computers, PDAs, or beam them to their Smartphones. Student can then use these notes to aid them in writing reports. Reading Pen II, a good device for dyslexic users, scans text and reads these scanned words aloud. Reading Pen also spells scanned words and has a dictionary containing 480,000 words. It defines words within the definition of the word. These devices both have assisted technology features such as large character readout and left-handed support.

Figure 13.9
QuickLink Pen Elite
(*Source:* Reprinted by permission of WizCom Technologies)

Figure 13.10
Reading Pen II
(*Source:* Reprinted by permission of WizCom Technologies)

PORTABLE KEYBOARDS

Neo (AlphaSmart Company), previously discussed in Chapter 2, is a powerful portable tool for students with and without disabilities. Students can use this type of portable keyboard (Figure 13.11) to learn keyboarding skills, write, take notes, and keep work organized.

Figure 13.11
A Student Using a Portable Device in the Classroom
(*Source:* Courtesy Vicki Sharp)

Portable keyboards can be used in the classroom, outside, or at home. The *Neo 2* runs on three AA batteries and provides 700 hours of writing time.

Neo also comes with sticky keys, **slow keys** (the computer recognizes only the key presses that are a certain length and disregards others), and auto-repeat control. There are four different keyboard layouts: QWERTY, Dvorak, left-handed, and right-handed. Students can use the keyboard to type their text, edit it, and then transfer it to a printer or directly to their computer for further modifications.

Visit the *Closing the Gap* Web site to learn more about assistive technology resources at http://www.closingthegap.com.

Universal Design for Learning

As you can see from reading these paragraphs, students come with different backgrounds and abilities. An increasing number of these students have learning disabilities. The question that is asked is how teachers can maximize instruction for all their students. The Universal Design field provides a foundation to facilitate this process.

Because teachers face many problems with the diversity of students they have in the classroom, teachers are applying these universal design principles for planning curricula. What this approach to learning does is "addresses diversity during all stages of course design and delivery, minimizing the need to make special arrangements for individuals" (Burgstahler, 2007). Guided by these principles, teachers can create courses with visual aids, videos, and printed materials accessible for the largest number of students possible. For example, a professor uses text-to-speech software on his Web site so that it is accessible to blind students. When he gives a PowerPoint presentation he uses captions for the student that cannot hear.

Universal design principles can be applied to the physical environment by making sure that students have access to materials, activities, equipment and taking into account their safety. To further aid students with disabilities, classroom furniture could be modified. Light switches could be lowered. The furniture should be arranged so teachers and students can move easily around the room.

We read about the importance of universal design for learning, but its significance does not register until we are faced with a real-life situation.

When our education building was constructed, the doors were so heavy it was impossible for students with physical disabilities to push them open. Furthermore, the ramps were not adequate. The administration fixed both problems. They installed enlarged buttons that enabled people to open the doors automatically. In addition, they corrected the ramps so that students with wheelchairs could readily use them. Such modifications in school building design were essential so that students with disabilities could have the same access as those without disabilities. These preceding modifications were designed for students with disabilities; however, many of these modifications also improved access for older individuals, those who are less strong, those carrying instructional material, and those pushing baby strollers. Because the doors were modified, everyone benefited.

Presently universal design concepts are incorporated into computer operating systems (for this example, see 266–267). Universal design concepts have been incorporated into software from companies such as Crick Software, Don Johnston, and Riverdeep. You have been reading about these accessibility options. Because of this development, individuals with disabilities do not have to give specialists money to make software modifications so that they can use these products. Center for Applied Special Technology (CAST) is in the forefront of this universal design movement.

 To learn more about this important topic, see CAST at **http://www.cast.org/**, visit our online site at **http://www.wiley.com/college/sharp**, and see the suggested references at the end of this chapter.

Software for the Special Education Classroom

Today, many software programs help students with disabilities learn, ranging from tutorials to drill and practice. In recent years, there has been an emphasis on software that aids students who are diagnosed with reading problems to improve their proficiency. Because of this emphasis, many software programs focus on building vocabulary and developing phonetics skills and decoding skills. Lets now look at a selection of programs that are especially useful to the special education teacher.

READING

Don Johnston offers a series of *Start-to-Finish Gold* books that motivate students who are struggling with reading. They are high-interest, controlled-vocabulary books that include abridged selections of classic literature, sports biographies, history biographies, original mysteries, and retellings of Sherlock Holmes mysteries. These books range from *The Red Badge of Courage* to the story of *Romeo and Juliet*. *Start-to-Finish* books help students who are two or more grades behind in reading or who are unsuccessful readers. They aid students with language disorders, students learning English as a second language, and those with spelling and writing difficulties. The program comes with a computer book, audiocassette, and paperback book. In Figure 13.12, a page from *I Have a Dream: The Life of Martin Luther King* is shown. The student has the option of listening to the book or reading silently. Students can use single switches to read the books by themselves. Don Johnston has expanded the series with the *Start-to-Finish Blue* books for more advanced students.

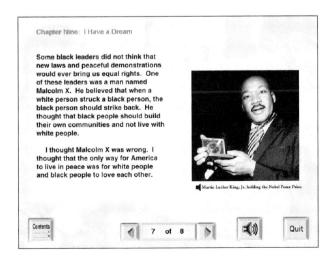

Figure 13.12
Start-to-Finish **Books**
(*Source:* Start-to-Finish® Books, Don Johnston Incorporated)

Along the same lines, Optimum Resources' *High School Reading Comprehension Series* reinforces reading comprehension, analysis skills, and evaluation abilities. This high-interest series features sound, music, and comprehension questions. One of the more popular topics included is fashion. Because of teenage interest in this topic, it encourages the reluctant teenage reader to read. In Figure 13.13, the reader answers a question about fashion and style.

Figure 13.13
Fashion and Style
(*Source:* © Optimum Resources, Inc.)

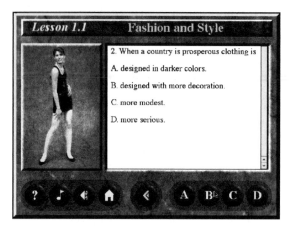

 To learn more about software, visit our online site at **http://www.wiley.com/college/sharp**. In a Podcast, Don Johnston discusses his special needs software products. Dr. Warren Buckleitner, who is an expert on software and technology, imparts his wisdom on educational software programs. Also refer to **www.littleclickers.com/** for a list of Web sites for elementary children. Dr. Buckleitner is editor of *Children's Technology Review*.

Edmark Reading Program Level 1 and 2 (Riverdeep) is designed for students (K–adult) who are struggling with basic reading skills. Using this program, students improve their sight recognition, learn the meaning of words, practice comprehension, and learn to use specific words in story content. The program uses short instructional steps, repetition, and positive reinforcement. Graphics can be turned off for the older student or adult. The management portion of the program is automatic so the individual student's progress is tracked. This program contains universal access features such as a touch window and single-switch compatibility. There is a choice of a standard interface or a simple interface for students who find it difficult to concentrate.

Simon S.I.O. (Sounds It Out), by Don Johnston, for pre-K to grade 2, is an interactive phonics tool designed to help students practice letter sounds. This program (Figure 13.14) features a helpful onscreen tutor, which is available for 31 levels of sounds and words. Colorful graphics, digitized sound, and animation motivate and entertain students during the learning process. *Simon S.I.O.* has a management component that enables the teacher to track the progress of multiple students and customize sound and word lessons. This product can be used with ESL students.

Figure 13.14
Simon S.I.O.
(*Source:* Simon S.I.O. ™, Don Johnston Incorporated)

WORD PROCESSING APPLICATIONS

Word processing is one of the most commonly used applications for students with learning disabilities (Holzberg, 1994). Students who have not written very much become motivated to write by word processing software. Talking word processors such as *Write:OutLoud* (Figure 13.15) can prove very beneficial for the student with learning disabilities. *Write:OutLoud* speaks letters, words, and sentences as they are typed. Students can then correct their writing. The word processor highlights text as it reads it.

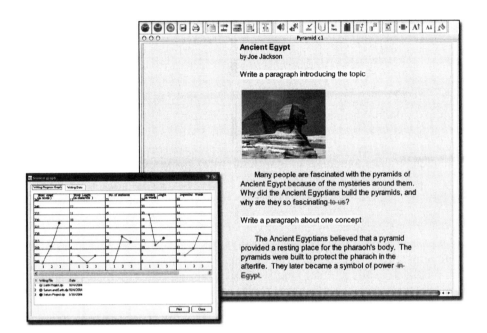

Figure 13.15
Write:OutLoud
(*Source:* Write: Outloud®, Don Johnston Incorporated)

Students can include graphics in their writing or import graphics from other sources. Onscreen tools with speech enable students to work without using menus. The word processor also comes with large font sizes to make the letters easier to read and a talking spell checker.

Another program that is helpful for writing is *CO:Writer*, a writing assistant with word-prediction capabilities that will work with any word processor. A student simply types a letter and *CO:Writer* suggests likely word choices and even reads the choices aloud (Figure 13.16). Students thus learn to make word choices. In addition, *CO:Writer* comes with built-in grammar prediction, which helps with such items as capitalization, spelling, and verb tense.

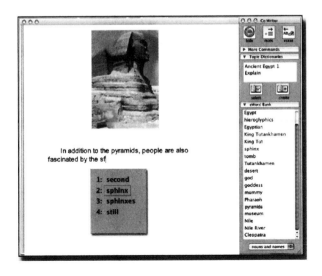

Figure 13.16
CO:Writer
(*Source:* Co: Writer®, Don Johnston Incorporated)

Also, *Clicker 5*, previously discussed in Chapter 6, is a writing and multimedia tool for students of all ability ranges. This talking word processor helps students write with pictures and words. *Wordbar* (Figure 13.17), Crick's writing tool for older students, gives point-and-click access to words, phrases, and Web addresses in all curriculum areas.

Figure 13.17
Wordbar
(*Source:* Crick Software, Inc/ Wordbar ™)

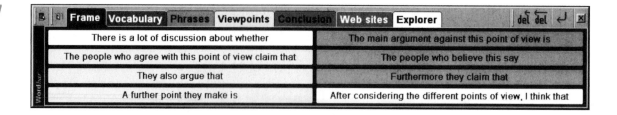

Finally, Aurora Suite 2005 (Aurora Systems) includes a screen reader, type and talk speech, and word prediction in one program. This expensive program has a whole array of features and it works with any application. It contains grammar rules, customizes spelling, and even has the ability to read menus and buttons on the screen. For more information on this program, visit its Web site (http://www.aurora-systems.com/).

MATH

Some programs use arcade-game formats to aid students in developing math skills such as adding and subtracting. These drill-and-practice programs are great ways of providing practice for students with learning disabilities. Some math tutorials give visual feedback to the student, and some simulation programs enable students to solve problems without personal risk.

Millie's Math House (Riverdeep) has been updated with expanded accessibility options for students in grades pre-K–2. This program contains nine activities that explore math concepts ranging from patterns (Figure 13.18) to counting. Drill-and-practice programs such as *Quarter Mile* (Barnum Software) and *Math-O-Matic: Arithmetic Flash Cards* (Math-O-Matic) are very useful programs for students with disabilities. These programs enable students to work at their own pace and receive immediate feedback on math skills.

Figure 13.18
Millie's Math House
(*Source:* ©2008 Riverdeep Interactive Learning Limited, and its licensors)

SCIENCE, SOCIAL STUDIES, AND MISCELLANEOUS PROGRAMS

There are many interesting programs in social studies and science. The new *Incite Learning* series, produced by Don Johnston, include titles such as *Lewis & Clark*

(Figure 13.19), *Middle Ages*, *Civil War: Life and Times*, and *World War II*. This series consists of short films with first-person narratives that aid students in understanding the subject matter and different points of view. The program is perfect for grades 4–9.

Figure 13.19
Incite! Middle Ages
(*Source:* Incite!™ Don Johnston Incorporated)

The *Incite* interactive lessons can be used with students at varying degrees of knowledge or reading levels. Each DVD contains five short original films that run 5–7 minutes, an instructional guide, thought sheets, sticky notes, an Anchor poster, and an Administrator's Walk-Through Guide.

Also, the newly updated *Sammy's Science House* (Houghton Mifflin Learning Technologies) for grades pre-K–2 helps students master elementary science concepts using seven different activities. Sammy shows students how to classify, sort, recycle, (Figure 13.20), construct, analyze, and more. This program also provides access to those with special needs.

Figure 13.20
Sammy's Science House
(*Source:* ©2008 Riverdeep Interactive Learning Limited, and its licensors)

MULTIMEDIA

Scratch (MIT Media Lab), and *Inspiration* (Inspiration) are two special programs that can help students with visual learning and multimedia authoring.

In collaboration with the UCLA Graduate School of Education and Information Studies, *Scratch* is designed by the Lifelong Kindergarten group at MIT Media Lab (http://www.media.mit.edu). *Scratch* (http://scratch.mit.edu/) is a free tile-based programming language that helps students from grades 3 and up to create interactive stories, games (Figure 13.21), animation, music, and art, and save these creations online. As they create they learn how to design, understand mathematical computation, collaborate, and analyze.

Figure 13.21
Scratch
(*Source:* Courtesy the Media Laboratory)

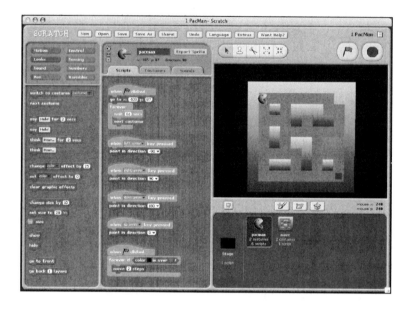

Inspiration is a powerful visual learning tool that helps students organize their thoughts (see Chapter 11). Students can visually map a story such as *Are You My Mother?* (Figure 13.22). In so doing they gain a greater understanding of the story's content.

Figure 13.22
Inspiration
(*Source:* Diagram created in Inspiration® by Inspiration Software®, Inc.)

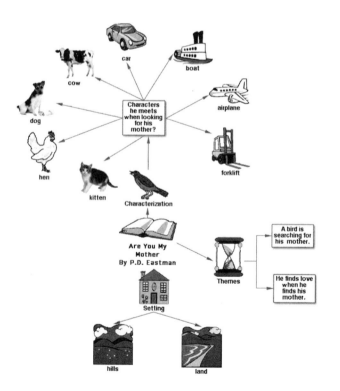

What follows is a checklist to use when evaluating assistive/adaptive technology.

Assistive/Adaptive Technology Checklist*

Directions: Examine the following items and determine which ones you feel are important for your class situation. Place an X on each line for which the software meets your needs.

Product Name_____ **Manufacturer**_____ **Grade Level**_____

Subject Area_____ **Skill Level**

Hardware

___ 1. Handheld devices

   ___ a. Scans type and edits text

   ___ b. Converts print documents into electronic format

   ___ c. Has outlining and word prediction capability

   ___ d. Exchanges files with PC and Palm applications

   ___ e. Uploads to printer and computer

   ___ f. Pronounces text, syllabication, spelling, and definitions

   ___ g. Has built-in loudspeaker and earphone jack

___ 2. Computer accessibility

   ___ a. Displays large type, reverses print color, offers varying grayscale, and uses sound in place of visual output

   ___ b. Alternative keyboard options include sticky keys and slow keys

   ___ c. Has mouse options and touch-free or alternative input devices

   ___ d. Is power activated with a single key

   ___ e. Translates text on screen into Braille

   ___ f. Prints out any size text or prints in Braille

___ 3. Ease of use

   ___ a. Memory requirements not too high

   ___ b. Is software and hardware compatible

   ___ c. Reasonable cost

   ___ d. Meets training requirements

Software

___ 1. Reading programs

   ___ a. Reads aloud individual words or whole passages

   ___ b. Has comprehension and analysis checks

   ___ c. Tracks progress of students and customizes lessons

   ___ d. Offers voice and corrective feedback

   ___ e. Creates personalized stories/movies

   ___ f. Includes pictures, graphics, digitized sound, and animation

   ___ g. Has high-interest stories with controlled vocabulary

   ___ h. Has universal access features

   ___ i. Has bilingual capabilities

___ 2. Speech products and synthesizers

   ___ a. Reads content from electronic documents/textbooks, word processors, and the Internet

   ___ b. Is downloadable to MP3 or WAV formats

   ___ c. Speaks Web page information and e-mail

   ___ d. Has voice recognition to create documents, browse the Web, e-mail, and navigate the desktop

   ___ e. Develops sound awareness and other aspects of voice

___ 3. Writing programs and word processing applications

   ___ a. Outlines and organizes writing

   ___ b. Has visual tools to map ideas and stories

   ___ c. Has speech/talking word processing capabilities

   ___ d. Imports graphics from other sources

   ___ e. Has word and grammar prediction capability

   ___ f. Writes with pictures and words

   ___ g. Has adjustable level of feedback and auditory support to help students self-correct

Rating Scale

Rate the program by placing a check in the appropriate line.

Excellent_____ Very good _____ Good _____ Fair _____ Poor _____

Comments:

*Courtesy of Sarah Hall

Laws Affecting Special Education

In 1949, no laws existed that required a school district to educate a student with special needs. If a student was diagnosed as having mental retardation, he or she usually was placed in a separate school or institution for children with disabilities. If there was no school or institution that could accommodate this student, the school district was not required by law to provide an education, and it was up to the parent or guardian to find a solution to the problem. Parent groups organized in response to the fact that their children were not being given access to a general education, and a movement to educate students with disabilities grew. At the same time, other factors contributed to the rise in the need for special education; these included changes in the economy, demographic shifts, changes in the family structure, and greater awareness of substance abuse and child abuse. As a result, laws were enacted to make sure that all students received optimal educational opportunities regardless of their disabilities. There were a number of key pieces of legislation that were important in ensuring that all students receive the same educational opportunities whatever their abilities.

Congress originally enacted the Individuals with Disabilities Acts in 1975. This particular act gave children with disabilities the opportunity to receive a free and appropriate public education (FAPE). This act has seen many revisions. The Technology-Related Assistance Act for Individuals with Disabilities, 1988 (Public Law 100-407) provided funding for assistance technology devices and services.

A key component of IDEA 1997 (Public Law 105-7) was that preschool, elementary school, and secondary schoolchildren receive FAPE. Schools are required to provide students with assistive technology (wheelchairs, switches, speech enhancement devices, etc.; (see http://idea.ed.gov/explore/home). The No Child Left Behind Act of 2001 (Public Law 107-110), commonly known as NCLB, had an impact by requiring that schools meet specific performance criteria. IDEA in 2004 promotes the use of technologies with universal design and assistive technology devices so children can participate in the general education curriculum and achieve. Because of the enactment of these laws, students with disabilities could no longer be separated from other students and be treated unequally.

To learn about these laws consult the Guide to Disabilities Rights Laws at http://www.usdoj.gov/crt/ada/cguide.htm and consult Individuals with Disabilities Education Act (IDEA) at http://www.nichcy.org/idea.htm.

Students with disabilities are now required to be placed in the regular classroom whenever possible. Schools have tried to provide such equal access through mainstreaming and inclusion.

Mainstreaming

After the passage of the 1975 Education for All Handicapped Children Act (PL 94–142), the term **mainstreaming** was adopted to refer to part-time and full-time programs that educated students with disabilities alongside their nondisabled peers. Students diagnosed with disabilities would be placed in regular classrooms all or part of the day. Students in mainstreaming programs might leave the general-education classroom for time in the resource room or for speech and language services. Special education teachers were in charge of these students, and the responsibility for their progress rested with them. Special education services did not have to be provided in the regular classroom. Often, the decision to place a student in a mainstreamed class was based on the educator's assessment of the student's readiness. Mainstreaming was broadly interpreted, which led to many different implementations.

Inclusion

Inclusion grew out of mainstreaming and shares many of its goals. **Inclusion** is based on the concept of the least-restrictive environment (LRE). LRE requires that schools make every reasonable attempt to educate students with disabilities with their peers who do not have disabilities. *Inclusion* has all students attending regular classes unless the school can show a reason this is not feasible. *Full inclusion* requires that all students be educated in a regular classroom regardless of the severity of disability. Currently students with disabilities are found in regular classrooms and they receive support from various personnel.

A successful inclusion program has a planned system of training and supports. Such a program usually includes the collaboration of a multidisciplinary team comprised of peers, classroom teachers, special educators, and family members. A disabled student is a full member of the classroom and receives special education within the regular classroom. For inclusion to be effective, teachers must be flexible and responsive to students' needs. There are drawbacks as well as advantages to this type of program. (See the PDF file online and the suggested readings and references at the end of the chapter.)

Adapting Classroom Lesson Plans for Students with Disabilities

By adapting classroom lessons, the teacher can meet the needs of the student with disabilities. The teacher should divide the class into small groups so that students can help each other. They then can work in pairs, complementing each other's strengths. Teachers can use a buddy system in which one student mentors another. If appropriate, teachers can use peer tutoring or cross-age tutoring. For any lesson, they can choose software that is auditory to help students who have trouble reading. The teacher can have someone read a written script to help with directions. Before writing a book report or composition, students might use a graphic organizer such as *Inspiration*, which visually represents the material and breaks it down into small steps. If the students need writing help, they can use a talking word processor or word prediction program.

SAMPLE CLASSROOM LESSON PLANS

I. USING FACE PUPPETS

Subject: Language Arts and Reading

Grade(s): 2–5

Objectives
Students will read a book, create a mask that portrays the main character in the story, and retell the story.

Standards
- NCTE English Language Arts Standards 3, 4
- ISTE NETS for Students 2, 3

Materials

You will need a program like the free Billy Bear program *Making Faces*. Use the following site to download this free program: http://www.billybear4kids.com/Learn2Draw/MakingFaces/Cartoons.html.

Procedures

1. Arrange the class into pairs in which the strengths of one student complement the strengths of the other.
2. Assign a short story for each pair to read and discuss.
3. Have students use a face-making program to print out a face to help illustrate their stories (Figure 13.23).

Figure 13.23
Making a Face
(*Source:* Courtesy of Vick Sharp)

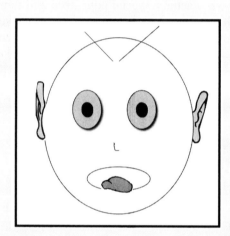

4. Next, have the students attach the faces to paper plates, sticks, or paper bags.
5. Ask students to share their stories with the class by retelling them.

Adaptation

If students have reading difficulties, simply tape-record or voice-record the story. This way a student can stop the recording when he or she wishes. There are numerous free library audiocassettes and CD-ROMs of books and short stories. You can also download audio books on your iPod. Furthermore, Don Johnston has a collection of *Start-to-Finish* books that can be used for this activity. For this series, there are audiocassettes, books, and CD-ROMs.

II. USING THE WEB TO DO HISTORICAL RESEARCH

Subject: Social Studies and History

Grade(s): 5–8

Objective

Using Internet sites such as *The American Civil War Homepage* (http://sunsite.utk.edu/civil-war/), students will learn about the Civil War.

Standards

- National Council for the Social Studies Curriculum Standards 2, 4, 5
- ISTE NETS for Students 4, 5

Materials

You will need an Internet connection and a word processing program.

Procedures

1. Arrange the class into pairs in which the strengths of one student complement the strengths of the other.

2. Have each group research some aspect of the Civil War. For example, a group could investigate the causes of the Civil War or contrast and compare the North and South.

3. Have the students search the Internet for information. Make sure they carefully document their research.

4. Ask students to use a word processor to create a paper explaining their findings.

5. Have the students discuss their papers in class.

Adaptation

If your students are visually impaired or blind, they can use a Web reader such as *Home Page Reader for Windows* (IBM). This program enables the student to open the Web page and listen to the page being read, including the text, data, and graphic descriptions. For students with visual impairments, teachers can print the material in large print. Teachers also can have students use keyboards with large-size letter stickers and software enlargement products.

III. WRITING STORIES

Subject: Language Arts and Writing and Planning

Grade(s): 2–6

Objective

Students will develop their language skills by writing a story.

Standards

• NCTE English Language Arts Standards 5, 12
• ISTE NETS for Students 2, 3

Materials

You will need a planner such as *Kidspiration* and a word processor such as *Write:Outloud* or a combination word processor and planner such as *Writer's Companion*.

Procedures

1. Arrange the class into pairs in which the strengths of one student complements the strengths of the other.

2. Have students use an organizer, such as *Kidspiration*, to plan their stories.

3. Ask students to use a word processor to type their stories.

Adaptation

Use large print for students with vision limitations. *Kidspiration* comes with a speech and recording feature so the students can record sounds and hear their planner. Use a word processor with speech output such as *Write:OutLoud* so the students can hear their stories and see them.

IV. TRAVELING TO DIFFERENT COUNTRIES

Subject: Geography

Grade(s): 2 and up

Objectives

Using the Internet, students will learn about a city, state, or region, and from this information create travel brochures.

Standards

- National Council for the Social Studies Curriculum Standards 3
- NCTE English Language Arts Standards 5, 12
- ISTE NETS for Students 3, 4

Materials

You will need an Internet connection and a print graphics program such as *Stationery Studio* (FableVision).

Procedures

1. Divide the class into small groups.

2. Have the students choose a city, state, or region.

3. Have the students pretend they are in charge of a tourist bureau for this area.

4. Ask students to research the region's geographic features, economy, restaurants, state capital, major attractions, hotel accommodations, camping facilities, and any other pertinent information. They can use the following Internet sites:

   a. State Report Information from Multnomah County Library in Portland, Oregon (http://www.multcolib.org/homework/)

   b. Sites with state facts information (http://www.multnomah.lib.or.us/lib/homework/state2hc.html#general)

   c. Yahoo! Get Local (http://local.yahoo.com)

   d. Hometown USA (http://www.hometownusa.com)

   e. Uscity.net (http://www.uscity.net)

   f. 411 Cities (http://www.411-cities.com)

   g. About.com's Cities/Towns (http://www.about.com/citiestowns)

   h. America.com (http://www.america.com)

   i. Travel.excite.com (http://www.travel.excite.com)

   j. Travelfacts.com (http://www.travelfacts.com)

5. If the students do not want to limit themselves to these sites, have them use search engines to find other sites.

6. Have students in lower grades use a program such as *Stationery Studio* (FableVision) to create a mini book and students in upper grades use a program such as *Microsoft Word* to create a travel brochure.

Adaptation

If your students are visually impaired, they can use a Web reader such as *Home Page Reader for Windows* (IBM). You can print the material in large print. You can also have students use keyboards with large-size letter stickers and software enlargement products.

V. THE ALPHABET

Subject: Language Arts and English

Grade(s): K–1

Objective

Students will develop their language skills by creating an alphabet book.

Standards
- NCTE English Language Arts Standards 3, 4, 7
- ISTE NETS for Students 2, 3

Materials

You will need a talking word processor.

Procedures

1. Divide the students into groups of two.

2. Tell each group to create an alphabet book.

3. Have each group use a talking word processor program such as *Write:OutLoud* to type a letter of the alphabet in a large font size. This word processor will speak the letter as it is typed.

4. Tell each group to find words to illustrate five letters of the alphabet. Students can look in books placed in the room.

5. When the students are finished, have them share the words they chose to illustrate the letters.

Adaptation

Students with handicaps may need an alternative keyboard with large numbers and letters such as *IntelliKeys* (IntelliTools). For students with learning disabilities, the computer should have speech output to read text. A tape recorder or voice recorder can be used to play the directions over and over.

VI. COMPARISON SHOPPING

Subject: Math and Problem Solving

Grade(s): 2–6

Objective

Students will learn how to shop by using a program such as *Ice Cream Truck* or *Hot Dog: Stand Top Dog* (Sunburst).

Standards
- National Council of Teachers of Mathematics Standards 6, 8
- ISTE NETS for Students 5, 6

Materials

You will need a program similar to *Hot Dog Stand: Top Dog*.

Procedures

1. Divide the class into small groups.

2. Have each group use *Hot Dog Stand: Top Dog* (Figure 13.24) to assume the role of the owner of a hot dog stand. Groups will begin with $5,000 and try to make as much money as possible.

3. Have the groups decide where they want the location of their stand, how much they want to charge, and how much product they wish to buy. These decisions are based on such factors as event calendar and temperature. They can analyze research data before they make any big decisions.

4. Ask the class to discuss strategies.

5. Have the students work on the project during the week.

6. At the end of the week, ask the students to discuss results.

Figure 13.24
Hot Dog Stand: Top Dog
(*Source:* Copyright Sunburst Technology
Corporation.)

7. To expand on the activities, have students conduct experiments to determine what is the best price to charge for their hot dogs and the best location.

Adaptation

For students with vision impairments, change the control panel to enlarge the text. The computer should have a voice synthesizer. Students with handicaps may need an alternative keyboard with large numbers and letters.

VII. BRUSHING YOUR TEETH

Subject: Science and Health

Grade(s): K and up

Objective
Students will learn how to create an instructional simulation.

Standards
• National Science Education Standards F1
• ISTE NETS for Students 2, 3

Materials
You will need *PowerPoint* or a similar program, a computer with sound capabilities, and a digital camera.

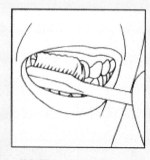

Figure 13.25
How to Brush
(*Source:* Image provided Courtesy of the
American Dental Association)

Procedures

1. Divide the students into small groups.

2. Instruct each group to create an instructional simulation. For example, one group may want to show the class how to brush their teeth properly.

3. Have students take pictures of each step that is required to complete the assignment.

4. After they save their pictures, ask them to copy and paste them into *PowerPoint*.

5. Next, have the groups record instructions for each slide. For example (Figure 13.25), students may start with "Place your toothbrush at a 45-degree angle against the gums" (American Dental Association, 2003). If the class is advanced, they may enhance the recording by identifying the different types of teeth (molars, incisors, etc.).

6. Have students share their presentations.

Adaptation

This activity can be used with students with developmental disabilities. However, the teacher should assemble the *PowerPoint* presentation. The students can take pictures and learn from the instructions. Wissick and Schweder (2001) wrote a creative article on making a grilled cheese sandwich. (See references at the end of the chapter for the complete citation.)

SUMMARY

The computer has been invaluable in helping special education students realize their potential. This chapter examined some of the key legislation affecting special education. We considered different ways of integrating technology into the classroom. In addition, we studied seven ready-to-use lesson plans for any student and how these lesson plans could be adapted for students with special needs. The chapter also reviewed some of the software and hardware that is available for these exceptional students. We explored terms such as *mainstreaming* and *inclusion*. Be sure to review the annotated list of award-winning special education programs on the Online Learning site.

STUDY AND ONLINE RESOURCES

CHAPTER 13 ONLINE RESOURCES

 In the **student section** of the book's online site at **http://www.wiley.com/college/sharp**, you will find templates and examples, video tutorials, PDFs, checklists, articles, Web sites, software reviews, and chapter quizzes. Access these resources to learn about technology and integrating it into the classroom.

CHAPTER MASTERY TEST

Lets check for chapter comprehension with a short mastery test. Key Terms, Computer Lab, and Suggested Readings and References follow the test.

1. How can the Internet be used to help students with special needs?

2. How does technology benefit students with special needs?

3. What is a *speech synthesizer*? What is the relationship between a speech synthesizer and voice input?

4. Distinguish between *mainstreaming* and *inclusion.*

5. Give two examples of output devices that help students with vision impairments or blindness overcome their disability.

6. What is *word prediction software* and why is it helpful for students with learning disabilities?

7. Why are the Individuals with Disabilities Education Act Amendments of 1997 (PL 105-17) important to students with disabilities?

8. What are some ways you can rearrange the computer equipment to make it easier for the student with special needs?

9. What is a *touch screen* and how can it be used to provide help to students with disabilities? List some advantages as well as disadvantages of this technology.

10. How can the computer enhance the development of reading skills for the child with learning disabilities?

11. Give two examples of input devices that help students with physical disabilities use the computer.

12. What is universal design for learning? Give an example.

KEY TERMS

Adaptive or assistive technology p. 269

Discover switch p. 270

Exceptional children p. 265

Inclusion p. 281

Keyboard emulators p. 270

Mainstreaming p. 280

Refreshable Braille display p. 268

Slow keys p. 272

Speech synthesis p. 267

Sticky keys p. 270

Touch screen p. 271

Universal design for learning p. 272

Voice recognition software p. 268

COMPUTER LAB: Activities for Mastery and Your Portfolio

13.1 Use a multimedia program to develop a presentation for the class with special needs. Watch the Video tutorial online and learn how to create a PowerPoint presentation.

13.2 Use the computer to visit the White House site (http://www.whitehouse.gov). What are some of the advantages and disadvantages of this trip for a student with special needs over a real-life visit to the White House?

13.3 Using word processing software, write a story for the special needs class using students' names. Illustrate this story with pictures and sounds. Print the story and read it to the class.

SUGGESTED READINGS AND REFERENCES

Alliance for Technology Access. *Computer Resources for People with Disabilities: A Guide to Assistive Technologies, Tools and Resources for People of All Ages (Computer Resources for People with Disabilities)*. Alameda, Calif.: Hunter House, 2004.

Allington, R. L. "You Can't Learn Much from Books You Can't Read." *Educational Leadership* 603 (2002): 16–19.

Beigel, Andrew R. "Assistive Technology Assessment: More Than the Device." *Intervention in School and Clinic* 35, no. 4 (March 2000): 237.

Bernacchio, Charlie, Flynn Ross, Kimberley Robinson Washburn, Jean Whitney, and Diane R. Wood. "Faculty Collaboration to Improve Equity, Access, and Inclusion in Higher Education." *Equity and Excellence in Education* 40, issue 1 (March 2007): 56–66.

Burgstahler, Sheryl. "Who Needs an Accessible Classroom?" *Academe* 93, issue 3 (May/June 2007): 37–39.

Cawley, John, Shari Hayden, Elsa Cade, and Susan Baker-Kroczynski. "Including Students with Disabilities into the General Education Science Classroom." *Exceptional Children* 68, no. 4 (Summer 2002): 423–435.

Dacey, M., K. Eichleay, and J. McCauley. "The Student Access Map (SAM): Ensuring Access to the General Curriculum." *Closing the Gap* 11, no. 3 (2002): 1, 8–9, 23.

Dolan, B. "Universal Design for Learning." *Journal of Special Education Technology* 15, no. 4 (2000): 44–51.

Downing, June E. "Meeting the Communication Needs of Students with Severe and Multiple Disabilities in General Education Classrooms." *Exceptionality* 9, no. 3 (2001): 147–156.

Edyburn. D. L. "Reading Difficulties in the General Education Classroom: Taxonomy of Text Modification Strategies." *Closing the Gap* 21, no. 6 (2003): 1, 10–13, 30–31.

Edyburn, D. L. "Assistive Technology and Students with Mild Disabilities." *Focus on Exceptional Children* 32, issue 9 (May 2000): 23–27.

Edyburn, D. L. "Introduction to the Special Issue." *Remedial and Special Education* 24, issue 3 (May/June 2003): 130–132.

Edyburn, D. L. "Technology Integration Strategies: Universal Design and Technology Integration, Finding the Connections." *Closing the Gap* 20, no. 1 (2001): 21–22.

Edyburn, D. L. "99 Essential Web Sites for Special Educators." *Special Education Technology Practice* (May/June 2002): 37–41.

Edyburn, D. L. "2001 in Review: A Synthesis of the Special Education Technology Literature." *Journal of Special Education Technology* 17, no. 2 (Spring 2002): 5–24.

Freedman, A. *The Computer Desktop Encyclopedia*. New York: American Management Association, 2007, at http://www.computerlanguage.com/techweb.html

Freedman, Vicki A., Linda G. Martin, and Robert F. Schoeni. "Disability in America." *Population Bulletin* 59 (September 2004): 1–32.

Heim, Judy. "Locking Out the Disabled." *PC World* 18, no. 9 (September 2000): 181.

Heward, William L. *Exceptional Children: An Introduction to Special Education, 8th ed.* Upper Saddle River, N.J.: Merrill, 2005.

Hitchcock, C., A. Meyer, D. Rose, and R. Jackson. "Providing New Access to the General Curriculum: Universal Design for Learning." *Teaching Exceptional Children* 35, no. 2 (2002): 8–17.

Holzberg, Carol S. "Technology in Special Education." *Technology and Learning* 14, no. 7 (April 1994): 18–21.

Keeler, Christy G., and Mark Horney. "Online Course Designs: Are Special Needs Being Met?" *American Journal of Distance Education* 21, issue 2 (July 2007): 61–75.

King-Sears. M. E. "Three Steps for Gaining Access to the General Educational Curriculum for Learners with Disabilities." *Intervention in School and Clinic* 37, no. 2 (2001): 67–76.

Lauffer, Kimberly A. "Accommodating Students with Specific Writing Disabilities." *Journalism and Mass Communication Educator* 54, no. 4 (Winter 2000): 29.

Male, Mary. *Technology for Inclusion: Meeting the Special Needs of All Students.* Boston: Allyn and Bacon, 2003.

Male, Mary, and Doug Gotthoffer. *Quick Guide to the Internet for Special Education.* Boston: Allyn and Bacon, 2000.

Mates, Barbara T., Doug Wakefield, and Judith M. Dixon. *Adaptive Technology for the Internet: Making Electronic Resources Accessible to All.* Chicago: American Library Association Editions, 2000.

McLeskey, James, and Nancy L. Waldron. "School Change and Inclusive Schools: Lessons Learned from Practice." *Phi Delta Kappan* 84, no. 1 (September 2002): 65–72.

Moore, Stephanie, David H. Rose, and Anne Meyer, "Teaching Every Student in the Digital Age: Universal Design for Learning." *Educational Technology Research and Development* 55, issue 5 (October 2007): 521–525.

Rea, Patricia J., Virginia L. McLaughlin, and Chriss Walther-Thomas. "Outcomes for Students with Learning Disabilities in Inclusive and Pullout Programs." *Exceptional Children* 68, no. 2 (Winter 2002): 203–222.

Rose, D., and A. Meyer. *Teaching Every Student in the Digital Age.* Alexandria, Va.: ASCD, 2002, at http://www.cast.org/teachingeverystudent/ideas/tes.

Smith, Tom E., Edward A. Polloway, James Patlon, and Carol Dowdy. *Teaching Students with Special Needs in Inclusive Settings, 4th ed.* Boston: Pearson/Allyn and Bacon, 2003.

Stanovich, Paula J., and Anne Jordan. "Preparing General Educators to Teach in Inclusive Classrooms: Some Food for Thought." *Teacher Educator* 37, no. 3 (Winter 2002): 173–185.

25th Annual Report to Congress on the Implementation of the Individuals with Disabilities Education Act to ensure the free appropriate public education of all Children with disabilities. Washington, D.C: U.S. Department of Education, Office of Special Education and Rehabilitative Services, 2005, at http://www.ed.gov/about/reports/annual/osep/2003/index.html

Webb, Barbara J. "Planning and Organizing—Assistive Technology Resources in Your School." *Teaching Exceptional Children* 32, no. 4 (March/April 2000): 50.

Wehmeyer, M. L., D. Lattin, and M. Agran. "Achieving Access to the General Education Curriculum for Students with Mental Retardation." *Education and Training in Mental Retardation and Developmental Disabilities* 36 (2001): 327–342.

Wilson, Elizabeth K., and Margaret L. Rice. "Virtual Field Trips and Newsrooms: Integrating Technology into the Classroom." *Social Education* 64, no. 3 (April 2000): 152.

Wissick, Cheryl, and Windy Schweder. "The Grilled Cheese Project: Using Presentation Software to Create Functional Software for Your Classroom." *Special Education Technology Practice* (March/April 2001): 32–36.

Zhang, Yuehua. "Technology and the Writing Skills of Students with Learning Disabilities." *Journal of Research on Computing in Education* 32, no. 4 (Summer 2000): 467.

Teacher Support Tools and Music, Art, and Graphics Software

Integrating Teacher Support Tools into the Classroom

Some computer software programs are especially designed for teachers. These programs can make a teacher's school year easier. They help the teacher plan everyday activities; design notes, letters, labels, and newsletters; and track information.

objectives

Upon completing this chapter, you will be able to do the following:

1 Discuss the features of a variety of teacher support software packages.

2 Identify teacher support tools that help teachers and students be more productive.

3 Describe three types of graphics software programs and how they are used in the classroom.

4 Explain the difference between paint programs and draw programs.

The teacher can utilize a variety of programs including grade-book programs, test makers, rubric creators, worksheet generators, crossword puzzle creators, certificate makers, and word searches. This chapter explores how to use these software programs to help students better accomplish educational objectives. In addition, we learn how the teacher and students can use graphics applications and art and music programs to improve students' performance in a variety of classroom situations.

Using the computer, students and teachers can do the following:

students can

- prepare a portfolio using a presentation package such as *PowerPoint*,
- create a newsletter on a current event topic,
- use a print software tool such as *Stationery Studio* to write a book report,
- create a sign for special events or as a public service warning, and
- create a time line banner using a program such as *TimeLiner.*

teachers can

- create history or spelling crossword puzzles,
- create a slide show to teach about a country,
- use a grade-book program to keep track of students' scores,
- use a flash card maker to help students with math skills,
- use a story starter program to give the class help in writing, and
- create personal name tags for classroom trips.

What Are Teacher Support Tools?

Teacher support tools (Figure 14.1) increase the classroom teacher's effectiveness (Moore, Orey, & Hardy, 2000). These programs are meant not for the student but for the teacher—to help in such tasks as recording grades, generating tests, making flash cards, generating puzzles and worksheets, and performing statistical analyses. These software tools save time and improve accuracy by assisting the teacher in chores that cannot easily be done otherwise. For example, a grade-book program can quickly weigh students' grades, calculate means and standard deviations, assign grades, and alphabetize the student list.

Figure 14.1
A teacher using support tools

Teacher Support Tools

When shopping for a utility program, a teacher should determine whether the program fits his or her needs, saves time, and results in student learning.

GRADE BOOKS

Teachers have different options when it comes to keeping track of their grades. They can use the old-fashioned pencil-and-paper grade book, input the data using a spreadsheet, or use an electronic program specifically designed for keeping track of grades. A spreadsheet is more difficult to use because it takes a longer time to set up. Electronic grade books enable teachers to quickly print reports, generate graphs, create seating charts, and track attendance. Furthermore, electronic grade books help teachers inform students, parents, and administrators about pupil performance in the classroom.

Lets examine one of these popular grade book programs to give you an idea of some of the features that these programs have. *GradeQuick* (Jackson Software) is an intuitive program created to look like a paper grade book (Figure 14.2). With this program you enter data directly into the grade book spreadsheet and display the information on one main screen.

Figure 14.2
GradeQuick
(*Source:* Edline - Heart of the Learning Community acohn@edline.com)

Name	ID	Facts-1	Facts-2	Apply₁	Compare₃	Total	Max	Avg	Grade
Long Name		Basic mat	Basic mat	Apply math	Compare				Yr
Term		1	1	1	1				
Category		Test	Test	Quiz	Homework				
Date		09/06/07	09/12/07	09/28/07	10/09/07				
Possible		100	100	50	50				
1. Adler, Leslie	1	100	100	45ᵢ	û+	389.5	400	97.37	A
2. Boyd, Jerry	18	**	75ₘ	32	ok	219.5	300	73.16	C
3. Chang, Julia	5	94	97	49	Good	371.0	400	92.75	A
4. Cohen, Josh	6	100	100	X	û	349.0	350	99.71	A
5. Denton, Bill	14	90	81	48	A	353.0	400	88.25	B
6. Flaherty, Sarah	7	88	84	45ᵢ	Fail	242.0	300	80.66	B
7. Gardner, Alex	4	92	76	50	NC	293.0	400	73.25	C
8. Guth, Michael	8	66	77	**	Good	257.0	350	73.42	C
9. Jackson, Martin	9	90	88	44	Pass	347.5	400	86.87	B
10. Johnson, Dave	2	NC	90	46	Failᵢ	216.0	400	54.00	F
11. Lansing, Eva	10	70ᵢ	88	30	A-	299.0	400	74.75	C
12. Lee, Thomas	13	97	55	38	Pass	304.5	400	76.12	C

GradeQuick - DEMOFILE.GBK

File Edit View Graph Grading Reports Edline Options Window Help

Attendance   Seating Chart   Reports   Student Information   Edit Skills   Lesson Planner   Memo   Send to Edline   Save to Edline   SupportLink Online   GradeQuick Web

View All Terms

Basic math facts subtraction 2 Avg: 79 Median: 85 High: 100

Press F1 for help.   C:\GQWin\DEMOFILE.GBK

You can customize this main screen and view any item by just clicking the mouse. For example, you may want to display statistics or show personal student data fields in addition to student averages and test scores. You have control over the content, style, and layout of this program. There is a wide selection of ready-to-print reports. The program displays statistics and will print them in any report. *GradeQuick* even comes with a seating chart feature that enables the teacher to display and print student pictures on the chart (Figure 14.3). With *GradeQuick* you can post attendance records, homework assignments, and grades on the Web. *GradeQuick* also lets you create colorful graphs to show students' progress.

Figure 14.3
GradeQuick Seating Chart
(*Source:* Edline - Heart of the Learning Community acohn@edline.com)

Some other standalone programs that are effective for the classroom teacher are *Making the Grade* (Jay Klein Productions), *Gradebook Plus* (SVE & Churchill Media), *Easy Grade Pro* (Orbis Software), and *Gradekeeper* (shareware). A useful site for reviews of the latest grade programs is http://www.educational-software-directory.net/teacher's/gradebook.html.

Note that many grade book programs are Web based. Teachers are using the Web to manage their grades, assignments, calendars, lessons, and attendance. For example, *ThinkWave Web Educator* (found at http://thinkwave.com/) handles these tasks easily. Using *ThinkWave*'s software, the teacher creates a grade book and selects the information to publish on the Internet. *ThinkWave* then creates student and parent accounts for each student in the teacher's class. Next, the teacher gives students and parents a start key and password so they can access the account. Students can log on to their accounts to see their individual class information. Parents can also log on to see their child's progress and communicate with the teacher.

Numerous school districts, colleges, and universities have adopted a student information system or student information management system designed for administrators, teachers, parents, students, and staff. This software application manages students' data. When these individuals use this management software package they each have their own unique Web portal transporting them to functions and information they need. Using a Web browser, they are able to access different modules such as a grade book, report card, attendance charts, report writer, portfolios, picture id, skill-based report cards, and schedules. Parents can access the site with a

To investigate different Web sites on teacher support tools, visit our online site at http://www.wiley.com/college/sharp.

password and see their child's information, and the teacher can log on to access their grades. A few of these systems are MMS Student Information Management System, Rediker Software's student information system, Infinite campus (http://www .infinitecampus.com), and Mac School. They also have online resources such as ready-to-use Web lessons, quizzes, and rubrics. These systems incorporate stand-alone grade book programs such as *GradeQuick* (Jackson) and *Making the Grade* (Jay Klein Productions).

TEST GENERATORS

A test-generating program resembles a word processor in that it comes with standard editing capabilities such as deletion and insertion. Many of these programs have font libraries from which you can select different typefaces. There are various test formats, including true/false, multiple choice, fill in the blank, short answer, essay, and matching. Some programs have graphics editors to help you integrate diagrams and pictures into your document. After entering your test questions, you can save them as a database file that can be retrieved on demand. Many programs enable you to randomize the order of the test questions and the arrangement of the possible responses to multiple-choice questions for makeup tests or alternate tests. The majority of programs enable you to print final copies of the tests along with answer sheets. An example of a test generator is *Test Creator* (Centron Software) Use this test generator to create multiple-choice, true/false, essay, and fill-in-the-blank questions (Figure 14.4). There are three versions of the program: one is the basic version, two is a network version, and three is an online version. The online version lets you send tests to anyone in the world.

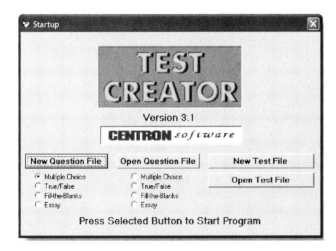

Figure 14.4
Test Creator
(*Source:* Centron Software, Inc. www. centronsoftware.com)

Many programs allow you to deliver Web exams online. For example, there are programs such as *Easy Test Maker* (http://www.easytestmaker.com/), *Test Generator* (http://www.testshop.com/), and *ExamView* (http://www.swlearning.com/examview/).

RUBRIC BUILDERS

Another great support tool for teachers is rubric builders or generators such as *Rubistar* (http://rubistar.4teachers.org/index.php) and *Rubric Generator* (http://teach-nology.com/). A rubric builder is an assessment tool that lets you evaluate the performance of your students. "The Rubric lists the criteria necessary to attain graduated levels of mastery" (Groeber, 2007). In Table 14.1 the student sees that he or she is to be evaluated on criteria such as organization, subject matter, and graphics. Each of these criteria has different levels of performance that range from level 1, "Audience cannot understand presentation because there is no sequence of information," to level 4, "Student presents information in logical, interesting sequence which audience can follow."

Table 14.1   Rubric Created by Caroline McCullen

Evaluating Student Presentations
Developed by Information Technology Evaluations Services, NC Department of Public Instruction

	1	2	3	4	Total
Organization	Audience cannot understand presentation because there is no sequence of information.	Audience has difficulty following presentation because student jumps around.	Student presents information in logical sequence which audience can follow.	Student presents information in logical, interesting sequence which audience can follow.	
Subject Knowledge	Student does not have grasp of information; student cannot answer questions about subject.	Student is uncomfortable with information and is able to answer only rudimentary questions.	Student is at ease with expected answers to all questions, but fails to elaborate.	Student demonstrates full knowledge (more than required) by answering all class questions with explanations and elaboration.	
Graphics	Student uses superfluous graphics or no graphics	Student occasionally uses graphics that rarely support text and presentation.	Student's graphics relate to text and presentation.	Student's graphics explain and reinforce screen text and presentation.	
Mechanics	Student's presentation has four or more spelling errors and/or grammatical errors.	Presentation has three misspellings and/or grammatical errors.	Presentation has no more than two misspellings and/or grammatical errors.	Presentation has no misspellings or grammatical errors.	
Eye Contact	Student reads all of report with no eye contact.	Student occasionally uses eye contact, but still reads most of report.	Student maintains eye contact most of the time but frequently returns to notes.	Student maintains eye contact with audience, seldom returning to notes.	
Elocution	Student mumbles, incorrectly pronounces terms, and speaks too quietly for students in the back of class to hear.	Student's voice is low. Student incorrectly pronounces terms. Audience members have difficulty hearing presentation.	Student's voice is clear. Student pronounces most words correctly. Most audience members can hear presentation.	Student uses a clear voice and correct, precise pronunciation of terms so that all audience members can hear presentation.	
				Total Points:	

The following example is found on Kathy Schrock's guide for educators site at http://school.discoveryeducation.com/schrockguide/assess.html. To learn more about rubrics, visit our Web sites online or read the suggested references.

PUZZLE MAKERS

Puzzle makers motivate students studying potentially unexciting topics such as state capitals and parts of the body. You can use such programs to develop a crossword puzzle for reviewing Spanish, generate a geographical crossword for studying Europe, or create a math quiz in which equations are clues to a mystery. There are many noteworthy puzzle generators for the classroom, including Teachers Value-Pak, which consists of *Puzzle Power*, *Test Creator*, and *Classroom*

Bingo (Centron), *Crossword Puzzle Maker* (http://www.teach-nology.com/web_tools/crossword/), *Crossword Compiler* (http://www.crossword.compiler.com/), and Discovery Education's *Puzzlemaker* (http://puzzlemaker.discoveryeducation.com). Figure 14.5 is a sample Civil War crossword puzzle generated from *Puzzle Power*.

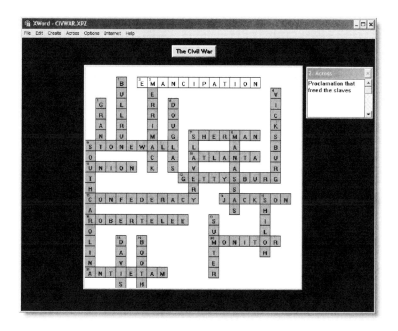

Figure 14.5
Puzzle Power
(*Source:* Centron Software, Inc. www.centronsoftware.com)

WORKSHEET GENERATORS, TIME LINERS, ORGANIZERS, AND OTHER SUPPORT TOOLS

Some programs such as *Worksheet Magic Plus* (Figure 14.6) (Gamco) and *Vocabulary 3* (Visions Technology in Education) produce worksheets in a variety of formats such as word searches, crossword puzzles, and fill-in-the-blank. Worksheet Magic Plus is simple to use, prints answer keys, and uses the *Word Works* Vocabulary

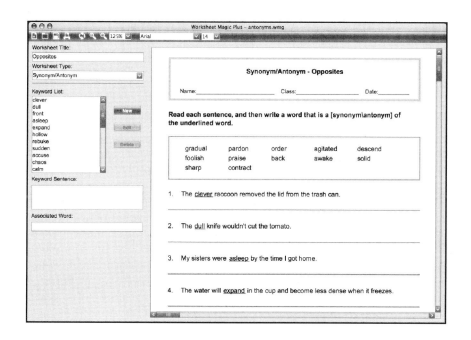

Figure 14.6
Worksheet Magic Plus
(*Source:* Centron Software, Inc. www.centronsoftware.com)

Series. *Vocabulary Companion 3* (Visions) (Figure 14.7) creates activity sheets, posters, and games and also uses a variety of activity sheets including crossword, word search, scrambled sentences, and flash cards.

Figure 14.7
Vocabulary Companion 3
(*Source:* Courtesy Visions Technology in Education)

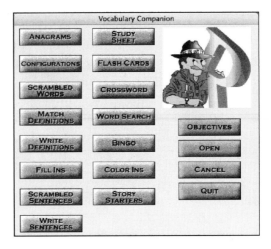

Other programs produce labels, time lines, attendance charts, flowcharts, and lesson plans. The latest version of *TimeLiner* (Tom Snyder Productions) enables you to design, illustrate, and print out time lines of any length in Spanish or English. You can add movies and sounds to make a true multimedia time line. There are also 100 ready-made activities (Figure 14.8).

Figure 14.8
TimeLiner XE
(*Source:* Courtesy Tom Snyder)

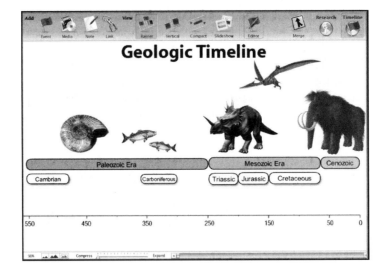

Write It Live (FTC Publishing) is a unique online writing tool that aids teachers, increasing the quantity and quality of writing. Using prompts, this product helps a student or class create reports or presentations. They can export reports or access these reports from any Internet browser. The teacher and students have two-way communication through inboxes. The teacher can make comments, grade reports, and return them immediately. With one click of the mouse, the teacher can distribute an assignment to anyone. To aid this process, *WriteIt! Live* has *Freewrite*, an online word processing application, and over 50 report templates (Figure 14.9).

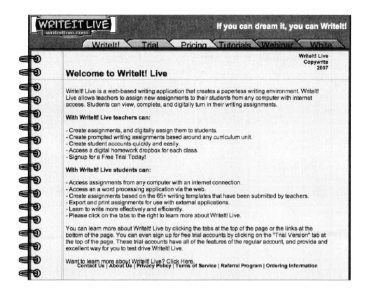

Figure 14.9
WriteIt! Live
(*Source:* Used with permission of FTC Publishing)

Another utility program from FTC Publishing for teachers is *PowerPak Plus for PowerPoint*. This program enables the teacher to design lesson plans and supplemental games for the whole class. All the work has been done for the teacher except for typing in the questions and answers. The program covers all curriculum areas and includes 12 interactive game templates such as Surgery (Figure 14.10).

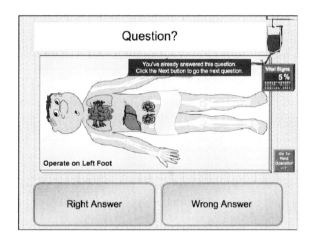

Figure 14.10
PowerPak Plus for PowerPoint
(*Source:* Used with permission of FTC Publishing)

Inspiration (Inspiration Software), a powerful visual thinking tool, helps students and teachers organize ideas and information. This program assists students in developing visual diagrams, flowcharts, and knowledge maps. It comes with an integrated outline view that helps teachers and students create concisely written proposals and reports.

Students can plan speeches, and they can use the program's checklist feature to complete tasks such as planning a multimedia presentation. Students are also able to brainstorm portfolios (Figure 14.11).

They can use the program to help students gain a deep understanding of scientific concepts such as global warming. In social studies they can show cause-and-effect relationships in historical events such as the French Revolution. In math they can explain math concepts such as factoring, addition, and subtraction. *Inspiration* can help teachers plan lessons for the classroom, prepare research papers, and create reports. Finally, teachers can use the *Template Wizard* to create customized learning activities for all curriculum areas.

Figure 14.11

Inspiration Portfolio Brainstorm

(*Source:* Diagram created in Inspiration(R) by Inspiration Software(R), Inc.)

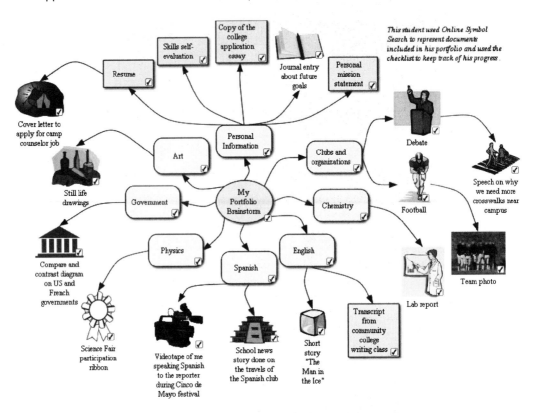

STATISTICAL PROGRAMS

In the past, if you wanted to do statistical analysis, you had to do the work by hand or on a mainframe at a university. Today, many microcomputer programs help the classroom teacher make calculations and analyze statistics. Most of these programs handle the simplest statistics, such as mean and standard deviation (Figure 14.12), but the more complex programs also handle multilinear regression and factor/time series analysis.

Figure 14.12

SPSS

(*Source:* Created with SPSS Inc. Copyright© 2008)

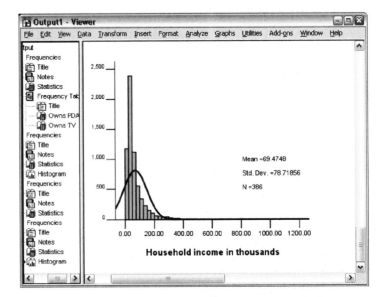

A few popular statistics programs are *SPSS* (SPSS Inc.; Figure 14.12), *GB Stat* (Dynamic Micro Systems), *NCSS Statistical Analysis* (Windows only), *Systat* (Systat Software, Inc.; Windows only), and *DeltaGraph* (Red Rock Software). You will find links to other statistical packages at http://www.stata.com/links/stat_software.html. In most cases, you will not need an expensive statistical package because many spreadsheets or grade book programs have sufficient statistics capabilities. However, if you are doing research or if your grade-management program does not provide statistics, then you will need this type of program.

Teacher Support Tools on the Internet

The Internet is a huge library where you can find teacher support tools and instructional material. There seems to be a limitless amount of resources available to the Web traveler. Many of these resources are free, and the ones that are subscription based usually have free resources for the teacher. There are Internet sites such as *TeAchnology* (http://www.teach-nology.com/) with free easy-to-use resources for teachers. There are also free resources such as *Moodle* where teachers can create online courses and online course management tools such as WebCT. Google has online tools for schools at http://www.google.com/a/edu.

There are many teacher resources found at *T.H.E. Journal's Educators Road Map to the Web* (http://www.thejournal.com/highlights/roadmap/). This site covers all the content areas. There are a tremendous variety of online references that a teacher can find by going to *Google* (http://www.google.com) and typing *reference sites* in its search engine. Especially good are *Refdesk* at http://www.refdesk.com/, the *University of Texas Library Online* at http://www.lib.utexas.edu/refsites/, *How Stuff Works* at http://howstuffworks.com (grades 8–12), and its companion site *How Stuff Works Express* (grades 4–8) at http://express.howstuffworks.com/Refdesk.com is a list of *Reference Resources*, ranging from a *Facts Encyclopedia* to *Essential Reference Tools*. The UT (University of Texas at Austin) library has a list of useful reference sites ranging from online dictionaries to encyclopedias. Finally, *How Stuff Works Express* and *How Stuff Works* lets you learn about mechanisms and workings of technology, natural phenomena, and scientific concepts. The sites discuss a range of topics including MP3 files, hurricanes, the United Nations, and computer viruses. In Table 14.2 you will see some other useful sites.

Table 14.2   Teacher Support Sites

Web Site	Description and URL
My Teacher Tools	http://www.myteachertools.com/ A directory of teaching tools, researched by teacher Rona Martin, ranging from a flipbook creator to Puzzle Makers.
Discovery School	http://puzzlemaker.school.discovery.com/ Lets teachers and students create and print word searches, math puzzles, criss-cross using their own word lists. If you click on **Kathy Schrock's Guide for Educators** you will find a list of useful sites.
4Teachers.org	http://www.4teachers.org/ Offers online tools and resources such as ready-to-use Web lessons, rubrics, calendars, and quizzes. *

(continued)

Table 14.2   continued

Web Site	Description and URL
The Math Worksheet site.com The Math Worksheet Site.com On-line Math Worksheet Generator Subscribe Forgot Password Log In	http://themathworksheetsite .com/5 Lets teachers create an array of math worksheets. This is subscription based, but there is also free material.
Internet4Classrooms: Teacher Tools Internet4Classrooms i4c Helping teachers use the Internet effectively Curriculum Management Gradebook Tools Glencoe FREE Professional Development with CEU's Success In The Classroom JOIN TODAY	http://www.internet4classrooms .com/teachertools.htm An array of teacher tools such as bulletin boards, flashcards, calendars, worksheets, and more.

(*Source:* 4Teachers.org 1995–2008. Copyright ALTECT at the University of Kansas
*Development of this educational resource was supported, in part, by the US Department of Education award #R302A000015 to ALTEC (Advanced Learning Technologies in Education Corsortia) at the University of Kansas.)

Electronic Portfolios

A **portfolio** is an organized collection of documents that is used by a student to reflect his or her knowledge, skills, and learning accomplishments. Portfolios constitute a valuable assessment tool for instructors. An **electronic portfolio** is one created on computer.

Many teachers find it helpful to use portfolio assessment as another means to keep track of a student's progress. They feel that testing only gives data on how well a student answers questions on a particular day in time. An electronic portfolio, on the other hand, gives the teacher insight into a student's personality and records his or her accomplishments over a period of time.

There are many different types of portfolios. For the purpose of this chapter we will classify these portfolios into three wide-ranging categories: personal, academic, and professional. **Personal portfolios** show a student's growth and development outside of school. The portfolio might include autobiographical data, information about hobbies and talents, awards, pictures, and goals. An **academic portfolio** (Figure 14.13) shows the student's academic performance and achievement. This portfolio might include a collection of a student's work in all subject areas over time. The academic portfolio may include book report lists, computer-generated examples of student work or projects, paintings, collages, photos, timed writings, letters, poems, and short stories.

Figure 14.13
Portfolio Builder for PowerPoint 2 by Dr. Arnie Abrams Visions Technology in Education

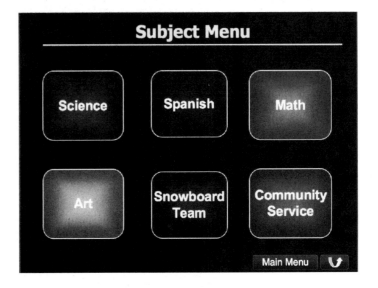

Finally, the **professional portfolio** might contain samples of a student's work that meet graduation requirements for high school or college admission. This portfolio can also be used for seeking employment, reflecting only the student's best academic work. Prospective teachers can prepare such professional portfolios before launching a job search.

To create a portfolio, students import work created with other software applications into a portfolio builder. They can import graphics, text, scanned images, full-motion video, and sound clips into portfolio builders such as *Portfolio Builder for PowerPoint 2* (Visions Technology in Education) or *Grady Profile* (Aurbach & Associates), or a Web-based electronic portfolio and program management systems such as *TaskStream* or an authoring program such as *PowerPoint* (see Chapter 11). In a program such as *PowerPoint*, they can manipulate images and sound, even add animation, and save the work as a presentation. The presentation can then be burned on a CD-ROM or DVD, stored on a USB drive, or placed on a Web page.

Academic institutions are moving toward Web-based portfolio systems such as *TaskStream*. *TaskStream* provides an integrated package of management tools that lets users build electronic portfolios that can be shared with other students for feedback, published online, and used for assessment (Figure 14.14).

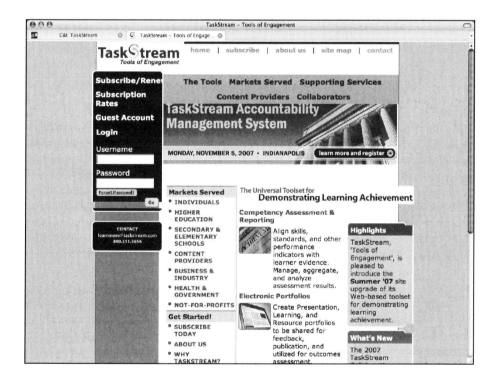

Figure 14.14
TaskStream
(*Source:* Reprinted with TaskStream Permission. All rights reserved.)

Using *TaskStream* the teacher can track and assess student work, produce reports, design customized portfolio templates, and add videos, file attachments, and images. To learn more about TaskStream, visit https://www.taskstream.com/pub/.

According to Barrett (2003, 2004, 2007), there are five basic steps that a person should go through in developing a portfolio. The five steps are (1) collecting or gathering material based on the purpose of your particular portfolio; (2) selecting or looking over what you have collected and choosing material based on educational objectives; (3) reflecting on the importance of the material in terms of learning objectives and revising if necessary; (4) projecting or thinking about the learning objectives for the future; and (5) celebrating or sharing the portfolio with others and receiving their comments.

After the portfolio is created, this author feels that a portfolio should be checked for the eight criteria as shown in the following checklist.

Portfolio Checklist

Is the portfolio

_____ 1. based on a standard or theme?		_____ 5. interesting?	
_____ 2. organized?		_____ 6. grammatically correct?	
_____ 3. easy to read?		_____ 7. free of spelling and syntax errors?	
_____ 4. understandable?		_____ 8. one cohesive unit?	

For further information on portfolios, see Dr. Helen Barrett's Web site, where you will find information about electronic portfolio development and numerous resources (http://electronicportfolios.org/). Also see Education World® Technology Center: Electronic Portfolios in the K–12 Classroom at http://www.educationworld.com/a_tech/tech/tech111.shtml, for information on developing a portfolio for the classroom. Finally, check out the American Association for Higher Education (AAHE) site (http://ctl.du.edu/portfolioclearinghouse/), which has a database of institutions that are working with portfolios and all sorts of resources.

Clip Art Collections

Clip art are "canned" images that the teacher can insert into documents such as portfolios, desktop publishing documents, presentation programs, word processing documents, authoring program files, or Web pages. For those of us who do not draw, these clip art libraries are an invaluable resource.

Using clip art saves the teacher or student the hours of time it would take to create images from scratch. At users' fingertips are hundreds of ready-to-use images. You can find clip art for any conceivable topic, from a beautiful photograph of Crater Lake to a detailed drawing of the human body. Teachers can buy clip art from companies such as Corel, Adobe, and IMSI. Teachers can also discover a vast array of clip art that is free online such as *Barry's Clip Art* (http://barrysclipart.com/), which offers thousands of clip art images.

Teachers can also pay for an online subscription service such as Clipart.com (http://www.clipart.com), a site that has over 6 million downloadable images. If you want to use the clip art from commercial sites, see if there are any restrictions such as written permission or payment. The majority of clip art packages provide their pictures in file formats such as JPEG, GIF, and EPS, which make them easy to insert in a variety of documents. Teachers can use graphic conversion programs such as *Graphic Converter* or programs such as *Photoshop Elements* to convert a file from one format to another format. However, the resulting image may not be the same as the original.

The Teacher Support Tools Checklist is an assessment form to use when evaluating electronic grade books and test generators.

Teacher Support Tools Checklist*

Directions: Examine the following items and determine which ones you feel are important for your current teaching situation. Place an X on each line for which the software meets your needs.

Electronic Grade Books

___ 1. Features

    ___ a. Has screen views by category, student, and assignment

    ___ b. Tracks attendance

    ___ c. Has seating charts with pictures

    ___ d. Sorts names alphabetically, numerically, or by class standing

    ___ e. Enters large numbers of students and grades

    ___ f. Flags students with problems

___ 2. Statistical capabilities

    ___ a. Averages grades

    ___ b. Scales scores (selects scores for student or class averages)

    ___ c. Weight grades according to value of assignment

    ___ d. Calculates pertinent statistics (range, mean, median, and standard deviation)

    ___ e. Compares individual students and class averages

___ 3. Output capabilities

    ___ a. Prints individual student and class reports

    ___ b. Generates graphs and tables depicting student/class performance

    ___ c. Saves information to disk

    ___ d. Has templates/reports in different languages

    ___ e. Posts information securely on the Web

___ 4. Utility

    ___ a. Is easy to use

    ___ b. Saves time

    ___ c. Is accessible at work, home, and on the Web

Test Generators

___ 1. Features for test creation

    ___ a. Has standard editing capabilities

    ___ b. Has font libraries with different typefaces

    ___ c. Integrates diagrams and pictures

    ___ d. Randomizes order of test questions and responses

    ___ e. Uses foreign languages

___ 2. Test formats

    ___ a. True/false

    ___ b. Multiple choice

    ___ c. Short answer

    ___ d. Fill in the blank

    ___ e. Matching

___ 3. Storing/retrieval

    ___ a. Items are saved in a database for easy retrieval

    ___ b. Creates quizzes, activity sheets, and other curricular materials

    ___ c. Prints final copies of tests and answer sheets

    ___ d. Accesses questions from publisher's database

    ___ e. Shares questions/tests with other teachers

Rating Scale

Rate the program by placing a check in the appropriate line.

Excellent_____ Very good _____ Good _____ Fair _____ Poor _____

Comments:

*Courtesy of Sarah Hill

Individualized Educational Plan Generators

To learn more about teacher support programs, visit our online site at http://www .wiley.com/college/sharp.

In the last 5 years politicians and the public have been calling for teacher and student accountability. This emphasis on accountability brings a need to track student progress and an increase in paperwork for the teacher. This has been especially true for the special education teacher with the enactment of the American Disability Act. This law requires that schools prepare an IEP (individualized education plan) for each special education student. To this end, teachers are using IEP programs such as *IEP Writer Supreme IIC* (SuperSchool) and *I-Plan* (http://www.schoolmax .net/). There is also open-source software like IEP-IPP (http://www.iep-ipp.com) and browser-based software like *IEPs PlaNET* (http://www.visionplanet.com) to help them prepare their reports and supply them with IEP forms.

What is Graphics Software?

Pictures shape our perceptions and help us communicate. When a biology instructor discusses the anatomy of the body, he or she finds it helpful to show a labeled drawing on a model. The businessperson uses graphics to make important presentation points. The engineer creates a scale drawing to guide the builders of a bridge. The statistician creates charts from data. In our society, people use pictures to educate, to communicate ideas and feelings, and to persuade. A picture is indeed worth a thousand words.

The term **computer graphics** refers to "the creation and manipulation of picture images in the computer" (Freedman, 2008). When discussing computer graphics, we are referring to computer-generated pictures on a screen, paper, or film. Graphics can be as simple as a pie graph or as elaborate as a detailed anatomical painting of the human body. Graphics software can help teachers and students communicate with images.

Graphics Software

There are many excellent software programs that can be used by teachers and students. We consider some of these programs, organized by broad category.

GRAPHING AND CHARTING SOFTWARE

In Chapters 8 and 9, we discussed databases and spreadsheets and their applications. It is not difficult to create graphs and charts from such databases and spreadsheets to illustrate presentations. These graphs and charts can take many forms, such as a bar graph (Figure 14.15). Anyone quickly looking at this data can see that Wentworth High has the highest test scores for grades 10 and 12, and Clayton High School has the lowest test scores for grades 10 and 12.

Graphs show a relationship among categories of data. This bar graph compares the results for four different schools at three different grade levels, with each color bar representing a different school. Other types of graphs could have illustrated the same data in different ways.

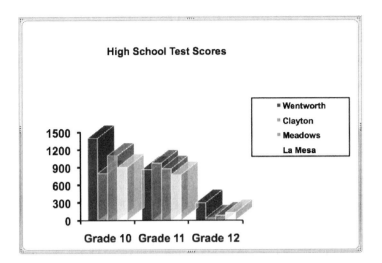

Figure 14.15
Excel Bar Graph
(*Source:* Courtesy Visions technology in Education)

You can use graphics to better understand a student's performance on a series of exams. In Figure 14.16, the teacher charts Jane Adams's scores on six math tests to grasp quickly the effect of an extreme score (0) on this student's performance.

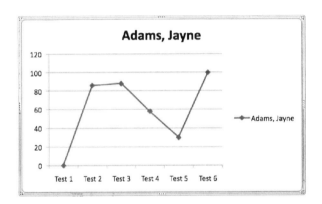

Figure 14.16
Excel Line Graph
(*Source:* Courtesy Visions technology in Education)

Graphing is a means of getting a clearer understanding of what the data represent. In education, graphing possibilities are unlimited. In science, students can graph the results of a series of plant experiments in which they alter variables such as temperature and water. In economics or social studies, the teacher might want the class to chart a stock's progress for a year or to graph voting trends. In English, the teacher can chart the incidences of certain words used in student writing to make a point about vocabulary. Graphic programs, such as *The Graph Club 2* (Tom Snyder Productions—Scholastic) and *InspireData* (Inspiration), are suitable for classroom use. If you do not want to buy a separate graphing program, you can use an integrated program such as *Microsoft Office*, which has graphing components.

InspireData enables students in grades 4–12 to improve their analytical skills. Students have access to 100+ content databases in all curriculum areas. To use *InspireData*, you simply enter data and then click on a graph icon to show the data graphically. You can represent your data in a variety of plot types such as a Venn, bar, stack, pie, and axis. Figure 14.17 is an example of a line chart of the January gasoline prices from 1976 to 2006. Using this program, you can export data into other applications. You can publish an online survey and collect data anytime with *InspireData*'s survey tool.

Figure 14.17
InspireData
(*Source:* Diagram created in InspireData[a]
by Inspiration software®, Inc.)

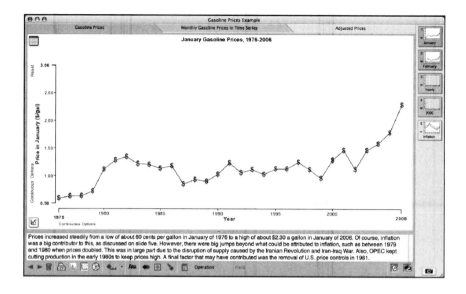

Presentation Graphics Programs

Presentation graphics programs have the capability of displaying charts, diagrams, special effects, predefined backgrounds, clip art, sound, transitions, and video in a computer-driven slide show. These slides are printable, but in most cases they are used to display material for a class or large audience. The teacher or students show their presentation on a regular monitor or a screen that is used in conjunction with a projector. An example of a presentation graphics program is *PowerPoint*. This program comes with art tools and templates that the user can incorporate into slide shows about everything from the anatomy of a heart (Figure 14.18) to the paintings of Van Gogh.

Figure 14.18
PowerPoint Human Heart
(*Source:* Courtesy Visions Technology
in Education)

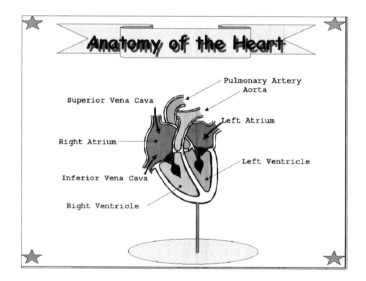

PowerPoint enables you to import content from other programs. At Microsoft's site (http://www.microsoft.com) you can download updated template and clip art. Refer to Chapter 11 for a discussion of presentation programs such as *Keynote* (Apple) and *HyperStudio* (Software Mackiev). Presentation graphics have become a substitute for the overhead projector. This software is replacing chalkboards and transparencies.

Print Graphics Programs

To create an award, a poster (Figure 14.19), a banner, a greeting card, or a certificate, you would use **print graphics** software. The best-known program is a classic called *Print Shop*, which came into existence in the 1980s. The most recent version is called *Print Shop* 2 (Software MacKiev) and it contains thousands of pictures to make your life easier.

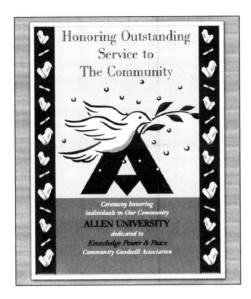

Figure 14.19
*Print Shop Version 2
Macintosh Version*
(*Source:* Courtesy Software MacKiev)

Stationery Studio (FableVision) is a perfect program for teachers or students in grades K–5. With this print graphic tool a student can print writing paper, templates for stories or reports, mini books, shape books, and much more. Visit our online site to see reviews of other programs.

ART SOFTWARE

Clearvue and SVE has a huge collection of art appreciation software covering art history and culture, art processes and design, and artists such as Henri Matisse, Pablo Picasso, and Leonardo da Vinci. However, most of their programs were produced in 2004 and earlier. The trend seems to be toward drawing and painting programs.

DRAWING VERSUS PAINTING TOOLS

When using a **drawing program**, you create illustrations that consist of mathematically defined curves and line segments called *vectors*. **Vector graphics** "is a technique for showing a picture as points, lines, and other geometric entities" (Freedman, 2008). What this means is that all elements of the picture can be isolated, moved independently, and scaled separately from one another (Figure 14.20). Vector graphics can be displayed or printed at any resolution or degree of sharpness or detail that a monitor or printer is capable of producing.

Some popular drawing programs are *Adobe Illustrator*, *Twist* (Tech4Learning), and *CorelDraw Graphics Suite*. With draw programs, students can draw geometric shapes, create designs, and construct miniature cities.

Figure 14.20
Vector-Based Drawing

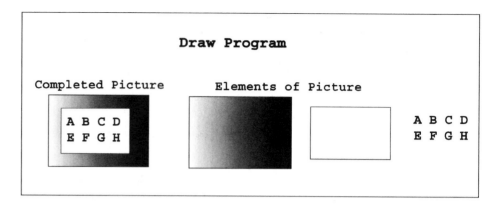

A **paint program** enables the student to paint on the screen with the use of a graphics tablet and a light pen (Figure 14.21) or a mouse.

Figure 14.21
Graphics Tablet and Light Pen
(*Source:* © 2008 Jupiterimages)

To learn more about paint programs, visit our online site at http://www.wiley .com/college/sharp.

Paint programs are art oriented rather than design oriented. The paintings are made up of dots or pixels. Each pixel consists of data describing whether the pixel is white or black or what level of color it has. Unlike draw programs, paint programs do not permit images to be scaled and separated from one another. Editing groups of pixels can alter the pictures you create with this format. Because images are resolution dependent, they will appear jagged and lose detail if you enlarge them.

The majority of paint programs mentioned in this book offer coloring and texturing capabilities. Most paint programs also feature brushes of different widths and shapes, drawing tools, a mirror-image function, different fonts, and an undo function. There are significant advantages to using the computer for painting. If the artist makes a mistake, he or she can easily correct it. There is no mess to clean up because there are no real paints or watercolors to spill, drip, or smear. The painter simply clicks the mouse to change the color, enlarge an image, or move an object. There are also disadvantages, including a possible failure to connect with traditional art media and the loss of the opportunity to have a hands-on experience with paint, clay, and other media.

The more advanced teacher, student, or professional will find paint programs such as *Adobe Photoshop* and *Corel Painter X* indispensable.

For less-talented artists like myself, programs such as *Microsoft Paint* and *Adobe PhotoShop Elements* will create beautiful pictures or designs that can be used in word processing and desktop publishing documents.

Two examples of paint programs especially appropriate for elementary school children are *Kid Pix Deluxe 3X* (Software MacKiev) and *Pixie* (Tech4Learning).

*Kid Pix Deluxe 3X (*Figure 14.22*)* has stamps, wacky tools, and sound effects. *Pixie* has an array of paintbrushes, an image scrambler, eyedropper, and a large sticker library collection.

Figure 14.22
Kid Pix Deluxe 3X
(*Source:* Courtesy Software MacKiev)

Computer-Aided Design Applications

Computer-aided design (CAD) assists in the design of objects such as machine parts, homes, or anatomical drawings. You must have the proper CAD program to accomplish such tasks. With CAD software, you can easily change or modify designs without having to create actual models, saving time, money, and effort. A few professional programs are *AutoCAD LT* and *AutoSketch* (both by Autodesk).

Many of the programs in this field are simulations that show the use of created models. For instance, CAD software enables an engineer not only to design a car, but also to test it and even rotate it in space to see it from all sides. *Car Builder Deluxe* (Optimum Resource Software) is a simulation for education with which students construct, modify, and test cars. In the process of constructing a car, students must select the chassis length, the type and size of the fuel tank, and the strength and size of the tires. When the mechanical selection is complete, students modify the body with data generated through a testing procedure that includes a wind tunnel and a test track. At the end of this testing session, students can save the specifications of the designed car on a disk (Figure 14.23).

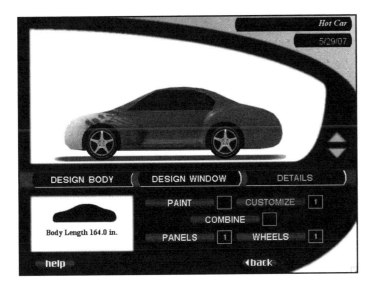

Figure 14.23
Car Builder Deluxe
(*Source:* CarBuilder® Optimum Resource, Inc.)

Sims and *SimCity Society* (Electronic Arts) are popular design programs using principles of CAD. *Sims* is for younger students, and *SimCity Societies* is for older students. Both programs are building games in which students create cities or neighborhoods.

With *Sims*, students design homes, furnish them, build neighborhoods, and take control of them. In *SimCity Societies*, students become planners and designers of their own kind of society and they may choose to create an industrial society with pollution or a police state (Figure 14.24).

Figure 14.24
SimCity™ *Societies*
(*Source:* © 2008 Electronic Arts, Inc. All Rights reserved. Use with permission. The Sims and SimCity are trademarks or registered trademarks of Electronic Art Inc. in the U.S. and/or other countries.)

Finally, *3D Railroad Concept & Design*, *Master 3D Railroad*, and *Train Engineer Deluxe* (The Liquid Ate Her.) are model railroad programs. These programs allow students to create model layouts, control trains, and build trains.

Music Technology

"After years of silence, the Internet is coming alive with sound and music. Students are getting their music from a variety of sources, giving small bands opportunities they never had before. Teachers can easily make collections of music, adding richness to their history and cultural discussions" (Dr. Jon Margerum-Leys, Professor at Eastern Michigan University). Students can now experiment with programs such as *GarageBand* (Apple) or *Mixcraft* (Acoustica).

In the early days of computing, it would take forever to download a music file, because of the slow speed of the Internet connection and the size of the music files. Most people today have fast connections to the Internet and the ability to download music files quickly with audio compression technology, which reduces file size without losing data. For example, **MP**eg Audio Layer **3** (MP3) is an audio compression technology that produces CD-quality sound while providing almost the same fidelity. People can download quality audio from the Internet quickly. In about five minutes, an hour of near–CD-quality audio can be downloaded. After the MP3 file is downloaded it is played through software such as WinAmp3 or iTunes or players such as the iPod (Apple), which is attached to the computer by USB or FireWire cable.

Among the programs available for creating classroom collections of music are *WinAmp* (Nullsoft; http://www.winamp.com) and *iTunes* (Apple; http://www. apple.com). These media players enable you to play MPEG-4 audio, MP3, Wav, and other audio formats; build custom playlists; and track your music by artist, track, song, music style, or whatever is important to you.

Recently there has been interest in music programs. Current programs give instruction in playing music, in music appreciation, and in composition and music theory.

eMedia Intermediate Guitar Method (eMedia) offers comprehensive, guided instruction in piano and guitar. Clearvue offers comprehensive music CD-ROMs on different musical periods, composers, and instruments. Still other music programs are sing-along adventures; they enable students to experiment with music, explore musical elements, and practice on musical instruments.

The award-winning *Music Ace Maestro* (Harmonic Vision) is wonderful for students from ages 8 to adult. The program introduces advanced concepts such as standard notation, rhythm, melody, and harmony in an engaging format. There are 48 lessons, thousands of musical examples, 48 games, and a composition tool. The interactive lessons come before each set of games. In Figure 14.25, the student is hearing an excerpt from Beethoven's Sonata Number 8, *Pathetique*. After listening, she chooses the correct tempo of the piece, in this case slow tempo.

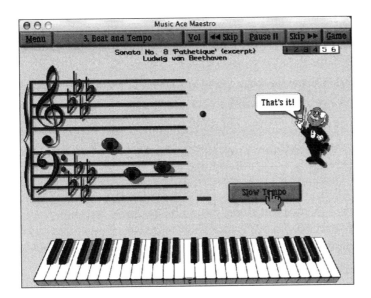

Figure 14.25
Music Ace Maestro
(*Source:* Courtesy Harmonic Vision)

SAMPLE CLASSROOM LESSON PLANS

I. PRESIDENTIAL ELECTION SURVEY

Subject: Social Studies

Grade(s): 2–8

Objectives

Students will learn how to do a survey and how to graph it using a bar graph and a pie graph.

Standards

• National Council for the Social Studies Curriculum Standards 3, 5
• ISTE NETS for Students 2, 3, 5

Materials

You will need a program that does graphics such as *InspireData*, *The Graph Club*, or *Excel* and one or more computers.

Procedures

1. Have the students work in teams to conduct a survey on the next presidential election.
2. Make sure they record information on socioeconomic level, education, voting preferences, and the like.
3. Have each team use the computer to create a bar graph of the results of its survey.
4. Finally, lead a discussion of the graphing results.

II. STATE DATA SHEET

Subject: Social Studies

Grade(s): 2 and up

Objectives

Students will read an almanac for information and learn how to graph their information using a bar graph and a line graph.

Standards

- National Council for the Social Studies Curriculum Standards 3, 5
- ISTE NETS for Students 3, 5, 6

Materials

You will need a graphing program such as *InspireData* or *Graph Club* and one or more computers.

Procedures

1. Have each student select three states and research the annual rainfall of those states.
2. Ask the students to create bar graphs on the computer comparing the three states.
3. Have students track down state rainfall statistics for three specific dates in the past.
4. Instruct students to construct line graphs showing the changes in the data for each state over a period of time.
5. Discuss with students what the graphs mean.

III. EDUCATIONAL SIGN ABOUT DRUGS

Subject: English

Grade(s): 2–12

Objectives

Students will use a print graphics program to design a sign, learn about design and placement of objects, and discuss the reasons for not taking drugs.

Standards

- NCTE English Language Arts Standards 8, 12
- ISTE NETS for Students 1, 2, 3, 5

Materials

You will need *Print Shop Version 2* or *Print Explosion Deluxe* and one or more computers.

Procedures

1. Discuss the reasons students should not take drugs.
2. Talk about placement and design with the students.
3. Instruct students to use a print graphics program to design a sign warning people not to take drugs.
4. After students have designed their signs, discuss what makes certain signs more appealing than others.

IV. MATH RIDDLE CARD

Subject: Math

Grade(s): 2–12

Objectives

Students will use a print graphics program to design a greeting card and practice solving math riddles.

Standards

- National Council of Teachers of Mathematics Standards 6, 8
- ISTE NETS for Students 5, 6

Materials

You will need *Print Shop Version 2* or *Print Explosion Deluxe* and one or more computers.

Procedures

1. Give each student a riddle or have students find riddles in books.
2. Tell the students to design a greeting card, putting the riddle on the cover and the answer on the inside of the card. An example is shown in Figure 14.26.

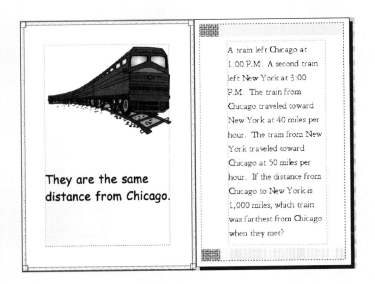

Figure 14.26
Print Shop Version 2
Greeting Card Cover
Software Mackiev

3. Now distribute the greeting cards and have the students solve the riddles.

V. GEOMETRIC PATTERNS

Subject: Math

Grade(s): K–3

Objectives

Students will use a paint program to make various geometric shapes, and they will learn about shapes.

Standards

• National Council of Teachers of Mathematics Standards 3, 8
• ISTE NETS for Students 1, 3, 4

Materials

You will need a paint program such as *Kid Pix Deluxe 3X* and one or more computers.

Procedures

1. Teach the students about different geometric shapes.

2. Show the students how to use the paint program to create these shapes. Figure 14.27 shows an example.

Figure 14.27
Shapes drawn in *KidPix Deluxe 3X*

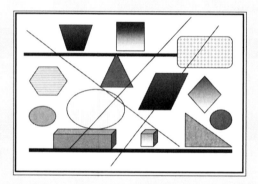

3. Explain how to fill the shapes with color and how to copy and paste shapes.

4. Have the students use the paint program to make abstract drawings without a fill pattern.

5. When they are finished, have them print out their shapes and color them, making sure all shapes of the same type are the same color.

6. Display these drawings on the bulletin board.

7. As a follow-up activity, have the students make collages with shapes or create faces.

VI. CELLS

Subject: Science

Grade(s): 5–8

Objectives

Students will use a draw program to illustrate the parts of an animal or plant cell and paste it in a report.

Standards

• National Science Education Standards C Life Science: The Characteristics of Organisms
• ISTE NETS for Students 1, 2, 3, 4, 5

Materials

You will need a drawing or painting program such as *Adobe Illustrator, Twist, Pixie,* or *KidPix Deluxe 3X* and one or more computers.

Procedures

1. Have students draw a cell on paper, labeling its parts.

2. Ask students to take turns using the computer to create their plant or animal cells.

3. Have students use a text tool to label each part of the cell.

4. Save this picture to a disk.

5. Tell students to prepare a report about animal cells or plant cells on the computer.

6. Have the students insert their pictures in their reports.

7. As a related activity, have the students draw the human body and label its parts.

VII. MAKING MUSIC

Subject: Music

Grade(s): 2 and up

Objective

Students will identify musical notes.

Standards

• ISTE NETS for Students 1, 2, 3

Materials

You will need a program such as *Morton Subotnick's Hearing Music* and one or more computers.

Procedures

1. Draw eight bars on the board to represent a scale.

2. Turn the computer monitor away from the students and have a student play six random notes.

3. Ask the students to listen carefully to the sounds and draw the bars and notes that represent the sound patterns.

4. Do this two more times so that students can check their work.

5. Now turn the monitor toward the class and play the pattern. Have them compare their patterns to the ones that are being played

SUMMARY

Teacher support tools can make a teacher more effective. One of the most popular tools is the electronic grade book, which lessens the time a teacher spends entering grades, computing averages, and informing parents about students' progress. Other tools that save time and reduce effort are test and worksheet generators, organizers, puzzle makers, and statistical packages.

A good paint program or draw program enables the user to draw without the fear of making a mistake, and a print graphics program enables those who are not artistically inclined to create visuals, from awards to posters. CAD programs are useful in designing room layouts, machine parts, and cars; presentation graphics produce charts and graphs that show relationships among categories of data. At the end of the chapter, we examined seven activities for integrating graphics art and music into the classroom. The Online Learning Center offers an annotated list of award-winning teacher support tools and graphics sites.

STUDY AND ONLINE RESOURCES

CHAPTER 14 ONLINE RESOURCES

 In the **student section** of the book's online site at **http://www.wiley.com/college/sharp** you will find templates and examples, video tutorials, PDFs, checklists, articles, Web sites, software reviews, and chapter quizzes. Access these resources to learn about technology and integrating it into the classroom.

CHAPTER MASTERY TEST

Lets check for chapter comprehension with a short mastery test. Key Terms, Computer Lab, and Suggested Readings and References follow the test.

1. What is the difference between a presentation graphics program and a paint program? Describe the major features of each.

2. How has the availability of paint programs on the computer affected the traditional way of drawing and painting?

3. Define *CAD* and discuss its primary use.

4. What is a *teacher support tool program*? Explain how it can provide individualized instruction for a class.

5. What is a *print graphics program*? Discuss two uses for this program in the school curriculum.

6. Define *computer graphics* and explain its importance in today's world.

7. Explain how graphics programs can be beneficial for the classroom.

8. What is an *electronic portfolio* and why is it useful for measuring student performance?

9. Your school will let you purchase only one graphics program. Will you choose a print graphics, presentation graphics, paint, drawing, or computer-aided design (CAD) package? Explain and justify your selection.

10. What is a rubric and why would you create one?

KEY TERMS

Academic portfolio p. 300

Computer-aided design (CAD) p. 309

Computer graphics p. 304

Drawing program p. 307

Electronic portfolio p. 300

MPEG Audio Layer 3 (MP3) p. 310

Paint program p. 308

Personal portfolios p. 300

Portfolio p. 300

Presentation graphics p. 306

Print graphics p. 307

Professional portfolio p. 301

Rubric Builders p. 293

Vector graphics p. 307

 COMPUTER LAB: Activities for Mastery and Your Portfolio

14.1 Create a basic database that can store a variety of information.

14.2 Determine which kind of software you should use for a given scenario.

14.3 Use a presentation graphics program to graphically represent Jane Smith's grades of 50, 60, 70, 88, 97, and 100. Watch the Video tutorial online and learn how to graphically represent these scores.

14.4 Use a print graphics program to produce (a) a riddle card, (b) a poster, (c) a calendar, and (d) letterhead stationery. Explain the educational value of each product. Watch the video tutorial online and learn how to create a letter.

14.5 Create a test for the class using a test-making program.

14.6 Evaluate three test-making programs, discussing their strengths and weaknesses.

14.7 Use one of the many puzzle utilities to create a product for class consumption.

14.8 Review three grade book programs and talk about their differences and similarities. Explain why you would choose one over the others.

14.9 Create an electronic portfolio as a website. Watch the video tutorial online use the powerpoint video tutorial online to help you with portfolio and Web page.

SUGGESTED READINGS AND REFERENCES

Archer, Jeff. "Digital Portfolios: An Alternative Approach to Assessing Progress." *Education Week* 26, issue 30 (March 29, 2007): 38–39.

Barrett, H. (2003, October). "*The portfolio: A revolutionary tool for education and training?*" Paper presented at the first International Conference on the e-Portfolio, Poitiers, France. Retrieved November 8, 2006, http://electronicportfolios.org/portfolios/eifel.pdf

Barrett, H. (2004). "*Electronic portfolios as digital stories of deep learning: Emerging digital tools to support reflection in learner-centered portfolios.*" Retrieved December 15, 2006, from http://electronicportfolios.org/digistory/epstory.

Barrett, Helen C. "Researching Electronic Portfolios and Learner Engagement: The REFLECT Initiative." *Journal of Adolescent and Adult Literacy* 50, issue 6 (March 2007): 436–449.

Freedman, Allan. *The Computer Desktop Encyclopedia.* Point Pleasant, Pa.: Computer Language Company, 2008.

Groeber, Joan F. *Designing and Using Rubrics for Reading and Language Arts, K–6,* 2nd ed. Thousand Oaks, Calif.: Corwin Press, 2007.

Guskey, Thomas R. "Computerized Grade Books and the Myth of Objectivity." *Phi Delta Kappan* 83, no. 10 (June 2002): 775–780.

Hale, Christy. "Art in the Classroom." *Instructor* 114, issue 5 (January/February 2005): 21–26.

Hartnell-Young, Elizabeth, and Maureen Morris. "Digital Portfolios: Powerful Tools for Promoting Professional Growth and Reflection." *School Library Journal* 53 (Fall 2007): 83.

Kilbane, Clare R., and Natalie B. Milman. *The Digital Teaching Portfolio Handbook: A How-to Guide for Educators.* New York: Allyn and Bacon, 2003.

Lacina, Jan. "Virtual Record Keeping: Should Teachers Keep Online Grade Books?" *Childhood Education* 82, issue 4 (Summer 2006): 252–254.

Lindroth, Linda. "Blue Ribbon Reviews." *Teaching PreK–8* 37, issue 8 (May 2007): 24–26.

Lindroth, Linda. "Hot Websites." *Teaching PreK–8* 37, issue 8 (May 2007): 28–30.

Lindroth, Linda. "ClozePro." *Teaching PreK–8* 37, issue 7 (April 2007): 22.

Moore, J. L., M. Orey, and J. V. Hardy. "The Development of an Electronic Performance Support Tool for Teachers." *Journal of Technology and Teacher Education* 8, no. 1 (2000): 29–52.

Schrock, Kathleen, and Sharron L. McElmeel. "Newsletter Design to Make Them Take Notice." *Library Talk* 13, no. 1 (January/February 2000): 36.

Sharp, Richard, and Vicki Sharp. *Best Web Sites for Teachers,* 7th ed. Eugene, Ore.: Visions Technology in Education, 2007.

Sharp, Vicki. *Make It with Inspiration.* Eugene, Ore.: Visions Technology in Education, 2004.

Snoeyink, Rick, and Joy Meyer. "Shaping Teacher Candidates' Digital Portfolios: What Administrators Want for Hiring." *Journal of Computing in Teacher Education* 23, no. 3, 89–96.

One Computer in the Classroom

The Computer and the School

There are many issues surrounding the use of computers in the classroom. Teachers, administrators, and parents must face the issue of having a single computer in a classroom of many students. Teachers in less-affluent neighborhoods, meanwhile, are lucky if they have even one computer in their classrooms. Whether a teacher has one or more computers in a classroom, the question becomes how this teacher can more effectively utilize this important resource.

Using the computer, students and teachers can do the following:

students can

- Use with oral reports,
- Display multimedia projects,
- Use computer encyclopedia for research, video, and sound clips,
- Create class newsletter,
- E-mail other students or classrooms,
- Use Internet to access libraries, databases, etc.,
- Create a class brochure,
- Create a class Web page.

teachers can

- Display quizzes and notes,
- Review information,
- To create charts for science and math,
- For educational resources,
- Write and receive e-mail from students,
- Use the computer to help students with writing skills.
- To create a professional Web page

objectives

Upon completing this chapter, you will be able to do the following:

1 List strategies for using one computer with 30 or more children in the math, science, social studies, and language arts areas.

2 Name two ways to integrate the computer into the classroom.

3 Explain the major advantage and disadvantage of a wireless mobile lab.

One Computer in the Classroom

The typical classroom used to have only one computer for 30 or more children. A recent survey, however, shows that the typical U.S. school today has one computer for every 3.8 students (Market Data Retrieval, Public School Technology Survey 2006, http://www.schooldata.com/). However, with this said the number of computers in the classroom fluctuates from state to state and the ratio for students in high-minority schools is not as favorable. Even with these computers in the classroom most of the time, however, they reside in a lab, are ancient, and lack software. Most classrooms still offer only a single computer. Some teachers move the one precious computer toward a back corner of the room and issue strict rules to govern its use, and others are afraid to use the computer at all.

We consider seven suggestions for better capitalizing on the computer's capabilities in the classroom: (1) select the software according to students' needs, (2) collect the appropriate equipment, (3) organize the classroom, (4) use the team approach, (5) know the software's time factor, (6) encourage group participation, and (7) integrate computer use into the curriculum.

SELECTION OF SOFTWARE

For good instruction, you adapt the material to students' needs. This principle holds for software as well. Students have varied abilities, interests, and preferences that warrant different teaching considerations and strategies. For example, if a student does not know how to type, he or she will have to search for the keys on the keyboard, thus becoming easily frustrated with the computer. At a third-grade level, a teacher's first strategy may be to instruct students in keyboarding skills, starting with the return, escape, and arrow keys.[1]

Another strategy for introducing the keyboard is to create a large keyboard and place it at the front of the room. Next, arrange students in pairs to practice the letter and number locations on seat copies of the large-size keyboard. After students have had the experience of helping each other explore the keyboard, direct the whole class in finding designated keys. Eventually, have the children close their eyes and continue to practice finding keys.

Typing programs such as *Type to Learn Junior—New Keys for Kids* (Sunburst), *Kid Keys* (Riverdeep), and *Keybo* (Heartsoft) provide excellent introductions to the keyboard.

Keybo is an adventure-typing program designed for students starting first grade. This program has over 30 tutorials with clever animation and audio feedback. Figure 15.1 shows a student learning how to type "j" and "f".

Figure 15.1
Keybo Typing Program
(*Source:* Heartsoft, LLC)

Once the children are skilled in locating keys, they are ready to work with more advanced typing programs such as *Mavis Beacon Teaches Typing Deluxe 16* (Riverdeep) and *Typing Tournament* (EdAlive).

If the students in the class need to improve their problem-solving abilities, there are a large range of programs available. For example, problem-solving software such as *Genui$: The Tech Tycoon Game* (Viva Media) works effectively with students in grades 8 and up. *Genui$: The Tech Tycoon Game* (Figure 15.2) is a simulation that combines historical events with science. You are in charge of a bicycle factory where you have to make the right decision for the factory to succeed.

You proceed by experimenting and creating different inventions. During the process you solve puzzles that apply to principals of electricity, optics, astronomy, and thermodynamics.

Another program of the same problem-solving genre is *Science Seekers: The Changing Earth* (Tom Snyder Productions–Scholastic) developed with the American Museum of Natural History. Using science seekers, students can collectively improve their critical thinking skills by taking notes, manipulating variables, analyzing the results, drawing conclusions, and offering solutions to problems. Students are

---

[1] One research scientist at SRI International recommends delaying the formal introduction of keyboarding until the third grade (Buckleitner, 2000).

Figure 15.2
Genui$: The Tech Tycoon Game
(*Source:* © Viva Media)

role-playing scientists on a special mission (Figure 15.3) where they have a problem that they must solve. Along the way, scientists help the students with their investigations.

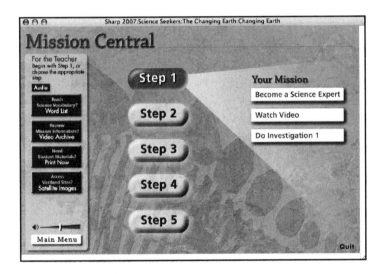

Figure 15.3
Science Seekers: The Changing Earth
(*Source:* Courtesy Tom Snyder)

If the class needs to study and research information about the United States, they can use a database software program like *Access* (Microsoft) or Bentō (Filemaker). The students create information sheets, compose questionnaires, and collect appropriate data for computer entry. Each student might research two states and input information about each state's population, capital, number of representatives, and main crop. After information is entered into the database, students might search for a state in which the main crop is corn. When the state appears on the screen, the student at the computer calls out its name, and the other students shade the state on a blank seat map. After the students find all the applicable states and shade them, the class might study the maps and discuss where the corn-producing states are located. From this class discussion, the students could learn about the Corn Belt and why this region produces the most corn.

A teacher might use a drill-and-practice program such as *Quarter Mile* to improve students' math skills. *The Quarter Mile* (Barnum Software) produces a series of these math programs that focus on a range of topics from whole numbers to equations for grades K–9. *The Quarter Mile* is designed so that users are in a competitive drag race with themselves. Students can opt to race "wild running horses"

(Figure 15.4) instead of cars. When they answer a problem correctly, the car leaves the starting line at 65 miles per hour. This math program can be used very effectively in a one-computer classroom. The teacher might organize students into groups of two or three and have the students compete with each other. The program not only lets you compare your top average scores with your previous scores, it also lets you compare yourself with others.

Figure 15.4
The Quarter Mile
(*Source:* Barnum Software & Quarter Mile Math™)

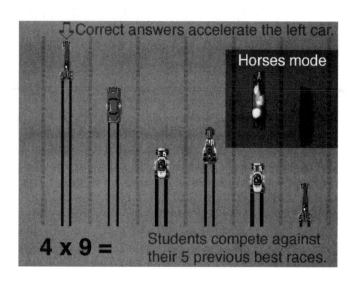

(*Source:* Courtesy InFocus Corporation)

Figure 15.5
InFocus Projector

COLLECTION OF EQUIPMENT

When there is only one computer in the classroom, you need additional equipment to make the computer screen visible to the whole class. Projectors such as *InFocus* (Figure 15.5) display enlarged images from a personal computer onto a wall screen.

Another alternative is a portable **liquid crystal display (LCD) projection panel** or an overhead projector that uses the personal computer to display enlarged images on a screen. If the district cannot afford a projector or projection panel, there are less expensive alternatives. An AT or Y adapter can split the signal coming from the class computer to display it on a larger television or monitor. A teacher can also use a **video scan converter** such as *TView Gold* to modify the personal computer or laptop output to display on a television or NTSC (National Television System Committee) monitor. (Refer to the online *Hardware Reference Guide for Teachers* for the rest of these hardware devices.) Many Macintosh computers have video out ports; you simply plug into that particular port for large-screen television reception capability. In most cases, these computers are ready for use with an additional monitor.

When you are cramped for space, you can improve the situation by elevating a large television or monitor to increase visibility. You also can tape a transparency on the TV screen (if it is not an LCD screen) and use a grease pencil to write on the screen to illustrate a point. Furthermore, you can create practice sheets that duplicate a screen from a computer program so that students can work along with the presentation.

CLASSROOM ORGANIZATION

Ask yourself questions to determine the best seating arrangement for viewing the computer. Are the students going to be in their seats or on the floor? Will the class be divided into small groups for discussion purposes? Will students be traveling to different learning stations in the room as they use manipulatives? Will they be using instruments such as a thermistor 2 to collect temperature data in different sections of the room?

Figure 15.6
Calahan Elementary School

TEAM APPROACH

Many students have been using computers since they were very young. If you have enough students who are familiar with the computer, organize them into a team. Under your tutelage, the team can practice giving directions, solving problems, and introducing new software. After the team is experienced, give the members identification badges and have them walk around the room answering questions on the current program. In addition to reducing the number of questions you will receive, this team method reaches a larger number of students.

SOFTWARE TIME FACTOR

For the computer program to be a success, you must know the program's time constraints. For instance, when the time frame is short, do not choose open-ended software, because the students will be unhappy when they have to stop prematurely. *Genui$: The Tech Tycoon Game* (Viva Media) takes at least 45 minutes to complete, and the students will object to quitting even though the program has a save function. *The Quarter Mile* (Barnum), on the other hand, is easier to stop and start with a class. Additionally, in selecting a program, check whether it saves the game or activity instantly or only at the end of a level. Software programs that require 15 or 20 minutes to finish a level might be inappropriate for some classroom situations.

GROUP INVOLVEMENT

Your interactions with a class are very important and will determine how free your students feel to participate in class lessons involving computers. At the introduction of a lesson, explain that there are many acceptable answers and that often there is no one solution to a problem. Try to reduce students' anxiety about evaluation. At first, involve the whole class in discussion; later, break the class up into smaller groups. Ask probing questions and ask students for their next move. Search for the reasons behind their answers and give them time to think. You should be a facilitator, letting the students do most of the talking and never imposing ideas on the class discussion. Try not to be judgmental in responding to students; they will pick up even on your body language. Encourage students to cooperate in order to promote learning and social skills. Advance students' thinking by making comments such as "That seems like a good idea, but expand on it." Help students practice problem solving by having them solve the same problem again, checking out their hypotheses and recording their collective answers. Give students objects to manipulate at their desks to help them answer the questions that the software is posing. For example, *Science Seekers: The Changing Earth* (Tom Snyder Productions–Scholastic) poses problems that has students manipulating foam, rocks, seashells, sand, and much more. The teacher distributes equipment to the class along with activity sheets to involve students in science investigations. The teacher can use these investigations as whole-class activities or divide the class into small groups.

To encourage group involvement, after you divide the class into small groups have them challenge each other to answer the most problems correctly. At the end of the day, have students work on the computer in pairs, one partner using the computer and the other coaching and recording. This pairing encourages students to develop strategies for handling problems inherent in the software. Organize the time the students spend at the computer with a schedule similar to the one in Figure 15.7. The students should work on a program for a designated time interval.

Figure 15.7
Computer-Use Chart

Computer Schedule		
Time	Teams	Finished
8:45–9:00	David/Richard	☑
9:00–9:15	Bobbie/Florence	☑
9:30–9:45	Bob/Karen	☑
9:45–10:00	Bobbie/Ruth	☑
Recess	Free Time	☐
10:30–10:45	Ken/Vicki	☐
10:45–11:00	Austin/Carolyn	☐

When their time is up, the next pair of students listed in the chart takes a turn. If a team is absent or busy, the next available partnership fills the void. This way the computer can be used by everyone in the class.

INTEGRATING THE COMPUTER INTO THE CLASSROOM

How do you make the computer an integral part of the core curriculum? The software should not substitute for the standard curriculum but rather should complement it on a regular basis. We look at five different software programs and how these programs can be included in classroom instruction. Then we consider two methods for extending the reach of the computer in the schools: computer labs and wireless mobile labs.

Kreative Komix Super Hero. If you want to improve students' writing skills, you might use a program such as *Kreative Komix* (Visions Technology in Education), which encourages creative writing and provides an opportunity for students to listen to their own written work and make revisions. Students can create comics, cutout puppets, slide shows, and greeting cards. When students use this program (Figure 15.8), they can write their own stories with sound, movement, and animation. Using this interactive writing tool they print out their comic book, and create stick puppets and a stage to act out their creation. Students can even share these animated stories with others on the Kreative Komix Web site. The teacher can make suggestions for scripts that include recent events, historical occurrences, stories read, or class science experiments. Each student can work at his or her own desk to develop ideas for scripts, and the class can collectively brainstorm these ideas. Then you and the class can discuss the characters, plot, purpose, and climax. The class then can form small groups to write their own scripts, and these scripts can be translated to the computer and viewed by the whole class.

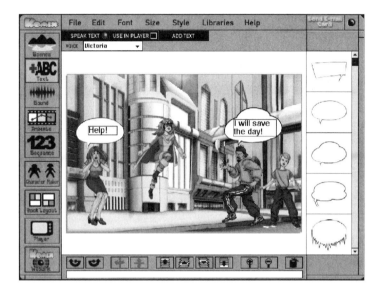

Figure 15.8
Kreative Komix Super Hero
(*Source:* Courtesy Visions Technology in Education)

World Book 2008.   For science and social studies this multimedia reference tool is perfect for any classroom. *World Book 2008* (MacKiev) is an encyclopedia for the Macintosh with animated thumbnails and thousands of articles that have audio, text, and video. There is also a Trivia Center with 500 questions and a "Just Listening Player" where you can hear music samples from classical to country. You can even export music samples to your iPod. Students can use the Trivia Center to play a Jeopardy game and they can use the Just Listening Player to try and guess the name of a particular musical composition. In a classroom the teacher can have students view videos as a group and then do group research on topics from antelopes (Figure 15.9) to presidents.

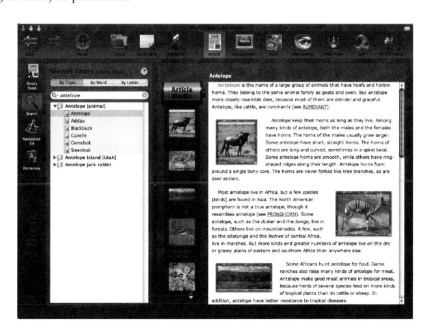

Figure 15.9
World Book Encyclopedia 2008
(*Source:* Courtesy Software MacKiev)

Crosscountry. For social studies, there is a truck-driving interactive simulation series entitled *Crosscountry* (Ingenuity Works), which includes such titles as *USA 2*, *Texas*, *Canada 2*, and *California*. The *Crosscountry* programs are effective for teaching map reading, geography, spatial relationships, and critical thinking skills. In *Crosscountry Canada 2* (Figure 15.10), students discover the geography of Canada by driving trucks to to pick up commodities that the teacher or computer has selected from a list of 50 possibilities. These commodities are located in 79 Canadian cities. You could divide the class into two competing trucking companies and send them on their missions. (If one trucking company chooses to pick up only four commodities, its mission will require about 40 minutes.) You can customize the operation of the program so that both companies have to travel the same distance. Each team decides when to eat, sleep, and get gas; which cities to travel to; and how to get to the final destination. Obviously, each team's objective is to pick up and deliver its loads before the other team does.

Figure 15.10
Crosscountry Canada 2
(*Source:* Use with permission of Ingenuity Works)

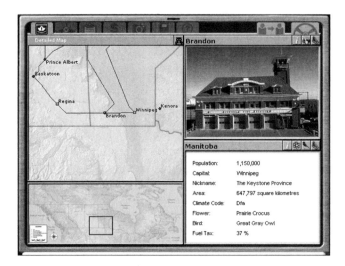

Members of the teams can record the trip routes, cities visited, population of those cities, locations, and other features. A winning team's strategy can be discussed, and each team can keep a journal of the journey.

Science Court. The *Science Court* series (Tom Snyder Productions) teaches science concepts to elementary and middle school students. The programs in the series cover, among other concepts and topics, sound, statistics, particles in motion, machines, the water cycle, fossils, and inertia. The program unfolds as a courtroom drama, and there are demonstrations and explanations as lawyers battle over a case. In *Science Court: Electric Current*, Mary Murray is accused of attempting to steal a Ping Pong trophy from Mr. Richman's mansion. During the trial, students work in cooperative teams. They review the facts, engage in hands-on activities, and predict what will happen next. As the case progresses, the students attempt to answer questions correctly (Figure 15.11). After the case is presented, students predict how the jury will vote. The teacher can lead interesting discussions about the trial. Members of the class can be encouraged to take notes and then share their notes with the class. During the course of the trial, the students learn about such things as electric circuit components and the difference between an open and closed circuit. They engage in hands-on experiments with open and closed circuits and comparing the electrical conductivity of different materials. Students also work as a team by listening and talking with others, sharing a goal, and becoming a member of a group. This series of programs is perfect for integrating the computer into the classroom.

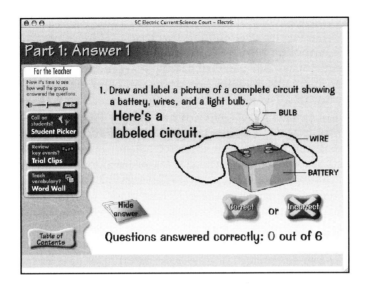

Figure 15.11
*Science Court: Electric
Current Version 2*
(*Source:* Courtesy Tom Snyder)

Finally, *High School Advantage 2008* (Encore) provides a resource center for 10 core subjects, a student planner, and SAT and ACT college test preparation. This program can be used as a learning station for individual students. They can be tutored on different subjects including Algebra II, Physics, and Biology (Figure 15.12).

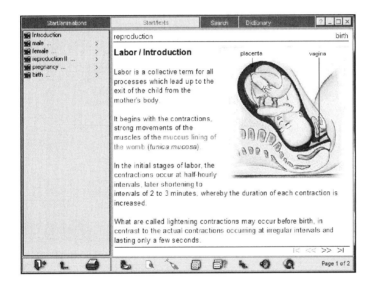

Figure 15.12
*High School Advantage:
Biology*
(*Source:* Advantage is a Trademark of Encore Software, Inc.)

In summation, you should select software that best satisfies students' needs. You should also take time to collect the appropriate equipment, organize the room, and put student experts to work. Learn the software, be aware of its time limitations, know how to integrate it into the classroom curriculum, and always encourage student participation by asking appropriate questions.

THE POTENTIAL OF A ONE-COMPUTER CLASSROOM

In the preceding paragraphs, we discussed different possibilities for utilization of a single computer in a classroom. These are but a few of the many possibilities that exist. They are "the tip of the iceberg." A resourceful teacher and motivated students can use a computer to enhance learning in a multitude of ways. In the paragraphs that follow, we touch on a few of these possibilities.

A teacher can use the computer for administrative tasks such as testing, a grade book, an attendance chart, and a seating chart. She can use this computer as a presentation tool on a variety of topics; for example, she can create a slide show for "Open House." She can also use the computer to write letters and create puzzles, lab handouts, bulletin boards, lesson plans, newsletters, announcements, and certificates. The teacher can use the computer to collect information or as a graphic organizer. For example, the teacher can use the graphic organizer *Inspiration* to outline material for a teacher demonstration. Teachers can use the computer to motivate students, provide information, demonstrate some concept, and role-play. They can improve themselves professionally using the Internet. Teachers can communicate with other instructors, principals, parents, and the class using e-mail. They can share lesson plans, class projects, and collaborative projects.

Students can use the computer as part of a learning center. At this learning center, they can use the computer as a tutor, for drill and practice, problem solving, or simulation. They can go online and explore the Internet, using it as a vast library of resources. They can use the computer as a creation tool. With this tool they can produce documents with a word processor, database, presentation tool, and spreadsheet. They can use the computer as a publishing center to produce newsletters and multimedia documents with graphics. They can produce class magazines, class presentations, Web pages, time lines, writing projects, and portfolios (Figure 15.13).

Figure 15.13
Make it with Office 2007
Portfolio
(*Source:* Courtesy Visions Technology in Education)

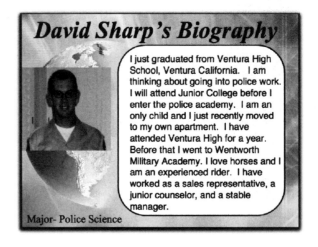

Computer Labs

With the paucity of computers in many classrooms and budget crunches, teachers may have to depend on computer labs. When setting up a computer lab the design is an important consideration. The computer lab's design is determined by the number of computers, room size, number of peripheral devices such as scanners and printers, and the instructor's teaching style. When the instructor demonstrates, it is important that students have an unobstructed view of the projection screen. If each computer station has a large desktop, students can work in pairs at each station. This is useful not only for collaborative activities, but also if some of the computers in the lab are not working. There are many advantages to using a computer lab. A computer lab is invaluable for teaching students word processing, desktop publishing, math, science, CAD, multimedia production, and report preparation. The computer lab is the perfect place for the teacher to do classroom demonstrations. In a computer lab you can share resources, and the students can work on projects simultaneously.

There are some drawbacks to computer labs. The computer lab costs more because it must have a technical staff to maintain its operation. The lab administrators must be able to fix and maintain the machines and make sure the network is operating properly. Lab rules (no eating or smoking near equipment) must be established and followed, computer use must be scheduled, security must be maintained, and the equipment must be protected from viruses.

The Wireless Mobile Lab

Because schools want to integrate the computer into the classroom more easily, there is a trend away from the standard computer lab toward the **wireless mobile lab**. A typical wireless mobile lab has 16, 24, or 32 laptops locked inside the cart's wireless hub. (The hub is plugged into the school's network by a regular network cable.) Companies such as Dell and Apple (Figure 15.14) are currently selling these mobile wireless laptop labs. They usually have a printer, and the laptops have CD drives or DVD drives.

Figure 15.14
iBook Wireless Mobile Lab
(*Source:* Courtesy Apple Computer, Inc.)

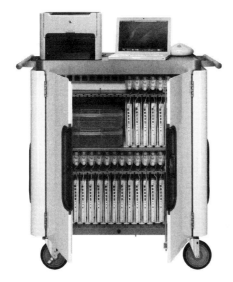

Using this kind of setup, a school can then provide computer workstations when and where they are needed. Each computer has a card inside that gives the student wireless access to the Internet and the school's network. Teachers can sign up to use the cart when they need it, and they do not have to march students to a separate lab. Also, this type of lab takes up less space than a standard lab.

A problem with these wireless networks is security. Whenever you use a wireless network your data can easily be intercepted (Shannon, 2007; Keizer, 2003; Brooks, 2002). Hackers can drive through your neighborhood, pulling access codes from your unsecured wireless network. It is easy to steal a person's Social Security number or banking account number and even place viruses on a network.

SUMMARY

In this chapter, we explored how to integrate the computer into the curriculum, select software according to the needs of pupils, collect the appropriate equipment, organize the classroom, and employ the team approach. We discussed the teacher's use of computer labs and wireless mobile labs.

STUDY AND ONLINE RESOURCES

CHAPTER 15 ONLINE RESOURCES

In the **student section** of the book's online site at **http://www.wiley.com/college/sharp** you will find templates and examples, video tutorials, PDFs, checklists, articles, Web sites, software reviews, and chapter quizzes. Access these resources to learn about technology and integrating it into the classroom.

CHAPTER MASTERY TEST

Lets check for chapter comprehension with a short mastery test. Key Terms, Computer Lab, and Suggested Readings and References follow the test.

1. Name two ways that the teacher can integrate the computer into the classroom.

2. Show three strategies for using one computer in the classroom.

3. Using one computer, how can the teacher increase group involvement in the learning process?

4. How can the teacher teach keyboarding skills effectively to young children?

5. Devise an organizational schedule for classroom computer use.

6. Name three activities that a student can do with only one computer in the classroom.

7. Name three activities that a teacher can do with only one computer in the classroom.

8. What is the major advantage and disadvantage of a wireless mobile lab? Explain your answer.

KEY TERMS

Liquid crystal display (LCD) p. 324

Projection panel p. 324

Video scan converter p. 324

Wireless mobile computer p. 331

 COMPUTER LAB: Activities for Mastery and Your Portfolio

15.1 Using the Internet evaluate different wireless mobile labs for the classroom. Watch the Video tutorial online and learn how to refine your Internet search.

15.2 Find three different ways to improve security when using a wireless mobile lab.

SUGGESTED READINGS AND REFERENCES

Brooks, Jason. "Wireless LAN Security Crackdown." *eWeek* 19, issue 18 (May 6, 2002): 45–47.

Buckleitner, Warren, ed. *The Complete Sourcebook on Children's Software* 8, New Jersey: Active Learning Associates (2000): 5.

Foster, Andrea L. "More Colleges Strive to Protect Data." *Chronicle of Higher Education* 53, issue 10 (October 27, 2006): A37–A45.

Hepp, Pedro and Laval, Ernesto. "Improving Literacy and Numeracy in Poor Schools: The Main Challenge in Developing Countries." *Education, Communication & Information* 4, issue 2/3 (May 2004): 332–336.

Keizer, Gregg. "WLAN Security: Reducing the Risks." *Tech-Web* (April, 13, 2003): http://www.techweb.com/tech/mobile/20030407_mobile.

Noon, Doug. "What Could Go Wrong?" *Teacher Magazine* 18, issue 4 (Jan/Feb 2007): 47–48.

Norris, Cathleen, Terry Sullivan, James Poirot, and Elliot Soloway. "No Access, No Use, No Impact: Snapshot Surveys of Educational Technology In K-12." *Journal of Research on Technology in Education* 36, issue 1 (Fall 2003): 15–27.

Rittner-Heir, Robbin M. "One Student One Computer." *School Planning and Management* 39, no. 5 (May 2000): 10.

Rivero, Victor. "Computer Labs: Here to Stay?" *American School Board Journal* 193, issue 10 (October 2006): 50–51.

Shannon, Meg McGinity. "Shannon's Eleven." Communications of the ACM (Association for Computing Machinery) 50, issue 1 (January 2007): 17–20 (http://www.acm.org.libproxy.csun.edu:2048/cacm/).

Siegel, Jack. "How One Class with One Computer Composed Music." *Teaching Music* 11, issue 5 (April 2004): 44–48.

Stone, M. David. "One Computer, Many Users." *PC Magazine* 19, no. 2 (January 18, 2000): 135.

Warwick, Sharon. "But I Only Have One Computer!" *School Arts* 106, issue 2 (October 2006): 35–36.

Wildstrom, Stephen H. Seeking Wi-Fi Security. *Business Week Online* (December 13, 2007): 5.

The Importance of Research and Computer Assisted Instruction

Learning theories and research are very important topics. Especially when learning theories shed light on how we should use computers in education. Computer research answers questions and raises numerous issues.

objectives

Upon completing this chapter, you will be able to do the following:

1 Explain the difference between the teacher-directed approach and constructivism.

2 Summarize the research findings on CAI and (a) gender differences, (b) science simulations, (c) word processing, (d) students with learning disabilities, (e) motivation, (f) attitudes, and (g) distance learning.

Using the computer, students and teachers can do the following:

students can

- prepare a PowerPoint presentation on two learning theorists,
- use the Internet to research Computer-Assisted Instruction, and
- find research on distance Learning.

teachers can

- show useful distance learning Internet sites,
- demonstrate how to research computer-instructed learning topics,
- explain learning theorist impact in education, and
- find lesson plans and instructional material.

Learning Theories and Technology Integration

Behaviorism, cognitive theory, constructivism, situated cognition, and other theories have been used to investigate the effect of the computer on teaching and learning. Learning theorists have disagreed about what strategies are most useful in achieving educational goals. From this disagreement has evolved a recent interest in two different approaches: teacher directed and constructivist (Roblyer, 2006). The teacher-directed approach is based on the behaviorism learning theory, and the constructivist approach comes from other branches of cognitive learning theory.

THE TEACHER-DIRECTED APPROACH

The **teacher-directed approach** is derived from the behavioral theories of B. F. Skinner (Figure 16.1), Edward Thorndike, Richard Atkinson, David Ausubel, Robert Gagné, and Lee Cronbach. These theories position the teacher as the manipulator of the classroom environment and the student as a receptacle for learning. Famous for his work in behavior modification, B. F. Skinner championed programmed instruction, in which lessons and drills are planned in small incremental steps to lessen the chance of incorrect responses on the part of the student. The idea is that the student will learn in a tightly structured environment. The teacher begins with lower-level teaching skills and builds to higher skills systematically. Clearly stated objectives are matched with test items. This approach stresses individual work and emphasizes traditional teaching and assessment methods, such as lectures and worksheets.

(*Source:* John WIley and Sons photo by Kathy Bendo)

Figure 16.1
B.F. Skinner

During the 1970s and 1980s, when computers first appeared in the classroom, behavioral theories were very popular. Software, which supported such theories, was based on programmed instruction. Today, thousands of educational software programs—such as *Physics Tutor* (Learning Interactive Company), *Elementary Advantage 2008* (Encore), *Quarter Mile* (Barnum Software), and *Fastt Math* (Tom Snyder Productions–Scholastic)—are based on the behavioral models of instruction. These programs use drill-and-practice and tutorial software. They diagnose student skills, monitor student performance, and make changes in instruction when necessary. The software usually generates student and class performance data for teacher use. Advocates of this approach praise the software for its individualized pacing, self-instructional sequences, and remediation, especially useful for a teacher whose time is limited. The software generally makes learning faster, especially the necessary basic skills. This software performs time-consuming tasks and frees the teacher to handle more complex student needs. Opponents of this type of software criticize its lack of flexibility and its foundations in preestablished curricula. They say it uses only one type of educational technology, whereas other approaches use a variety such as multimedia and telecommunication.

THE CONSTRUCTIVISM APPROACH

The **constructivist approach** evolved from the work of developmental theorists such as Jerome Bruner, Jean Piaget, Lev Vygotsky, Seymour Papert, and Howard Gardner (Figure 16.2). The constructivist feels that learning occurs when the learner controls his or her own acquisition of knowledge. Constructivist models pose problems and involve students in searching for answers through exploration or discovery learning. Assessment involves student portfolios, performance checklists, and tests with open-ended questions and narratives.

Howard Gardner proposed the concept of multiple intelligences. He argued there is not one single measure of intelligences, but that humans have a family of seven intelligences, as shown in Table 16.1.

Figure 16.2
Howard Gardner
(*Source:* Jerry Bauer/AFP/Getty Images)

Table 16.1 **Howard Gardner's Seven Intelligences**

1. Visual/spatial intelligence	5. Interpersonal intelligence
2. Musical intelligence	6. Intrapersonal intelligence
3. Verbal intelligence	7. Bodily/kinesthetic intelligence
4. Logical/mathematical intelligence	

Gardner believed that our educational system is not addressing all the intelligences. He pushed for teachers to break free from the teacher-directed approach's emphasis on testing, focusing instead on other sources of information about how students develop skills that are important in real life.

The constructivist model differs widely from the teacher-directed model, especially in its emphasis on group work over individual work. Students play an active rather than passive role, and they work to solve problems through cooperative learning activities.

One of the main technological approaches to constructivist teaching is the computer simulation. The application of simulations can be traced to 17th-century war games in which participants set up mock battles. In the mid-1950s simulations were introduced in business training, and in the 1970s the popular simulation program *Lemonade Stand* by Minnesota Educational Computing Corporation (MECC) was introduced to run on the Apple II computer. Today, programs such as *Sims 2* and *SimCity Societies* series (Electronic Arts) teach complex concepts such as supply and demand by asking players to make decisions about cost, production, price structure, and advertising. A further innovation in this field is virtual reality, in which the student enters an artificial environment, such as *Myst V* (Ubisoft) (Figure 16.3).

Figure 16.3
Myst V—The Bridge
(*Source:* Courtesy of Ubisoft)

Other constructivist-based technologies are more recent developments than simulation software. Annotated movies and hypertext, for example, engage students in highly meaningful and active learning. Advocates of constructivism say that it teaches skills more relevant to students' experiences by anchoring tasks in real-life situations. Students address problems through interactive situations and play active rather than passive roles. They work together in groups to solve problems. This software stresses high-level skills as well as low-level skills.

Both constructivist and teacher-directed approaches attempt to identify what Gagné (1985) calls the "conditions of learning," or the circumstances that influence learning.

Both approaches are based on work done by respected psychologists and learning theorists, and the approaches differ only in the ways they describe the environment in which learning occurs. Table 16.2 compares the characteristics of the teacher-directed model with those of the constructivist model.

Table 16.2 Teacher-Directed versus Constructivist Instructional Models

Teacher Directed	Constructivist
Based on worksheets and textbooks	Based on manipulatives and primary sources
Curriculum is fixed	Curriculum is flexible
Teacher transmits knowledge	Approach develops concepts
Instruction is didactic	Student explores and discovers knowledge
Results in one correct answer	Results in acquisition of large concepts
Stresses individualized work	Stresses cooperative group work
Poses questions for students to answer	Engages students in interactive activities
Concerned with information acquisition	Concerned with the process of learning
Assessment is by testing	Assessment is by student products and student observation

Since this textbook is not an instructional theory textbook, we did not explore this topic in depth.

Computer-Assisted Instruction Research Findings

Computer-assisted instruction (CAI) has been used for over 27 years. It is sometimes referred to as computer-based instruction (CBI), computer-assisted learning (CAL), or computer-based learning (CBL). CAI refers to "using the computer for training and instruction" (Freedman, 2008). In CAI, students receive feedback from the computer, which controls the sequencing of the subject matter. Because of increased access to computers, teachers are concerned about the effects the computer has on instruction. The research literature contains many studies related to computer-assisted instruction, and this section highlights some of these research findings.

 If you want to more thoroughly examine the different learning theories, refer to Dr. David Kretschmer's article, which appears on our online site at http://www.wiley.com/college/sharp. For your convenience, the PDF file can be downloaded and printed. Dr. Kretschmer is the Chair of the Elementary Department at California State University, Northridge. He has written articles in the field of education.

ACHIEVEMENT

Numerous studies have compared the achievement scores of students using computer-assisted instruction with the achievement scores of students receiving regular instruction. Generally, the results indicate that CAI produces equal or greater achievement (eNews, 2007; Timmerman & Kruepke, 2006; Atkinson, 2004; Traynor, 2003; Bayraktar, 2002; Wong, 2001; House, 2001).

Gene Glass (1976, 1977) introduced a technique called **meta-analysis**[1] in order to generate a clearer picture of the effects of computer-based treatments. Other researchers followed and compiled meta-analysis studies in the area of instructional computing. Kulik's series of meta-analysis studies were the most comprehensive (C. C. Kulik, J. A. Kulik, & Cohen, 1980; J. A. Kulik, Bangert, & Williams, 1983; C. C. Kulik, J. A. Kulik, & Shwath, 1986; J. A. Kulik & Chen-Lin, 1987; C. C. Kulik, Chen-Lin, & J. A. Kulik, 1991). These studies showed that students who were taught using the computer scored higher on achievement tests than did those students who were taught using other methods. The Kulik studies also showed that this analysis produced different results, depending on the grade, ability level, and type of instruction.

---

[1] Meta-analysis is a statistical technique that enables researchers to summarize the results of a large group of research studies and identify general effects.

Roblyer, Castine, and King (1988) summarized previous literature reviews on the educational effectiveness of instructional computing before they presented their meta-analysis of studies. Here is a brief rundown of their findings: (1) There are higher achievement results for college-age and adult students than for elementary and secondary students; (2) the computer produces the greatest achievement gains in science, with math, reading, and cognitive skills yielding about half the effect; (3) computer-assisted instruction software programs are all of approximately equal effectiveness; and (4) lower-achieving students show more gains with CAI than do students who are achieving at grade level, but these gains are not statistically significant.

Using a meta-analysis approach, Khalili and Shashaani (1994), Mann and Shakesshaft (1997), Christmann, Badgett, and Lucking (1997), Sivin-Kachala (1998), Schacter (1999), Bayraktar (2002) concluded that CAI was effective in improving students' academic achievement.

In addition to his finding is a Cisco Systems and Metiri Group report called "Technology in Schools: What the Research Says." It summarized certain trends in regard to television, video use, calculators, handheld devices, whiteboards, and virtual learning. The report stated that technology did produce significant but small gains across all content areas (eNews, 2007).

On the other hand, Clark's review of CAI in meta-analytical studies in 1985 was critical of the research and suggested that studies by the Kuliks and others overestimated CAI's benefits because uncontrolled instructional methods were embedded in the instructional treatments. Clark (1991, 1994) felt that the existing evidence did not indicate that computers yield learning benefits. Also, Rachal (1995) reviewed studies on adult reading achievement and CAI. He found that most of these studies did not show a significant difference between CAI and conventional approaches. In an eastern Canada high school study, Liu, Macmillan, and Timmons (1998) found computer integration produced no significant effect on achievement and there is no change in student attitude toward computers. Finally, Batchelder and Rachal (2000) did an experimental study that examined the worth of computer-assisted instruction on inmates who were participating in a prison education program. They studied the achievement scores of a group who received CAI and traditional instruction and a control group that just received the traditional method of instruction. The results showed no statistically significant difference between the groups.

As you can see from this discussion, recent research findings on CAI suggest that CAI produces achievement equal to or greater than traditional teaching even though there is still a lack of consensus among some researchers on the value of CAI.

GENDER DIFFERENCES

Most gender studies try to get at the reasons for males using the computer more than females. Collis and Ollila (1986) examined gender differences in secondary school students' attitudes toward writing on the computer. Females were significantly less positive than their male counterparts on every item that related to computers. Swadener and Hannafin (1987) studied the gender similarities and differences in sixth graders' attitudes toward the computer. They found that boys with higher achievement levels in mathematics also had a high interest in computers. The boys with low scores had low interest in computers. This finding is completely opposite for females, with the low-achieving female students having the most interest in the computer. Siann et al. (1988) studied gender stereotyping and computer involvement. They suggested there are some encouraging trends, but males still use computers more than females do. Williams et al. (1994) examined the effects of factors such as past experience and sex-role stereotyping on computer-interaction tasks completed by 154 male and 223 female college students. The results of the study did support the pattern of male advantage, but they also highlighted the complex factors involved in computer interactions. Makrakis and Sawada (1996) surveyed 773 ninth-grade students in Tokyo, Japan, and Stockholm, Sweden. They found that, regardless of the country surveyed, males reported higher scores on computer aptitude and enjoyment than females did. Whitley (1997) did a meta-analysis of studies of gender differences in computer attitude and found that males showed greater sex-role stereotyping of computer use, higher computer self-efficacy, and more positive attitudes toward computers than did females. The largest differences were found in high school students; most other differences were small. Liao (1999) did a meta-analysis on the effect of gender differences on attitudes toward computers. These results too suggest that male subjects have a slightly more positive attitude toward computers than female subjects. Young (2000) used a student computer attitude survey with 462 middle and high school students. The results of the study showed greater confidence among male students in regard to the computer and the perception of computers as a male domain supported by males. In a study involving 104 first-year teacher education students in Brunei Darussalam, Khine (2001) found that female students showed higher anxiety toward using computers as compared to their male counterparts. Finally, Cooper (2006) in an overview of the research, found that females are at a disadvantage compared to men when using computer-assisted instruction.

The majority of studies on gender differences seem to point to males having a more positive attitude toward computers than females. There are many possible reasons: (1) most of the computer games are violent and appeal to the male population; (2) computers are linked to math and science, fields that show an overrepresentation of males; (3) magazines and newspapers depict men using the computer more than women; (4) when women are associated with the computer it is in a secretarial role; and (5) many teachers encourage boys to use computers but discourage girls from doing so.

SCIENCE SIMULATIONS

Generally, students learn very well with science simulation software. Moore, Smith, and Avner (1980) found higher student achievement with computer simulations when students had to interpret the results of the experiments to make decisions. If the students only had to follow directions and calculate the results, there was no difference between the experimental and control groups. Summerville (1984) and Fortner, Schar, and Mayer (1986) noted similar findings. Linn (1986) conducted an experiment in which 8 eighth-grade science classes used computers as lab partners for a semester. The students learned to use the computer to collect and display data and save and print out their reports. They used tools such as temperature and light probes that were attached to the computer, and the results were displayed on their computer screens. Linn found that the students instructed in the microcomputer-based labs outperformed 17-year-olds who took a standardized test on scientific knowledge. In addition, the computer-taught students demonstrated a very positive attitude toward experimentation.

Farynaiarz and Lockwood (1992) examined the impact of microcomputer simulations on environmental problem solving among community college students. The students showed a highly significant improvement in problem-solving skills after being exposed to three simulation models on lake pollution.

Rueter and Perrin (1999) tested the effect of using a computer simulation to teach the concept of a food web to nonbiology majors in an introductory course. They concluded that the use of the simulation resulted in significantly better performance on an open-ended essay question for students using the software, and the average student generally scored higher. Bayraktar's (2002) meta-analysis study investigated how effective computer-assisted instruction was on student achievement in secondary and college science classes compared to regular instruction. The result showed positive results for CAI used for science simulation. Finally, Shim et al. (2003) did a study on virtual reality technology (VRT) learning programs for middle school students. Their study reported that VRT simulations increase students' interest and understanding of scientific concepts. The results of the science simulation studies continue to be promising. Even a study that shows no significant difference between students who use the traditional method and students who use the computer is encouraging. Such a finding means that simulations can substitute for laboratory experiments, which is advantageous because science simulations are less dangerous, less time-consuming, and less expensive than actual lab work. They encourage student involvement in the learning process and enable teachers to give students access to situations that ordinarily would be impossible.

WORD PROCESSING

Many studies deal with word processing and its effect on the quantity and quality of student writing, but the evidence is contradictory (Sharp, & Trotter, 2007; Penuel, 2006; Li & Cumming, 2001; Gupta, 1998; Owston & Wideman, 1997; O'Brien, 1994; Jones, 1994; Bangert-Drowns, 1993; Morehouse, Hoaglund, & Schmidt, 1987; Feldman, 1984). The research was conducted in a variety of settings. Researchers David L. Silvernail and Aaron K. Gritter conducted a study on an educational program in Maine that supplied their seventh and eighth-grade students with computer laptops. They found that these students' writing scores improved on the state's standardized tests (Sharp & Trotter, 2007). In 2001, Li and Cumming did a study of adult male Mandarin speakers learning English as a second language (ESL). They studied whether using the computer for writing improved the quality of the revisions and the quality of the students' compositions. The results of the study showed that when the learners used the computer they stayed on task longer and they produced higher-level revisions.

However, Daiute (1985) found that students wrote less with a word processor. Kurth (1987) found no differences in quality of writing or revisions between a secondary school group that used word processing for their writing and a secondary group that used pencil and paper. Hawisher (1986) and Bangert-Drowns (1993) reviewed the research on word processing and noted that implementation differences among the various studies could affect their outcomes. Seawell et al. (1994) compared the effects of computer-based word processing and writing by hand on third and fourth graders' attitudes and performance in writing. The third graders made more revisions and edits when using word processors, whereas the fourth graders made more changes in their handwritten drafts. Reed (1996) found that the type of word processor that is used affects the students. For example, younger students need more prompts, but older ones find this inhibiting. Jackowski-Bartol (2001) investigated the impact of word processing on middle school students. Their study found that when students used the computer they had trouble with hand–thought coordination for typing, and that computer composition time exceeded that of traditional composition.

These criticisms highlight the problem, not only for word processing studies but also for other research concerning computer applications. The inconclusive nature of these studies may be due to the difficulty of quantifying the assessment of writing.

STUDENTS WITH LEARNING DISABILITIES

Most research indicates that those with learning disabilities (LD) benefit from involvement with CAI. At the Open University of Israel, Klemes, Epstein, Zuker, Grinberg, and Ilovitch (2006) showed that using a computerized learning environment helped students with learning disabilities enrolled in a distance-learning course. Ortega-Tudela and Gomez-Ariza (2006) worked with children with Down Syndrome and investigated whether computer-assisted teaching helped these children learn basic mathematical concepts and skills. They found that the computer-assisted group performed better than the paper-and-pencil–assisted group on different tasks. They concluded that there appears to be a relationship between the teaching method used and the mathematical learning of these children. In 2002, Blair et al. studied 24 eighth-grade students with mild disabilities, and they found that these students improved their organization and writing performance with computer technology. During a one-month summer school remedial program, students with mild disabilities were taught writing strategies using word processors and a visual planning software program called *Inspiration*. The students were tracked on their attitude toward writing and the quantity and quality of their writing compositions. As the students progressed, they engaged more in planning their writing, their objections to writing decreased, and positive attitudes toward writing increased. There was a slight increase in the quality of their writing and an increase in the amount of writing. Students enjoyed the computers and improved their keyboarding skills.

Zhang (2000) found similar results when he conducted a year-long research study involving fifth-grade students with learning disabilities. He used a specially designed computer program as a writing tool to assist these students with a weekly writing curriculum. The study showed that students had positive gains in their writing behaviors and their written products. Xin and Jitendra (1999), in a meta-analysis study on the effectiveness of instruction in word-problem solving for students with learning problems, found that computer-assisted instruction was most effective for group-design studies and long-term intervention effects. McNaughton et al. (1997) investigated the impact of integrated proofreading strategy training on LD secondary students. This training consisted of using a computer spelling checker and student strategies for proofreading. Students showed an increase in strategy use and percentage of spelling errors corrected on student compositions and proofread material. Every method improved writing accuracy.

MOTIVATION AND ATTITUDE

Teachers face the challenge of motivating students and fostering in them a positive attitude to improve their chances for success in school. For example, an essential element in improving students' spelling is keeping interest high (Ruel, 1977). Many studies report students' positive attitudes toward the computer and how computers motivate students and help them maintain high interest in academics and a better attitude toward learning (House, 2007; Glickman & Dixon, 2002; Lim, 2002; Kosakowski, 2000; Yildirim, 2000; Hatfield, 1996; Terrell & Rendulic, 1996; Richman, 1994; Clement, 1981). A few of these studies are summarized in the following paragraphs.

Daniel House (2007) conducted a reading study using students in Hong Kong and the United States. He examined the relationship between using computer activities and instructional strategies and student motivation. He found that students who used the computer more often to look up information and write reports have a greater interest and enjoyment of reading.

In 2002, Glickman and Dixon studied community college intermediate algebra students. They found that students taught by CAI significantly outperformed on conceptual measures than students taught with a lecture approach. Furthermore, they saw significant improvement in mathematics attitudes from start to finish of the semester.

Yildirim (2000) examined the changes in attitude of 114 preservice and inservice teachers toward computers after they participated in an educational computing class. The results indicated that the teachers' attitudes (anxiety, confidence, and liking) significantly improved after this computer literacy course. Mitra and Steffensmeir (2000) found that, if students did not have ready access to computers, their attitudes toward teaching and learning did not change. However, if these students had easy access through a networked institution, this fostered a positive attitude toward computers in teaching and learning. Hatfield (1996) examined the effective use of computer stations across the curriculum and found overall increased computer use and increased student motivation and interest. Terrell and Rendulic (1996) did a comparative study of elementary school students and found evidence that the use of computer-managed instructional feedback can have a positive effect on student motivation and achievement. Richman's (1994) study showed how innovations in educational technology contributed to motivation and achievement of at-risk students in New York's Berkshire Union Free School District. Robertson (1978) found that children who had experienced failure in the past responded positively to computer-assisted programs. She concluded that the children involved in the study did not experience a sense of failure over an incorrect response.

In a departure from the other studies, McKinnon, Nolan, and Sinclair (2000) found that an increase in access to computers resulted in a decrease in favorable attitudes toward the computer. The findings seem paradoxical because the decrease in positive attitudes toward computers was accompanied by an increasingly positive attitude toward school and the integrated curriculum program in which computers were a major element. In a 1998 study, Liu, Macmillan, and Timmons found that there was no significant effect of computer integration on achievement, and there was no significant change in student attitude toward computers after computer integration. Generally, students perceived that using computers had a positive effect on their learning. Some researchers have tried to find out if students prefer computer-based methods simply because a computer is involved. Other research has focused on the computer's influence on student attitudes toward school and curriculum.

Generally, the CAI studies that focused on students' attitudes toward themselves and school learning were positive. However, the results are inconclusive on the effects of computer instruction on motivation and school achievement. One reason for this finding might be that achievement in school is not based on a simple set of variables but is the result of a complex set of factors.

DISTANCE LEARNING RESEARCH

In the literature from the mid-1950s to the present there are numerous studies comparing distance learning with traditional learning. The majority of these studies found that there is no significant difference between distance learning and traditional classroom learning (O'Dwyer, Carey, & Kleiman, 2007; Yu-Chiung & Ya-Ming, 2005; Person and Bond (2004); Simonson, Smaldino, Albright, and Zvacek, 2003; Allen, Bourhis, Burrell, & Mabry, 2002; Merisotis & Jamie, 1999). Even a finding of no significant difference between students who use the traditional method and students who use distance learning is optimistic. Such a finding means that distance learning can substitute for the traditional classroom experience. The research also shows that distance learners have a better attitude toward learning than do traditional learners. Distance learners feel they learn just as much as a traditional classroom learner (Simonson, Smaldino, Albright, & Zvacek, 2003; Bisciglia & Monk-Turner, 2002; Grenzky & Maitland, 2001; Inman, Kerwin, & Mayes, 1999). Furthermore, a distance learner has greater satisfaction when there is more interaction between the teacher and the students. In distance learning the student must be able to communicate with the instructor (Simonson, 2000; Fulford & Zang, 1993; Westbrook, 1997). In a 1997 study, McHenry and Bozik found distance learners need a sense of community in order to be successful. If a distance learner perceives there is a decrease in interaction, this affects his or her coursework satisfaction. The research also shows that a successful distance learner is usually an abstract learner who is inwardly motivated (Osborn, 2001; Wang & Newlin, 2000; Song, 2000; Bures, Abrami, & Amundsen, 2000). Even with all this research on distance learning, there is a need for further research on distance learning's effect on K–12 students. For more insight into distance learning, consult Kerry Lynn Rice's 2006 journal article, "A Comprehensive Look at Distance Education in the K–12."

PROBLEMS WITH THE RESEARCH

Although a considerable amount of research has been done since the early 1980s, the research is problematic. Many CAI studies were conducted before microcomputers were readily available. In addition, many studies are not thoroughly reported in the literature, so it is impossible to determine whether the conclusions drawn by the investigators are supported by the data. The meta-analysis that Roblyer et al. (1988) performed included 38 studies and 44 dissertations from a possible 200. The rest of the studies were eliminated because of reasons such as methodological flaws or insufficient data. A good portion of CAI research is anecdotal, based on experiences and not on experimental design.

Educators are now beginning to understand what role the computer could play in educating students. However, we still do not know if computers are the best way to foster learning. There definitely is a need for higher-quality computer research to get substantive answers to our many questions.

RESEARCH GENERALIZATIONS

Even with these problems, some relevant generalizations can be made from the research:

1. In science, the computer is a useful tool for simulations. The Army and Navy use war-game simulations. Chemistry instructors can use computer-based simulations as substitutes for lab work. Flight instructors can use flight simulation software instead of putting novices at the controls of actual planes. A simulation program is generally less dangerous, less expensive, and less time-consuming than the real experience.

2. The computer is helpful for individualization. Students working with computers can progress at their own pace. If they need help with math facts, they can turn to the computer for individualized tutoring, freeing the teacher to work with other students or on other academic areas. This type of individualization spreads the range of abilities in a class and enables some students to move ahead.

3. The computer changes attitudes toward the computer, school, and school subjects. The computer does motivate children, and there is speculation that it might improve the dropout rate.

4. There is no strong body of evidence supporting the notion that a positive attitude toward the computer will result in improved achievement.

5. Generally, the results indicate that CAI produces equal or greater achievement.

6. There is no significant difference between distance learning and traditional classroom learning.

7. Distance learners have a better attitude toward learning than do traditional learners.

8. Word processing motivates children to write. However, there is no difference between the quality of writing produced using a word processor and that generated with pencil and paper.

9. Gender studies have found that boys work more frequently with the computer than do girls. This finding appears to be a socially developed difference.

SUMMARY

We discussed the learning theories that shed light on how we should use computers in education. The chapter concluded with a brief rundown of some of the important research studies on computer-assisted instruction.

STUDY AND ONLINE RESOURCES

CHAPTER 16 ONLINE RESOURCES

 In the **student section** of the book's online site at **http://www.wiley.com/college/sharp** you will find templates and examples, video tutorials, PDFs, checklists, articles, Web sites, software reviews, and chapter quizzes. Access these resources to learn about technology and integrating it into the classroom.

CHAPTER MASTERY TEST

Lets check for chapter comprehension with a short mastery test. Key Terms, Computer Lab, and Suggested Readings and References follow the test.

1. Discuss the findings of three research studies on CAI.

2. Does CAI research show that science simulations are more effective than laboratory experiences? Explain your answer.

3. Who was B. F. Skinner and what was his contribution?

4. What was Howard Gardner's major contribution?

5. As a teacher are you more comfortable with teacher-directed or constructivist strategies?

6. Name three characteristics associated with the constructivist learning model and three characteristics associated with the teacher-directed model.

KEY TERMS

Computer-assisted instruction p. 337

Constructivist approach p. 335

Meta-analysis p. 337

Teacher-directed approach p. 334

 COMPUTER LAB: Activities for Mastery and Your Portfolio

16.1 Using one of the research topics, write a paper discussing its implications for education. Watch the Video tutorial online and learn how to refine your Internet search.

16.2 Discuss any learning theorist and what implications his theory has to educational technology.

SUGGESTED READINGS AND REFERENCES

Allen, Mike, John Bourhis, Nancy Burrell, and Edward Mabry. "Comparing Student Satisfaction with Distance Education to Traditional Classrooms in Higher Education: A Meta-Analysis." *American Journal of Distance Education* 16, no. 2 (2002): 83–98.

Atkinson, Stephanie. "A Comparison of Pupil Learning and Achievement in Computer Aided Learning and Traditionally Taught Situations with Special Reference to Cognitive Style and Gender Issues." *Educational Psychology* 24, issue 5 (October 2004): 659–679.

Badgett, Christmann E. J., and R. Lucking. "Progressive Comparison of the Effects of Computer-Assisted Instruction on the Academic Achievement of Secondary Students." *Journal of Research on Computing Education* 29, no. 4 (1997): 325–337.

Bain, Connie D.; Rice, Margaret L. "The Influence of Gender on Attitudes, Perceptions, and Uses of Technology." *Journal of Research on Technology in Education* 39, issue 2 (Winter 2006): 119–132.

Bangert-Drowns, R. "The Word Processor as an Instructional Tool: A Meta-Analysis of Word Processing in Writing

Instruction." *Review of Educational Research* 63, no. 1 (1993): 69–93.

Batchelder, John Stuart, and John R. Rachal. "Efficacy of a Computer-Assisted Instruction Program in a Prison Setting: An Experimental Study." *Adult Education Quarterly* 50, no. 2 (February 2000): 120–133.

Bayraktar, Sule. "A Meta-Analysis of the Effectiveness of Computer-Assisted Instruction in Science Education." *Journal of Research on Technology in Education* 34, no. 2 (Winter 2001–2002): 173–188.

Bisciglia, Michael, and Elizabeth Monk-Turner. "Differences in Attitudes Between On Site and Distance-Site Students in Group Teleconference Courses." *The American Journal of Distance Education* 16, no. 1 (2002): 37–52.

Blair, Regina B., Christine Ormsbee, and Joyce Brandes. "Using Writing Strategies and Visual Thinking Software to Enhance the Written Performance of Students with Mild Disabilities." ERIC_NO: ED463125, 2002.

Bures, Eva Mary, Philip C. Abrami, and Cheryl Amundsen. "Student Motivation to Learn via Computer Conferencing." *Research in Higher Education* 41, no. 5 (October 2000): 593–621.

Christmann, Edwin, John Badgett, and Robert Lucking. "Progressive Comparisons of the Effects of Computer-Assisted Instruction on the Academic Achievement of Secondary Students." *Journal of Research on Computing in Education* 29, no. 4 (Summer 1997).

Clark, Richard E. "Evidence for Confounding in Computer-Based Instruction Studies: Analyzing the Meta-Analysis." *Educational Communication and Technology Journal* 33, no. 4 (Winter 1985): 249–262.

Clark, Richard E. "Media Will Never Influence Learning." *Educational Technology, Research and Development* 42, no. 2 (1994): 21–29.

Clark, Richard E. "When Researchers Swim Upstream: Reflections on an Unpopular Argument About Learning from Media." *Educational Technology* 31, no. 31 (February 1991): 34–40.

Clement, Frank J. "Affective Considerations in Computer-Based Education." *Educational Technology* (April 1981): 228–232.

Collis, B., and L. Ollila. "An Examination of Sex Difference in Secondary School Students' Attitudes Toward Writing and the Computer." *Alberta Journal of Educational Research* 34, no. 4 (1986): 297–306.

Cooper, J. "The Digital Divide: The Special Case of Gender." *Journal of Computer Assisted Learning* 22, issue 5 (October 2006): 320–334.

Daiute, C. *Writing and Computers.* Reading, Mass.: Addison-Wesley, 1985.

eNews. "The Case for Ed-Tech Efficacy." *eSchool News* 10, no. 6 (June 2007).

Farynaiarz, Joseph V., and Linda G. Lockwood. "Effectiveness of Microcomputer Simulations in Stimulating Environmental Problem Solving by Community College Students." *Journal of Research in Science Teaching* 29, no. 5 (May 1992): 453–470.

Feldman, P. R. "Personal Computers in a Writing Course." *Perspectives in Computing,* Spring 1984, 4–9.

Fortner, R., W. Schar, and J. Mayer. *Effect of Microcomputer Simulations on Computer Awareness and Perception of*

Environmental Relationships Among College Students. Columbus, Ohio: Ohio State University, Office of Learning Resources (ERIC Document Reproduction Service No. ED 270–311), 1986.

Fulford, Catherine P., and Shuqiang Zhang. "Perceptions of Interaction: The Critical Predictor in Distance Education." *American Journal of Distance Education* 7, no. 3 (1993): 8–21.

Freedman, Allen. *The Computer Desktop Encyclopedia.* New York: American Management Association, 2008.

Gagné, Robert M. "The Conditions of Learning and Theory of Instruction." 4th edition. New York: Holt, Rinehart, and Winston, 1985.

Glass, G. V. "Integrated Findings: The Meta-Analysis of Research." In *Review of Research in Education,* ed. L. Schulman. Itasca, Ill.: Peacock, 1977.

Glass, G. V. "Primary, Secondary, and Meta-Analysis of Research." *Educational Researcher* 5 (1976): 3–8.

Glickman, Cynthia L., and Juli Dixon. "Teaching Algebra in a Situated Context Through Reform Computer Assisted Instruction." *Research and Teaching in Developmental Education* 18, no. 24 (Spring 2002): 57–84.

Grenzky, Janet, and Christine Maitland. "Focus on Distance Education." *NEA Higher Education Research Center Update* 7, no. 2 (March 2001).

Gupta, Renu. "Can Spelling Checkers Help the Novice Writer?" *British Journal of Educational Technology* 29, no. 3 (July 1998): 255–266.

Hasselbring, Ted S. "Remediating Spelling Problems of Learning-Handicapped Students Through the Use of Microcomputers." *Educational Technology,* April 1982, 31–32.

Hatfield, Susan. *Effective Use of Classroom Computer Stations Across the Curriculum.* ERIC Document No. ED396704 RIENOV96, Dissertations/Theses, Research Technical, June 30, 1996.

Hawisher, G. E. "The Effects of Word Processing on the Revision Strategies of College Students." Paper presented at the annual meeting of the American Educational Research Association, San Francisco (ERIC Document No. ED. 268–546), April 1986.

House, J. Daniel. "Relationships Between Computer Use, Instructional Strategies, and Interest in Reading for students in Hong Kong and the United States: Results from the Pirls 2001 Assessment." *International Journal of Instructional Media* 34, issue 1 (2007): 91–104.

Inman, Elliot, Michael Kerwin, and Larry Mayes. "Instructor and Student Attitudes Toward Distance Learning." *Community College Journal of Research and Practice* 23, no. 6 (1999): 581–591.

Jackowski-Bartol, Tillary R. "The Impact of Word Processing on Middle School Students," ERIC No. ED 453825, 2001.

Jones, I. "The Effects of a Word Processor on the Written Composition of Second-Grade Pupils." *Computers in the Schools* 11, no. 2 (1994): 43–54.

Khalili, A., and L. Shashaani. "The Effectiveness of Computer Applications: A Meta-Analysis." *Journal of Research on Computing in Education* 27, no. 1 (Fall 1994): 48–61.

Khine, Myint Swe. "Attitudes Toward Computers Among Teacher Education Students in Brunei, Darussalam." *International Journal of Instructional Media* 28, issue 2, (2001): 147–153.

Klemes, Joel, Alit Epstein, Michal Zuker, Nira Grinberg, and Tamar Ilovitch. "An Assistive Computerized Learning Environment for Distance Learning Students with Learning Disabilities." *Open Learning* 21, issue 1 (February 2006): 19–32.

Kosakowski, John. "The Benefits of Information Technology." *Educational Media and Technology Yearbook* 25 (2000): 53–56.

Kulik, C. C., C. Chen-Lin, and J. A. Kulik. "Effectiveness of Computer-Based Instruction: An Updated Analysis." *Computers in Human Behavior* 7 (1991): 75–94.

Kulik, C. C., J. A. Kulik, and P. Cohen. "Instructional Technology and College Teaching." *Teaching of Psychology* 7 (1980): 199–205.

Kulik, C. C., J. A. Kulik, and B. J. Shwath. "Effectiveness of Computer-Based Adult Learning: A Meta-Analysis." *Journal of Educational Computing Research* 2 (1986): 235–252.

Kulik, J. A., R. Bangert, and G. Williams. "Effects of Computer-Based Teaching on Secondary School Students." *Journal of Educational Psychology* 75 (1983): 19–26.

Kulik, J. A., and C. Chen-Lin. "Review of Recent Literature on Computer-Based Instruction." *Contemporary Education Psychology* 12, no. 3 (July 1987): 222–230.

Kulik, J. A., and C. C. Kulik. "Timing of Feedback and Verbal Learning." *Review of Educational Research* 58, no. 1 (1988): 79–97.

Kurth, R. J. "Using Word Processing to Enhance Revision Strategies During Student Writing Activities." *Educational Technology* 27 (1987): 13–19.

Li, Jiang, and Alister Cumming. "Word Processing and Second Language Writing: A Longitudinal Case Study." *International Journal of English Studies* 1, no. 2 (2001): 127–152.

Liao, Cliff Yuen-Kuang. *Gender Differences on Attitudes Toward Computers: A Meta-Analysis.* ERIC No. ED 432287, Clearinghouse Number IRO19657, 1999.

Lim, Kee-Sook. "Impacts of Personal Characteristics on Computer Attitude and Academic Users' Information System Satisfaction." *Journal of Educational Computing Research* 26, no. 4 (2002): 395–406.

Linn, C. "Learning More—with Computers as Lab Partners." Paper presented at the annual meeting of the American Educational Research Association, San Francisco, April 1986.

Liu, Xiufeng, Robert Macmillan, and Vianne Timmons. "Assessing the Impact of Computer Integration on Students." *Journal of Research on Computing in Education* 31, no. 2 (Winter 1998): 189–201.

Makrakis, Vasilios, and Toshio Sawada. "Gender, Computers and Other School Subjects Among Japanese and Swedish Students." *Computers and Education* 26, no. 4 (May 1996): 225–231.

Mann, D., and C. Shakeshaft. *The Impact of Technology in the Schools of the Mohawk Regional Information Center Area.* Technical Report, 1997. ERIC Document No. ED 405893, (800) 443-ERIC.

McKinnon, David H., C. J. Patrick Nolan, and Kenneth E. Sinclair. "A Longitudinal Study of Student Attitudes Toward Computers: Resolving an Attitude Decay Paradox." *Journal of Research on Computing in Education* 32, no. 3 (Spring 2000): 325–335.

McNaughton, David, et al. "Proofreading for Students with Learning Disabilities." *Learning Disabilities Research and Practice* 12, no. 1 (1997): 16–28.

Merisotis, Jamie P. " 'What's the-Difference?' Debate." *Academe* 85, issue 5 (September/October 1999): 47–52.

Moore, C., S. Smith, and R. A. Avner. "Facilitation of Laboratory Performance Through CAI." *Journal of Chemical Education* 57, no. 3 (1980): 196–198.

Morehouse, D. L., M. L. Hoaglund, and R. H. Schmidt. *Technology Demonstration Program Final Evaluation Report.* Menononie, Wis.: Quality Evaluation and Development, February 1987.

O'Brien, P. "Working at Home." *PC Novice,* September 1994, 61.

O'Dwyer, Laura M.; Carey, Rebecca; Kleiman, Glenn. "A Study of the Effectiveness of the Louisiana Algebra I Online Course. *Journal of Research on Technology in Education* 39, issue 3 (Spring 2007): 289–306.

Ortega-Tudela, J. M.; Gomez-Ariza, C. J. "Computer-Assisted Teaching and Mathematical Learning in Down Syndrome Children." *Journal of Computer Assisted Learning* 22, no. 4 (August 2006): 298–307.

Osborn, Viola. "Identifying At-Risk Students in Videoconferencing and Web-Based Distance Education." *American Journal of Distance Education* 15, no. 1 (2001), 41–54.

Owston, Ronald D., and Herbert H. Wideman. "Word Processors and Children's Writing in a High-Computer-Access Setting." *Journal of Research on Computing in Education* 30, no. 2 (1997): 202–220.

Penuel, William R. "Implementation and Effects Of One-to-One Computing Initiatives: A Research Synthesis." *Journal of Research on Technology in Education* 38, issue 3 (Spring 2006): 329–348.

Person, C., and N. Bond. "Online Compared to Face-to-Face Teacher Preparation for Learning Standards-Based Planning Skills." *Journal of Research on Technology in Education,* 36, no. 4 (2004): 345–360.

Rachal, J. R. "Adult Reading Achievement Comparing Computer-Assisted Instructional and Traditional Approaches." A Comprehensive Review of Experimental Literature. Reading and Research, and Instruction, 34, no. 3 (1995): 239–258.

Reed, W. M. "Assessing the Importance of Computer-Based Writing." *Journal of Research on Computing in Education* 28, no. 4 (1996): 418–437.

Rice, Kerry Lynn. "A Comprehensive Look at Distance Education in K-12." *Journal of Research Journal of Research on Technology in Education* 38, no. 4 (Summer, 2006): 425–448.

Richman, John A. "At-Risk Students: Innovative Technologies." *Media and Methods* 30, no. 5 (May–June 1994): 26–27.

Robertson G. *A Comparison of Meaningful and Nonmeaningful Content in Computer-Assisted Spelling Programs.* Saskatchewan, Canada: Saskatchewan School Trustees Association Research Center, 1978.

Roblyer, M. D., W. H. Castine, and F. J. King. *Assessing the Impact of Computer-Based Instruction: A Review of Recent Research.* New York: Haworth Press, 1988.

Roblyer, M.D. "Integrating Educational Technology in Teaching." Fourth Edition, Pearson, Columbus, New Jersey, (2006): 38–52.

Ruel, Alfred A. *The Application of Research Findings.* Washington, D.C.: National Education Association, 1977.

Rueter, John G., and Nancy A. Perrin. "Using a Simulation to Teach Food Web Dynamics." *American Biology Teacher* 61, no. 2 (February 1999): 116–123.

Russell, Ben. "Slow Achievement Causes Concern." *Times Educational Supplement* issue 4219 (1997): 23.

Schacter, J. *The Impact of Education Technology on Student Achievement: What the Most Current Research Has to Say.* Santa Monica, Calif.: Milken Family Foundation, 1999.

Sharp, David, Trotter, Andrew. "Maine's Laptop Program Found to Aid Student Scores in Writing." *Education Week* 27, issue 10 (October 31, 2007): 11.

Shim, Kew-Cheol, Jong-Seok Park, Hyun-Sup Kim, Jae-Hyun Kim, Young-Chul Park, and Hai-Il Ryu. "Application of Virtual Reality Technology in Biology Education." *Journal of Biological Education* 37, issue 2 (Spring 2003): 71–75.

Siann, G., A. Durndell, H. Macleod, and P. Glissov. "Stereotyping in Relation to the Gender Gap in Participation in Computing." *Educational Research* 30, no. 2 (1988): 98–103.

Simonson, Michael, Sharon Smaldino, Michael Albright, and Susan Avacek. *Teaching and Learning at a Distance.* Upper Saddle River, N.J.: Merrill, Prentice Hall, 2003.

Simonson, Michael. "Myths and Distance Education: What the Research Says (And Does Not Say)." *Quarterly Review of Distance Education* 1, no. 4 (Winter 2000): 277–279.

Sivin-Kachala, J. *Report on the Effectiveness of Technology in Schools, 1990–1997.* Washington, D.C: Software Publishers Association, 1998.

Song, Sang Ho. "Research Issues of Motivation in Web-Based Instruction." *Quarterly Review of Distance Education* 1, no. 3 (Fall 2000): 225–229.

Summerville, L. J. "The Relationship Between Computer-Assisted Instruction and Achievement Levels and Learning Rates of Secondary School Students in First Year Chemistry." *Dissertation Abstracts International* 46, no. 3 (1984): 603a (University Microfilms No. 85–10891).

Swadener, M., and M. Hannafin. "Gender Similarities and Differences in Sixth Graders' Attitudes Toward Computers: An Exploratory Study." *Educational Technology* 27, no. 1 (1987): 37–42.

Swan, K., F. Gueerero, N. M. Mitrani, and J. Schoener. "Honing in on the Target: Who Among the Educationally Disadvantaged Benefits Most from What CBI?" *Journal of Research on Computing in Education* 22, no. 4 (1990): 381–404.

Terrell, Steve, and Paul Rendulic. "Using Computer-Managed Instructional Software to Increase Motivation and Achievement in Elementary School Children." *Journal of Research on Computing in Education* 26, no. 3 (Spring 1996): 403–414.

Timmerman, C. Erik; Kruepke, Kristine A. "Computer-Assisted Instruction, Media Richness, and College Student Performance." *Communication Education* 55, issue 1 (January 2006): 73–104.

Traynor, Patrick L. "Effects of Computer-Assisted-Instruction On Different Learners." *Journal of Instructional Psychology* 30, issue 2 (June 2003): 137, 144.

Wang, Alvin Y., and Michael H. Newlin. "Characteristics of Students Who Enroll and Succeed in Psychology Webbased Classes." *Journal of Educational Psychology* 92, no. 1 (2000): 137–143.

Westbrook, Thomas S., and Donald K. Moon. "Lessons Learned from the Delivery of a Graduate Business Degree Program Utilizing Interactive Television." *Journal of Continuing Higher Education* 45, no. 2 (1997): 25-33.

Whitley Jr., Bernard E. "Gender Differences in Computer-Related Attitudes and Behavior: A Meta-Analysis." *Computers in Human Behavior* 13, no. 1 (January 1997): 1–22.

Williams, Sue Winkle, et al. "Gender Roles, Computer Attitudes, and Dyadic Computer Interaction Performance in College Students." *Sex Roles: A Journal of Research* 29, no. 7–8 (June 1994): 515–525.

Wilson, Jan. "The Power of Distance Learning, Guest Editorial." *Education* 122, issue 4 (Summer 2002): 638–640.

Wong, Chi Kuen. "Attitudes and Achievements: Comparing Computer-Based and Traditional Homework Assignments in Mathematics." *Journal of Research on Technology in Education* 33, no. 5 (Summer 2001).

Xin, Yan Ping, and Asha K. Jitendra. "The Effects of Instruction in Solving Mathematical Word Problems for Students with Learning Problems: A Meta-Analysis." *Journal of Special Education* 32, no. 4 (1999): 207–225.

Yildirim, Soner. "Effects of an Educational Computing Course on Preservice and Inservice Teachers: A Discussion and Analysis of Attitudes and Use." *Journal of Research on Computing in Education* 32, no. 4 (2000): 479–495.

Young, Betty. "Gender Differences in Student Attitudes Toward Computers." *Journal of Research on Computing in Education* 33, no. 2 (Winter 2000): 204–213.

Yu-Chiung Hsu; Ya-Ming Shiue. "The Effect of Self-Directed Learning Readiness on Achievement Comparing Face-to-Face and Two-Way Distance Learning Instruction. *International Journal of Instructional Media* 32, issue 2, (2005): 143–156.

Zhang, Yuehua. "Technology and the Writing Skills of Students with Learning Disabilities." *Journal of Research on Computing in Education* 32, no. 4 (Summer 2000): 467–478.

17 The Future

Schools of the Future

Future technology breakthroughs will make it easier to integrate the computer into the classroom. The majority of students will be distance learning, using wireless communication, using robots to aid them in the instructional process, working with virtual keyboards, downloading interactive books, and wearing their computers. Using virtual reality, students will visit museums, visit different countries, listen to chamber groups in concert, learn how to fly airplanes, work in science labs, and engage in all sorts of exciting educational experiences.

Using the computer, students and teachers can do the following:

students can

- Use the Internet to learn about the different computer trends,
- Evaluate different sites on robotics,
- Prepare an electronic report on the emerging technologies in education, and
- Show a picture presentation of the different technologies.

teachers can

- Define terms such as mesh network, Artificial Intelligence, virtual keyboards,
- Show students quality companies producing emerging technologies,
- Find lesson plans and instructional material that are relevant, and
- Discuss future trends in education.

objectives

Upon completing this chapter, you will be able to do the following:

1 Discuss some of the future computer trends in Education.

2 Explain what OLED displays are.

3 Discuss the advantages and disadvantages of electronic books in the classroom.

4 Explain how robotics is being used in the classroom.

5 Be familiar with emerging technology such as wearable computers, wristwatch video conferencing, Clickers, Microsoft Surface, and Mesh Networks.

Future Trends

Examining the research leads to some natural questions: What will the future bring? What are the trends for microcomputer development? Will we have more artificial intelligence applications? Will we have networking in every school? Will we have helper robots? Will there be more emphasis on distance learning and video conferencing? Will there be further developments in multimedia technologies? How will these new developments affect teaching? Lets use our crystal ball—an electronic one, of course— to try to answer some of these questions.

COMPUTER HARDWARE

Recent developments such as the wireless computer and wireless computer network, distance learning, and flash memory chips will play a more prominent role in the computer's future. The cathode ray tube (CRT) monitor is almost a dinosaur. We now see large liquid crystal displays and plasma displays. We're now beginning to see plastic screens called OLED. An **OLED**, or **organic light-emitting diode display**, "is a thin-film, light emitting device that typically consists of a series of organic layers between two contacts (electrodes)" (Freedman, 2008). OLEDs are prepared using either low molecular-weight organic materials or polymer-based materials. An advantage of the OLED display is it will not break when dropped. Also, OLEDs generate their own light, and they save on energy. The problem with this display is the organic material used decreases in brightness over a period of time. This cheap alternative to silicon will result in very tiny transistors, wall-size displays, or rolled-up pen displays. Eastman Kodak Company and Sanyo had a working color OLED flat panel display in 2002. At the 2008 Consumer Electronics show in Las Vegas, Nevada (Figure 17.1), Sony showed off an OLED 27-inch panel that will be used in future television sets.

(*Source:* Ronda Churchill/Bloomberg News/Landov LLC)

Figure 17.1
—Sony OLED Flat Panel Display

Future displays will feature poster-size screens as well as screens that can be hung on the wall or unfold from our pockets. Displays will evolve from two-dimensional displays into large three-dimensional displays. If we want to access the Internet, we can use the pocket Net computer, a computer that fits in a pocket, to log on anytime from anywhere. Figure 17.2 shows Universal Display Corporation concept of a pen with a roll-up screen using OLED technology. This pen is so small you can easily slip it in your pocket. In the future our computer displays could come from an ordinary spray can. You could spray a video display from a can on any surface and be able to print it out. In 2005, E Ink Immediate Technology started producing paper-thin displays consisting of liquid ink embedded in paper-thin plastic sheets. E Ink created electronic books with flexible plastic pages that could display downloaded text and erase and reprint themselves. Sony's Reader, Amazon's Kindle and Readius® (Polymer Vision) are electronic readers that are now using these displays.

(*Source:* Courtesy Universal Display Corporation)

Figure 17.2
OLED Roll-up Pen

ELECTRONIC BOOKS

The electronic book, or **e-book**, may someday replace the traditional paper book or textbook. The e-book displays electronic versions of books, enabling you to set bookmarks, perform keyword searches, and make notes in margins. Already, many portable devices enable you to download books from the Internet: palm handhelds, pocket PCs, tablet PCs, portables such as the *iPod Touch*, and readers such as the Sony Reader (Figure 17.3a), and Amazon's new reader "Kindle" (Figure 17.3b). People seem to be reading their e-books with cell phones, portable media players, and tablet PCs.

Figure 17.3
Sony Reader (a);
Kindle (b)

(*Source:* NewsCom)

(*Source:* Courtesy Amazon.com)

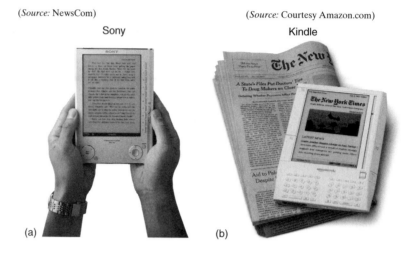

(a) (b)

A number of excellent subscription-based Web sites enable you to download books, ranging from the classics to popular nonfiction. For example, Palm Digital Media Inc. (www.palmdigitalmedia.com) offers great classics collections and eBookMall (www.ebookmall.com/), offers books ranging from best sellers to children's books. For a fee, students, teachers, and administrators have access to a large number of e-books during the school year. The books can be loaded on a school's Web site, from which users can download them to their portable devices.

In January 2008, Eindhoven, The Netherlands, Polymer Vision, inventor of rollable displays, showed an exciting new product called Readius® (Figure 17.4). This product will be officially introduced in mid 2008 (http://www.polymervision.com). What is unique about this mobile device is that it merges e-reading technology with the mobile phone. You no longer have a small screen, a battery that runs only two hours or a heavy bulky phone. The Readius® is one-third the average weight of an e-reader, equal to the average size of a mobile phone closed, battery life of 30 continuous hours, and twice the display of the average cell phone. Readius® lets you make a world wide call with simple touch buttons and do high speed updates on the Internet. "The Readius® also features audio capabilities, including MP3 for podcasts, audio books, and music." Students and teachers can use this versatile device for reading newspapers, personal information, talking, searching the Internet, music, books and much more.

Howard Strauss's statement in 2003 of another alternative to a standard textbook or novel doesn't seem so unrealistic. He predicted that textbooks or novels would be stored in a standard format from which students could access with a variety of pocket-size devices such as a wristwatch. The wristwatch will only require a small screen because it will be a text-to-speech device. The device will be capable of storing thousands of books that can be read by the wearer. The voices may be customized. To read the text, a student will connect it to a laptop or PDA. With all the different devices ranging from *iPod Touch* to *Palm* handhelds, it is only a matter of time before we see a wristwatch that has the same functions and more.

Figure 17.4
Readius®
(*Source:* Courtesy Polymer Vision)

HANDHELD COMPUTERS

As you learned in Chapter 2, handheld computers have made inroads into the classroom. They are popular because of the cost factor and their wide range of capabilities. Students can take notes and start papers and reports that can be transferred to their desktop computers. They can also collect experimental data in the field and check sites on the Internet. They can use the device as a reference tool, a calculator, for drill and practice, and for graphing.

In the future *all* handheld computers will be easier to use and feature wireless Internet access, easier transfer capabilities, built-in cameras, virtual keyboards, and speech-recognition capabilities.

COMPUTER DESKTOP REPLACEMENTS

Displays.   There is a trend toward smaller, faster, and easier-to-use computers. Earlier, we talked about OLED displays and how this technology will make it possible to have smaller computers. These displays will be incorporated into thin laptops that will replace desktop computers. Sony has developed a small prototype OLED portable display computer (Figure 17.5) that is wafer thin.

Power.   These future computers will not only be thinner and smaller; they also will be more powerful. Nanotechnology and quantum computing are two areas in which researchers are trying to supplant the silicon chip. These technologies use molecular or subatomic particles as logic components. A powerful microscopic computer that used the position of individual atoms or spinning electrons to calculate numbers would leave today's machine in the scrap bin.

Portability.   Microscopic computing would require very little power, and it would be perfect for wearable computers such as wristwatches. Researchers predict that, in a few years, advances in such technologies could produce a powerful watch-size computer that would require minimum battery power. Resembling a Dick Tracy two-way wrist radio, this device would work with voice commands, feature wireless Internet access, and have holographic projection displays. Every child in a classroom could then have a personal computerized watch. Currently there is a wristwatch videoconferencing computer (Figure 17.6) that runs on a GNU Linux operating system.

In 2005 Xybernaut produced wearable PCs, which enable people to perform a wide range of mobile tasks easily and safely. This wearable PC is small and lightweight, but powerful (Figure 17.7).

A monitor is mounted on an eyeglass frame. A handheld mouse and the CPU are located on a belt. Computers can be touch or voice activated. This computer enables users to surf the Internet, edit documents, and dictate while in motion.

In 2003, the Boston Public Schools received seven mobile/wearable computers codeveloped by Xybernaut Corporation and IBM. The *Mobile Assistant*, as the computer is called, is as powerful as a desktop computer and weighs only 2 pounds. Students can easily place it in a backpack or pocket. This wearable computer has a viewing screen that can be readable in any lighting situation, and it is touch sensitive. The computer comes with software specifically designed for education. It features voice-recognition applications, touch-activated icons, an onscreen keyboard, and handwriting recognition. This system is especially useful for students with disabilities (Figure 17.8; http://www.xybernaut.com/). Other wearable computer prototypes come in the form of undetectable glasses, wristwatches and belt clips.

Figure 17.5
Sony OLED Portable Display

Figure 17.6
Wristwatch Videoconferencing
Computer (http://www
.linuxjournal.com/article/3993)
(*Source:* Courtesy Steve Mann)

Figure 17.7
Wearable Computer
(*Source:* Getty Images)

Plastics.   Soon plastic transistors will change the way we see computing forever. Using plastics, engineers will be able to sew entire computer systems into a person's clothing. Hewlett-Packard has even designed a yellow biodegradable computer made from corn-based plastic.

Speed.   At the very least, plastic transistors will make computers smaller and faster. Every time we turn around, someone has introduced a new computer that is quicker and can run more complex programs. The speed keeps changing. Today, machines run at a trillion cycles per second.

Printers.   Improved color inkjet printers will continue to figure prominently in the printing device market. Furthermore, color laser printers are becoming increasingly popular because of their superior printing capabilities and their reduced price.

Design.   Apple Computer forever changed the design of new computers with its iMac. This computer is not bulky, and it houses the components of most desktop computers inside its base (Figure 17.9). Computer design will continue to change and the next computer could have interchangeable parts.

Memory.   The memory needed to run different applications has increased. In the early 1980s, most microcomputers needed only 16K of random access memory (RAM) to run the available educational software programs. Today, it is not uncommon to see a machine with 8 GB of RAM, and in a few months this requirement will be much higher. Because of their large memory, new microcomputers are much more powerful and can perform myriad tasks. The price of the memory chip has decreased and will continue to do so in the next few years.

Storage.   Not only has memory size increased, but storage devices have increased their capacity to store data. The $5\frac{1}{4}$-inch floppy disk faded into oblivion, and the $3\frac{1}{2}$-inch disk also has disappeared from sight. Hard drive capacity has increased, and many new machines have hard drives that hold over 640 GB. Next year this will probably be the standard. Now online subscription storage depots such as *.mac* (http://www.mac.com/), *IBackup* (https://www.ibackup.com/), and *Xdrive* (http://www.xdrive.com/) provide online storage. This enables the user to store material quickly at one location and travel to another to retrieve it.

The 750-MB Iomega removable *Zip disk* has become a popular option for storage. The *USB flash drive*, which can hold as much as 64 GB (see Chapter 3) and portable hard drives are just a few of the other options that are available. The trend is toward smaller disks that hold more information, such as the 1.8-inch disks already available for some portables. CD-ROM discs and laser discs have been replaced by DVDs that are the same size as CD-ROMs, but capable of holding 17 GB of data with digital images equal to those of laser discs.

Future storage might also occur in another dimension. Holographic storage disks, for example, could hold millions and millions of holograms, and the transfer rates could reach 1 GB per second. This technology holds promise for interactive video. These advances are just the tip of the iceberg—in the near future this huge amount of storage capacity will seem minuscule.

Input Devices.   Along with changes in storage devices are changes in input devices. The movement is away from the keyboard as the primary input device. Touch screens, optical pens, variations on the mouse, and virtual keyboards will replace the keyboard. The virtual keyboard projects an LED image of a keyboard on a flat surface such as a desk. An infrared motion detector senses the movement of the fingers on the keyboard. The *Canesta* virtual keyboard (shown in Figure 17.10) has mouse and touch-pad controls. Companies such as BT Exact, part of British Telecommunications, are working on developing touch over the Internet. This new technology uses a 3-D scanner and special touch monitors, which could eliminate the need for monitors, keyboards, mice, and other peripherals. Microsoft's Surface Computing is multitouch computing that makes the mouse unnecessary (Figure 17.11). Eric Horvitz, Microsoft's principal researcher, demonstrated at the Gartner Symposium/ITxpo how you could convert any surface into an interactive

Figure 17.10
Canesta Virtual Keyboard
(*Source:* ©AP/Wide World Photos)

Figure 17.11
Microsoft Surface

(*Source:* Courtesy Microsoft)

surface by putting a gismo down on its surface. The surface is then able to pull images from all sorts of devices—for example, a digital camera—and these images can then be manipulated by hand. Eric also showed how individuals separated by distance could work simultaneously on a document (http://www.news.com /1606-2_3-6180198.html). Shortly Microsoft will release a computer that uses a tabletop that is able to recognize items located on its surface.

WIRELESS NETWORKS IN THE SCHOOLS

In Chapter 3 we defined *wireless networking* and discussed its increased use in schools across the country. There are great possibilities for this technology in years to come. In the near future, we will most likely see wireless wearable networks that are always in use. When you wake up in the morning, a panel that is installed in your house will tell you the time and alert you to the weather conditions outside. When you drive along the freeway, a device in your car will tell you the traffic conditions and immediately tell you the best route to travel. Microsoft Research has developed **Smart Personal Objects Technology (SPOT)**, a technology that implants

wireless connectivity that is always on in devices such as watches and necklaces (Figure 17.12).

Each SPOT device has its own identifier so that your location can always update the watch or necklace with the local weather, time, or traffic conditions (Kaplan, 2003). Using a low-bandwidth data channel on local radio, SPOT broadcasts data to receivers in your wearable gadgets. (Presently, this system is one-way, so it rules out the possibility of my checking on my son's whereabouts!)

The **mesh network**, funded by the Defense Advanced Research Projects Agency and named *Sensit*, is the next development in wireless networks. This network is built on thousands of tiny acoustic sensors that can distinguish sounds ranging from that of a falling ball to that of a shot fired by a soldier (Rupley, 2003). The *Sensit* wireless network is very reliable because it is not dependent on one central device. Universities and colleges are converting campuses to mesh networks.

VOICE RECOGNITION SYSTEMS

In the future, we will no longer need a keyboard to communicate; we will use speech instead. **Voice recognition systems** have come a long way from the system introduced by Convox in 1991. The *Voice Master Key System II*, as it was called, could recognize only 64 words. Users typed in the words they wanted the system to listen for, spoke each twice, and then typed in the desired keyboard responses. After this programming, users only needed to say a command to direct the computer to execute it. This type of voice recognition was *discrete voice recognition* because it required a pause between each word.

From this type of voice recognition system we moved to *continuous-speech systems*, or systems that understand natural speech without pauses. The new voice recognition systems are speaker independent; that is, they do not require user training. These products are still not 100 percent accurate, but shortly we will see breakthroughs in speech recognition technologies.

In a few years, you will not have to speak a foreign language when you visit a foreign country. You will order meals easily or ask for directions with Yuqing Gao's *Multilingual Automatic Speech Translator* (MASTOR). Using a speech recognizer based on IBM's *Via Voice Gao*, a speech recognition expert at IBM Research's Watson Research Center has turned spoken words into text. A machine translator converts this text into a language, and a speech synthesizer converts it into audible words. Currently this program runs on a laptop or handheld computer (Metz, 2003; IBM, 2006), http://www.ibm.com/news/us/en/2006/11 /2006_11_10.html. Robots will make communication between people of different countries easier.

ARTIFICIAL INTELLIGENCE

Artificial intelligence (AI) is a range of computer applications that are designed to simulate human intelligence and behavior. For instance, with AI, a machine or robot can recognize pictures and sounds. In the future, we may be able to walk up to any computer or robot, ask it for help, and receive information useful in solving a problem. The RIDC-01 (Robotics Industry Development Council) Japanese robot made by Tmsuk can recognize a variety of human voices and speech and responds in Japanese. It also cleans floors ("The Robot Butler Cometh," 2007).

In a short amount of time, the differences between a machine and an intelligent person will be reduced drastically. At UCLA and other universities, scientists are working on computer programs and, in some instances, on robots that will respond to conditions of animal life such as evolution.

AI systems designed for particular fields make evaluations, draw conclusions, and provide recommendations. They help doctors make diagnoses on diseases and treatments, they help drill oil wells, and they aid stockbrokers in making analyses.

This type of software will have a similar impact on education. Teachers are already demanding and using programs that have been made more interactive through artificial intelligence. The AI language will definitely increase the number of programs that respond in human ways. The software we will be using in the near future will tackle concepts and ideas. This software will accept a range of English-language commands and be easier to use. In the future, you will be able to converse with the average computer and ask for help. The computer will automatically bring up the appropriate application to aid you in solving your problem. We will see real AI, as Alan Turning, a well-known mathematician, defined it: "A machine has artificial intelligence when there is no discernible difference between the conversation generated by the machine and that of an intelligent person" (Hodges, 1992).

 It is important that you read Dr. Kenneth Berry's article on robotics online at **http://www.wiley/college/sharp**. He is a professor at California State University, Northridge and is an expert on robotics.

ROBOTS

Robotics is "the art and science of the creation and use of robots" (Freedman, 2008). A **robot** is a computer system that performs physical and computational activities. The robot can be created in human form; however, industrial robots are not designed this way. The advantage of a robot is that it can perform many different human jobs, often better than a person might perform them, or at least more efficiently or quickly. Robots are being designed with artificial intelligence features so they may respond more effectively to unusual situations. In the future, robots may be in the classroom serving as teachers' aides. Robots will spend time with students, individually drilling them on math skills. In the chemistry lab, robots will handle dangerous chemicals. Robots will also help students with disabilities do their homework. Robots will be used to greet parents and show them around a school.

As the average age of the population increases, the need for and cost of assisted care will increase. Robots will escort patients to restrooms, to activity rooms, to meals, and on shopping outings. Robots can help people by carrying foods and other items that they need for home care. Robots will reach items on top shelves, respond to voice commands, push wheelchairs, and walk dogs.

Robots already spray chemicals, chase birds, and serve as tour guides. There are robot vacuum cleaners such as *Roomba* and robot dogs for recreation. Jean-Claude Latombe, chairman of the computer science department at Stanford University, says, "One of the fastest-growing areas for robotics today is robot-assisted surgery." Stanford is doing brain surgery with robots (Kaplan, 1994). Robots are also being used as targets in weapons training. K. G. Engelhardt, formerly manager of Robotics for the NASA Regional Technology Transfer Center and director for the Center for Human Service Robotics at Carnegie Mellon University, has been developing robots for many years. She has written a program that introduces teachers to robots. The *Teachers Corps* program utilizes robots and robotics-related technologies to teach scientific, biological, and engineering concepts (http://www-robotics.usc.edu/).

Robots in the Classroom.   Students and teachers are programming robots such as *Roamer. Roamer* (Terrapin Software; Figure 17.13) is an easy-to-use robot that introduces kindergarten and first-grade students to Logo commands. *Roamer*, which is in the form of a turtle, contains a computer that is dedicated to Logo. Students can see, touch, and follow the Logo turtle as it moves around the room. Students can easily use the colored touchpad to give *Roamer* single-keystroke commands. *Roamer* is battery powered and lightweight, offering students hours of fun. *Roamer* can play music, and it has accessories that enable users to customize it. For example, you can add a nose, ears, or tail and change its color. If you place a marker pen into the pen pack attachment, you can even watch *Roamer* draw designs. You can also connect *Roamer* to the computer and upload computer programs, as well as merge them with other programs.

Figure 17.13
Students Using *Roamer* Robot
(*Source:* Courtesy Valiant Technology)

In addition, you can write programs on the computer and download them to *Roamer*. Sixteen story-based activities help students learn problem solving, programming, spatial concepts, and mapping. The activities integrate the *Roamer* floor turtle with the onscreen *Roamer* (http://www.terrapinlogo.com/). Using Lego kits, students can build machines in the form of a car, a camera robot, a tower (Figure 17.14), and a truck that includes motors, sensors, and gears. After these machines are built, students connect them with an interface to a computer that speaks the proper dialect of Logo. Using a few simple commands, students write computer programs to control the machines. These commands turn the motors off and on and send them in various directions. These robotic construction kits are really a relic of the early days of Logo programming when the experimenters with Logo used a "floor turtle," a mechanical robot connected to the computer by a cord.

Figure 17.14
Students Using *Lego* Robots
(*Source:* Courtesy Vicki Sharp)

A Lego package usually includes an assortment of gears, wheels, motors, lights, and sensors. Students can send commands to Lego motors and lights and receive information from Lego sensors. *Terrapin Logo* can make a robot turn to the right or reverse direction when it touches a wall. Students can engage in all kinds of experimentation, and they can learn the importance of changing only one variable at a time. They can use the scientific method as they invent their machines, and when they have problems with their inventions, they can develop hypotheses and test them. When students use this computer-based system, they engage in data gathering, record keeping, and brainstorming.

The Artificial Intelligence Laboratory at MIT is working with robots. The researcher's goal is to make these robot have the thinking abilities of a 3-year-old, which requires a lot of programming. Cynthia Brazeal is the director of MIT Media Lab's Robotic Life Group,

As you can see, robots of the future will not just be doing repetitive tasks; they will also have personality and be able to think, hear, see, and communicate. Advances in face and object recognition and voice processing will make such robots a reality (Fordahl, 2006). They will not only take care of performing household chores such as vacuuming, lawnmowing, home protection, and dusting, but they also will be nannies, perform brain surgery, gather things from the ocean, teach, and help the elderly dress, wash, and take medicine.

VIRTUAL REALITY

Virtual reality (VR) is "an artificial reality that projects the user into a 3-D space generated by the computer" (Freedman, 2008). (See Chapter 11 for a more detailed explanation of virtual reality.) The future promises VR technological breakthroughs to help the student with disabilities function better in the classroom. VR technology enables the student with physical disabilities to interact with information being presented in all subject areas. Students can immerse themselves physically in different environments and experience life on a different intellectual plane.

VRML (virtual reality modeling language), a 3-D graphics language, is currently used on the World Wide Web. When you download a page containing VRML, you see scenery and objects that you can rotate. Students can walk through simulated rooms such as a gallery in an art museum.

IBM researchers recently developed a virtual interpreter for the deaf in the form of an animated avatar. The avatar can translate the spoken words into sign language in real time when an interpreter is not available. Currently the system is a prototype but soon we will see it in college lecture halls where deaf individuals will see a digital character projected on a screen behind the teacher, interpreting his or her speech during a lecture (Bergstein, 2007).

At Hewlett-Packard (HP) Labs, Norm Jouppi and his team have developed a system called **eTravel** that enables a person to be in two places at the same time. The system is based on technology known as **mutually immersive mobile telepresence**, in which a robot substitutes for the individual.

The robot is capable of moving from one room to another, viewing what is at the location, making eye contact with the people in the room, and whispering in people's ears. You can be in Rhode Island and see, hear, and talk to people in California. This robotic device has cameras and microphones that provide a 360-degree video and audio view of a location. It displays the user's head on a flat panel display (Figure 17.15; Janowski, 2003). The educational implications for this technology are endless. You could explore the Art Institute in Chicago while in a different location, view an operation, and participate in a classroom when you are sick at home http://www.hpl.hp.com/news/2003/jan_mar/norm_jouppi.html.

Figure 17.15
Mutually
Immersive
Mobile
Telepresence

(*Source:* Courtesy Hewlett-Packard Company)   (*Source:* Courtesy Hewlett-Packard Company)

This technology surpasses current video conferencing. With this new technology, you become a part of the remote environment. What you see is lifelike, with colors that are vibrant. You can make eye contact with people at the remote location. As you participate, you can see physical nuances you might miss if you were just using video conferencing.

HP has also developed HP Halo Telepresence Solutions (Figure 17.16), which are the future of collaboration. HP Halo Telepresence Solutions are end-to-end

Figure 17.16
Halo Collaboration Suite
(*Source:* Courtesy Hewlett-Packard
Company)

collaboration technologies that bring people from across the globe into an environment that looks, sounds and feels as if they are just across the table. Participants see each other in life-sized images projected on high-resolution displays and can communicate with no perceived delays, regardless of how far apart the teams may be. This experience creates a live, virtual meeting room providing the clarity to work face-to-face and eye-to-eye, read body language and foster stronger business relationships, while reducing the personal cost, time and stress of business travel.

COMPUTER USE BY PEOPLE WITH DISABILITIES

Many devices are currently available to aid students with disabilities. These include Braille keyboards and computer-operated telephone devices for the deaf and screen reading programs for the blind. (Many of these devices were mentioned in Chapter 13.) Screen reader programs such as *Job Access* (Henter-Hoyce, Inc., a division of Freedom Scientific) for Windows computers or *OutSPOKEN* (ALVA Access Group) for Macintosh computers enable the blind to surf the Web. Using speech synthesizers, the software reads text in a computerized voice and names the icons as the individual encounters them. The blind person then uses the keyboard to navigate, and the software interprets whether a user has tabbed to a button or graphic or other element. People can wear talking PDAs around their necks. Scotland's University of Glasgow introduced a talking computer mouse that was able to convey graphic shapes on a computer monitor. Products for those with speech impairments such as *Speech Enhancer Spectrum VP* (Electronic Speech Enhancement, Inc.), use the latest voice processing technology to turn unclear speech into sound that can be understood by any person. Until this development, the only help for those with speech impairments was the amplifier, which did not improve voice clarity. IBM's *Blue Eyes* research program is working on a face-recognition system. Using this technology, the computer can recognize faces, track gazes, and even sense moods. For gaze tracking, a computer camera is mounted on the user's computer display, and this camera follows the user's iris. Depending on where the person focuses his or her eyes, the monitor senses what information is wanted and calls it up. In addition, face-recognition systems may be used for security. The keyboard locks out any unauthorized person who tries to use your computer.

Jordy devices, which have goggles with tiny screens that enable people with impaired vision to see clearly with their own eyes, are commercially available. The *tactile graphics display* (TGD) enables students who are visually impaired to feel an image. Using TGE, for example, a student could run his or her fingers over a picture of a bed of pins and feel pinpricks (Kushner, 2003).

TECHNOLOGY CLASSROOMS

Smart Classrooms.   The Hueneme School District, located in Ventura County, California, was one of the first to receive international recognition for its leadership in developing technology. According to superintendent Dr. Ron Rescigno, students have made marked improvements in their achievement. The district offers technologically designed classrooms, called *smart classrooms*, organized by curriculum area.

Twenty-First-Century Learning Environments.   Creative Learning Systems, of Longmont, Colorado, has pioneered the whole-laboratory approach to technology education, introducing the *Technology Lab 2000* in 1987 as the first such system ever sold. This company currently provides custom and semi-custom learning environments to middle and high schools under the trade names of *SmartLab*. Creative Learning Systems emphasizes the following core principles in its learning environments:

- learning facilitation model, not stand-and-deliver teaching;

- learner-focused instruction, which engages young people and helps instill in them the love of learning that is so necessary to creating communities of lifelong learners;

- constructivist approaches, which allow learners to make meaning out of their experiences;

- portfolio-based assessment, not prescriptive "single-answer" testing;

- project work that requires collaboration;

- learning that is self-directed;

- cross-curricular project work (to better reflect the real world), rather than separate, arbitrary subject matter; and

- a brain-based system of learning.

The environment is a total integrated system of furnishings, equipment, computer-mediated instruction, software, and hands-on computer-based learning. The instructional resources are self-paced, interactive tutorials. The materials launch learners into a variety of technological experiences and support self-designed projects that expand students' understanding of technological phenomena. *SmartLab* gives learners access to information in areas such as robotics, audio engineering, Web design, entertainment engineering, multimedia production, satellite technology, and lasers, to name just a few.

Island-like arrangements of versatile, leading-edge laboratory furnishings form a series of activity zones within which students work and learn collaboratively. Each station is also reconfigurable to accommodate new activities or advanced explorations (Figure 17.17). Learner teams participate in computer-integrated enterprises in which all phases in the creation of a product are linked and interdependent.

Figure 17.17
Team Workstation
(*Source:* Courtesy Creative Learning systems, Longmont, CO)

Math-, science-, and technology-related areas of study are presented in an integrated curriculum. The power of the *SmartLab* is realized when the vast array of activities are seen not as finite exercises, but rather as open-ended investigations, each leading to the next, linked by the common thread of curiosity.

One of the greatest changes in this new mode of learning is the teacher's role. The teacher is no longer the all-knowing instructor, but rather a facilitator of learning. The teacher-facilitator is freed to circulate, to facilitate creative contributions, and to help learners make connections and develop higher-order critical thinking skills.

Ventura Adult and Continuing Education. Students who attend the Ventura Adult and Continuing Education school can earn a high school diploma and receive preparation and testing for General Educational Development (GED), for vocational education, and for much more. The programs at the Technology Development Center (TDC) are oriented toward employment in tomorrow's world. TDC covers a wide range of disciplines, including computer systems technology, medical programs, business, digital multimedia, TV production, and computer-aided design (CAD). Because of this modern orientation, this center has the most up-to-date technology. Over 90 percent of the students attending this school work with computers. Students are expertly trained to survive in today's digital world. Students have access to high-end Apple multimedia computers and state-of-the art drafting tools. They are trained to produce digital music videos in a multimedia class. This school responds to what employers want, upgrading to the best technology.

Furthermore, students at this school have access to a stunning new technology called *rapid prototyping*. Using this technology, they can print three-dimensional objects. Student projects include chess figures, tiny human skulls with sinus cavities and brains, and complex interior displays. The items on the table in Figure 17.18 were the result of a computer-aided design drafting class. To produce these items, students feed digital images into a machine that looks like a photocopier.

Figure 17.18
Computer-Aided Design Drafting
Class Products

Figure 17.19
Clicker

Emerging Technologies in Education

There are many emerging technologies in education. For the purpose of this Chapter I discuss four: (1) clickers, (2) open journaling, (3) screencasting, and (4) remote instrumentation.

Clickers. A clicker is an audience response system that consists of handheld gadgets that look like a remote control for a television (Figure 17.19).

These handheld transmitters gather student input and software collects and tabulates the data for display on a monitor or screen (Bush & McLester, 2007).

Students are utilizing these remote devices (Figure 17.20) to respond in college and university and high school course quizzes. Students are able to respond to yes and no questions, for example, "Would you vote for a woman president?"

The clickers can be registered to a student if the instructor wishes. These devices provide a way for the teacher to have immediate feedback on their lecture and motivate students while the students actively participate in the class.

Open journaling is trying to replace traditional peer-reviewed journals. Using the Web, authors are able to follow their submissions through the review process and access reviewers' comments and revise their articles and resubmit them. An example of a popular open online journal system is *Open Journal Systems*. For a representative list of other open online journals systems, see http://pkp.sfu.ca/ojs-journals.

Screencasting refers to capturing the actions of a computer screen with audio. A screen shot like those appearing in this book are inert whereas a screencast involves movement and is a video that usually has a teacher explaining a topic. For example, the video tutorials that are on our site at http://www.wiley.com/college /sharp are small screencasts that demonstrate how to do things such as create a newsletter. Screencasts have become very popular in distance learning. Many professors are using them as tutorials for the classroom. The advantage of a screencast is that students can see the teacher demonstrating the material over and over until they feel they understand what is being said.

Remote instrumentation lets teachers and students control scientific instruments from a distance. It enables colleges and universities to share their resources and it provides a unique learning experience for students. Students can conduct experiments using rare scientific instruments and can do this outside of specified lab times. Remote instrumentation eliminates the individual traveling to the place where the equipment is stored.

Software

Software manufacturers are producing high-quality multimedia programs that follow sound educational principles. Programs such as *World Book*—which combines sound, still sequences, animation, and full-motion video, photographs, and simulations—are the norm. Software is now more interactivity and problem solving. For the classroom, there is a problem-solving and creative storytelling program called *Scratch* that MIT

Media Lab produces (see Chapter 13.) This program can be downloaded from from http://scratch.mit.edu/. Many programs contain elements of artificial intelligence and are now found online; for example, programs such as *Gnu Chess* contain elements of artificial intelligence.

Virtual reality is also being integrated into every software package through *QuickTime VR* (see Chapter 11 for a full discussion). Online *Second Life* allows architectural students to build virtual houses, clothing design students to hold virtual fashion shows, and business students to start companies without risking a dime. *Sims 2* (Figure 17.21) is software that merges the user into a 3-D visual world that works on problem solving and planning. You feel like you are living in this world of people and decisions. "The World Wide Web will soon be absorbed into the World Wide Sims: an immersive, 3-D visual environment that combines elements of social virtual worlds such as Second Life and mapping applications such as Google Earth" (Roush, 2007). As you can see, software has come a long way and it is impossible to predict what the future will hold.

Figure 17.21
Sims 2
(*Source:* Electronic Arts)

Trends and Interesting Developments

For this edition, I had Anthony Nguyen, Director of Technology at California State University, Northridge, reflect on some of the trends and interesting developments in educational technology. Mr. Nguyen's insights follow.

TRENDS

• We will see the proliferation of mobile Internet access via WiMax. Companies, such as Clearwire, are teaming up with large carriers, such as Sprint, to deploy wireless Internet access in wide area networks. See http://wimaxforce.com/ca/. Many cities plan to provide wireless Internet access free of charge.

• We will see social networking sites keep growing at breathtaking speed: Youtube, Facebook, Myspace, etc.

INTERESTING DEVELOPMENTS

1. Good Web Sites for students practicing tests and for teachers to monitor classroom progress is practiceplanet.com (free for 90-day trial for the whole school), for example.

2. Educational games: *World of Warcraft* (helps with analytics, thinking skills); *Railroad Tycoon* (helps with building general knowledge of history, economics, science); *Secondlife.com* (online society emulation, teaches social skills).

3. E-mail harvesting like Ada Email Address Search XP, bulk mailer programs such as http://www.adanw.com/, and e-mail prevention programs such as email masker http://mindprod.com/applets/masker.html.

Concluding Thoughts

We would all like to see technologically advanced computer labs such as *Smart Lab 2007*. Furthermore, we want every student in our classrooms to have a computer that is connected to a wireless network. If a robot aide could decrease our workload, most of us would order one tomorrow. Many of the items on our wish lists may never materialize. Unfortunately, schools do not have the money to buy the equipment to implement a technology-based program. The more sophisticated computer equipment will be found primarily at the college and university level. Elementary and secondary schools will not be able to afford this costly hardware. But there is another problem: lack of teachers trained to manage this new technology. Still, most states now require that teachers complete a computer course for certification. Because of this requirement, eventually there will be more trained teachers who can integrate the computer in the classroom.

It is important that you read Dr. David Moursund's article on the future of technology online at **http://www.wiley /college/sharp**. He is a leader in technology and has authored or co-authored more than 30 books and numerous articles on information technology in education.

What does the future hold? Computers will become cheaper and more affordable. Computer use will increase, and computers will be smaller, faster, more efficient, and less expensive. More emphasis will be placed on computer ethics, and the Internet will be available to all schools. Multimedia software will be even more sophisticated, offer speech recognition, be less expensive, and more transparent. Computer storage capacity will be improved, and optical drives will enable teachers and students to access software more easily. More networkable machines will be available; advances in networking will lead to better communication among classrooms, schools, and school districts. One classroom will be networked with another classroom on a national or state database. Eventually, classrooms will be networking with classrooms in other countries. Students and teachers will commonly use desktop video conferencing and publishing programs as well as scanners, digital cameras, and fax machines to import pictures and graphic images into their documents.

Teachers will be "teaching" less because the computer will have a more prominent role in the classroom. Computers will enable teachers to assume the role of facilitators, designing learning experiences and individualizing instruction. There will be less drill and practice and more problem solving and real, meaningful learning activities. Many more of our universities will offer virtual degree programs, giving classes via the Internet. Books are still going to exist but maybe as a supplement to technologies such as the Internet. There may be only electronic books in our future, with the traditional book disappearing forever. Ahead of his time, one Illinois state superintendent of schools wanted laptop computers in his school instead of books. The computer is a remarkable invention. Its possible impact on the curriculum is staggering, but it needs to be given a chance to show what it can do for children in the schools. It is up to educators to inspire, motivate, and excite students and colleagues about this remarkable instrument for learning.

Lessons We Have Learned

We have learned quite a few things from our experiences with computers. History has taught us that technology will not solve all our educational problems. Programming or networked computers do not offer quick answers to the question of how to educate students. The computer is an especially useful tool when applied to students with learning disabilities (see Chapter 13). We are living in a society where technology is constantly changing and the skills that students need to compete are ever changing. These skills differ according to a student's needs and competencies. Educators generally want technology integrated into the classroom, but there are no firm guidelines for accomplishing this task. Stand-alone computers and networked computers each have their advantages and disadvantages. Networked computers enable teachers to standardize material across schools, districts, and classrooms. Stand-alone systems enable teachers to individualize the curriculum and control scheduling. We have learned that teachers usually do not have the time to develop computer materials or curricula.

Distance learning has enabled people to attend class and conferences online, without having to travel to other locations. However, there is still something wonderful about face-to-face instruction. From the history of educational computing we can see that technology is developing faster than teachers can keep abreast of these changes. Teachers can no longer use the same handouts, homework, worksheets, or lecture notes. Educators must continually change to take advantage of technological advances. Finally, even in this new-technology world, teachers will always be essential, and their understanding of how to use this technology in the classroom is indispensable.

SUMMARY

Computers are not just a passing fancy; they will be with us for a long time. They have made life both easier and more complicated. We can accomplish a great deal more by using a computer, but we have to work harder to keep up with the technology. In the end, we must consider the future of this exciting technology. We will definitely have smaller, faster, easier-to-use, and more powerful computers. Future software and hardware will accommodate multimedia, involve virtual worlds, be networkable, include voice recognition, be based on artificial intelligence, and involve robots. Education will integrate computers into the curriculum as much as possible, but problems with funding and a lack of adequately trained teachers may limit what is accomplished in classrooms. We can only speculate on what will happen in the future. What we do know is that the coming years will be exciting!

STUDY AND ONLINE RESOURCES

CHAPTER 17 ONLINE RESOURCES

In the **student section** of the book's online site at **http://www.wiley.com/college/sharp** you will find templates and examples, video tutorials, PDFs, checklists, articles, Web sites, software reviews, and chapter quizzes. Access these resources to learn about technology and integrating it into the classroom.

CHAPTER MASTERY TEST

Lets check for chapter comprehension with a short mastery test. Key Terms, Computer Lab, and Suggested Readings and References follow the test.

1. What are two lessons we have learned from our experiences with educational technology?

2. Why is the voice recognition system the wave of the future?

3. Define *artificial intelligence* and speculate on how it could be used in the classroom.

4. How can the computer help children with disabilities?

5. What has slowed the use of computers in the schools? How can these obstacles be overcome?

6. Explain how computers in the classroom will change the traditional roles of teachers, students, and parents.

7. What are some future directions for computer use in the classroom? Defend your choices.

8. Explain what the OLED display is and why it would be valuable in the classroom.

9. Explain what the mesh network is and why it is important.

10. Explain the following terms: *open journaling*, *clickers*, *remote instrumentation*, and *screencasting*. How are they being used in education?

KEY TERMS

Artificial intelligence (AI) p. 354

Clickers p. 360

E-book p. 349

eTravel (mutually immersive mobil telepresence) p. 357

Halo telepresence solutions p. 357

Mesh network p. 354

Microsoft Surface p. 353

Organic light-emitting diode display (OLED) p. 348

Open journaling p. 361

Remote instrumentation p. 361

Robot p. 355

Smart Personal Objects Technology (SPOT) p. 353

Screencasting p. 361

Voice recognition systems p. 354

COMPUTER LAB: Activities for Mastery and Your Portfolio

17.1 Find out how you can keep up with the constant changes in technology.

17.2 Using the Internet, research and write about a future development in Educational Technology. Watch the Video tutorial online and learn how to refine your Internet search.

SUGGESTED READINGS AND REFERENCES

"100 New Products Go Back to School with the Latest Tools." *Technology and Learning* 28, no. 1 (August 2007): 28, issue 1 20–34.

"A Device That's On a Roll." *PC Magazine*, March 2007, p. 21.

"An Interesting Read, But No Page-Turner." *PC Magazine*, December 5, 2006, p. 42.

Bergstein, Brain. "IBM Develops Virtual Deaf Interpreter." *Ventura County Star*, October 1, 2007, p. D1.

"Bomb-Sniffing Bot." *PC Magazine*, October 3, 2006, p. 20.

Bush, Susan, and Susan McLester, "Clickers Rule!" *TechLearning and Learning* 28, issue 4 (November 15, 2007). Page 8.

DuBois, Grant. "Membership Swells for the E-Book Club." *EWeek* 17, no. 41 (October 9, 2000). Page 55

Fordahl, Matthew. "Developing Robots as Social Companions." *ACM TechNews* 8, issue 892 (January 20, 2006).

Freedman, Alan. *Computer Desktop Encyclopedia*. Point Pleasant, Pa.: Computer Language Company, 2008.

"High School Students Get Laptops." *Education Week* 27, issue 12 (November 14, 2007): p. 5.

Hodges, Andrew. *Alan Turning: The Enigma*. London: Vintage, 1992.

Hof, Robert D. "The Quest for the Next Big Thing." *BusinessWeek*, August 18–25, 2003, pp. 91–94.

Janowski, Davis D. "Silicon Photonics." *PC Magazine*, July 2003, p. 100.

Kaplan, Jeremy. "Microsoft SPOT." *PC Magazine*, July 2003, p. 102.

Kaplan, Karen. "Robots Roll up their Sleeves," *Los Angeles Times* (March 10, 1994): 1D.

Knowles, John. "E-Bombs." *PC Magazine*, July 2003, 86–88.

Kushner, David. "They Give Sight to the Blind." *Los Angeles Times: Parade*, September 7, 2003, pp. 6–8.

Levine, Jessica. "OLED Displays." *PC Magazine*, July 2003, p. 98.

Marx, Patricia. "Tech Stuff," *New Yorker* 84, issue 4 (March 10, 2008): 82–87.

McDonald, Glenn, and Crotty Cameron. "The Digital Future." *PC World*, January 2000, pp. 116–134.

Metz, Cade. "Carbon Nanotubes." *PC Magazine*, July 2003, pp. 83–84, http://www.pcmag.com.

Metz, Cade. "Plastic Transistors." *PC Magazine*, July 2003, p. 94.

Miller, Michael J., et al. "The Next 25 Years in Tech." *PC Magazine*, January 2008, p. 73–86.

Mutschler, Ann Steffora. "Intel Unveils Teraflop Programmable Processor." *Electronic News* 53, issue 8 (February 19, 2007): 13.

Neel, Dan. "Wearable PC Goes to Work." *InfoWorld* 22, no. 47 (November 20, 2000): 10.

Niederhauser, Dale S., and Niki Davis. "Virtual Schooling." *Learning and Leading with Technology* 34, no. 7 (April 2007): 11–15.

Port, Otis. "Cheap, Pliable, and Powerful." *BusinessWeek,* August 15, 2003, p. 104.

Ribbens, Eric. "Why I Like Clicker Personal Response Systems." *Journal of College Science Teaching* 37, issue 2 (October/November): 60–62.

Roush, Wade. "Second Earth: What Happens When the Virtual and Real Worlds Collide?" Technology and Learning 28, issue 4 (November 15, 2007): 48. http://www.techlearning.com /showArticle.php?articleID=196604812

Rupley, Sebastian. "Mesh Networks." *PC Magazine,* July 2003, p. 104.

Rupley, Sebastian. "Talking Bot." *PC Magazine* (February 7, 2007): 25, issue 2, 21.

Simkins, Michael. "Supersmart Robots." *Technology and Learning* 28, issue 7 (February 2008): 40.

Stowell, Jeffrey R. and Jason M. Nelson. "Benefits of Electronic Audience Response Systems on Student Participation, Learning, and Emotion." *Teaching of Psychology* 34, issue 4 (November 2007): 253–258.

Strauss, Howard. "Reflections: Another Look at Education Technology." *Syllabus* (April 2003): 41–42.

Taylor, Peter Shawn. "Can Clickers Cure Crowded Classes?" Maclean's 120, issue 26/27 (July 9, 2007): 73–75.

"The Robot Butler Cometh." *PC Magazine*, February 26, 2007, p. 21.

"Toward Intelligent Machines." *PC Magazine*, January 2006, p. 21.

Ulanoff, Lance. "Cognitive Machines." *PC Magazine,* July 2003, pp. 118–120.

"User Interface Microsoft Surface." *PC Magazine*, December 4, 2007, p. 98.

Viscusi, Vance. "21st Century Classroom." In *Computers in Education, 8th ed*. New York: Dushkin/McGraw-Hill, 2002, pp. 31–33.

Williams, Peter E. "Will a Digital Textbook Replace Me?" *T.H.E. Journal* 30, no. 10 (May 2003): 25–26.

Withrow, Frank B. "Technology in Education and the Next Twenty-Five Years." *T.H.E. Journal* 24, no. 11 (June 1997): 59–62.

Wolfson, Oliver. "10 Tech Trends That Will Shape What You Buy This Year." *MacWorld*, January 2007, pp. 51–60.

"$100 Laptops to be sold in U.S." *eNews* 10, no. 11 (November/December 2007): 6–7.

Active Learning Associates, Inc.,
120 Main Street,
Flemington,
NJ 08822
Warren Buckleitner, Editor
800/993-9499

A.D.A.M. Software, Inc.
1600 RiverEdge Parkway, Suite 100
Atlanta, GA 30328
800/408-2326
404/980-0888
404/955-3088 (fax)
www.adam.com/

Addison-Wesley, Boston office
75 Arlington Street, Suite 300
Boston, MA 02116
617/848-7500
www.aw.com/

Adobe Systems, Inc.
345 Park Avenue
San Jose, CA 95110-2704
800/833-6687
408/537-6000 (fax)
www.adobe.com/products/main.html

AlphaSmart (a subsidiary of Renaissance Learning)
http://www.alphasmart.com/

Apple, Inc.
1 Infinite Loop
Cupertino, CA 95014
800/767-2775
408/996-1010
www.apple.com

Aurbach & Associates, Inc.
8233 Tulane Avenue, Suite B
St. Louis, MO 63132
800/774-7239
314/432-7577
314/678–0869 (fax)
www.aurbach.com/

Avanquest Software (Dorling Kindersley)
23801 Calabasas Road, Suite 2005
Calabasas, CA 91302
818/591-9600 x404
818/591-8885 (fax)
http://www.learnatglobal.com/
www.DorlingKindersleySoftware.com

Barnum Software
1910 Lyon Avenue
Belmont, CA 94002

800/553-9155
650/610-9034 (outside Canada)
800/553-9156 (fax)
www.thequartermile.com/
mail@TheQuarterMile.com

Bias
140 Keller St
Petaluma, CA 94952
707/782-1866
800/775-BIAS (2427)
707/782-1874 (fax)

Blue Squirrel (ForeFront)
686 E 8400 South
Sandy, UT 84070
800/403-0925
801/352-1551
www.bluesquirrel.com

Bytes of Learning
445 Apple Creek Blvd., Suite 204
Markham, ON L3R 9X7
CANADA
Phone: +905-947-4646
800/465-6428
905/475-8650 (fax; no solicitations please).
www.bytesoflearning.com/

Centron Software, Inc.
760 Monticello Dr.
Pinehurst, NC 28374
800-848-2424
910-215-5708
http://www.centronsoftware.com/

Children's Technology Review
Over 7,000 reviews of pieces of software
http://www.childrenssoftware.com/

Classroom Connect
8000 Marina Blvd., Suite 100
Brisbane, CA 94005
650/589-8326
888/877-1565 (fax)
www.classroom.net/

Clearvue/eav
6465 North Avondale Avenue
Chicago, IL 60631
800/CLEARVU (253-2788)
773/775-9433
800/444-9855 (fax)
www.clearvue.com/

Cognitive Technologies Corporation
MathRealm
5 Sotweed Ct.

Potomac, MD 20854
800/335-0781
301/299-0523 (fax)
www.mathrealm.com/

CompassLearning (formerly Josten)
203 Colorado Street
Austin, TX 78701
800/232.9556
www.compasslearning.com/

Compu-Teach, Inc.
PMB 137
16541 Redmond Way, Suite. C
Redmond, WA 98052
800/448-3224
425/885-0517
425/883-9169 (fax)
www.compu-teach.com/

Corel Corporation
1600 Carling Avenue
Ottawa, ON K1Z 8R7
Canada
800/772-6735
613/761-9176
www.corel.com

Crick Software
14687 N.E. 95th Street
Redmond, WA 98052
866/33-CRICK
425/467-8260
425/467-8245 (fax)
www.cricksoft.com

Critical Thinking Books & Software
800/458-4849
831/393-3288
831/393-3277 (fax)
www.criticalthinking.com/

Digital Frog International
Trillium Place
RR #2, 7377 Calfass Road
Puslinch, ON N0B 2J0
Canada
519/766-1097
519/767-9994

Discovery Channel Multimedia
800/889-9950
multimedia.discovery.com/

Disney Interactive
800/328-0368
818/846-0454 (fax)
disney.go.com/DisneyInteractive/

DK Publishing, Inc. (see Avanquest Software)
375 Hudson St.
New York, NY 10014
800/631 8571
800/788-6262
201/256-0017
201/256-0000 (fax)
us.dk.com/

Don Johnston, Inc.
26799 West Commerce Drive
Volo, IL 60073
800/999-4660
847/740-0749
847/740-7326 (fax)
www.donjohnston.com

Edmark Corporation (see Riverdeep)

Edware Interactive Learning
Mount Dreoilin
Prosperous
Co. Kildare
IRELAND
+353 86 1794731 (international)
+353 1 6335760 (international)
info@edware.ie

Electronic Arts
866/543-5435
www.ea.com/

Encore, Inc.
999 N. Sepulveda Blvd., Suite 700
El Segundo, CA 90245
800/507-1375
310/768-1800
310/768-1822 (fax)
www.encoresoftware.com

Equilibrium
3 Harbor Drive, Suite 100
Sausalito, CA
415/332-4343
415/331-8374 (fax)
www.equilibrium.com/

FableVision
308 Congress Street, 6th floor
@ Boston Children's Museum
Children's Wharf
Boston, MA 02210
617/956-5700
617/956-5766 (fax)
www.fablevision.com/

FileMaker, Inc.
5201 Patrick Henry Drive
Santa Clara, CA 95054
800/325-2747
408/987-7000
www.filemaker.com/

FTC Publishing Group
P.O. Box 1361

Bloomington, IL 61702
888/237-6740
309/663-5025 (fax)
sales@ftcpublishing.com
www.ftcpublishing.com/

Gamco
325 North Kirkwood Road, Suite 200
St. Louis, MO 63122
888/726-8100
314/984-8063 (fax)
888/351-4430
800/896-1760 (fax)
www.gamco.com/

Grolier Interactive (see Scholastic)
Heartsoft, LLC
8252 S. Harvard Ave., Suite 100
Tulsa, OK 74137
800/285-3475
800/285-4018 (Fax)
support@heartsoft.com
www.heartsoft.com/

Harmonic Vision
630/584-8513
800/474-0903 (U.S. only)
630/584-7828
info@harmonicvision.com

Houghton Mifflin Company Headquarters
222 Berkeley Street
Boston, MA 02116
617/351-5000
www.hmco.com/

IBM Software
1 New Orchard Road
Armonk, NY 10504-1722
(888/SHOP-IBM) 888/746-7426
800/246-6329 (fax)
www-306.ibm.com/software

Ignite It Inc.
866/464-4648
www.squibs.com/

Ingenuity Works, Inc.
325 Howe Street, Suite 407
Vancouver, BC V6C 1Z7
Canada
800/665-0667
604/484-8053
604/484-8096 (fax)
www.ingenuityworks.com/

Inspiration Software, Inc.
9400 SW Beaverton-Hillsdale Hwy,
Suite 300
Beaverton, OR 97005-3300
503/297-3004
800/877-4292
503/297-4676 (fax)
www.inspiration.com/

Intego
500 North Capital of Texas Highway
Building 8-150
Austin, TX 78746
512/637-0700
512/637-0701
http://www.intego.com/

Interactive Learning, Inc.
P.O. Box 718
Westtown, PA 19395
610/399-4959
610/399-4924

Interactive Learning, Inc.
23 Indian Pipe Drive
Wynantskill, NY 12198
518/283-6900
518/283-5589 (fax)
www.highergrades.com/

Jackson Software
361 Park Avenue, Suite B
Glencoe, IL 60022
800/850-1777
847/835-1992
847/835-4926 (fax)
www.jacksoncorp.com/

Jay Klein Productions, Inc.
118 N. Tejon Street, Suite 304
Colorado Springs, CO 80903
719/599-8786
719/380-9997
www.gradebusters.com/

Knowledge Adventure
6060 Center Drive, 10th Floor
Los Angeles, CA 90045
800/545-7677
800/871-2969
310/258-0744 (fax)
www.knowledgeadventure.com/

The Learning Company (see Riverdeep)
www.riverdeepinet/learningcompany/

Learning Enhancement Corporation
200 S. Wacker, Suite 3100
Chicago, IL 60606
877/LEC1-10 (877/272-4610)
brainware@lecforyou.com

Logo Computer Systems, Inc. (LCSI)
P. O. Box 162
Highgate Springs, VT 05460
800/321-5646
514/331-1380 (fax)
info@lcsi.ca
www.microworlds.com/

MacKiev Software
http://www.mackiev.com/

Mainstay
1320 Flynn Road, Suite 401

Camarillo, CA 93012
800/362-2605
805/484-9400
805/484-9428 (fax)
www.mstay.com/

McAfee.com
3965 Freedom Circle
Santa Clara, CA 95054
866/622-3911
www.mcafee.com

Microsoft Corp.
1 Microsoft Way
Redmond, WA 98052-6399
800/MICROSOFT (642-7676)
425/93-MS FAX (936-7329)
www.microsoft.com/

Milliken Software
3190 Rider Trail South
Earth City, MO 63045
314/991-4220
800/325-4136
314/991-4807 (fax)
www.millikenpub.com/

MindPlay
440 S. Williams Blvd., Suite 206
Tucson, AZ 85711-4403
800/221-7911
520/888-1800
520/888-7904 (fax)
www.mindplay.com/

Neufeld Learning Systems
7 Conifer Crescent
London, ON N6K 2V3
Canada
866/429-Math
519/657-9334
519/657-3220 (fax)
www.neufeldmath.com/

Nordic Software, Inc.
P.O. Box 5403
Lincoln, NE 68505
800/306-6502
402/489-1557
402/489-1560 (fax)
www.nordicsoftware.com/

Optimum Resource, Inc.
18 Hunter Road
Hilton Head Island, SC 29926
843/689-8000
843/689-8008 (fax)
stickyb@stickybear.com
www.stickybear.com/

Pearl Software
64 East Uwchlan Avenue, Suite 230
Exton, PA 19341

800/732-7596
www.pearlsw.com

PLATO Learning
10801 Nesbitt Avenue South
Bloomington, MN 55437
800/44.PLATO
800/681.4357
952/832-1270 (fax)
info@plato.com
www.plato.com

The Princeton Review
2315 Broadway, 3rd Floor
New York, NY 10024
800/738-4392
800/Review 2
212/874-8282
212/874-0775 (fax)
www.princetonreview.com/

Quark, Inc.
1800 Grant St.
Denver, CO 80203
303/894.8888
www.quark.com/

Renaissance Learning, Inc.
P.O. Box 8036
Wisconsin Rapids, WI 54495-8036
800/656-6740
715/424-4242 (fax)

Riverdeep, Inc.
100 Pine Street, Suite 1900
San Francisco, CA 94111
415/659.2000
415/659.2020 (fax)
info@riverdeep.net
www.riverdeep.net

Scholastic, Inc.
557 Broadway
New York, NY 10012
800/541-5513
800/724-6527
212/343-6100
www.scholastic.com/

Software MacKiev Online Store
www.mackiev.com

Sunburst Technology
1550 Executive Drive
Elgin, IL 60123-9979
888/492-8817
888/800-3028 (fax)
www.sunburst.com/

Symantec Corp.
20330 Stevens Creek Blvd.
Cupertino, CA 95014
800/441-7234

541/984-8020 (fax)
www.symantec.com/

Teacher Support Software (Gamco)
325 North Kirkwood Road, Suite 200
Kirkwood, MO 63122
888/726-88100
800/896-1760 (fax)
www.tssoftware.com

Tech4Learning, Inc.
10981 San Diego Mission Road, Suite 120
San Diego, CA 92108-3233
877/834-5453
619/563-5348
619/283-8176 (fax)
sales@tech4learning.com
www.tech4learning.com/

Terrapin Logo Software
955 Massachusetts Ave. #365
Cambridge, MA 02139
800/774-LOGO
508/487-4141
508/487-4147 (fax)
www.terrapinlogo.com/

Tom Snyder Productions (Scholastic)
100 Talcott Avenue
Watertown, MA 02472-5703
800/342-0236
617/926-6000 ext. 276
800/304-1254 (fax)
ask@tomsnyder.com
www.teachtsp.com/

Ubisoft
888/824-7038,
ushop.ubi.com/

Ventura Educational Systems
P.O. Box 1622
Arroyo Grande, CA 93421-1622
800/336-1022
800/493-7380 (fax)
www.venturaes.com/

Visions Technology in Education
P.O. Box 70479
Eugene, OR 97401
800/877-0858
541/349-0905
541/349-0944 (fax)
www.toolsforteachers.com

Viva Media
580 Broadway, Room 604
New York, NY 10012
212/431-4420, ext. 207
877/848-6520
212/431-4537 (fax)
www.viva-media.com

Academic Superstore
2101 E. Saint Elmo, Suite 360
Austin, TX 78744
800/817-2347
512/450-0263
www.academicsuperstore.com

Amazon.com, Inc.
www.amazon.com/

Attainment Company (special education)
504 Commerce Parkway
P.O. Box 930160
Verona, WI 53593-0160
800/327-4269
608/845-7880
800/942-3865 (fax)
www.attainmen.company.com/

CCV Software
P.O. Box 6724
Charleston, WV 25362-0724
800/843-5576 (East)
800/541-6078 (West)
800/321-4297 (fax—East)
800/457-6953 (fax—West)
www.ccvsoftware.com

CDW
200 N. Milwaukee Avenue
Vernon Hills, IL 60061
800/750.4239
847/465.6800 (fax)
www.CDW.com/mac

Educational Resources
1550 Executive Drive
P.O. Box 1900
Elgin, IL 60121-1900
800/860-7004
800/624-2926
800/610-5005 (fax)
custserv@edresources.com
www.edresources.com/

Education Software Cooperative
www.edu-soft.org/index.php

Educational Software Directory.net
www.educational-software-directory.net/

Education Works Inc.
shop.store.yahoo.com/educationworks/

eToys.com
www.etoys.com/

Funschool
www.funschool.com/

Goggle Directory
www.shop.store.yahoo.com/
educationworks/

Interact CD-ROM Store
www.interacted.com/

KBkids.com
1099 18th Street, Suite 1000
Denver, CO 80202
877/452-5437
303/228-9000
www.kbkids.com/soft/

Kids Click
www.kidsclick.com/

Learning Services
P. O. Box 1036
Eugene, OR 97440
800/877-9378 (West)
www.learningservicesinc.com

MacConnection
730 Milford Road
Merrimack, NH 03054-4631
800/986-4420
www.macconnection.com

MacMall
2555 W. 190th Street
Torrance, CA 90504
800/622-6255
www.macmall.com

MacWarehouse (see CDW)

MacZone
1102 15th St SW, Suite 102
Auburn, WA 98001-6509
800/454-3686
800/750-4923
800/417-1993 (fax)
www.maczone.com

MicroWarehouse (PCs) (see CDW)

PC Connection
730 Milford Road
Merrimack, NH 03054-4631
888/800-0323
www.pcconnection.com

PC Mall
2555 W. 190th Street
Torrance, CA 90504
800/555-6255
www.pcmall.com

PC Zone
707 South Grady Way
Renton, WA 98055-3233

800/408-9663
www.zones.com

Smart Kids Software
888/881-6001
www.smartkidssoftware.com/

Software Express, Inc.
4128-A South Blvd.
Charlotte, NC 28209
800/527-7638
704/522-7638
704/529-1010 (fax)
www.swexpress.com

Softwareoutlet.com
www.softwareoutlet.com/

Studio eWorks
Bonnie Saliba
1038 Riverside Drive
Holly Hill FL 32117-2836
Toll-Free: 800-432-2082
Phone: 386-257-9398
Fax: 386-257-2530
http://www.studioeworks.com

SuperKids
www.superkids.com/

Surplus CD-ROM Family Software
www.surpluscdrom.com/

TigerDirect.com
7795 W. Flagler Street, Suite. 35
Miami, FL 33144
800/800-8300
888/278-4437
305/415-2202 (fax)
www.tigerdirect.com/

Tucows
800/371-6992
96 Mowat Avenue
Toronto,
ON M6K 3M1
Canada
416/535-0123
416/531-5584 (fax)
www.tucows.com/

Yahoo! Shopping: Internet Marketing Associates
877/275-9955
813/571-7631
http://shop.store.yahoo.com/meter/
http://search.yahoo.com/bin/search?
p=educational+software

ZDNET Reviews (Ziff Davis Software Library)
www.zdnet.com/products/stories/reviews/

GLOSSARY

Abacus An ancient calculating device consisting of beads strung on wires or rods that are set in a frame.

ABC An abbreviation for the Atanasoff-Berry Computer, the first electronic digital computer.

Academic portfolio Shows the student's academic performance and achievement.

Access time The time a computer needs from the instant it asks for information until it receives it.

Active matrix A screen, generally used in portable computers, in which each pixel is controlled by its own transistor.

Ada A high-level programming language developed in the late 1970s and named after Augusta Ada Byron, Countess of Lovelace and daughter of Lord Byron.

Adaptive technology (also referred to as assistive technology) Refers to using technology to provide equal access for students with disabilities.

Algorithm Generally a set of instructions for a person to follow in order to solve a problem. A computer program is an algorithm that tells the computer what to do in a step-by-step manner—in a language that it comprehends.

Analog device A mechanism that handles values in continuous variable quantities such as voltage fluctuations.

Analytical engine A sophisticated mechanical calculating machine designed by Charles Babbage in 1833. Conceived before the technology was available, it was to have been capable of storing instructions, performing mathematical operations, and using punched cards for storage.

Applet In Java, a small program that is embedded in a Web page and, when downloaded, is started by the browser.

Application program or software A program written for a certain purpose, such as word processing.

Archie server Finds files stored at an anonymous FTP site.

Arithmetic logic unit (ALU) The central processing unit component responsible for the execution of fundamental arithmetic and logical operations on data.

Artificial intelligence (AI) Use of the computer to simulate the thinking of human beings.

ASCII The American Standard Code for Information Interchange, a standard computer character set that facilitates efficient data communication and achieves compatibility among computer devices.

Assembler A computer program that converts assembly language programs into executable machine language programs.

Assembly language A low-level programming language that uses mnemonic words and in which each statement corresponds directly to a single machine instruction.

Assistive technologies Equipment that increases, maintains, or improves the capabilities of individuals with disabilities.

Authoring language A computer language used to create educational software, such as drill-and-practice lessons.

Authoring system A program requiring little knowledge, used to create computer-based lessons and tests.

Backup disk A second copy of a program or document.

Bandwidth The amount of data that can be transmitted through a communication network.

Bar code reader An input device that scans bar codes and converts the bar codes into numbers that are displayed on the screen.

BASIC Beginner's All Purpose Symbolic Instruction Code, one of the most commonly used high-level programming languages.

Baud rate The speed at which a modem can transmit data.

Binary notation The number system a computer uses. It has only two digits, 1 and 0.

Bit An abbreviation for *binary digit*, either 1 or 0 in the binary number system.

Blog (See Weblog)

Bookmark manager A software program that enables you to organize and collect Uniform Resource Locators (URLs) in a hierarchical manner.

Boolean algebra Devised by George Boole, a system of algebra that uses the operations of informal logic.

Booting the system The process of starting the computer.

BPS An abbreviation for *bits per second*, the measurement of data transmission speed. Presently, the fastest modem transfer over phone lines is 56 kilobits per second (kbps).

Broadband Refers to high bandwidth that transmits 1.5 Mps over fiber optic cables.

Browser Software that enables users to surf the World Wide Web. *FireFox* and *Internet Explorer* are the two most popular browsers.

Bug A mistake or error in a computer program.

Bulletin board system (BBS) A computer that serves as a center for exchange of information for various interest groups.

Bus network A network with a single bidirectional cable or bus line that carries messages to and from devices. Each workstation can access the network independently.

Buttons "Hot spots" that are clicked to initiate an action.

Byte A unit of computer storage that consists of eight binary digits (bits). A byte holds the equivalent of one character, such as the letter C.

C A computer language developed by Bell Labs for the UNIX operating system.

Cable modem A modem that uses a cable TV service to provide high-speed access to the Internet.

Card A rectangular box on the screen that contains text, graphics, sound, and animation. A bunch of cards are referred to as a stack.

Cathode ray tube (CRT) The basis of the television screen and the typical microcomputer display screen.

CD-ROM (compact disc–read only memory) A means of high-capacity storage (more than 600 megabytes) that uses laser optics for reading data.

Cell In an electronic spreadsheet, the intersection of a row and a column.

Central processing unit (CPU) The "brains of the computer," where the computing takes place. The CPU is also called the *processor*. It is made up of a control unit and the arithmetic logic unit.

Chat room A real-time Internet discussion on some topic.

Circuit board A board onto which electrical components are mounted and interconnected to form a circuit.

Clickers When a teacher asks questions, students respond by using these remote control devices (clickers) to send their answers wirelessly to the teacher's computer.

Clipboard A temporary memory storage area where text or graphics can be copied from a document and stored until pasted elsewhere in a document.

Clock speed (clock rate) Refers to the speed at which the computer performs basic operations.

COBOL Common Business-Oriented Language, a high-level programming language used for business applications.

Collaborative editing Lets people use editing tools to simultaneously edit a document using different computers.

Compiler A program that translates the source code of a program written in a higher-level language such as BASIC into a machine-readable, executable program.

Composite color monitor A monitor that accepts an analog video signal and combines red, green, and blue signals to produce a color image.

Computer A machine that accepts information, processes it according to a set of instructions, and produces the results as output.

Computer chip A piece of semiconducting material, such as silicon, with transistors and resistors etched on its surface. The formal name for a computer chip is integrated circuit.

Computer conferencing Communication between two or more computers in real time.

Computer graphics Using the computer to create and manipulate pictures.

Computer literacy The basic knowledge that one needs to work independently with the computer.

Computer-aided design (CAD) Use of the computer for industrial design and technical drawing.

Computer-assisted instruction (CAI) Use of the computer as an instructional tool.

Computer-managed instruction (CMI) A computerized record-keeping system that diagnoses a student's progress, provides instruction, and analyzes progress.

Connect time The time spent online between logging on and logging off.

Constructivism A learning theory emphasizing experience-based activities.

Control unit The component of the central processing unit that receives programmed instructions and carries them out.

Cookie A text file that a server writes to a person's hard drive without his or her knowledge. The purpose is to track the individual's computer usage.

Copyright The laws that protect people who own creative works such as music, art, text, software, and other products of this nature.

CPS An abbreviation for *characters per second*, a term used to describe the number of characters printed per second by a printer.

Cursor The blinking light that shows the user where he or she is working on the computer screen.

Cyberspace The use of computer technology to create virtual space.

Daisy-wheel printer An impact printer that produces typewriter-quality print. This printer has its type characters set around a daisy wheel, similar to a wagon wheel minus an outer ring.

Database A collection of information organized according to some structure or purpose.

Database management system Application software that controls the organization, storage, and retrieval of data in the database.

Debug To find errors in a computer's hardware or software.

Delete To remove information from a file or disk.

Demodulation Used in telecommunication, the process of receiving and transforming an analog signal into its digital equivalent, which can be used by the computer.

Desktop A computerized representation of a person's work as if he or she were looking at a desk cluttered with folders.

Desktop publishing (DTP) The use of the personal computer in conjunction with specialized software to combine text and graphics to produce high-quality output on a laser printer or typesetting machine.

Desktop publishing software Applications that enable the computer to be a desktop publishing workstation, such as *Microsoft Publisher*, *Adobe PageMaker*, and *QuarkXpress*.

Desktop video conferencing Refers to using a personal computer to do video conferencing.

Digital camera A portable camera that records images in digital format.

Digital computer A computer that operates by accepting and processing data that has been converted into binary numbers.

Digital divide A term that refers to the gap between those who have access to computer technologies and those who do not have access.

Digital storytelling- Refers to telling a story using sound, text, voice, music, video, and animation.

Digital subscriber line (DSL) Digital technology that offers high-speed transmission over standard copper telephone wiring.

Digitizer A device that translates analog information into digital information for computer processing. Examples include scanners and digital cameras.

Discover switch An "intelligent" switch that enables people with physical disabilities to use a variety of software programs that feature single-switch scanning.

Display The representation of data on a screen in the form of a printed report, graph, or drawing.

Distance education The delivery by institutions or instructors of knowledge via telecommunication or remote capabilities. (See **Distance learning**.)

Distance learning The receiving of training from a remote teaching site via TV or computer.

Documentation The set of instructions, tutorials, or reference materials that is required for a computer program to run effectively. Documentation can be in the form of online help or printed material.

DOS (disk operating system) A program that enables the computer to control its own operation. This program's major task is to handle the transfer of data and programs to and from the computer's disks.

Dot pitch The smallest dot that a computer monitor can display. The smaller the dots, the higher the resolution.

Dot-matrix printer An impact printer that produces characters and graphic images by striking an inked ribbon with tiny metal rods called *pins*.

Download The process of sending information from a larger computer to a smaller one by means of a modem or network.

Drag-and-drop A technique that uses the mouse to drag objects on a computer screen.

Drawing programs Programs that use vector graphics to produce line art.

Drill and practice A type of computer instruction that enables students to practice information with which they are familiar in order to become proficient.

DVD-RAM (digital video disc–random access memory) The read/write version of DVD-ROM.

DVD-ROM (digital video disc–read only memory) Similar to CD-ROM in appearance, this disc format has the capacity to hold 17 gigabytes.

E-book A handheld computer, similar in size to an organizer, that displays electronic versions of books, enabling users to set bookmarks, do keyword searches, and make notes in margins.

eTravel A system developed by Hewlett-Packard in which a robot substitutes for the individual and enables this individual to be in two places at the same time.

Educational technology Technology that aids the teaching and learning process.

Electronic mail, e-mail A system of transmitting messages over a communication network via the computer.

Electronic portfolio A representative collection of an individual's work that shows his or her talents and is presented electronically by a presentation program or displayed on a Web site.

E-mail address A name and a computer location (often referred to as a *host*). An example is vicki.sharp@csun.edu, in which vicki@sharp is the name and csun is the location.

Encryption The process of coding information so that it cannot be understood unless decoded.

Encyclopedia database (See **Free-form database**.)

Ergonomics The science of designing computers and furniture so that they are easy and safe to use.

Ethernet One of the most popular types of local area network connections.

Execute To carry out the instructions given in machine language code.

Expansion slot A slot inside the computer that accepts boards that add to the computer's capabilities and features.

Fair use The part of copyright law that tells when it is legal to copy another's creative work.

FAQs (frequently asked questions) Files found at Internet sites that answer frequently asked questions. It is a good idea to check for FAQs and read them.

Fax machine An input/output device that enables the user to transmit text and images between distant locations.

Fiber optics A medium consisting of glass fibers that transmit data using light.

Field A record location in which a certain type of data is stored.

File A collection of related records.

File server A powerful computer that stores information and programs that users share.

Filtering software A program that tries to prevent the user from accessing adult material on the Internet.

Finger server Finds out information about another Internet user, including the name of the person behind the user identification name.

Firewall A security system that protects a network against threats from hackers from other networks.

FireWire A high-speed serial bus that connects up to 63 peripheral devices such as digital cameras and printers.

Flame An argumentative posting of an e-mail message or newsgroup message in response to another posting.

Flat file database A simple database that works with only one data file at a time, with no linking to other data files.

Floppy disk Covered with magnetic coating, such as iron oxide, the mass storage device used primarily with microcomputers.

Flowchart A graphical representation of the flow of operations that is needed to finish a job. It uses rectangles, diamonds, ovals, parallelograms, arrows, circles, and words to represent different levels of operations.

Font A group of letters, numbers, punctuation marks, and special characters with the same typeface, style, and weight.

Footer In word processing, repeated text such as a title that appears at the bottom of a page.

Format To prepare a disk so the user can store information on it. During the formatting process, the computer's disk drive encodes a magnetic pattern consisting of tracks and sectors.

FORTRAN FORmula TRANslator, one of the oldest high-level programming languages, suited for scientific and mathematical applications.

Frame In desktop publishing, a movable and resizable box that holds graphics and text.

Free-form database A database that enables the user to enter text without regard to its length or order.

Freeware Software that is given away at no charge.

FTP (File Transfer Protocol) The basic Internet function that enables files to be transferred between computers. It can be used to download files from a remote host computer as well as to upload files from a computer to a remote host computer.

Function key A key located on the keyboard that the user programs to perform a specific task.

Gigabyte A unit of measure that equals approximately 1 billion (1,073,741,824) bytes.

Google jockeying A participant in a class who uses a search engine like Google to search for ideas or Internet terms while the presenter talks.

Gopher A program that enables the user to browse the Internet using menus.

Graphic organizer A visual communication tool that enables users to organize their ideas using symbols.

Graphical user interface (GUI) An interface that differs from a character-based computer interface such as MS-DOS. An example of a popular graphical interface is the Macintosh operating system.

Graphics tablet A plotting tablet that the user draws on to communicate with the computer.

Gutenberg, Johannes The inventor of movable type.

Hacker A computer expert; sometimes one who illegally accesses and tampers with computer programs and data.

Halo collaboration suites Refers to video conferencing rooms where people from the either sides of the ocean come together as if they were sitting across from each other.

Handheld computer A small mobile computer that enables the user to write onscreen with a stylus. This device provides tools for everyday use such as a notepad, word processor, appointment calendar, address book, and fax modem.

Hard copy Computer output that is on paper, film, or another permanent medium.

Hard disk One or more disk platters coated with a metal oxide substance that enables information to be magnetically stored.

Hard drive The computer's main storage device.

Hardware The physical components of the computer system, which include the computer, monitor, printer, and disk drives.

Header In word processing, repeated text such as page numbers that appear at the top of the page.

Hierarchical database A database that stores items in a top-to-bottom organizational structure.

High-level language Language that is further away from the machine's operation and approximates human language. Low-level language is nearer the machine's operation.

Home page The main page in a Web site, at which you find hyperlinks to other pages.

Host The computer that serves as the beginning point and ending point for data transfer when accessing the Internet.

Hub A central connecting device in a computer network that joins communication lines together on the network.

HyperCard An authoring tool that enables the user to organize information and retrieve onscreen cards that contain text, graphics, sound, and animation.

Hyperlink A graphic, an icon, or a word in a file that, when clicked, automatically opens another file for viewing.

Hypermedia A system nearly synonymous with *hypertext* (however, it emphasizes the nontextual components of hypertext) that uses the computer to input, manipulate, and output graphics, sound, text, and video in the presentation of ideas and information.

HyperTalk The programming language that is used with *HyperCard*.

Hypertext Nonsequential associations of images, sound, text, and actions through which the user can browse, regardless of the order. An example of hypertext is a computer glossary from which a user can select a word and retrieve its definition.

Hypertext Markup Language (HTML) The basic language that people use to build hypertext electronic documents on the Web.

Identity theft The illegal gathering of information about a person and its use for the successful impersonation of this person by mail, over the telephone, in person, or online.

Inclusion or inclusive education Education of students with disabilities with those who do not have disabilities.

Initialize (See **Format**.)

Inkjet printer A nonimpact printer that uses a nozzle to spray a jet of ink onto a page of paper. These small, spherical bodies of ink are released through a matrix of holes to form characters.

Instant messaging A service that tells users when their friends are online and enables them to exchange information in real time.

Integrated circuit (IC chip) (See **Chip**.)

Integrated learning system (ILS) A central computer with software consisting of planned lessons in various curriculum areas.

Integrated program An application program such as *Microsoft Works* that combines several tasks such as word processing and database management in one package and facilitates the free interchange of information among applications. These applications do not offer as much capability as a single application.

Interactive video A system consisting of a computer, videodisc player, videotape, and software that provides the student with immediate feedback. It includes management features so lessons can be customized to specific student needs.

Interface The place at which a connection is made between two elements so they can work together harmoniously. In computing, different interfaces occur, ranging from user interfaces, in which people communicate with programs, to hardware interfaces, which connect devices and components in a computer.

Internet A system of worldwide networks that enables a user to send electronic mail, conduct research, chat, and participate in newsgroups.

Internet 2 The second generation of the Internet, designed primarily to exchange multimedia data in real time at high speeds.

Internet appliances Low-cost devices that handle e-mail and Web browsing and perform this job faster than an ordinary modem connection.

Internet relay chat (IRC) A real-time Internet service that enables users to do conferencing all over the world.

Internet service provider (ISP) An organization that charges a fee for users to dial into its computer for an Internet connection.

Interpreter A high-level program translator that translates and then executes each statement in a computer program. It translates a statement into machine language, runs it, then proceeds to the next statement, translates it, runs it, and so on.

Java A programming language designed by Sun Microsystems to write programs that can be downloaded from the Internet with a Java interpreter. Many World Wide Web pages on the Internet use small Java applications, or applets, to display animations.

JavaScript A scripting language for Web publishing.

Joystick A small, boxlike object with a moving stick and buttons used primarily for games, educational software, and CAD systems.

Kbps An abbreviation for *kilobits per second*, a computer modem's speed rating, measured in units of 1,024 bits. This is the maximum number a device can transfer in one second under the best of conditions.

Kerning In typography, the adjustment of space between pairs of characters, as in "B A," to enhance the appearance of the type or to enhance readability.

Keyboard An input device similar to a standard typewriter but with extra keys, such as function keys and a numeric pad.

Keyboard emulator A device that exists inside a computer or is connected to a computer that imitates the computer keyboard's performance.

Kilobyte (K) A unit of measure for computers that is equal to 1,024, or 210, bytes.

Laser disc A large optical disc that utilizes laser technology for the purpose of video.

Laser printer A printer that produces high-quality text and graphic output by tracing images with a laser beam controlled by the computer.

Leading In typography, the vertical spacing between lines of type that is measured from baseline to baseline.

Light pen An instrument, used in conjunction with a video display, with a light-sensitive, photoelectric cell in its tip that sends an electrical impulse to the computer, which identifies its current location.

Light-emitting diode (LED) When charged with electricity, a semiconductor diode that gives off light.

Linotype machine The first successful automated typecasting machine.

Liquid crystal display (LCD) A display that uses a liquid compound, positioned between two sheets of polarizing material squeezed between two glass panels.

Liquid crystal display projection panel A projector that receives computer output and displays it on a liquid crystal screen placed on an overhead projector. The projector displays on a large screen the program that the computer generates.

Local area network (LAN) A network that provides communication within a local area, usually within 200 or 300 feet, as found in office buildings.

Logo A high-level programming language designed for children that contains many functions found in List Processing (LISP).

Low-level language A programming language, like assembly language, that is close to the machine's language.

Machine language A programming language composed of a pattern of 0s and 1s that is far removed from the language understood by human beings. This is the only language that computers understand.

Macro A group of routines or commands combined into one or two keystrokes.

Magnetic disk A device that stores data magnetically in circular tracks that are divided into sectors.

Magnetic ink character recognition (MICR) A character recognition system that reads text printed with a special magnetic ink. All the checks issued by banks are coded with this special ink and characters so that an MICR unit can read them.

Magnetic tape A reel of tape that is usually around 1/2-inch wide that can store about 25 megabytes of data magnetically in a linear track.

Mail merge A word processing feature that prints customized form letters.

Mainframe computer A high-level computer designed for sophisticated computational tasks.

Mainstreaming Refers to part-time and full-time programs that educate students with disabilities with their nondisabled peers.

Mapping mashups Refers to using an Internet service such as Google to put together map information from more than one source.

Mark I An electromechanical calculating machine designed by Howard Aiken at Harvard University and built by IBM.

Megabyte (MB) A unit of measure that equals approximately 1,048,576 bytes.

Megahertz (MHz) A measure of frequency equal to 1 million cycles per second.

Megapixel A megapixel is equal to 1 million pixels, which defines a digital image's resolution.

Memory The circuitry inside the computer that enables it to store and retrieve information. Generally, *memory* refers to the semiconductor storage (RAM) that is directly connected to the microprocessor.

Mesh network An Internet-like communication network that has at least two pathways to each node. In a completely meshed network every node has a direct connection to every other node.

Microcomputer system A computer that uses a single-chip microprocessor, one that is less powerful than that of a minicomputer.

Microprocessor chip A chip that contains the central processing unit of the computer.

Microsoft Surface A Microsoft product that turns a tabletop into an interactive surface.

Microworld The Logo environment in which a child freely experiments, tests, and revises his or her own theories in order to create a product.

MIDI (Musical Instrument Digital Interface) A protocol that enables individuals to exchange musical information between musical instruments, computers, and synthesizers.

Millisecond (ms) Equivalent to $10{-}3$, or one-thousandth, of a second.

Minicomputer A midlevel computer whose capabilities are between those of a mainframe and a microcomputer.

Modem Short for MOdulator/DEModulator, a device that enables two computers to communicate with each other via telephone lines.

Modulation In telecommunication, the means that a modem uses to convert digital information sent by computer to its analog form, so that the information can be sent over telephone lines.

Monitor A video display that resembles a television set, designed to handle a wider and higher range of frequencies.

Morphing A special effect that changes one image into another image.

Mouse A popular input device that is used instead of a keyboard to make menu selections.

MPEG Audio Layer 3 (MP3) A Moving Pictures Experts Group (MPEG) audio format that produces CD-quality audio using a 12:1 compression rate.

Multimedia A subset of hypermedia that combines graphics, sound, animation, and video.

Nanosecond (ns) Equivalent to $10{-}9$, or one-billionth, of a second.

Napier's rods A device used for multiplying large numbers, invented by John Napier, a Scottish mathematician, in 1617.

Netiquette The etiquette used in cyberspace.

Network Computers that share storage devices, peripherals, and applications. A network can be connected by telephone lines, satellites, or cables.

Network database Works the same as a hierarchical database except that a record can belong to more than one main group.

Newsgroups Electronic bulletin boards where you can read messages that others have written and contribute to the discussion.

Online The status of a computer interacting with an online service or the Internet.

Online help The capability of a program to display onscreen guidance while an individual uses the computer.

Online service Any commercial service, such as *America Online* (AOL), that gives access to electronic mail, news services, and the Web.

Open journaling. Using the Web, authors are able to follow their submissions through the review process and access reviewers' comments and revise and resubmit their articles.

Open source Refers to a program whose software code is available to anyone that wants to use or change it.

Operating system (See **DOS.**)

Optical character recognition (OCR) A device that recognizes printed or typed text.

Optical disc A round platter that has information recorded on it with laser beam technology. It is capable of storing large amounts of information.

Optical mark reader (OMR) A device that reads penciled or graphic information on cards or pages. Lamps furnish light reflected from the card or paper; the amount of reflected light is measured by a photocell.

Organic light-emitting diode display (OLED) A technology pioneered by Kodak. This display typically consists of a series of organic layers between two electrical electrodes. The display is brighter than the current liquid crystal displays.

Output After processing, the information that is sent from the computer to a peripheral device.

Page layout In desktop publishing, the process of arranging text and graphics on the page.

Paint programs Graphics programs that enable individuals to simulate painting on the computer screen with the use of a mouse or graphics tablet. Paint programs create raster graphic images.

Pascal A high-level structured programming language, designed by Niklaus Wirth in the late 1960s.

Peripheral The devices that are connected to the computer under the microprocessor's control, such as disk drives, printers, and modems.

Personal data assistant (PDA) A small, handheld computer that accepts input on the screen from a stylus.

Personal portfolio Shows a student's growth and development outside of school.

Phishing Refers to e-mail scams that attempt to get your credit card numbers, Social Security numbers, and personal passwords.

Piracy The act of copying software illegally.

Pixel Short for *picture element*, a linear dot on a display screen. When this dot is combined with other dots, it creates an image.

Plagiarism The taking of the graphic representation, writings, or ideas of another person and using them as one's own.

Plasma display A display produced by a mixture of neon gases between two transparent panels, giving a very sharp, clean image with a wide viewing angle.

PLATO Programmed Logic for Automatic Teaching Operations, an early computer system developed by the University of Illinois and Control Data Corporation and designed for instructional use.

Plug-ins Programs built to extend a browser's capabilities. Plug-ins enable users to see and hear video, audio, and other kinds of multimedia files.

Podcast Refers to an audio broadcast that can be listened to on a computer or digital music player such as an iPod.

Portal A Web site that acts as a starting point to the Internet, usually on a specific subject area.

Portfolio An organized collection of documents that is used by a student to reflect the student's knowledge, skills, and learning accomplishments.

Predetermined functions Ready-made formulas that enable the user to solve problems quickly.

Presentation graphics Combining text and images, software that produces and displays graphic screens.

Print graphics Has many of the same characteristics as presentation graphics: clip art, image manipulation; however, its focus is on creating products for printout.

Printer A device that produces computer output.

Problem-solving software Computer-assisted software that helps students develop critical thinking skills with the intent that these skills will transfer to other areas of the curriculum.

Professional portfolio Could contain samples of students' work that meet graduation requirements for high school or college admission.

Program A series of instructions designed to make a computer do a given task.

Protected and hidden cells A spreadsheet program feature that protects a group of cells from being altered or erased.

Public domain software Software that is not copyrighted and can be copied freely and distributed without payment or permission.

QuickLink pen A device that scans printed text, printed Internet links, charts, tables, books, and magazines. Students can then transfer this information to their computers to aid them in writing their reports.

QuickTime A program designed by Apple to show small movies on the computer screen.

QuickTime VR An extension of *QuickTime* that enables the user to view onscreen movies in 3-D space.

Quicktionary Reading Pen A device that scans printed words, displays them in large characters, pronounces them aloud, and defines them at the touch of a button.

Random access memory (RAM) Volatile memory. Whenever the computer is turned off, information stored in RAM is lost.

Raster graphics or bit-mapped graphics Images made up of a pattern of pixels or dots. These images are limited to the maximum resolution of the computer display or printer.

Read-only memory (ROM) Memory that retains its contents when the power supply is turned off. Often referred to as *hardwired, internal memory*, it cannot be altered or changed.

Real time The immediate processing of data as it becomes available. In telecommunication, a person online can be connected to others who are online at the same time.

RealAudio A plug-in that enables users to listen to live or prerecorded audio transmissions on the World Wide Web.

Record A collection of related fields that are treated as a single unit.

Red, Green, and Blue (RGB) monitor A CRT (cathode ray tube) monitor that uses three electronic guns to generate red, green, and blue.

Refreshable Braille display A device that is added to a computer system to translate text on the screen into Braille.

Relational database Links files together that enables the user to work with more than one file at a time.

Remote instrumentation Devices that let teachers and students control scientific instruments from a distance.

Repetitive stress or strain injury An injury caused by the repeated use of muscles, ligaments, tendons, tendon sheaths, and nerves, often during computer use.

Resolution The clarity or degree of sharpness of a displayed character or image, expressed in linear dots per inch.

Ring network A group of computers that communicate with each other in a ring, without a file server.

Robotics A branch of engineering that is concerned with the training and creation of robots.

Router A device that forwards data packets from one network to another.

Rubrics Refer to clearly stated criteria that are used to evaluate students' work.

Satellite data service Uses a satellite dish to connect to your computer.

Scanner A device that digitizes photographs or line art and stores the images as a file that can be transferred into a paint program or directly into a word processor.

Screencasting Refers to making a video recording of the computer screen, which is in reality a video Podcast.

Search engine A program that enables a user to find information on the Internet.

Second Life A virtual 3-D world created by Linden Labs where individuals can meet people, create an identity, buy land, and design their own creations.

Shared-bus network A network where a single bidirectional cable carries messages to and from devices.

Shareware Copyrighted software that is distributed free but must be paid for if the customer is satisfied.

Simulation Software that approximates the conditions of the real world in an environment in which the user changes the variables.

Site licensing A software licensing system in which a person or organization pays a set fee to run copies of a program on a large number of computers.

Slow keys Enable the computer to recognize only the key presses that are a certain length and disregard others.

Smart card A credit card with an embedded microprocessor that provides information about its user's identity.

Social bookmarking Using social bookmarking, individuals take their favorite bookmarks and download them to a site like del.icio.us (*http://del.icio.us*).

Social networking A Web site that lets individuals of similar interests spend time together.

Software A program that instructs a computer to perform a specific job.

Software suite A collection of programs that are usually sold individually (e.g., *Microsoft Office*).

Sorting An operation that reorders data in a new sequence, usually alphabetically or numerically.

Spam Unsolicited messages sent via the Internet.

Speech recognition A computer program that can decode human speech into text.

Speech synthesizer An output device that generates sound. This chip gives the computer the ability to search for words and their pronunciations in a database.

Spider programs Automated electronic software programs that follow the links on a page and put all the text into one huge database.

SPOT A technology that implants wireless connectivity that is always on in devices such as watches and necklaces.

Spreadsheet A computerized version of a manual worksheet, with a matrix of numbers arranged in rows and columns, that facilitates calculations.

Star network A communications network in which all the computers are connected to a file server or host computer.

Sticky keys Certain keys that lock in place—allowing a user with a disability to press combination key strokes without having to press multiple keys simultaneously.

Streaming audio Compressed audio that is sent in real time via the Internet.

Streaming video Compressed movies that are sent in real time via the Internet.

Style sheet A file that contains instructions that apply character, paragraph, and page layout formats to desktop publishing and word processing documents. Style sheets include settings such as tabs, margins, columns, and fonts.

Supercomputers The largest and fastest of the mainframe computers with the most advanced processing abilities.

Surge suppressor Also known as a *surge protector*, a device that protects the computer from damaging electrical surges.

Switch A network device that forwards traffic at very high speeds.

Teacher-directed approach A learning theory that emphasizes that the teacher is the manipulator of the class environment and the student is the receptacle.

Telecommunication The electronic transmission of information, including data, television pictures, sound, and facsimiles.

Telnet A commonly used protocol on the Internet that enables users to log onto a remote computer to run a program.

Template A predesigned document that includes text or formulas that are needed to create a standard document.

Terabyte A unit of measurement that equals roughly 1 trillion bytes (actually 1,099,511,627,776 bytes).

Thermal printer A printer that uses heated wires to burn dots into special paper.

Time bomb A computer virus that is programmed to go off on a specific day and time.

Touch screen A display that has a pressure-sensitive panel mounted in the front. The user makes choices by touching the screen in the correct location.

Touch-free switch An input device that enables users to trigger a mouse click without applying any pressure.

Trackball A movable ball that moves the cursor on the screen as it is manipulated.

Trackpad or touchpad A pressure-sensitive pad that is smaller and more accurate than the trackball.

Transistor An electronic gate that bridges the gap between two wires and enables the current to flow.

Tutorial Similar to a tutor, a program that explains new material and then tests the student's progress.

Uniform Resource Locator (URL) A site address on the World Wide Web. For example, the URL for the California State University home page is *http://www.csun.edu*.

UNIX Originally developed by AT&T Bell Laboratories, an operating system used on different types of computers that supports multitasking.

Upload Transfer of information from one computer to a remote computer.

USB drive (flash drive) A flash memory card that plugs into the user's USB port.

Usenet A leading network system of bulletin boards that services more than 1,500 newsgroups.

User friendly A term that means "easy to learn and use."

User group A group of users of a specific type of computer who share experiences to improve their understanding of the product.

Utility programs Programs that perform a variety of housekeeping and control functions such as sorting, copying, searching, and file management.

Vector graphics Images made up of independent objects that can be sized, moved, and manipulated.

Video blog (Vlog) A Web blog that uses video content to communicate. (See **Weblog**.)

Video conferencing A multiuser chat in which the live images of the users are displayed on each participant's computer screen.

Video RAM (VRAM) A chip used to transfer and hold an image on a computer screen.

Video scan converter A device that changes personal computer or laptop output so it can be displayed on a television monitor.

Videodisc A read-only optical disc that uses an analog signal to store and retrieve still and moving pictures, sound, or color.

Virtual meetings Real-time encounters that take place on the Internet using audio, video, and chat tools.

Virtual reality (VR) A computer-generated world in which a person is able to manipulate the environment. The user generally wears a head-mounted device and special sensor gloves.

Virus A program that infects computer files by duplicating itself.

Voice recognition software or system A system that converts the spoken word into binary patterns that are computer recognizable; it understands human speech.

Warping A process similar to morphing, involving the altering and manipulation of a single image.

Web 2 A term used to talk about the second generation of the Web which contains blogs, social networks, Wikis, and more.

Weblog A method of expressing oneself using a personal online diary on a Web site.

Webcam A small camera, usually a video camera, whose images are seen over the World Wide Web.

Web page An HTML document that displays information on the World Wide Web.

WebQuest Bernie Dodge defines a WebQuest as "an inquiry-oriented activity where most or all of the information that the students use comes from the Web."

Web site A collection or related Web pages on the Internet that contains information about instructional material, services, products, and so on.

Whiteboard A device that is connected to a teacher's computer that enables users to see what the instructor writes and that captures the information that is written into a computer file.

Wide area network (WAN) A network that uses long-distance communication or satellites to connect computers over greater distances than a local area network does.

Wikis A Wikis is a Web site where individuals can view, edit, and add to the information.

Wildcard character A character such as an asterisk that is used to represent one or more characters.

Window An onscreen frame in which users can view a document, database, spreadsheet, or application program.

Windows A graphical interface developed by Microsoft Corporation for IBM and IBM-compatible computers.

Wireless communication A method of linking computers with radio waves or infrared. There are no interconnecting cables or wires.

Wireless network A network that enables users to transmit information by infrared, microwave technology, or radio waves instead of by wire.

Wizard A small program that enables the user to input information to create a customized template.

Word processor A software program designed to make the computer a useful electronic writing tool that can edit, store, and print documents.

Word wrap In word processing, when words go beyond a margin, the process of automatically pushing them to the beginning of the next line.

World Wide Web (WWW) An Internet service that enables users to navigate the Internet using hypertext documents.

Worm A program that can run by itself and replicate a full working version to other computers. After the worm is finished with its work, the data are usually deleted.

YouTube Refers to a Web site where people are able to share their videos.

INDEX